People-Centric Security

Transforming Your Enterprise Security Culture

Lance Hayden

New York   Chicago   San Francisco
Athens   London   Madrid   Mexico City
Milan   New Delhi   Singapore   Sydney   Toronto

Cataloging-in-Publication Data is on file with the Library of Congress

McGraw-Hill Education books are available at special quantity discounts to use as premiums and sales promotions, or for use in corporate training programs. To contact a representative, please visit the Contact Us pages at www.mhprofessional.com.

People-Centric Security: Transforming Your Enterprise Security Culture

1 2 3 4 5 6 7 8 9 0   DOC DOC   1 0 9 8 7 6 5

ISBN   978-0-07-184677-6
MHID   0-07-184677-8

Sponsoring Editor Meghan Manfre
Editorial Supervisor Janet Walden
Project Manager Anubhooti Saxena,
            Cenveo® Publisher Services
Acquisitions Coordinator Amy Stonebraker
Technical Editor David Phillips
Copy Editor William McManus

Proofreader Lisa McCoy
Indexer Claire Splan
Production Supervisor James Kussow
Composition Cenveo Publisher Services
Illustration Cenveo Publisher Services
Art Director, Cover Jeff Weeks
Cover Designer Jeff Weeks

To Jayne and Wyatt, because everything.

About the Author

Dr. Lance Hayden is a managing director in the Technology Advisory Practice of BRG, an international strategy and research firm. Dr. Hayden's security career spans 25 years across the public, private, and academic sectors. His interest in human security behaviors and culture began while a HUMINT operations officer with the Central Intelligence Agency, and continued in security roles at companies including KPMG, FedEx, and Cisco. Dr. Hayden provides expert advice and consulting on information security strategy, measurement, and culture to companies and governments around the globe. In addition to *People-Centric Security*, he is the author of *IT Security Metrics: A Practical Framework for Measuring Security and Protecting Data*, also from McGraw-Hill Education. Lance received his PhD in information science from the University of Texas, where he also teaches courses on security, privacy, and the intelligence community. He lives in Austin.

About the Technical Editor

David Phillips has been protecting clients' IT systems for over 20 years, including technical mitigation, information security risk programs, IT network security architecture, and regulatory compliance. David developed a growing professional service business inside a multinational networking corporation focused on cybersecurity, protecting clients' intellectual property and customer data, and securing networks to allow for resilient IT infrastructure in the face of cyberattacks. His clients have included multibillion-dollar businesses in the retail, finance, manufacturing, energy, and healthcare verticals. David has worked with global enterprises to measure and mature their security capabilities across people, process, and technology, spanning levels from technology management to security awareness and security cultural transformation. David lives outside of Austin, Texas.

Contents at a Glance

Contents

Part I   Understanding Your Security Culture

Part II   **Measuring Your Security Culture**

Foreword

After having worked in information security for over 20 years, I have come to a simple conclusion: unless we move beyond technology alone and start addressing the human element, we are in a no-win situation. Technology is where every organization should start when managing its cyber-risk, but technology can only go so far. We have hit that point of diminishing return. We can no longer ignore the human factor in information security. Lance's book is a breath of fresh air. He creates a new chapter in how organizations should manage their risk, not just at the technical level but at a human level. What makes Lance's book so powerful is that he not only backs the book with tremendous research and academic studies, but also brings in real-world application.

I first met Lance through his previous book, *IT Security Metrics*. It was one of the few books I had found that attempted to measure the human side of information security. He went beyond just hard numbers and acknowledged the softer side of our world. Since then, I have been working with Lance and have come to recognize and respect the unique traits he brings to our community. As a PhD in social science, Lance brings academic rigor to our world, but even better, he brings the skills necessary to understand *how* people and cultures work. Combined with more than 25 years of real-world, global experience in the information security field, his philosophy and practice bring immense wealth to the security sector.

What I love most about this book is that anyone can read it. Lance helps you understand what culture is and why it is an issue for information security, ultimately providing a framework to manage and measure it. I hope you are as excited as I am about this opportunity to both better understand a challenge we all face and leave this book better armed to do something about it.

–Lance Spitzner
Research & Community Director, SANS Securing The Human

Acknowledgments

A lot of people had a hand in making this book happen, both directly and indirectly, and I want to try to acknowledge all of them. I owe so much to Meghan, my editor at McGraw-Hill Education, who took a chance on an idea that she believed in and fought for. There would be no book without her. I also want to thank David, my friend and mentor for so many years. I like to tell my son that he'll have lived a fortunate life if he has a friend as good as David has been to me.

I am indebted to the entire team at McGraw-Hill Education, especially those who supported getting this book out the door. Amy, Janet, Brandi, Jared, Bill, and Anubhooti, you made this experience rewarding and challenging, and I can't tell you how thankful I am for your help and your insights. Thanks as well to the many people behind the scenes at McGraw-Hill Education who I never got to know personally, but who contributed their own efforts to this project. Big shout-outs go to Lance Spitzner, for contributions of both words and deeds as I was putting this book together. To Ira, who always gives me his honest opinion on everything, which I value more than I tell him. To Ric, for walkabouts and conversations all over the world. And to Ken, Mike, Pablo, Steve, and Troy, for being true friends in good times and bad. Also my gratitude to Dr. Phil Doty, one of the smartest people I have ever met, who first suggested I read Karl Weick all those years ago.

There is very little truly original knowledge in the world, and scholars and researchers everywhere create new contributions by mining the efforts of others who have gone before them. I am a prime example, and I want to acknowledge the work and contributions of all the academics and practitioners cited, quoted, and adapted in this book. Thank you so much for lending me such excellent shoulders to stand upon as I looked around.

Finally, a dedication is not quite enough. My wife and son deserve the last word. They gave me space and freedom, without complaint, to take on one of the most consuming activities I have ever experienced. And they did it not once, but twice. Thanks, you two.

Introduction

The origins of this book are diverse. It comes from several different ideas I've explored or been interested in over the years, ideas that traced their own individual orbits inside my head and then gradually came together into a concept I felt compelled to write about. I decided I wanted to write a book about security culture not long after I finished my first book, *IT Security Metrics*. I didn't call it "security culture" at the time or think about in those terms. I just knew after I finished the first book that I wasn't actually finished.

A good friend commented to me after reading *IT Security Metrics* that he thought one of my most important points was how valuable qualitative data and measurement can be to information security programs. It made me glad to hear him say that, because it was one of the reasons I had written the book in the first place. I wanted to add something new to a conversation that was already taking place in our industry. Having recently finished a dissertation in the social sciences, one that relied on both quantitative and qualitative research methods, I thought the security metrics literature was overemphasizing quantitative inquiry and analysis and missing out on the value of qualitative approaches. Often, security professionals I encountered criticized qualitative data and downplayed its usefulness, but these same folks many times didn't even use the term "qualitative" correctly or understand how qualitative research actually works.

In *IT Security Metrics*, my advocacy for qualitative approaches was deliberately gentle and conciliatory, toned down in the hopes that I might get some readers interested but not alienate too many of them. I still gave quantitative approaches top billing, which was fine. The book seemed to have the intended effect. Some people wanted to explore qualitative information security metrics more deeply, while those who did not could safely ignore those particular chapters.

In the years since I finished the first book, a lot of things have happened and a lot of things have changed. Perhaps the two most impactful events as far as *People-Centric Security* is concerned were a global financial crisis and a crisis of confidence in the information security industry. The former has passed, although we still feel its lingering aftermath, while we are still smack in the middle of the latter. In the case of the financial meltdown, a complex global system that had become opaque and automated broke down as a direct result of irrational human behavior. Safeguards that were meant to prevent such collapses didn't work. In the case of information security, a similarly complex global system that is also highly dependent upon technology solutions seems to be breaking down. The collapse is not as spectacular or compressed as the financial crisis was, but it still feels pretty catastrophic when every week seems to bring news reports of millions of people's data being stolen, public accusations of spying and sabotage against governments and criminal organizations alike, and trade conferences where the industry that makes security products will be the first to tell you it has failed and that literally everyone has already been successfully "owned" by the bad guys.

I found at the center of all these things interesting questions of complexity, of the limits of technology solutions, and of the power of human behavior for good and for bad. Society is becoming more technical and more social, each driving and extending the other. Social networking, sharing economies, and the Internet of Things (or Everything) promise to make our world more interconnected and more complex than ever in human history. They also promise to make the idea of people and machines being separate more meaningless than ever before. We're not exactly at the point where everyone becomes a cyborg, but in a world of wearable technology, amazing prosthetics controlled by the user's mind, and body implants with embedded computing and Wi-Fi capabilities, the idea isn't exactly hyperbole.

What happens when you can no longer tell the human infrastructure from the technology infrastructure? That's a question that has as many philosophical implications as practical ones. I'm not trying to address the philosophical points in this book. But I am going to draw a bit of a line in the sand on the practical side of the question, specifically the one that we face in information security. Culture has long been a word associated with how a particular group of people sees the world, including what that group believes and how those beliefs influence the way the group lives. Culture functions at different levels, including geographical, ethnological, and religious levels. Culture also functions at the level of organizations, such as companies and governments, which are perhaps more artificial and less organic than families, tribes, and religions, but which have come to dominate our world just as much. The company I work for has a culture. So does the information security industry. And those cultures, as much as anything else, drive why people do what they do. Our culture has become technological, so we have to understand technology to decipher it. But our technology has also become cultural. If you want to know why a technology system succeeds or fails, whether it be a financial system or an IT system, you have to also understand people.

Which brings me, if in a roundabout way, to this book. InfoSec has always preached the triad of "people, process, and technology" as essential for good, effective security. My experience in the industry has been that technology always comes first, followed by process when we can manage it, and people when we get around to them. The main role people play in information security tends to be that of a problem waiting to happen, an insider threat, a negligent user, or just an annoyance to be automated out of existence as best we can. This book is my attempt to invert that, to put people in the center of information security programs and practices. Sometimes people will be threats, but more often they will be the untapped resources with the solutions to many of security's current challenges. Thankfully, I'm not alone in believing that people-centric security is the future. The security industry is beginning to realize that technology can only take us so far. As InfoSec programs hit the point of diminishing returns on their technology investments, they must look for other reserves of effectiveness and value. I hope this book helps, in some way, to facilitate the realization of that value.

Who Should Read This Book?

I wrote this book for everyone who has ever wondered why, despite our best efforts and most sophisticated technology solutions, information security seems to be failing more now than ever. InfoSec has become so big and so dispersed across different specializations and disciplines that there's not really even a single field anymore. We have information security, IT security, information assurance, cybersecurity, and others all maybe referring to the same thing, but maybe not. As an example, throughout this book I'll refer to our field as information security, or InfoSec for short, which is indicative of my own professional history, preferences, and experience. At the leadership level, however, no matter what you call it, chief information security officers (CISOs) have to run their programs as a business, in partnership with other, non-security executives. At other levels, practitioners will have their own preferences and opinions of what constitutes our field. Everyone has their own concerns about the best way to protect the information assets that are crucial to enterprise success. That being said, there are several groups I can mention who might find value in ideas about how to measure and change security culture.

CISOs

I use "CISOs" as a catch-all to include any organization's InfoSec leadership, regardless of official title. If you're in charge of managing security for your company, you are the chief no matter what your job title is. As leaders, CISOs are the people best positioned to actually manage and change an organization's culture, including its information security culture. But you can't manage what you can't measure, so having a way to analyze and articulate security culture becomes central to impacting and improving it. The techniques and methods I lay out in this book can give CISOs that analytical capability, enabling them to add InfoSec culture to their strategic objectives and roadmaps.

Non-security Organizational Leadership

For every senior executive or board member who has struggled to understand what a CISO is talking about or to make sense of the fear, uncertainty, and doubt over security breaches bombarding them in the media, I hope this book helps to break down how security professionals think. If you can understand what motivates a person, you can find a way to work with them, to compromise for mutual benefit, and to resolve conflicts before they become dangerous. This book talks a lot about the competition between values and cultures within an organization, including values and cultures outside of the InfoSec program. My sincere hope is that non-security leaders and managers can use this book as a way to better understand information security, and where the security team is coming from in terms of values and priorities. Even better, maybe these same non-security professionals will be better able to explain to security practitioners where everyone else in the organization may be coming from, especially when those values and priorities clash. InfoSec programs are often seen as impeding rather than enabling the business, which leads to tension and conflict between stakeholders. This is, at heart, a cultural challenge, one I hope this book can help people to overcome.

Training and Awareness Teams

In the book, I refer to security training and awareness teams as the "tip of the spear" for cultural transformation in the industry today. I have a great deal of respect for anyone who takes on the challenge of educating and mentoring others, and when the subject is protecting and preserving an organization's information and technology assets, that challenge can be even greater, the stakes higher. This book is not a training and awareness book, but the methods and tools provided in the book can absolutely help security awareness programs. One major contributor to security incidents and data breaches today is that we don't include enough human and organizational behaviors in our repertoires of risk. The frameworks I offer here can help expand that knowledge base and give training teams more options and more areas of focus with which to be successful.

Security Operations

Again, I talk about "security operations" generally, as a blanket reference to all the people responsible for keeping the InfoSec program running. Whether you are an analyst, an incident response manager, a developer, or some other information security specialist, you are part of what creates and transmits your organization's security culture. That means you have power, even if it doesn't always feel that way.

This book can help give information security professionals a language with which to express what they do and why, and to communicate with others who may not understand or agree with them. I don't expect people to read this book out of some appeal to the cliché that "everyone is responsible for information security," although that's true. Instead, I would encourage you to read the book for the most self-serving of reasons, namely to be able to justify why you do things a certain way and to explain to others why they should give their support (financial, political, time) to help you get them done. The most common question I get asked by customers is if I can help them justify information security measures, activities, and budgets to upper management. In my experience, senior business leaders speak the language of culture and organizational behavior more fluently than they speak the language of technology and security. This book can help translate the cryptic dialect of InfoSec into speech that business stakeholders understand.

I have drawn on years of consulting experiences in developing the case studies and stories in this book. Names, details, and circumstances have been altered to protect the identities of specific organizations.

Companion Website

Accompanying this book are templates that you can use in your own organization to transform your information security culture. To call your attention to these templates, the Download icon has been included where these templates are referenced throughout the book. These templates, as well as other resources on organizational and InfoSec culture, are available to you for download from http://lancehayden.net/culture. The templates are fully customizable so that you can use them to their best effect within your organization.

A note on URLs. Throughout the book, I use only top-level URLs, even when pointing readers to specific documents or web pages. This is deliberate. In this age of e-books, a broken link can be troublesome, sometimes even resulting in a book being made unavailable through some vendors. To avoid this problem, I have avoided links that are more likely to change or die. In all cases, it should be a simple matter to search the site I give in the link, or the Internet more generally, for titles and authors. I apologize for any inconvenience this may cause.

Understanding Your Security Culture

Information Security: Adventures in Culture Hacking

You don't have to go digging through technology news feeds for evidence that the world of information security is in a state of crisis. Data breaches are all over the mainstream media. Enormous in scale and frightening in their implications, major security incidents seem to be happening with alarming regularity. When it is not shady criminal hackers perpetrating the theft, we worry that it might be a hostile government gearing up for a new kind of warfare, or even our own government embracing a new age of Orwellian surveillance possibilities. And the message that resonates from the pages of information security industry magazines and websites to the keynote speeches of industry conferences and the marketing brochures of product and services vendors is, *InfoSec is broken somehow—it doesn't seem to work anymore.*

Maybe. Society has undergone profound changes with the widespread adoption of digital, networked information technologies. Some theorists speculate that these changes are structural, representing not just new features of traditional society, but new definitions of society itself. In this view, we are going through changes like those that happened when human beings stopped being nomadic and established agriculture and villages, or like the transformations that took place during the Enlightenment, or as a result of the Industrial Revolution.

Such evolution means that everyone, including the information security industry, better be ready for changes unlike anything we've previously experienced. Technology has become social, centered around people, and information security must become equally people-centric if it hopes to succeed. We not only have to do things better, but we have to invent whole new ways of doing them. That means looking at things that have traditionally made security experts, especially technologists and engineers, uncomfortable. Things that are hard to measure or automate. Things like people, including their beliefs and assumptions as much as their behavior. Things like culture.

Burnt Bacon

I first realized the power of culture in information security a few years ago at a supplier conference hosted by a customer. Dozens of reps from different vendors filled a large hotel ballroom reserved by our host. After we had all grabbed our coffees and sat down, the executive running the event called the meeting to order with a safety briefing. He introduced us to our safety officer, let's call him Bob, who also worked for the customer. Bob was not an executive or even a manager. But before turning over the microphone to Bob, the executive made it clear that, in terms of our physical safety and security, for the next two days Bob might as well be the CEO.

I had not expected the briefing, but I wasn't very surprised. The company running the conference operated in several hazardous industries and prided itself on the "culture of safety" it instilled in employees. Bob spent about five minutes running us through a review of safety protocols for the event, pointing out all the exits, telling us which we should use in the event of an emergency, and even declaring a rallying point across the street. Should something happen that required us to leave the building, everyone was required to meet at the rallying point for a headcount prior to returning or taking whatever other actions Bob deemed appropriate. Once he had finished, Bob took his post at the back of the ballroom and the day's activities commenced.

I *was* surprised when we returned from the first day's lunch break and the executive again handed Bob the mike so that he could repeat the same briefing we had listened to only four hours before. "Wow," I thought. "These people take safety seriously." I had never experienced that kind of briefing before at any of my own company's meetings, much less two in the same day at the same event!

Coincidence is a funny thing. Just over an hour after our post-lunch briefing, the hotel fire alarm began to wail. On reflex, everyone turned around to look at Bob, who immediately slipped out of the room. Within a minute, the alarm stopped. A minute or two later Bob returned with one of the hotel managers in tow, who was obviously trying to explain something. I watched Bob shake his head "no," prompting the manager to leave. Ten minutes later, I was standing with my fellow vendor representatives across the street as Bob took a head count.

We found out later that the manager had contacted Bob to tell him the fire alarm had been triggered by a small grease fire in the kitchen, but that it had been contained and posed no danger to our meeting. Bob had not bought the explanation and had triggered an evacuation anyway. We were the only ones to leave the hotel after the alarm, and we caught more than a few curious glances from people passing by. Once Bob was satisfied everyone was present and that the hotel was not actually on fire, he gave the all clear and we filed back into our seats in the ballroom. Despite the minor nature of the fire and the fact that unnecessarily evacuating had cost us nearly an hour of our packed schedule, the executive never gave a hint of annoyance. Instead, he called us back to order by spending another few minutes praising Bob's decision and reminding us that, for his company, safety came before anything else.

The second morning of the conference consisted of breakout sessions scattered in smaller rooms throughout the hotel conference center, but they began only after our morning safety briefing was complete. We broke again for lunch, and when we returned to the ballroom in the afternoon, the executive was waiting for us. He was not happy. Standing in front of the room, he held up one of the vendor packets each of us had received at the start. Stamped "Highly Confidential" on every page, the packets were the blueprints of the company's forward-looking IT strategy, including strategic competitive differentiators enabled by technology adoption.

Waving the packet slowly so that we all could see it, the executive chewed us out, describing how the document he held had been discovered in one of the empty breakout rooms during lunch, left there by someone in the room. He explained with obvious irritation that such blatant disregard for protecting sensitive corporate data was unacceptable, especially in a room that included many information security professionals. If it happened again, he warned us, there would be hell to pay. And with that, we started up again, beginning once again with our mandatory safety briefing.

Safe and Not Secure

An important characteristic of culture is that it tends to be invisible, functioning just below our conscious awareness of its influence. But that often changes when we find our own cultural norms challenged, and suddenly we see patterns and conflicts jumping out at us from the shadows. Take, for example, the stark contrast between my customer's *safety* culture, where the response to the possibility of an incident brought all business to a stop and triggered emergency action plans, and the customer's *security* culture, where an actual security incident resulted in nothing more than a stern talking-to. The two completely divergent responses to essentially the same thing, a failure incident, made the differences between the safety and security cultures of my customer stand out from one another like black and white. "Wow," I thought, "one of these things is not like the other." It was astounding.

My customer believed they had a strong culture of safety. They also believed they had a strong information security culture. But culture is defined by behaviors, not beliefs. The completely different behaviors they exhibited between the two incidents showed where their priorities really lay. Had the executive treated the failure to secure sensitive information like Bob had treated a burnt rasher of bacon, we would have stopped the proceedings immediately until he resolved the problem. Instead of ordering an evacuation, he would have ordered everyone in the room to hold up their vendor packets. The documents were controlled, and at least one person would not have had one.

What Were You Thinking?

I found myself obsessing over the experience for the rest of the day. It distracted me from focusing on the presentations and the interactive sessions. I was distant and disengaged. Why had the executive just let that security incident slide so easily? He had been visibly angry over it, but he could have done much more than scold us. Was he worried about embarrassing people? Had the evacuation thrown us so far off schedule that he was just trying to make up for lost time and not delay the event further? Thinking that maybe he intended to follow up later and try to track down the perpetrator some other way, I checked for unique identifiers on my packet that could have tracked it back to me directly. I found nothing of the sort.

For a little while, I got depressed. I had traveled a long way to attend a meeting that was all about how important security was to this company, only to watch a senior executive get upstaged by a junior employee when it came to taking action in the face of risk. The response to the security incident called into question the whole purpose of the conference. If the company wasn't going to take action when faced with a security breach involving one of their own information security vendors, how were they ever going to protect themselves from the real bad guys? It would all be technology products and lip service. They didn't care enough to make a real change. I found myself thinking, "They should put Bob in charge of information security."

Then I realized something else. I considered the real, physical harm that I knew this company had seen as a result of lapses in workplace safety. People had been injured on the job, had even died, in the decades that the firm had been working in the industry. I knew the firm had also experienced information security breaches in the past, but my impression was that these failures had rarely risen above the level of a moderate inconvenience. People had a bad day, to be sure, but at the end of it everyone went home safely. If the information security culture was not as strong as the safety culture, it was because the world of information security just didn't *feel* as dangerous as the world of workplace safety. No matter what they said, this company could not think about data security the same way they thought about physical safety. Those cultures could exist side by side, but the assumptions and beliefs that drive behavior, born of experience and observation, were just not the same. I was fascinated and, once more able to focus on the customer, made a mental promise to research the topic further.

So here we are.

Culture Hacking

This book is about culture. It is about understanding it and about transforming it. You can even say it's about hacking it. And when I say *hacking*, I mean hacking in an old-school sense, the hacking that Steven Levy described in *Hackers: Heroes of the Computer Revolution*. Before the term evolved (some might say devolved) into today's more familiar usage, with all its implied negativity and criminal inferences, hacking described a process of gaining knowledge about a system by exploring and deconstructing it. This knowledge would then be put to use to make that system better, more innovative and elegant. The MIT hackers that Levy wrote about dealt in computer software, the programs and digital code that define how those systems function. But systems, code, and hacking don't stop there.

Software of the Mind

Researchers and experts in organizational culture talk about their topic in ways that would not be completely unfamiliar to computer engineers. There are many frameworks and metaphors for describing organizational culture, but all converge on the idea that culture is a shared set of norms, values, and routines that serves to define how people behave together in organized group settings. If you have ever started a new job, then you have probably experienced a cultural shift as you had to learn how things were done at your new organization, and maybe some of those things were completely foreign to you. But as you learned the ropes, as the culture was transmitted to you and you became part of it, things that you had to think about became automatic and unconscious behaviors. It's almost like the organization programmed you to function within it.

Geert Hofstede, one of the more influential scholars in the field, talks about organizational culture in just this way. For Hofstede, culture is "software of the mind" that allows individuals to align their thoughts, beliefs, and actions in order to solve specific problems. Nowhere does Hofstede, or any other culture researcher I am familiar with, claim that people are programmable in the same way computers are. But these experts do look at organizations as complex systems that share similarities with computers and networks.

By using metaphors drawn from software and computing, we can conceptualize and identify means of understanding how culture can be observed, measured, and changed. Thinking about organizational culture as a different kind of software, with its own codes and programming techniques, makes the hacking analogy a lot more applicable. In fact, the security industry already uses the analogy all the time when talking about social engineering. The idea of hacking people is not new or even very controversial in our industry. But social engineering has always focused primarily on individuals, treating each potential victim as an independent system that must be exploited. You can automate social engineering, as does an attacker who conducts mass phishing attempts by using automated group e-mail tools, but this only allows the attacker to target individuals more quickly and efficiently. It's simply a question of scale.

Hacking culture is different from hacking computers. It means understanding and exploring the relationships between people, the drives and motivations that cause many unique individuals to behave in very similar ways, as a group. Instead of trying to affect the behavior of individual people making specific decisions, a culture hacker is more interested in understanding and changing the entire group's behavior, by changing what that group thinks and believes. Part of hacking is about elegance and efficiency, the ability to produce the greatest effect with the least effort. If you focus on my individual behaviors, trying to change them one at a time, you will be lost in an infinity of inputs and outputs. But if you are able to understand and change my beliefs and assumptions, you will have tapped into the programming that drives all my decisions.

Hacking a person's belief systems may seem kind of creepy, and culture hacking can certainly be put to evil uses. But hacking has never just been about breaking into computer systems illegally or immorally for illicit gain. That's a narrow definition that has, unfortunately, come to be the most associated meaning of the word, thanks to the media and, ironically enough, the security industry. But hacking is much more than that, with a longer history than the one information security has tried to impose on it. Culture hacking is similar. I didn't invent the concept, and it's been around for a long time. I just believe it's a very useful way to think about the challenge of people-centric security.

A Brief History of Culture Hacking

The first people to call themselves culture hackers came from the worlds of activism, fashion, and art. They wanted to shape the way the world looked at itself, to shake up the status quo, and to pull the curtains back on people's preconceived notions. For Mike Myatt, a leadership expert and author, hacking in organizations involves breaking down existing codes and complexity, finding alternatives, and replacing out-of-date or inefficient processes. That's old-school hacking.

Culture hacking is pre-digital, going back to practices like billboard jamming, literally changing the messages on real-world roadside billboards from advertisements to more ironic or anti-corporate messages. These techniques date back to the 1970s, developing in parallel with phone phreaking and the beginning of computer hacking. It wasn't about stealing or defacing private property; it was about retaking control of the system from those who had corrupted it, to make it free again. This was the '70s, remember.

Though it started out fueled by flower power, culture hacking has proven remarkably resilient. As the world changed, so did the focus of the movement. Culture hacking and technology merged with the creation of groups like the

Adbusters Media Foundation, which both uses and critiques digital technologies. In 2011, Adbusters was central in creating the Occupy Wall Street movement. Throughout its history, the mission of culture hackers was to reshape behavior by targeting basic social programming, usually with an anti-authoritarian and anti-corporate bias, just like many of the early computer hackers.

Whether or not you grok the whole anti-establishment theme, hacking (computers or cultures) is a set of techniques and tools for exploring and deconstructing complex systems for the express purpose of changing them, making them work differently, evolving them. Depending on what side of the fence you are on, this can be a process of innovation or a process of manipulation and abuse. But then again, you can say that of just about any tool. A hammer can easily become a nasty weapon.

Security Culture: Hack or Be Hacked

I believe that culture is the single most important untapped resource for improving information security today. Security is not a technology challenge. If it were, technology would have fixed the problems a long time ago. Security is a people challenge, a social and organizational challenge. It's a cultural challenge.

People, and how to deal with them, seem to especially baffle information security professionals, to the point where we have trouble even talking about the human beings that make up our organizations as anything other than problems to be dealt with, insider threats to be identified and managed, or risks to be mitigated, preferably by automating them away. When we do think about people, we tend to think of them as targets for attack or accidents waiting to happen. Steeped as the industry is in a background of engineering and applied technology, we can be deeply ambivalent about the qualitative, the emotional, or the political—in other words, all the things that make up the organizational cultures in which information security has to operate. Given the industry's mistrust of people in general, it's not very surprising that the idea of people-centric security has taken a while to gain traction.

The industry is changing, becoming more cognizant of the importance of people to the successful protection of information assets and information supply chains throughout the global digital economy. We're not changing because we have suddenly seen the light and developed a new appreciation for the chaotic and irrational human networks we must secure. We're changing, at least in part, because we've tried everything else, it's still not working, and we're desperate. And that's okay. Sitting in my vendor conference, I had the epiphany that my hosts didn't take information security seriously because they had never experienced any really serious problems related to it, certainly not like they had with physical accidents and losses. I was sure that as soon as they did experience a catastrophic information security event, they would attack the problem with the same commitment and zeal that had created their impressively formidable safety culture. Today's information security environment is changing dramatically. Today you either hack your own culture or you wait for someone to do it for (or to) you.

Who's Hacking Your Security Culture?

Think for a moment about the culture hackers in your own security program. They may not be immediately apparent. Your first thought might be the security awareness team, if your organization has one. These brave souls are presently the tip of the spear when it comes to security culture transformation, although we will see in later chapters that the challenge they face is often impossibly idealistic. But if you are looking for those folks beating the behavioral drum and trying to change the way the entire company thinks about security, awareness teams are top of mind.

Security awareness managers are probably not the only ones socially engineering your organization's security beliefs and practices. Think about your auditors, for example. Audits, particularly those for regulatory or industry standards like the Payment Card Industry Data Security Standard (PCI DSS) or Sarbanes-Oxley, have a material effect on a company's ability to do business. Internal audit and compliance teams are responsible for making sure the company doesn't fail audits, and they do their best to transmit and instill certain beliefs and rituals into the larger enterprise. A strong audit culture is unlikely to believe, for instance, that documented processes are unnecessary or that every employee should have complete access to every system in order to stay agile. Given the importance of maintaining compliance, auditors also typically have the power to reprogram the organization's focus and activities, even if only temporarily.

Finally, think about the project manager or line manager who has no direct responsibility for security but can reward or punish his employees based on their job performance, through promotions and pay raises, or even by firing poor performers. Every organization has priorities, and these do not always align. In fact, they can compete directly, a situation we often see in information security as a sort of Rubik's Cube effect, in which improving one part of the problem makes another part worse.

Imagine our project manager running a software development team working on a new product. Bringing the project in on time and on budget is a major priority for the company. So, too, is ensuring that the product does not have security vulnerabilities. What happens when there is not enough time to do both? For example, suppose a developer realizes she has seven days to finish her work before deadline but that a full security review will take ten days. She could go to her manager and tell him that she will complete the review, because security is a priority, but that the project will be late to market. Her manager's response will be key. Whether he gives her praise, like Bob received when he put safety first and evacuated over a minor incident, or punishes her with the loss of a bonus or maybe even her job for delaying the project, he will show everyone what the company values most. When that choice comes up again, everyone will know what to do.

Now imagine that you are the security awareness manager for this example firm, or another member of the security team. If the cultural bias is toward deadlines, how can your values compete? Security awareness suddenly becomes more complex than just making sure all the developers know the policies on secure coding and testing. Our developer was already aware of her responsibility for security. But if management rewards and punishes based on project deadlines, or budgets, or some other factor, no amount of handwringing, training sessions, or posters on the wall will change a developer's empirical understanding that security comes second. That's cultural engineering.

Security, Hack Thyself

You don't have to have a graduate degree in organizational psychology to become a culture hacker, any more than you need one in computer science to become a technology hacker. What you do need is a new way of looking at your organizational environment and the people in it, which requires imagination and a willingness to experiment. Technology hackers don't let others tell them what the system can or cannot do, but instead figure it out for themselves by exploring the system. If you want to hack culture, you have to learn how the culture really works, not just what everyone thinks or expects of it.

The closest this book gets to a manifesto—and a first principle that anyone seeking to transform their security culture must become comfortable with—concerns the role of people in information security. In a people-centric security program, human beings matter every bit as much as technology, and probably quite a bit more. Technology enables people, not the other way around. Technology neither cares nor suffers if it is hacked or compromised, at least not yet. If you were to throw every IT asset your company owns out the window tonight, tomorrow morning when everyone shows up for work you would still have an organization.

Kick out all the people, on the other hand, and tomorrow you will have a warehouse full of stuff with no one left to care about whether or not it's secure.

Computer systems are immensely complicated, designed and built from hardware and software, governed by extraordinarily intricate architectures and millions of lines of programmatic code. For all that, computers have finite limits to their capabilities. People define what computers can do, and they do only what they have been programmed to do, even in situations where those possibilities are not what the programmers expected or intended. There are always clear reasons for a computer's behavior, at least once you have tracked down those reasons to root causes. But complexity is different. Complex systems produce emergent behaviors, an infinite possibility of outcomes that is impossible to predict. Those behaviors may not be consistent, or even rational. People and social systems are complex in ways that a computer can never be just on its own. But plugging a computer into a social system like a company or a government creates new avenues for complexity and emergent behavior. People-centric security recognizes that focusing on technology systems alone will always be a losing battle because technology-centric security is invariably outflanked by emergent human behavior. The moment you think you're covering all the angles, someone will figure out how to square a circle and produce four more new angles where none previously existed.

Hacking your security culture, as opposed to hacking your IT infrastructure, means digging into the forces that motivate people's security-related behaviors within your organization. You have to analyze not only what your systems do, but what people are doing with them, how they are adapting them to new and innovative purposes. Some of these new uses will create risk, but also opportunity. Culture defines the interface between users and systems. If you want to transform your organization's security culture, to make it better and more efficient at protecting organizational assets, you have to pull apart the people system as well as the process and technology systems, so that you know all of them inside and out. It isn't enough to just observe what people do, or do with the technology at their disposal. You have to understand why they do it, and try to consider all the possible alternative decisions they could have made, rather than just the one that may seem obvious or expected.

In the years since I sat in that hotel conference room and realized the differences between a culture of safety and a culture of security, I have observed dozens of other organizations' InfoSec cultures. Every one has had something to teach me. Even when I cannot get a customer to think about culture as much as I might like, they always manage to keep me thinking about it. And I can tell you that culture hacking in the security space is a zesty enterprise, regardless of whether the organization is even aware they are doing it.

Culture Hacks: The Good

It's always great to work with an organization that takes culture seriously, without discounting it as too vague or paying lip service to its importance but never really trying to change it. I've even encountered a few organizations that embraced the cultural transformation of information security full on, with all the messiness and uncertainty that come with that sort of work. In the case of one particular organization, I had come in to help them define a new enterprise security framework, a governance program that would tie together all the disparate and sometimes dysfunctional silos and pockets of security ownership that had grown up organically over the life of the company. As we walked through the various options for designing the new program, the security team kept trying to articulate what they really were trying to achieve. They had needs and requirements that spanned people, processes, and technology, and our conversations often got specific and detailed on one or more desired outcomes, but nothing ever seemed to completely hit the mark. "Yes," they would say, "we need that. But we need much more."

The organization was intrigued by ISO 27001, the international standard for security program management, and asked me a lot of questions about what I thought of it. I told them I thought very highly of ISO 27001. When properly and conscientiously implemented, ISO 27001 can function as a very powerful governance framework, one that I also think happens to be the most people-centric security standard out there today. I told my customer so.

"But ISO isn't for everyone," I cautioned. "It's not about technology or even controls. The standard is about changing what your whole organization thinks and believes when it comes to information security. Implementing ISO to me is about driving a process of cultural transformation in regard to security across the entire enterprise."

The team members' eyes lit up. Eureka! That was exactly what they had been struggling to articulate. They didn't just want a new security program, they wanted a whole new security culture. "We don't want to just change the mechanics," they explained, "or to switch out one set of controls or one best practices framework for another. We want to change what security means to the company, and we want to change it for every single person who works here regardless of rank or role." Amen, I thought.

That's a good culture hack, or at least the beginning of one. The security team wanted to change behavior, but recognized that behavior grew out of something deeper. That was where they wanted to concentrate their efforts. It helped that the company was already a self-consciously strong culture. The idea of social identity and shared beliefs permeated its business. The security team already had a template and a language that were familiar to them. Believing in the power of culture in general makes it a lot easier to see the benefits of improving security culture in particular.

Culture Hacks: The Bad

Not every organization thinks in terms of transforming their information security program or culture. Some security teams are so swamped just keeping on top of operational activities and deadlines that thinking about why they do things the way they do, or whether they could do them better, seems like a luxury. It's hard to think about a five-year improvement plan when the auditors are coming next week. In fact, compliance drives so much security activity today that it's probably the main motivation companies have for taking security as seriously as they do. ISO 27001 is a voluntary security standard, but most companies are dealing with the nonvoluntary sort. PCI DSS for credit card processors, Sarbanes-Oxley internal control requirements for publicly traded companies, HIPAA regulations in healthcare, along with a slew of other local, national, and transnational regulatory regimes may put constant demands on the attention of the Chief Information Security Officer (CISO).

Security compliance efforts are a bit of an attempt at culture hacking themselves. Regulators and industry groups develop compliance requirements as a means of forcing organizations to take security more seriously. This is great insofar as it improves the final product. But when compliance replaces security as the goal, cultural transformation backfires. It's like the old Zen warning not to mistake the finger pointing at the moon for the moon itself. Compliance is not the same thing as security, as has been made painfully clear by recent security incidents where auditors had previously signed off on the very systems that ended up being compromised.

I've observed more than one organization where the security culture has been trained and conditioned by compliance programs to equate successful audits with good security. Even when certain folks inside the organization know better—and often these are the security operations people, who know how the sausage is made, so to speak—the shared assumption is that if the auditors are happy, the organization must be secure. That, too, is a form of cultural transformation, just not a good one.

Culture hacks are bad when they make the system easier but don't actually solve the problem. Knowledge of the system is partial or incomplete, making a culture hacker feel like they have accomplished something more than they actually have. To extend the metaphor, those who put total faith in a one-size-fits-all compliance checklist are like cultural script kiddies, interested more in quick results than in deep and lasting change.

Culture Hacks: The Ugly

Even when the efforts at cultural change are unsophisticated or incomplete, the people trying to change things usually have good intentions. Most security teams are passionate about what they do and are deeply concerned with making their systems safer and stronger. But there will always be outliers, individuals and organizations whose security behaviors are so egregious that you almost have to think they want to fail.

I visited an organization once where the security management team members were some of the most arrogant jerks I had ever met. Even though I had been hired to help them, they belittled and second-guessed everything I or my team said. When we asked if they had a particular control or process, they would roll their eyes. "Of course we have that," was the answer. "That's security 101. Is that all you smart consultants can ask us?"

In the organization's defense, it did have a formidable set of controls in place. A lot of highly sensitive data passed through its systems, and the information security team made it difficult within those systems to share the data without jumping through administrative hoops. "We lock our people down tight," senior leaders bragged to us. "No one gets up to any funny business."

When we moved on from the leadership and started interviewing employees who were lower on the organizational chart, we asked about the intense levels of control the organization had put in place. Many of our interview subjects grinned at the questions, then told us stories of how much of a pain it was to share information efficiently.

"Those senior guys you talked to," one employee told us, "all have personal webmail accounts they've set up. When they want to share things quickly, they just bypass the controls and attach stuff to their personal e-mails and share it."

We were shocked. "But they said you guys couldn't do anything like that," we protested.

"Oh, sure. We can't. They don't trust us, and they think everyone who is not a manager is an idiot. But it's not a problem for them. That's just the way things work around here."

Security Is People!

This book is about giving organizations and the people responsible for securing them a new set of concepts and techniques. I'm not trying to replace technology or process as effective tools that are needed in information security. But I am trying to give people, the often neglected third leg of the people-process-technology triad, their proper place. People-centric security means looking at the human element of data protection as more than just another threat vector. People-centric security implies that without people there is no security, nor any need for it. Process and technology are there to support people, both from a security perspective and for the entire organization. Nobody starts out with security but no information to protect. Security needs are born when an organization's information supply chain starts producing valuable assets that demand protection. People define when that occurs, people make protection happen, and people are responsible when security fails.

Culture acts as a powerful engine of organizational security, and in subsequent chapters I'll go into lots of detail about what culture is and how it drives human behavior. But the core premise of everything that will follow is this: if you want to really change how security works, you have to change the culture operating beneath it. Just because security has struggled with the human equation in the past doesn't mean it must continue to baffle us in the future. In fact, it can't. Our world is social, and our technologies are increasingly social. Our security must be social too, retirement puns notwithstanding. People-centric, then. Security is people!

Further Reading

▶ Adbusters: Journal of the Mental Environment. Available at www.adbusters.org.

▶ Hofstede, Geert, Gert Jan Hofstede, and Michael Minkov. *Cultures and Organizations: Software of the Mind.* 3rd ed. New York: McGraw-Hill, 2010.

▶ Levy, Steven. *Hackers: Heroes of the Computer Revolution.* 25th Anniversary Edition. Sebastopol, CA: O'Reilly, 2010.

▶ Myatt, Michael. *Hacking Leadership: The 11 Gaps Every Business Needs to Close and the Secrets to Closing Them Quickly.* Hoboken, NJ: Wiley, 2013.

Strategy for Breakfast: The Hidden Power of Security Culture

For an industry that is so grounded in engineering and technology, information security can appear quite unscientific to those outside of the field. Your organization's information security team can probably inundate you with reams of data about security operations and posture, including product performance benchmarks, security event logs, patches applied, and events counted. But the industry struggles to satisfactorily answer the question of why one organization's security strategy seems to protect the organization, while another's efforts fail miserably. It's almost like fate or the wrath of the gods is involved. We seem to know everything about how information security works except how it actually works. That is not because information security is inherently mystical or more art than science. Security fails because strategy is not enough. Management guru Peter Drucker summed up the problem in a phrase: "culture eats strategy for breakfast." Too often, security programs searching for the reasons why they failed in their technology or their strategy are simply looking in the wrong place for answers.

Why Security Fails

I have a presentation I often give to customers and deliver at industry conferences, a thought exercise to demonstrate how security can fail even in the face of controls and commitment to ensuring that it does not. It's a naturally visual thought experiment, but I'll try to commit to something more narrative in the following pages. You can find an actual video presentation at http://lancehayden.net/culture.

We Start with a Design

Suppose we want to build a new system, or maybe protect an existing one. It can be a technology system or an organizational system, a machine or a corporate process, or even a global financial system…it doesn't matter. We begin with a design for the system. In the case of a new system, we create that design. If the system already exists, we may just document the existing design. However we do it, we end up with something we'll call System 1. Now, we may know only a little about this system or a lot, but one thing we always know for certain is that there are conditions under which the system will fail. We may not know exactly when or how such failure will occur, but we know it is inevitable given the right circumstances. We may, in some cases, be able to test for failure, but in many other cases that won't be possible. Failure in this system is like a cliff in the dark, a precipice at night that we can't see until it is too late and we are about to tumble over it. We're afraid of it, waiting for us out there in the darkness, and all we know is that we never want to get too close in our wanderings. See Figure 2-1 for a simple picture of this scenario.

To make the metaphor concrete, let's extend an example I touched on briefly in Chapter 1. Imagine a company that produces commercial software products. The design we are interested in is the production system that makes the programs the company sells. The system is made up of people, processes, and technologies, all existing within the context of software development. Engineers and developers write the code that goes into the company's products. Managers supervise the engineers and developers. Customers depend on the end products that the company sells. Within this system is Clara, a developer who has worked for the company for several years.

There are many ways the software production system might fail, but we'll concentrate specifically on security events. Narrowing our focus even further, we know that mistakes Clara might make while writing her code could have deleterious effects, perhaps by introducing vulnerabilities into the company's

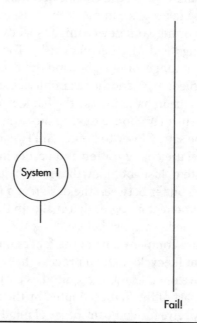

Figure 2-1   *System 1 and the failure line*

software products, to use one example. If a product hits the market with a serious vulnerability, one that results in a zero-day exploit being created that completely compromises the software, then the development system will have experienced a major failure. But that edge is extremely difficult to see, and Clara's company may only find out it is in a state of free fall when journalists or law enforcement agencies start calling.

Warning Signs

If we were dealing with a real cliff, we might put up a fence. We could build it far enough back that there would be no danger of people getting too close to the edge as they wander around at night. We could hang lighted warning signs saying, "Danger! Go No Further! Cliff!" And, having done this, we could reasonably expect that we have managed the risk of someone having an unfortunate accident.

It turns out we do very much the same thing in other systems that we design. Not knowing exactly where the failure point is, we *hedge*, putting in place thresholds and boundaries that we believe provide a healthy buffer between us and our theoretical point of no return. We call this our *risk tolerance level*, and it is a measure of the risk we can live with, the chance of failure that we find acceptable.

As mentioned, hedging takes place in many systems. For example, the manufacturer of a server or network device might specify a temperature range outside of which operating the device becomes risky. The device may work just fine at the extremes of that range, or even beyond them, but pushing the limits is like dancing on the cliff edge. As another example, a banker might decide to keep a certain ratio of assets on hand in case the bank experiences losses or a run on the bank occurs, and she may choose to keep more on hand than she thinks she'll ever need, just to be safe. Closer to home, an IT manager might implement controls in the form of secure configuration and hardening standards that apply to any production IT system. Just about anything can be made to play the role of the fence when building a buffer between the design and its failure, including the same people, processes, and technologies that make up the system. Figure 2-2 illustrates this protective hedge against failure.

In our example software company, one of the fences built for security purposes is a software development lifecycle (SDLC) process that explicitly includes security reviews. Our developer, Clara, is required as part of her job to perform certain security tests as part of the SDLC adopted by the firm. These tests, among them a source code review, give the company peace of mind that reasonable measures are in place to keep failures associated with vulnerable code from happening.

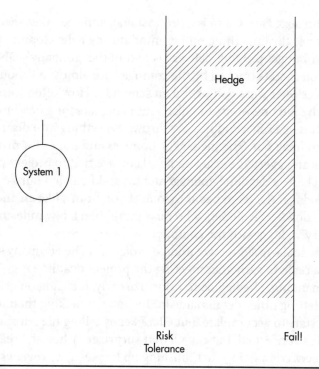

Figure 2-2   *Risk tolerance and hedging against failure*

Doing More with Less

Now everything looks good for our example software company. The company has a system designed to produce quality software for its customers. Part of that quality is a commitment to security. And the company has designed protective processes into the system in the form of SDLC security to make sure that Clara never gets too close to the cliff. Management sleeps well at night.

The problem with this happy scenario is that it rarely plays out so perfectly in the real world. For Clara, working in a high-speed software company is rewarding, but stressful. Like most organizations, Clara's company does not have unlimited resources and has high expectations of employee productivity. The development team seems to be constantly short a couple of software engineers, and the market is always demanding new and improved versions of the company's products. Project deadlines for code delivery can be brutal, and Clara's job sometimes feels like she's running one marathon after another, sprinting to the finish line just in time to start the next race. Clara is a professional, and she takes security seriously. But security is not the only thing on her mind during a development project.

On-time, on-budget product delivery is part of the company's DNA. Clara knows this. Project stats tracked by the company are almost all about completion. How many milestones were completed on schedule? How often were they completed early? No one wants to talk about being late for a deadline. Missing project deadlines by even a couple days throws everything into disarray and causes management to freak out. The managers' bonuses and hopes for promotion, just like Clara's and everyone else's on her team, are tied to project performance metrics. If you blow a deadline, management is suddenly in your face, and even your friends on the team begin to look at you funny, like an anchor that is dragging them down. Developers who miss more than a few milestone deadlines tend not to survive long with the company.

During a particularly aggressive update project for the company's flagship product, Clara realizes early that meeting the project deadline is going to be extremely demanding. She begins to prioritize early, focusing on critical-path activities and letting other details slide in the hope of picking them up later. SDLC security tasks start to accumulate, but Clara keeps telling herself she'll get caught up later. So she's concerned, but not all that surprised, when she realizes ten days before the project completion that finishing up her security reviews and testing is going to take two full weeks. Now Clara has a decision to make. She knows how important security is to the firm, and to her personally. She *wants* to tell her boss the deadline will need to slip to accommodate the SDLC requirements, but she also knows that doing so could mean the end of her career at the company. Clara feels as though she's caught between two opposing forces. The SDLC is like a barrier in front of her, holding her back until she finishes the whole job. But behind her is a crowd of people, surging and pushing her against that barrier unrelentingly, trying to force it to give so that she can finish on time. Figure 2-3 illustrates the forces acting on Clara.

In the end, the pressure of the deadline overwhelms the influence of the SDLC security review policies. Clara likes her job, and she needs that bonus for a long-overdue tropical vacation. So she crosses her fingers and chooses. She'll complete as much of the security review as she possibly can in ten days, but then she's handing off that code.

Who Moved My Fence?

Unless someone notices and calls Clara out on her incomplete review, it's unlikely that anything bad will happen. In Clara's company, the SDLC is a set of guidelines

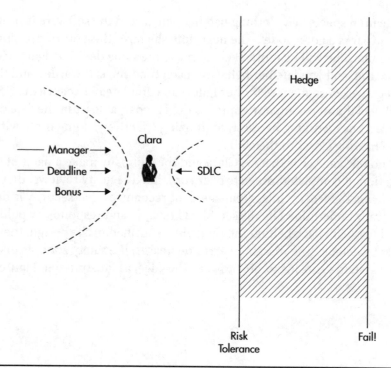

Figure 2-3   *Opposing forces influencing Clara's decision*

and policies. The developers hold themselves accountable for compliance, with some periodic spot checking by management and auditors. The odds are in Clara's favor. No one notices that she's cut a few corners on the security reviews. In fact, life for Clara is good. Her boss is giddy that his team managed to pull off such an aggressive update on time. Sales is happy to have a product to deliver. The customer is satisfied with the new features. Once again, the company has lived up to its reputation for reliable delivery. Clara gets a good bonus and lots of praise for balancing priorities effectively.

Clara regrets that she skimped on security, but it's obvious to her that she made the right decision. If she had delayed delivery to dot all the security i's and cross all the t's, the whole situation would have ended differently, and probably badly for her. She's pretty sure she wouldn't be flying to Maui at the end of the month.

Clara has experienced a powerful feedback loop, created by the requirement for her to manage two opposing sets of expectations. Living up to one set meant everything worked out and Clara prospered. Now her boss thinks she's a rock star, and her team respects her. Nothing bad happened, and the software is probably fine, since Clara's a good coder. The next time she faces this sort of decision, Clara will remember. She will be more likely to make the same decision again. Her peers will notice too, and emulate her behavior. Each time she is rewarded and there are no negative consequences for her failure to complete her security reviews, Clara will feel that the company approves of her lapse, at least in the face of the alternatives. She's working her best, optimizing effectively, doing more with less. She's also moving closer to the cliff.

What no one can see is that, as Clara and the company make a habit of the prioritization of completed projects over completed security reviews, they are slowly moving the fence. Unless management recognizes that security is being systematically undermined by missed SDLC reviews and responds by pulling Clara and her team back behind the safety line specified in the design, then that line shifts by default. The margin of error decreases, the safety zone shrinks, and the whole system drifts inexorably toward the edge, as illustrated in Figure 2-4.

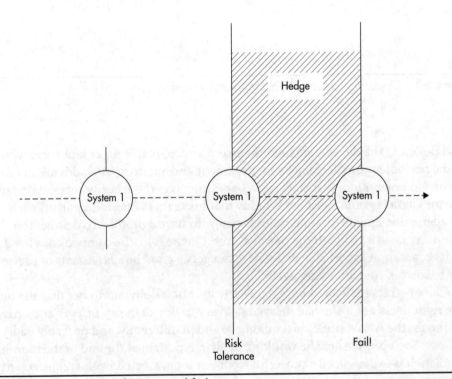

Figure 2-4   *The system drifting toward failure*

Look Out Below!

Then the day comes when a vulnerability in one of the company's products spawns an exploit that is used to attack a customer, resulting in a very public security breach. In the ensuing investigation and root cause analysis, the failure is traced back to code Clara developed. People start demanding explanations. How could this happen? How could the company, and Clara in particular, be so negligent? Investigators and auditors begin to ask, "Don't you have processes in place to review the security of your code?" "Well of course we do," the company responds. "But in this case they were not followed appropriately." Further digging reveals systematic problems. Many SDLC-mandated security reviews were never completed. The risk management design—the fence that people depended on and assumed was functioning properly—existed only on paper. Overnight, Clara goes from being a model employee, rewarded and admired, to being incompetent, negligent even, and perhaps worse. No one is singing her praises now, as everyone looks for a scapegoat. Her manager says he never knew Clara had violated policy, which was supposed to make security reviews automatic. Clara will be lucky to keep her job.

The company's management, now faced with a crisis that is more than just a one-off fluke, decides that the system itself is flawed and needs to be changed. "We need a completely new SDLC system," they say to one another, "maybe one that is fully automated." The CIO puts out an RFP for consulting to help them rebuild the broken processes. The result, after six months and a large bucket of money? System 2, which is better and is designed to overcome the weaknesses that got Clara into trouble. Of course, no system can be perfect, and knowing that this new system will also have a failure point, one that is hard to predict, hard to see until you've gotten too close, the company makes sure to build in appropriate levels of risk tolerance, key controls to make sure that security is properly prioritized, and up goes a bright, shiny, new fence to keep everyone back from the edge...

Getting the Drift

The phenomenon this case study describes is what failure studies scholar Sidney Dekker calls "drifting" into failure states, and it has nothing to do with any deliberately bad behavior on the part of Clara or anyone else. On the contrary, up to the point of failure, Clara was doing everything right. Faced with competing priorities and insufficient resources to accomplish everything that was expected of her, Clara had to make trade-offs. Her environment was a complex system, full of intertwined demands and emergent consequences for each decision.

By focusing on the design of a strategy to prevent failure, rather than the incompatible and unresolved demands on Clara's time that actually led to the failure, the company should really have zero confidence that System 2 will escape the same eventual fate.

When I give this presentation, I often see heads nodding in agreement in the audience. The drift analogy obviously resonates with people I talk to, who see within it their own situations and struggles. But drift explains more than just information security's struggle to maintain effective protective postures over time. Dekker explored failure in everything from commercial aviation to financial crises. Security is not unique; it's just another complex system. And this type of slow movement toward failure, brought about by competing imperatives that prove incompatible with all of an organization's strategies and goals, can be seen in any complex system. As one goal is optimized, the risk of failure increases for another. As the system produces success in one area, it creates failure in another, like a byproduct.

The Opposite of Monoculture

The idea of the monoculture, a low-diversity environment where everything is the same, has gotten some attention in security. Specifically applied to technology, it means that if you depend too much on one technology product, you can be widely vulnerable if that technology fails or is compromised. Monocultural vulnerabilities may apply to software vendors, but they rarely exist when it comes to people and social systems. If anything, the opposite is true. Organizations have so many different microcultures operating within them, each with its own beliefs and ways of doing things, that they can impact performance if they don't get along.

Think for a moment about the differences between groups of people within your own organization. Do the people in the IT support department experience the world the same way as the people in the finance organization? In some ways, they probably do. For example, they probably speak the same national language, or at least agree to work in the same language when doing business. But even if everyone speaks English, people in the different groups likely speak very different languages in the context of their jobs, with different terminology and communication styles that characterize their business functions. Beyond language, there can sometimes seem to be worlds of difference between how one group thinks and behaves compared to another. Engineers don't worry about employee retention like HR managers do. The custodial staff does not obsess over quota retirement like the sales team does. Managers and executives stress over political rivalries that many individual contributors couldn't care less about.

Microcultures are inevitable when you have different specialized groups populating the large organizations that define modern society. Everything has become too complex for one person to be able to have all the competencies necessary to achieve our organizational objectives. So we divide up the work and everyone provides their unique contributions to the overall goal. We've even developed specialization to enable some people to manage all the moving parts strategically, even if they don't understand everything about how those parts operate.

But our collective activity doesn't always work, despite all our efforts. We can't herd the cats, can't get all the different teams to play nicely together. Our strategic planning may be stymied when all of the groups necessary to achieve the goals don't perform the way we have predicted or expected. If we ask "ordinary" people within the organization about why a strategy didn't work out, we often get surprisingly honest answers:

> "Oh, I could have told you that software implementation wasn't going to work from the beginning. They just set it up to fail."

> "The new executive staff just doesn't get it. They think they are going to magically change company performance overnight. You don't turn an oil tanker on a dime."

> "You know, we try reorganizing around smaller teams every few years, but it never takes. That's just not the way we do things here."

When Drucker coined his phrase, the previous examples are exactly the sorts of scenarios he was talking about. (As an aside, although the quote is attributed to him, Drucker never actually wrote "culture eats strategy for breakfast" in any of his books; see the reading suggestions at the end of the chapter for a good article that quotes it.) Organizations make plans and formulate business strategies all the time. Those plans and strategies emerge from more or less rational consideration of the requirements and challenges facing the organizations, and the organizations devote extensive time and energy to writing them down, organizing them into initiatives and projects, setting up teams, and executing on milestones to achieve their goals. And, when those strategies sometimes fall short, when they fail to succeed for no apparent reason, organizations have a difficult time articulating what exactly went wrong. Organizations talk about culture, and they go to great lengths to emphasize their unique cultures, but talking about something isn't the same thing as doing it, and more effort is put into doing strategy. Organizations don't put the same emphasis on understanding culture, working to change it, and setting goals for it. That's a problem because, as Drucker pointed out, culture is fundamental to strategic success.

Cultural Traits in Information Security

Security organizations aren't different than other organizations when it comes to specialization and subcultures. Information security often functions as a subculture of information technology, while also possessing its own specializations and microcultures at the corporate, professional, and individual levels. You can find very different types of people in information security, with completely separate skill sets and experiences, yet all of them identify themselves as belonging to the same industry or field. And the field of information security most definitely has a shared culture all its own. Inside a company, InfoSec may be a specialized subculture within IT, which cohabitates and constructs the general enterprise culture, along with other specialized communities like HR, Legal, or Physical Safety and Security. Figure 2-5 illustrates this relationship in a simple way. As I described in my story about the difference between physical security and information security in Chapter 1, even two subcultures that are both dedicated to the same purpose, protecting corporate assets, can be quite different in what they believe is important and in the decisions that they make about how to achieve their ends.

In information security, even though there are many different roles, each requiring specialized skills, the culture shares some common characteristics and values that everyone in the culture more or less accepts. Defining and analyzing these shared beliefs and assumptions is a core requirement for understanding and eventually transforming security culture. Through my career experience I have identified four cultural traits that I believe are important to recognize

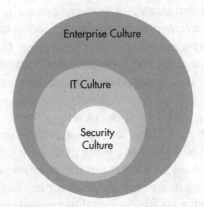

Figure 2-5   *Security as a subculture*

when trying to understand why security struggles to succeed. These traits are not the only characteristics that define our culture, and obviously not everyone in the industry exhibits every trait or shares them to the same degree. But as general principles, I often see these traits drive the thinking and decisions of organizations, their vendors and suppliers, and even regulators and policymakers trying to solve information security's more contentious problems.

Techno-romanticism

It's right there in the name. Technology is front and center in security today, both as the potential problem and as the likely solution. But what do I mean by techno-romanticism as a cultural trait? This means that, all things being equal, we tend to default to prioritizing technology over everything else. Actually, we do it even when all things are not equal. When we identify a problem, the first place we usually go looking for a solution is technology. That this is the way the industry works is not really very surprising. We have more than our fair share of engineers in the industry, people who come from their own technology-centric cultural background. And security product vendors have a vested interest in encouraging and maintaining a system in which automation and infrastructure are believed to be the most important aspect of security.

Cultural values empower people by giving them a common frame of reference. But they can limit people, too, by closing minds to alternative ways of thinking about a problem. Psychologist Abraham Maslow captured the concept in his famous saying, "I suppose it is tempting, if the only tool you have is a hammer, to treat everything as if it were a nail." This can be a problem in security when technology eclipses everything else. I frequently talk to security professionals who not only believe that most security problems can be best solved with technology solutions, but also believe that if technology cannot solve a problem, the problem is inherently unsolvable and there's no point in putting further effort into it. For them, technology is not just the best solution, it is the only real solution.

Monocultures are a problem not only when they have too much of one kind of technology, but also when technology is all they have. One of my hopes for this book is that it begins to point to a demonstrably effective approach to people-centric security that can help alleviate our unhealthy dependence on technological solutions.

Defeatism

This cultural trait seems to have evolved pretty recently, but it has quickly gone viral. Within the last few years, the general message you will hear transmitted in marketing materials, at conferences, and in trade magazines has changed from one of how to keep your security from failing, to the need to accept that it has already failed. Even if you don't know it, the extreme version of this meme goes, *The bad guys have won. You are already owned. All you can do is try to contain the damage and clean up the mess.*

When I came into the industry decades ago, the general consensus was that security was winning. Sure, there were threats and challenges, but the dominant analogy was that of the Wild West. And information security was like the Texas Rangers, riding across the land protecting citizens from marauding bandits and outlaws as the modern world of law and order took root. Today, we still live in the Wild West, but now it seems we identify more with the defenders of the Alamo. Surrounded on all sides by the bad guys, everything has become an existential threat, and heroic as our efforts might be, it's only a matter of time before we get overrun and slaughtered.

Exceptionalism

Talk to many security professionals today and you'll hear that there is absolutely nothing that represents a greater menace to the well-being of society than cyber threats. In addition to thinking that security is the *biggest* problem the world faces in a world full of problems, the industry often acts like the security problem is also *unique*—no one has faced anything like it before, so no one can understand what it is like to be responsible for information security. When you combine this sense of exceptionalism with the sense of embattled defeatism, you can start to understand why security experts look at you like a suicidal idiot when you suggest that it might be cool to be able to use your personal iPhone at work.

There's nothing particularly exceptional about information security's sense of exceptionalism. Every field thinks it's different. We'd be more exceptional if we recognized as an industry that we are not unique. The problems we face, even technical problems that seem impossible without the presence of advanced IT systems, can be traced back historically to the telephone, the telegraph before that, and probably all the way back to when some Neanderthal snuck into a rival clan's cave and exfiltrated the secret of making fire by copying a drawing from the wall. What our exceptionalism does a much better job of explaining is why it can be so difficult for the security programs in many organizations to get people to listen to them. It can be hard to get someone to agree with your answer when you continually act as though they are incapable of really understanding the nature of the question in the first place.

Paranoia

Although we might not be as exceptional as we like to think we are, InfoSec does do some things quite differently from other professions, so much so that we sometimes look at the world one way while wearing our security glasses, and a different way when looking at it through a business or even personal lens. Consider the case of risk. When working with clients, I often find that a cognitive dissonance exists around risk, a state where the security professional I'm talking with holds differing and contradictory ideas about the same concept simultaneously. When they discuss risk in the context of security, they give a definition that essentially characterizes it as potential loss or downside. They may define it as a formula, such as likelihood × severity, or as a statement of things that can go wrong. But risk is almost always perceived as negative and almost always something to be avoided or, if it is not possible to avoid altogether, managed in a way that minimizes it.

But if I ask that same professional some probing questions about how they invest for retirement, or what they like to eat or do for fun, or which companies they admire most, it can be like talking to a completely different person. Are they keeping their portfolio exclusively in safe, low-yield investments? Most say "no." Do they smoke, drink, or eat things that are bad for them? Many do. And the companies they get excited about are usually startups and innovative trendsetters, not the boring, dependable sorts of companies that would attract Warren Buffet's eye. Risk, it seems, means something remarkably different when they are not talking about security.

These differences between how InfoSec professionals address security as opposed to other things in their lives speaks to another cultural trait, a sometimes pervading sense of paranoia. We are so used to watching things go wrong and to understanding all the things that can go wrong, that we "accentuate the negative." The benefits of all this IT infrastructure we have built tend to fade into the background when it runs smoothly, and we take it as a given. At least until it breaks. Since security is usually front and center when it does break, both as the means to a fix and a potential target of blame, it's no wonder that some security professionals develop an obsessively glass-half-empty worldview. It's the nature of the beast. But it doesn't always help us relate to other parts of the organization that don't necessarily share our feeling that everything is a security incident waiting to happen.

"I Just Know What They *Could* Do..."

One of my best friends is a security expert who has performed penetration tests for years. On a trip to do a joint consulting engagement, I stopped by his room as we were leaving the hotel just in time to find him locking his toothbrush and several other personal grooming items in the hotel safe, along with his valuables.

"What are you doing?" I asked. His passport and iPad, I understood. But his toothbrush and comb?

"I never leave that stuff out," he said, entering a new code into the safe. "Do you?"

"Yeah," I laughed. "What, you think the cleaning staff wants to mess with your stuff?"

"I don't care what they want," he replied, shooting me a look. "But I've been screwing with people's systems for long enough to know it's not about what they want to do. I just know what they *could* do, if they wanted to. Think about that."

I did. And to this day, I lock up my toothbrush every time I stay in a hotel.

Competing Values and Security Threats

Clara's case earlier in the chapter is an example of a situation where one cultural value (the desire to produce a finished product quickly) created a direct threat to another cultural value (the desire to make sure that product did not contain security flaws). These conflicts occur all the time in business and in life. They are at the core of Dekker's concept of drift, because individuals are forced to choose between competing priorities that all have the potential to cause failure. The priorities that end up being chosen, and whether those decisions are then rewarded or punished, represent the real-world operationalization of an organization's values. Security may have been a priority in Clara's company, but when pressed, when there was not enough time or money to do everything, as in Clara's case, the company's most important cultural imperative was to get products to market on time. That's what the company most cared about. Cutting a security review short was lamentable, but blowing the production deadline was unacceptable.

Much of the rest of this book will be devoted to hunting down the hidden threats posed by competing cultural values and replacing values that degrade security with those that improve it. Many, if not most, security incidents can be traced back at least in part to competing values that led to conflicts in behavior, which in turn created risk. These risks cannot be easily managed by just identifying a threat and avoiding or controlling for it. The threat is also intrinsic to the system. It is the Rubik's Cube effect I mentioned in Chapter 1, where making something more secure means making something else less successful, maybe less efficient or less productive. If the organization puts a greater priority on that success than on information security, security will lose. The only surefire control is to increase resources so that both priorities can be achieved. Since that's not usually going to happen, the only realistic option is to discover these threats and make the competing values that initiate them visible to all the stakeholders involved. You don't solve the problem this way, but you allow people to have an honest conversation about those priorities and give the organization the opportunity to accept risk in an informed way, rather than the blind acceptance of letting it continue to exist, invisible and dangerous.

When leaders impose strategies on an organization without understanding the cultural dynamics in place, or in spite of those cultural dynamics, they make the mistake of expecting a boulder to roll up hill. You can certainly make a boulder roll up a hill, but not by just declaring that is where it must go. Defying gravity requires planning, force, and engineering efforts to create what feels like a very unnatural outcome. Execution is the boulder. Culture is the hill. Gravity and inertia are always on its side, and left to its own devices, culture always has the final say.

The Change Agents of Security Culture

So who makes security culture work? Who is responsible for changing it, for hacking it like I encouraged in Chapter 1? Who is best positioned to transform the system? The cliché answer is *everybody*. An organization's culture is created by the everyday decisions and interactions and beliefs of the people in it. But we can narrow that down a little and identify different folks with the best chance of leveraging cultural change. Let's start at the very top, with senior leadership.

The C-Suite

Leaders are in a unique position to affect culture, because they can help create it through their influence and their examples. In information security, the CISO is the senior security-specific leader, but companies have become painfully aware that the effects of a breach can reverberate far beyond the CISO's office, affecting the entire C-Suite of chief executives. So security leadership and organizational leadership are sort of synonymous these days. They all have a stake in success.

Changing culture is hard. The most important thing senior security stakeholders, both inside and outside the formal security program, can do is to recognize that transforming security culture means changing the way people think, not just how they behave. And that starts with the leaders themselves. They may have to change completely the way they think about security, and they will certainly have to accept that solving the human equation is the only way to make their strategies successful. You can dictate a strategy, but you cannot dictate the culture you need to make it work.

Security Awareness Teams

I mentioned security awareness teams in Chapter 1 in the context of culture hacking, and I have to put them front and center again here. More than anyone else outside of senior leadership, the security awareness managers and trainers in an organization are best positioned as cultural change agents. One reason is that, even more than senior leadership, security awareness professionals have already bought into people-centric security. A great part of their raison d'être is the exploration and management of human behavior, including the motivations and hidden drivers of it.

What I have seen security awareness teams struggle with is the lack of a good knowledge base and maturity in the industry for understanding organizational and human behavior in general. While there are lots of tactical approaches and methods for improving security awareness, I often see security awareness teams looking for more strategic and theoretic resources that can help inform their efforts and carry them to new levels of efficacy and reach. Given the relative youth and inexperience of information security as a formal discipline (a few decades for us compared to generations or even centuries for law, insurance, and finance), this should be unsurprising. And we are at the point in our profession's evolution where we move from practicing what we do to theorizing about how and why we do it, so those conversations are beginning to happen. I'm writing this book in my own minor attempt at contributing to and influencing that conversation.

Security Researchers

I'm not the only curious soul in the security industry, fortunately. One thing that makes me proud of being part of information security is that we seem to have more than our share of smart, curious researchers who enjoy thinking about things in new ways. That includes the bad guys as well as the good guys, but if you can judge people by the quality of their enemies, information security is a dynamic and innovative place.

The industry's love affair with technology puts a premium on engineering and product research, and there's no question that InfoSec researchers in this space do some amazing things. But that same techno-romanticism has made security pretty weak in the social sciences, by comparison. I encounter a lot of bias and condescension directed toward "subjective" approaches and qualitative research methods commonly used by social science researchers such as anthropologists, sociologists, and economists. Security pros will use such approaches and methods, but only as necessary evils when "objective" and quantitative methods aren't possible. The fact that the industry often shows a lack of understanding of what these terms actually mean can be annoying, but I like to think of it as an opportunity.

This book is about culture, so it is unashamedly grounded in the social sciences, in the ostensibly second-tier subjective and qualitative methods many in the industry mistrust. One of my hopes is that readers find the techniques I include intriguing, maybe even capable of answering, at least in part, questions they thought impossible to answer before. I am convinced that more social science research in information security—explorations of sociology, of psychology, and of human relationships in general—has the capability to transform not just security culture but the entire way we operate as a discipline.

Security Practitioners

From software developers to firewall administrators to the analysts manning the security operations centers, practitioners make the daily work of information security happen. You don't change security culture without them. But practitioners are not just passive targets of transformational efforts. These stakeholders are perhaps best positioned to understand and explore security culture because they live it every day.

Security practitioners can contribute to security cultural change in at least two ways. First, they can act as a source of data on how the security culture functions, what it is, where it works, and where it does not work. Researchers and specialists who are trained to elicit this information can help the security culture become more self-aware. Once self-knowledge takes root, practitioners can then become more active participants in changing their own environment. As we'll see, much of the process of cultural transformation relies on these sorts of bootstrapping efforts, people recognizing good and bad habits, cultivating the former and working to modify the latter.

Making Security Cultural

A people-centric approach to security does not mean addressing the human threat. People-centric means, literally, putting people at the center of the whole security challenge and emphasizing the ways in which they are central to solving problems rather than how they contribute to them. People-centric security means that security leaders such as the CISO have to look beyond the immediate needs of a security program team and take into account other stakeholders and their needs and priorities. People-centric security means the entire industry recognizes that not everyone shares in their belief that security is the world's biggest problem, that technology is the best way to escape that problem, and that information security has a privileged and unique insight into how the world operates.

Instead, a people-centric security perspective embraces the values and priorities of those who are outside the information security field as the best way of helping security be successful and compete in an active marketplace of values and ideas. People-centric security is political and humanistic, and it is the only way for security to thrive in today's environment. FUD, the use of fear, uncertainty, and doubt to push our agenda, is no longer sustainable. We need to reexamine our own beliefs, question everything that we have come to understand about information security, and see if those values still hold up. Where they do not, we must change them. Our end goal will be to transform information security culture for entire organizations, but before that happens, we will have to transform our own, and that requires learning a bit about how organizational culture functions.

Further Reading

▶ Aulet, Bill. "Culture Eats Strategy for Breakfast." *TechCrunch*, April 12, 2014. Available at http://techcrunch.com/.

▶ Dekker, Sidney. *Drift into Failure: From Hunting Broken Components to Understanding Complex Systems.* Burlington, VT: Ashgate, 2011.

CHAPTER 3

Organizational Culture: A Primer

I'm going to make the case in this book that security culture is fundamental to security performance and offer a path to transforming your organization's information security culture as a way to reduce risk, increase value, and avoid security incidents. But to make that case, I need to demonstrate that the critical link between organizational culture and organizational performance is not a new idea in industry, just one that is pretty new to InfoSec. Studying organizational and corporate culture as a means to making companies perform better in competitive and volatile circumstances has a rich history in both business and academia. In this chapter I will draw on some of this research to help you understand the groundwork that has already been established, even if only at a very high level.

The Cultural Success of Apple

It's almost a cliché to hold up Apple as an example of a successful organizational culture, but probably more than any other company in recent memory, including other wildly successful technology firms, Apple remains unique as a cultural case study. It succeeded wildly, then nearly failed, only to pull off one of the most amazing comeback stories in history. The near cult of personality that developed around Steve Jobs, who was instrumental in Apple's return to glory, made his style of leadership synonymous with Apple's culture. And the company has literally changed global society with its hardware and software, all while maintaining an aura of style and continuous innovation that few of its peers can match.

Much ink, real and digital, has been spilled trying to deconstruct Apple's culture, including whether the company is as magical as its hardcore fans believe it to be. But you don't have to love Apple to appreciate the power of its employees' and customers' sense of identity and near worship of core tenets like design, simplicity, and novelty. Culture is about shared values and beliefs. Whatever one thinks about Apple as a company, no one can say that the company's culture has little to do with Apple's success.

The Field of Organizational Culture

The study of organizational culture grew out of the study of culture at a more general level. Sometimes the two fields still overlap. Some researchers engage with cultures that exist within organizations, as I do in this book, and some study how organizations work across and between cultures (for instance, in the case of multinational corporations). I don't put as much emphasis on this latter aspect, although it still can hold implications for information security.

Origins

The first scientists to study culture, the ones who invented the word in the first place, were anthropologists. In the nineteenth century, social scientists were concerned with how societies and civilizations developed and evolved. Specifically, they wanted to know how entire belief systems could be transmitted and maintained from generation to generation. What made one society so very different from another, and what made those differences stick over time? A full examination of the evolution of cultural anthropology is way beyond the scope of this book; the pertinent point here is that early anthropologists recognized that something, some phenomenon, allowed differing groups of people to share common social attributes

Security and Global Culture

Cisco is a global technology company with offices and customers all over the world. In addition to managing a diverse and multicultural workforce across dozens of countries, Cisco has sponsored dedicated research into the ways that different cultures engage in information security. A study commissioned by Cisco in 2008, resulting in a series of white papers titled *Data Leakage Worldwide*, specifically targeted human information security behaviors across cultures, identifying patterns and differences around security practices from country to country. The results pointed to interesting, culturally specific ways that security practices differ depending upon the unique beliefs and social values of the societies in which those practices exist. The *Data Leakage Worldwide* white papers can be found by searching on the Cisco homepage at www.cisco.com.

and behaviors, and that this phenomenon could act as a powerful force in shaping the lives of a group's members across both space and time.

With the rise of large, bureaucratic organizations designed to facilitate business, governance, and other strategic social goals, the world began to witness different enterprises growing as complex and as geographically distributed as some nations or peoples. As these organizations expanded and thrived across space and time as well, maintaining the same structures and processes well beyond the lifetime of any single individual member, a new generation of researchers took notice. Business scholars and organizational theorists borrowed the concepts invented by the social scientists and anthropologists and began to apply them to companies and other large organizations. It took a while. The field of organizational studies has also been around a long time, evolving separately from anthropology and dating back to the Industrial Revolution. But it was only in the second half of the twentieth century that researchers merged the two disciplines and began specifically looking at culture in the context of businesses and other large, organized enterprises.

Whereas the anthropologists were concerned with understanding what made a society tick, the organizational culture researchers were often more concerned with what made organizations, particularly businesses, successful. Why did one company do so much better in its industry (or so much worse) than another? How could one company completely reinvent itself to overcome a market challenge while a peer struggled and ultimately failed to change the way it did business? Often, the differences between competitor firms seemed to boil down to things that seemed intangible. What did the leadership believe? How did the organization treat its members? What were the most important symbols, values, and rituals in the daily lives of all the members?

Outcomes

The end result of these studies is an academic field of its own (several, actually), as well as an industry of management theorists and business consultants who have attempted to unlock the secrets of culture and put them to productive use in improving organizational performance. There are theories and frameworks to explain culture, as well as disagreement and debate about what it all means, but at the core of the discipline are a number of powerful common themes that you will find over and over again. These commonalities are what we need to focus on in order to understand what organizational culture can do for IT and information security.

The Cultural Failure of Enron

If Apple is a go-to example of successful organizational culture, the scandalous Enron culture easily qualifies as an obvious opposing example. In 2001, the energy and commodities company imploded as it became apparent that the entire enterprise was built upon a systemic culture of corruption, deceit, and fraud. Where Apple changed the world by creating the iPhone, thus ushering in the age of mobile smart devices, Enron changed it by calling into question virtually the whole accounting industry and ushering in the age of Sarbanes-Oxley (SOX) compliance.

Enron did not fail because its culture was weak, at least not in the sense that people didn't share common values. The big problem was that the common values shared by senior management and pushed throughout the company were reprehensible and ethically bankrupt. Enron's culture was about pushing to the edge and beyond, beginning with innovations in commodities trading and energy markets, before ending with debt, oversight, and the law. Enron was not the last of the corporate governance scandals in that period, and several high-profile companies followed the firm into ignominious failure as a result of their own toxic cultures, while simultaneously poisoning the reputations of the accounting firms that managed their books. In the case of Enron's own accounting company, Arthur Andersen, the damage proved fatal and that company ceased to exist along with its disgraced client.

The Culture Iceberg

Organizational culture lends itself to the iceberg metaphor. Read a few books on corporate culture and what immediately comes through is the sense of things hidden below the surface. No matter what you can see superficially, you can be sure there is much more going on below that you cannot observe. In fact, in the grand scheme of things, the iceberg you see is really just the tip.

In Chapter 2, I quoted Peter Drucker's prediction that strategy will lose out to culture in nearly every contest. The iceberg metaphor helps to explain why. When a strategic initiative focuses only on the part of a challenge or problem that is visible and easily identified, it's like hooking a rope between the iceberg and a rowboat and telling the crew to tow it. It may not look like such a big job from the surface, but that's only because you can't see the enormity of what you are trying to move. People can row really hard and everyone may applaud their efforts, but that one little rowboat is not going to alter the iceberg's course, no matter how great the exertion. The reality is it's the mass under the waves that actually determines the iceberg's course through the sea, the part that remains hidden from you, untouched and unaffected. There might not be a boat big enough to change that thing's direction.

With culture, the part of the whole that is analogous to the visible ice above the surface is the collection of observable behaviors occurring within the organization every day. What people do, what they say, what they wear...these are all more or less visible decisions. And we tend to talk about culture in terms of these behaviors, choices, and decisions. We might say an organization has a formal culture if we observe that everyone wears a suit and tie to work, or a casual culture if everyone comes to the office in shorts and flip-flops. Based on an organization's behavior, its culture may be described as cutthroat compared to one that is collegial; or open and trusting as opposed to highly controlled. We even see cultures that we would describe as toxic or unhealthy and that corrupt or harm the people within them. But all of these behaviors are driven by motivating factors that are happening underneath the things we are seeing in front of us, as illustrated in Figure 3-1.

Hidden Aspects

The first principle experts recognize in organizational culture is that observable behaviors are superficial. They are always connected to underlying assumptions and beliefs that remain hidden in the sense that everyone simply takes them for granted. People don't often spend a lot of time thinking about why they believe something. They are usually too busy doing things, living their lives. But the things they do are driven, at least in part, by what they believe. Culture is the same way, and scholars from Edgar Schein to Geert Hofstede to Karl Weick have explored and documented the way organizational culture functions as a sort of collective unconscious for the organization. It would be incredibly difficult for a company to do business if everyone in it had to ask "why do we do this?" before making a decision. Companies will actually go to great pains to articulate aspects of the culture—posting signs around their offices, making cards to wear with peoples' badges, running awareness campaigns—to encourage certain types of behaviors. They want to make those hidden assumptions more visible. Ironically, this attempt to help people understand why they are expected to behave in a certain way is also intended to make such behavior more automatic and reflexive.

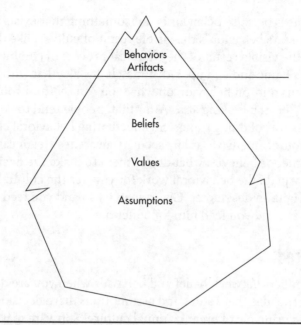

Figure 3-1   *The iceberg metaphor of culture*

So any understanding of security culture has to take into account all the assumptions, hidden beliefs and motivations, and unconscious rituals that have been ingrained into the organization as a whole. The example of Clara in the previous chapter illustrates this idea. Encouraging a specific security behavior was very important to the company. No one would have suggested otherwise, and there were numerous policies and processes in place to enforce that behavior. But lurking under the surface were other beliefs and assumptions, ones that directly competed with Clara's security responsibilities. No one really questioned them, or the resulting incompatible relationship. And, at the end of the day, Clara believed more strongly that she would be rewarded or punished for one behavior than she would for another. After the customer breach occurred that exploited her coding mistake, the company retroactively attempted to make her decision to forego final security checks look negligent and wrong. But the fact was, at the time, *she did exactly what the system had trained and conditioned (and even rewarded) her to do.*

A difficulty of analyzing culture is that it involves more than just differentiating between what a person does and the motivations behind (or beneath) those actions and decisions. Almost all researchers into organizational culture share the opinion that culture can be very difficult to change (a topic I'll cover a bit later in the chapter). This is because behavior is not something that exists independently of culture. A person's behavior is the visible result of culture, like the flame on a matchstick is the visible result of the chemical process of combustion. You can't start with a flame and end up with a match. It's like that with behavior and culture, too. Focus only on behavior, on what you can see, and you might change it, at least until you stop looking at it. After that, people tend to go back to their old, unconscious way of doing things. So effectuating behavioral change alone is extremely resource intensive, as any security awareness team can tell you. But change what someone believes, what drives them to make the decision in the first place, and they will do the behavioral work for you. It's the cultural equivalent of the ancient Maimonides quote, "Give a man a fish and you feed him for a day; teach a man to fish and you feed him for a lifetime."

People Powered

You only get conflicts between belief and behavior when you are dealing with human beings. The idea that values and assumptions drive decisions and actions is a second basic principle of organizational culture. Software may have hidden bugs, your firewall may have hidden rule conflicts, but technology doesn't have hidden motivations. It can't experience cognitive dissonance or get conflicted about the right thing to do in a difficult situation. People are the only ones who experience these things, and people-centric security means first and foremost recognizing that culture drives behavior. Policies don't. How many of us can think of a policy that we know is in place in our organization yet we don't follow or obey it, maybe because it's silly, maybe because we know that the company doesn't enforce it, or maybe because it conflicts with a more important policy?

Diving into the organizational culture literature, you will find an overwhelmingly diverse exploration of the ways in which people create the organization and how they change it for the good or for the bad. Insights can range from the existence of mythologies and stories to define how culture works, tales of heroes and monsters straight out of Joseph Campbell, to clinical psychology, diagnosing behavior as though an organization itself could be mentally ill. But at the heart of everything is the recognition that without people, you have no organizational culture, or even an organization.

The ease with which culture can overwhelm and confound organizational strategy is one of the power lessons for people-centric security. Information security is beginning to hit a wall in terms of what it can hope to accomplish with strategies based primarily on tools and technology products. This is not because we don't have great tools and technologies, but because we are reaching a point where we cannot do more without the express cooperation and collaboration of the rest of the organization, who have their own great tools and technologies, many of which conflict with security. Increasingly, the potential success or failure of information security is a joint partnership with people elsewhere in the system, whether they are the executives who set strategy and direction, the budget gatekeepers who fund things, the managers who keep it all running on the front lines, or the individual users who make the everyday choices that mean the difference between deterrence and disaster.

The Organizational Cultural/Organizational Performance Link

Another common theme in organizational culture research, and the one that resonates most with corporate executives, is the link between organizational culture and organizational performance. Does an organization's culture exert a positive or negative impact on how successful that organization is in its industry or how effectively it achieves its goals? The answer is an unqualified yes. Evidence ranges from "common sense" anecdotal stories, to business school case studies, to longitudinal studies of corporate performance stretching over years. But the bottom line, figuratively as well as literally, is that an organization with a dysfunctional culture is never going to perform as well as it could. What constitutes good or bad when it comes to culture, what makes one culture strong and another weak, is a stickier problem. Different cultures are appropriate for different industries, and what works for one organization won't necessarily generate success in another. But if your culture holds you back, it can be like running a race with weights tied to your organization's legs.

One of the most impressive examinations of the culture–performance link is John Kotter and James Heskett's book, *Corporate Culture and Performance*, which describes their research studies spanning multiple companies over several years. Empirical and nuanced, Kotter and Heskett's work explores theories of why and when culture either helps or gets in the way of a company's success. They show that it is not as easy as saying a "strong" or a "weak" culture makes your organization successful. Many organizations with strong, forceful cultures that are transmitted and enforced among members have failed, sometimes spectacularly, while seemingly weak or less entrenched cultures have thrived. Instead, it seems that the secret to success is one of harnessing culture to serve the business, just like any other resource. The cultures that do the best appear to be the ones that have the best "fit" for the industry and the challenges they face, including the capability to respond and adapt to change.

Culture can be disruptive just like markets, business models, and technologies. Many of the case studies you will find that describe how culture is linked to performance will not be about any particular culture type, but about how an organization adapted itself to new challenges and used its culture to help it do so. Failure becomes more likely when a culture that seemed to work yesterday no longer "fits" its environment. In these situations the organization can find itself outmaneuvered by other, more responsive cultures. Cultures can also compete within the same organization, as my examples have shown, and this can lead to degrading capabilities as the enterprise has to compete with other organizations while also addressing internal conflicts that distract and sap resources.

The Cultural Migration of PayPal

A fascinating example of the power of organizational culture can be found in the so-called PayPal Mafia, a term that refers to the founders and early employees of digital payment pioneer PayPal. After eBay's acquisition of PayPal in 2002, many of those founders and employees left to go start other companies. These individuals, including billionaire entrepreneurs Reid Hoffman (LinkedIn), Elon Musk (Tesla and SpaceX), and Peter Thiel (Clarium Capital and Facebook), are often credited as starting a new Silicon Valley resurgence. The common threads of the story, beginning with reported clashes between the PayPal founders and their more corporate and conservative new owners, have to do with a set of brilliant and restless people literally sharing a vision of reshaping the world, not just facilitating online financial transactions.

Culture is not only powerful and malleable. It is portable and potentially contagious. Created by people organizing in complex, interdependent ways, culture can produce effects that ripple and transmit through an entire social network. In the case of the PayPal Mafia, normal startup visions were not even enough. More than building a company, they were (and still are in many cases) driven to change society altogether, from space travel to electric vehicles to finding a cure for death. And they had no intention of allowing the status quo, even one that made them fabulously wealthy, get in the way of their vision for a new, more functional system. That's culture hacking.

The implications of the culture–performance link for information security are pretty clear. InfoSec usually exists as a separate subculture within an organization, maybe even removed from the rest of IT. And information security cultures tend to be strong, in opinion and motivation if not always in political power. If information security is not a good cultural fit within the organization, if it conflicts or competes with other cultural groups, then it is going to be very difficult to maximize the InfoSec program's effectiveness. Consequently, performance may degrade, or at least may not be as effective as it could be, and this leads directly to increased security risks.

Assessing and Measuring Culture

The idea of culture having a causal link to company performance makes the idea of measuring and analyzing organizational culture very important. You are not going to successfully change or manage something that you cannot define, observe, and assess; in other words, something you cannot measure. Researchers have responded by developing instruments and techniques for measuring culture and its impact on an organization's effectiveness.

Qualitative vs. Quantitative Measurement of Culture

As anyone who knows me or has heard me speak publicly can tell you, I have a problem with the information security field's use of the term *qualitative*. In InfoSec, referring to data as qualitative implies that the data should be considered subjective and less reliable, as opposed to quantitative data, which are seen to be more objective and trustworthy. This creates all sorts of challenges for security professionals who are trying to measure the results of their activities. Our industry's bias toward numbers limits the measures and approaches we can use. It also encourages us to engage in "statistical alchemy," which is the process by which we take things that are not quantitative and assign numbers to them in an attempt to make them appear more rigorous. What we end up with is not only an attempt to compare apples to oranges, but a formula by which apples are multiplied by oranges, then weighted using a system of bagels. In other words, nonsense dressed up as science.

I regularly see security teams get into trouble statistically, usually when they feel the need to create metrics that will impress senior management. Asking individual members of the security team whether risks and costs are high, medium, or low is a staple of information security risk assessments. The resulting red, yellow, and green heat maps can come across to some audiences as simplistic, because they usually are. But changing high, medium, and low to a range between 1 and 100 (or corresponding arbitrary financial figures) doesn't make a measurement quantitative. It just means that you are asking for an opinion expressed as a number rather than a word. You're still getting people's opinions about the truth rather than actually measuring what's true. But this nevertheless allows many security teams to claim that they have stopped collecting fuzzy "qualitative" data in their assessments in favor of those that are more quantitative.

In the social sciences, including fields like anthropology and sociology, where culture can be of primary interest, qualitative data means something very different. Simply put, data are qualitative when you cannot easily count them. Good examples include a story told during a staff meeting, the transcript of a response to an open-ended interview question, a video recording of a sales meeting, or the photograph from your last team-building event. My example of the security team's opinions regarding risk is another example of qualitative data. Qualitative data are empirical, meaning you can observe them. They just don't immediately lend themselves to statistical analysis, assuming that's what you want to do. But is statistical analysis the only way we can obtain truth or knowledge? When your significant other, or your child, tells you they love you, do you insist on verifying that assertion through a two-tailed t-test or linear regression? Do our favorite movies and novels speak to us because we appreciate that they follow a verifiable Gaussian probability distribution? Clearly, numbers can't tell us everything that is worth knowing.

Qualitative Measures and Techniques

Culture is about beliefs and assumptions, about motivations and values that may not even be explicit within an organization or conscious on the part of its members. Culture tends to stay hidden below the surface, unless you deliberately seek it out. Yet you can't just go out and start counting culture. People's behaviors are more directly observable and lend themselves to more quantitative analysis, but knowing who did what and when and where they did it, does not tell you how or why they behaved that way. These questions of how and why, which are more important when attempting cultural transformation, are the domain of qualitative research and analysis. Qualitative researchers use surveys, interviews, and other interactions between people to facilitate understanding of the topics they explore.

Lord Kelvin's "Meagre Understanding"

When I wrote my book *IT Security Metrics* a few years back, it was fashionable among some security metrics proponents to quote Lord Kelvin's adage on measuring something, "when you can measure...and express it in numbers, you know something about it; but when you cannot measure it, when you cannot express it in numbers, your knowledge is of a meagre and unsatisfactory kind." I would usually ask whoever threw out the quote to express the measurement reasoning behind it in the form of a number. I never got one. Instead, I got stories and anecdotes that demonstrated both the "meagre understanding" of Kelvin's claim as well as the incredible utility of qualitative data such as stories and anecdotes.

Different traditions of qualitative research methods have developed in various fields. Table 3-1 lists the major qualitative research approaches. Some of these are going to look a bit strange to an information security professional with an engineering background, although they might look less so to anyone who has studied psychology or business administration. In fact, all of these research approaches are used in industry in one form or another. The fact that information security has not made much use of them says more about the inadequacy of our own research methods and our bias against qualitative research than it does about the effectiveness of qualitative techniques.

I've gone into some detail in Table 3-1 about these qualitative techniques because they are often the only way to measure and understand organizational culture. As such, they belong in the conceptual toolkit of every organization looking to improve and transform security culture and make it people-centric. You do not have to be a Ph.D. anthropologist to do basic qualitative research. You just have to recognize that sometimes you are not going to find the answers you are looking for in any way other than talking with people, listening to what they say, and looking for the meaning you seek in the stories they tell.

Culture by the Numbers

Although qualitative data and analysis play a big role in understanding culture, that does not mean that quantitative measurement is off the table. Quantitative

Qualitative Research Approach	Description	Industry Applications
History & Biography	Focuses on comprehensively understanding events and people over time. Researchers are typically outsiders.	Companies and individuals use historical and biographical studies to apply lessons from the past or to emulate desired personal qualities. Walter Isaacson's biography of Steve Jobs is a good example.
Ethnography	Focuses on a deep social and behavioral understanding of a group or culture. Researchers typically embed as neutral "participant observers" for an extended period.	Ethnographical studies are used to gain an "insider's view" of an organization or industry. Examples include Tracy Kidder's *The Soul of a New Machine* (about Digital Equipment Corporation) and Michael Lewis's *Moneyball*.
Grounded Theory	Focuses on creating theories from observations in an inductive, "bottom up" way, instead of developing the theory first and deductively testing it with observed data. Researchers may be insiders or outsiders.	Grounded theory has been used to study B2B interactions, to theorize customer expectations, and to understand how R&D groups share knowledge across enterprises.
Action Research	Focuses on gaining scientific or theoretical knowledge while simultaneously creating organizational change. Researchers are active insiders, applying what they learn to what they are trying to accomplish.	Action research has been used to develop management frameworks, strategy planning tools, and innovation initiatives. One famous example is Robert Kaplan's use of action theory to develop the Balanced Scorecard methodology.

Table 3-1 *Major Qualitative Research Approaches*

and qualitative techniques are often both necessary to understand what is going on under the surface. Many researchers use qualitative techniques, such as interviews, participant observation, and the analysis of artifacts, to lead them to patterns and relationships that can be quantified. Let's again consider Clara and her development team. What if a researcher or a consultant came in and began interviewing all the developers, collecting stories about times they neglected or failed to complete their security reviews, and asking them to talk about why they made those decisions.

As different reasons were given, the consultant might begin putting together patterns such as deadline pressures being a primary cause. These reasons might correlate to certain types of software development projects that had a tendency to run into other delays, maybe even in a statistically significant way that proved these projects were more likely to have security vulnerabilities in the code when shipped. Now we're talking real numbers and quantitative insight, but none of it would be available without the qualitative data contained in those interviews.

Kotter and Heskitt did similar combining of qualitative and quantitative data when they measured the link between culture and performance. By collecting qualitative data from industry analysts about perceived corporate cultures and comparing those data to the hard numbers of company financial performance, they were able to draw conclusions about how and when culture affected the bottom line. Other researchers have attempted even more specific quantitative measures of culture, although the more statistical the measures get, the more they tend to focus with laser intensity on describing specific attributes of culture rather than exploring how to change it.

Challenges of Cultural Transformation

If nothing else is clear at this point, it should be apparent that understanding and managing corporate culture is hard work. We take culture for granted because we are immersed in it. We live it. And like other parts of our lives that we might want to change for the better, it's easier to say we are going to change our culture than to actually effect that change. Cultural transformation initiatives in many organizations are something like the New Year's resolutions we make each year. They are expressions of hope and optimism. And without commitment and hard work, many of them don't make it out of January alive.

Organizational culture experts prescribe many differing ways to transform culture, but, like their understanding of culture in general, there are several common themes that emerge from their advice. These include

▶ Culture can be changed in a variety of ways.

▶ Culture is inclusive, so cultural change must be too.

▶ Consensus building allows for the creation of new shared beliefs.

▶ Cultural change cannot be taken for granted.

▶ Leaders must set an appropriate example.

There's No One Right Way to Change Culture

If an algorithm for creating the perfect culture existed, every organization would be equally innovative and adaptable to shifts in its business, every member would function efficiently and effectively to achieve the organization's goals, and performance would be maximized across all industries. The fact that this utopia has not come to pass is proof enough that no one has discovered the secret, claims by consultants and management gurus notwithstanding. Researchers and theorists of organizational culture will tell you as much. The point is not to create some mythical perfect culture, but rather to shoot for the best culture your organization can have given its members, the environment in which it finds itself, and the goals and strategies it wants to achieve. This being said, successful cultural transformation will depend on a few key strategies, described in the following sections.

You Have to Include Everybody

Any cultural transformation is highly unlikely to succeed unless the process is deliberately inclusive. Since everyone in an organization helps to create and transmit the culture, everyone has to have a stake in changing it. This really means everyone, from the top of the organizational chart to the bottom. Inclusiveness also means direct involvement. Many frameworks for culture management are formed around representative teams made up of people from all over the organization, all of whom contribute to planning and formulating the changes and then go back to their own roles as champions and change agents to help ensure that the efforts are adopted into daily behaviors. The ultimate oxymoron in cultural transformation is the top-down "cultural change" strategy, where leadership expresses dissatisfaction with the existing culture, defines unilaterally what the new culture will be, and then demands everyone get with the new program.

You Have to Build Consensus

Getting everyone involved in cultural transformation is only the first step. Since an organization's culture is a reflection of the deep-seated beliefs and assumptions held by its members, you cannot simply dictate that everyone will now believe something different, or even what the new beliefs should be based upon. When was the last time you successfully argued that someone was wrong based on the fact that you really felt you were right? Most organizational change research emphasizes the need for some level of consensus building in identifying the current culture in place, as well as any changes that need to be made.

Information security is particularly vulnerable to a lack of cultural consensus. When talking with CISOs and other security stakeholders, I hear time and again that one of their greatest struggles is to make people outside of the InfoSec program care about security like members of the program do, to take it as seriously as everyone who is tasked with protecting company information assets. Without that consensus, security professionals must spend a lot of time explaining and justifying their work. Of course, it doesn't help when security teams can come across as not caring very much about the priorities and concerns of those stakeholders outside the security team. But in organizations where other business units and executives wield more political clout than the CISO or the security owner, the burden of consensus building falls on the security team, if for no other reason than they have to sell security transformation to stakeholders who may not even understand security, and certainly don't prioritize it over their own unique challenges and concerns. In the wake of the massive security breaches of recent years, it's getting less difficult to convince these stakeholders that security is important. But what is the best way to do security, and what is the best way to allocate resources that will have to come out of other people's budgets? Those remain hotly divisive issues that the security team is going to have to deconflict.

You Have to Evaluate the Outcomes

A common trap that organizational culture experts often warn of in the literature can be characterized as a "fire and forget" approach to transformational change. In other words, we make some attempt to change our culture, but then never follow up to see if what we did had any effect. One origin of this trap is the general belief that culture is difficult or impossible to measure, so you can't know whether efforts to change culture have been effective anyway. I have described a number of ways that organizations can and do measure their cultures, but not everyone is familiar or comfortable with these approaches. A more pernicious contributor to the trap could be described as general laziness. It is a lot easier to hire consultants to conduct a survey, to adopt the framework they recommend, to print up motivational posters encouraging everyone to adhere to the framework, and then to declare the cultural transformation initiative a success than it is to forge ahead and measure whether the culture has actually been transformed. Doing the investigative legwork to determine what, if any, effect all this activity had is time consuming, it's tedious, and it always carries the risk that maybe your slick internal awareness campaign really didn't convince anyone that they should start looking at the world differently.

But why should the organization care enough to devote the time and resources necessary to actually evaluate whether or not the culture changed? Here we must look back to the culture–performance link. Organizations don't worry about changing their culture just because they want to experiment with social theory. They do it because the research has shown that better culture equates with better business outcomes. Evaluation is then key for two crucial reasons. First, if performance improves only when the culture improves, you need to be sure the culture is actually improving. Second, you need to evaluate the link itself to understand how much moving the culture needle corresponds to moving the performance needle. Without this insight, there's no point in trying to change your culture at all.

You Have to Have Good Leadership

The last common thread I'll discuss is the universal importance that organizational culture research places on leadership. Leadership plays a central role in just about every study of organizational culture you will find. In some cases, culture and leadership almost become synonymous, given that few entities within an organization have the same opportunity to set cultural direction as those who set both the direction and the example.

Leadership is a double-edged sword as well. Business books are littered with cases where an organization brings in a new leader in an effort to improve performance only to watch them fail miserably either because they could not adapt to the existing culture or were so arrogant that they believed they could just change it by force of will. Over my own career I've personally experienced several painful periods where I found myself transitioning through a management change that seemed designed to cause as much disruption to the existing culture as possible. In the worst cases, the transition felt less like a reorganization and more like a coup d'état, where the existing management team was demoted or even fired, often for no other reason than they represented the old way of doing things. In spite of study after study showing that promoting insiders tends to produce better results than recruiting outsiders, many companies still operate under an apparent assumption that radical change of culture, quickly accomplished, is the only way to improve. Much of the organizational behavior research would seem to indicate that this very sense of insecurity and desperation is a symptom of a culture that may have already begun to degrade.

An Ocean of Research

If organizational cultures are like icebergs, the study of them is like an ocean of research and insight that spans academia, industry, and government. This chapter has necessarily been little more than a glimpse into that ocean. My intent was not to provide a comprehensive survey of the field, as there are plenty of great books that do this better than I ever could (and you'll find a list of just a few of these books in the "Further Reading" sections throughout the chapters). But to understand how information security culture works and how it can be transformed, it is necessary to at least understand that the broader and well-established fields of organizational culture and organizational behavior have already explored, debated, and maybe answered many of the questions that apply to information security culture. People-centric security is one of the more demanding developments in our industry today, not because it is so much more difficult to do than process or technology, but because it is equally difficult and we have so little experience doing it compared to the other two areas of focus. But we can take comfort in the knowledge that so much work has been done for us, blazing a trail that we can follow in order to apply these insights to the cultural challenges facing our own industry.

Further Reading

▶ Cohen D., and B. Crabtree. "Qualitative Research Guidelines Project." July 2006. Available at www.qualres.org.

▶ Kotter, John P., and James L. Heskett. *Corporate Culture and Performance.* New York: The Free Press, 1992.

▶ Myers, Michael D. *Qualitative Research in Business and Management.* 2nd ed. Thousand Oaks, CA: SAGE, 2013.

▶ Schein, Edgar. *Organizational Culture and Leadership.* San Francisco: Jossey-Bass, 2010.

Cultural Threats and Risks

Having covered the ground of the previous three chapters, we're left with a lot of circumstantial evidence regarding the relationship between information security and organizational culture. But where does the rubber hit the road? Where is the tangible, empirical interface between culture and security that allows us to imagine, observe, and design around the challenges and opportunities of our own security cultures?

Cultural Threat Modeling

In recent years the security industry has taken an interest in threat-centric security approaches, which attempt to address the actors responsible for security incidents instead of focusing on the weaknesses that such actors might exploit (vulnerability-centric approach) or the things they want to attack (asset-centric approach). To this end, methodologies for modeling security threats are in demand. The recent success of Adam Shostack's *Threat Modeling: Designing for Security*, including being nominated as one of the best security books for 2014, demonstrates the popular interest within the security community.

Threat Modeling is predominantly technology-centric, but Adam does go out of his way to explore human factors, a topic he also emphasized in his previous book, *The New School of Information Security*. Obviously interested in behavioral and social models and their applicability to the security industry, Adam catalogs and describes several theories, applying them at a high level to our field. And he explicitly recognizes and articulates the need for improved models to better describe how people "do" security, as well as the value of bringing in other research traditions such as sociology, anthropology, and psychology into our efforts. *Threat Modeling* never directly applies to people the STRIDE methodology that Adam helped to create, but the book serves as a tantalizing endorsement of more cultural threat modeling techniques to complement the technology- and actor-centric models the industry depends on today.

Today's threat modeling techniques all more or less assume a bounded information system or asset that is somehow faced with attack or other compromise. This lends itself very well to a specific product or system, but the threat modeling breaks down if you try to apply it to something less circumscribed, like human behaviors or social systems. Unfortunately, those of us responsible for security don't live in a world where the only concern is a technology system. In the complex web of real-world relationships, technology systems interact with, influence, and are shaped by other actors and events, including people, forces of nature, and other complex systems. The resulting emergent behaviors make the establishment of boundaries around any particular element of the system artificial at best, although assuming such arbitrary boundaries becomes somewhat obligatory for breaking down and analyzing challenges that would otherwise defy analysis. Applied to threat models, this just means we have to get comfortable with replacing hardware, software, and networks with more abstract boundaries like the person, the social group, and the organization, something social scientists are adept at doing.

Covert Processes and Cultural Risk

Modeling security threats involving an organization's culture really is not that different from modeling security threats involving software or hardware. At the core is a basic exercise in exposing the non-obvious, making it observable and tangible in a way that can be properly analyzed in order to properly manage or mitigate the threat. The differences are less conceptual than operational. Not every software application will be modeled in the same way, and hardware and software threats can be very different from a threat modeling perspective. Modeling cultural threats is just a further variation on this theme. There will be different sources of threats, different ways of describing them, and different approaches to managing them.

Since traditional threat modeling is about making visible the hidden relationship between those responsible for security failures and the means by which security fails, we can attempt to replicate that approach for culture. As it turns out, there is research available in this area. *Covert processes*, a concept first developed by organizational development scholar Bob Marshak, are organizational forces and dynamics that are hidden but exert powerful effects on our communications and efforts to achieve goals. We experience covert processes as hidden agendas, unspoken rules, or organizational taboos. Many of the examples I've given so far in this book are evidence of covert processes functioning within an organization. They are also at the heart of cultural risk from a security perspective.

Covert processes, and the behaviors they create, are difficult to recognize and address because they typically are camouflaged by appeals to a much more overt process, rational logic. Returning to the iceberg metaphor of culture and behavior, supposedly logical and objective decision making is one of the more visible aspects of organizational activity. We make plans and build strategies for activity based on our analyses of what we believe needs to be accomplished for organizational success. This is, arguably, the primary job of managers and leaders in an enterprise. They debate requirements and desired outcomes, lay out the best rational path for getting there, and set the conditions by which the organization will execute on their strategy. Usually that process of reason (singular) generates lists of reasons (plural) why the strategy is the right thing to do, which are communicated throughout the organization in the form of vision statements, plans, policies, and other artifacts.

Organizational leaders, having undertaken logical and rational deliberation to develop the best strategy, tend to expect everyone else in the organization to buy into their plans. To not do so would be irrational; it literally would not make sense. And that which does not make logical sense has no place in the management of the organization. After all, how can you respond to someone who is being unreasonable? But rationality is only one organizational dynamic, just as reason coexists in individuals along with physical, emotional, and psychological factors that can and do overpower our reason all the time. By ignoring everything but logic, organizations often deny themselves the insight they would need to understand why a strategy failed.

Inspired by Adam Shostack's work, and drawing from the literature on covert processes, I've developed a simplified threat model for security culture. Since we love acronyms and mnemonics in security, and the threat modeling literature has its fair share in methods such as STRIDE, DREAD, and OCTAVE, I decided to continue the tradition and searched for a good mnemonic. The acronym gods smiled on me. People are at the heart of cultural threats, both as actors and as targets. And political, emotional, psychological, and logistical threats are often core covert processes that create risks within an organization. Thus my cultural threat model, PEPL, was born.

Getting to Know PEPL

PEPL threats affect desired security outcomes rather than bounded systems. These security outcomes are desirable because of some rational, logical deliberation on the part of the organization that defined them as the way things should function. An outcome will almost always be a combination of people, process, and technology, and threats may exist to some or all of these elements. Good examples of outcomes would be bringing a software product to market that has no hidden security flaws, or an organization not getting hit with a massive data breach due to a compromised system. As in traditional security threat modeling, the threat relies on some vulnerability in the system, although I prefer to refer to these as "weaknesses" to avoid confusion with technical vulnerabilities. Table 4-1 describes and defines the specific PEPL threat along with the likely target of the threat and examples of specific cultural weaknesses and their effects on security outcomes. Of course, the ultimate effect is a security failure leading to an incident, often brought about by an inability to realize the desired outcome.

Threat	Definition	Motivations	Targets	Weaknesses Exploited	Effect on Outcomes
Political	Unique needs and interests of individuals and groups within the organization that may or may not align with established organizational interests.	Political motivations relate to position, authority, status, ownership, budget, resources, and general organizational control or influence.	Policies, decisions, resource allocations, technologies, people, and groups	Lack of controls or policy enforcement; resource shortages and conflicts; personal and professional relationships	Security strategies can be undermined or sabotaged in part or completely; security silos can develop; new IT projects or mergers can fail to achieve desired levels of protection
Emotional	Nonrational, affective responses to security planning related to feelings (fear, sadness, anger) that may not correspond to rational or logical arguments.	Emotional motivations relate to nonrational responses to desired security outcomes that may not be considered or appreciated by organizational planners.	Compliance with security policies or directives; adoption of processes or technology products; cooperation with auditors or security stakeholders	Organizational inability to control all activity; expectations of rational behavior and decision making	Security outcomes can be impaired or made inefficient and less effective; security problems and failures can be hidden deliberately or as part of a "rational bias" that ignores or depreciates emotional response
Psychological	Responses to security planning that develop out of cognitive or subconscious conditioning and reactions that limit the possibilities for acceptance and cooperation.	Psychological motivations relate to mental states and skills that have a direct effect on a person's ability to realize a desired security outcome.	Similar to the targets of emotional threats (policies, technologies, cooperation), but emerging from inability and anxiety related to cognitive skills	Improper communications or training; memory of individual or organizational trauma; insufficient education or technical skill sets	Security outcomes can be made inefficient and less effective; assumptions regarding individual capabilities may be inaccurate or false, leading to security failures
Logistical	Responses to security planning that are structural but not obvious, embedded into the existing people, processes, and technologies already in place within the organization.	Logistical motivations relate to the incompatibility of existing organizational structures and dynamics with the desired outcomes of security plans and strategies.	Security operations and designs; adoption of specific technologies or processes; compliance with policies and regulations	Existing incompatibility between systems; perceived inefficiency or problems associated with new security objectives	The organization may struggle to achieve desired security outcomes without significant compromises and exception processes

Table 4-1   *PEPL Threat Model*

Like other threat modeling frameworks, PEPL is primarily a brainstorming tool. It can generate a large set of potential problems for the security outcomes your organization hopes to achieve, much larger even than a traditional model focusing on a bounded system. While it is easy to apply PEPL to those same bounded systems (software applications, hardware systems, even a department or function), often the resulting threats will be functions of the organization as a whole. The culture that ends up defining the use of a people, process, or technology system is the culture of everyone who depends on it, whether or not they are immediate members of the information security teams.

Political Threats

Political threats happen when interests and agendas collide within an organization in a way that damages organizational effectiveness. Politics is everywhere in business, and political rivalries, alliances, and conflicts between individuals and groups are so common that we take them for granted even as we complain about their effects. What makes politics a covert process is not our lack of awareness that political behaviors exist, but rather our reluctance to admit just how much they play a role in our business decisions. Professional politicians, of course, have less problem admitting to overt political maneuvering, but employees and managers who behave this way can find themselves accused of manipulation or "playing politics" instead of putting the needs of the business first. Individual political ambitions and motivations are often seen as unprofessional and incompatible with good governance practices. Business stakeholders are supposed to plan and set strategy rationally, on the basis of objective evidence, not out of personal ambition or rivalries. The result is often a situation where the political dimensions of a planning or decision activity are not admitted to or are camouflaged within rationalizations that are more professionally acceptable. This drives political motivations into the background and people may be discouraged from addressing them openly. The result: people pretending to do something for business reasons when those reasons are actually personal and political can have a pernicious influence on organizational culture.

Turf Wars

Turf wars are a staple of organizational politics. They occur when actors within an organization (or sometimes between collaborative organizations) engage in competition over areas of bureaucratic control, resources, or advancement of goals and objectives (individual as well as organizational). This competition diverts energy and effort from other endeavors while creating tension and social friction between rival actors. Turf war combatants may deliberately withhold resources and information from one another, or may use their organizational authority to weaken or counter demands and requirements imposed by other groups. In highly pathological turf wars, organizations can fracture completely as actors and their representatives attempt to deliberately stymie or sabotage the efforts of internal competitors.

As a cultural threat, turf wars involving security can result in a breakdown of posture that introduces significant risk to the organization. Silos and organizational fiefdoms may develop outside the influence or reach of central security management. In some cases, central management may cease to exist or may be relegated to a small security team with no real authority to impose security related to people, process, or technology on any other part of the organization. Decentralized security is not necessarily a product of turf wars, as there are many reasons organizations may wish to federate or devolve security efforts. But in situations where security becomes a mechanism by which actors fight for turf, the organization's overall protective posture can be impaired, sometimes severely.

A Battle for Control

The following example illustrates the perverse threat of a turf war.

A customer once contracted my company to conduct a penetration test on their network. Unfortunately, we did not realize that Security Operations, the internal sponsor of the test, was engaged in a turf war with Network Operations, which still owned security responsibility for the company's network infrastructure. Security Operations hoped to use the pen test to show how poor security was on the network, then make a claim for authority over those resources (including the enormous budget for security technology that Network Ops controlled). But the Network Ops team was no slouch when it came to monitoring and protecting their domain. Three days after the start of the test, armed corporate security guards showed up at the conference room where the pen testers had set up shop, threatening to kick them all out of the building and notify the authorities. The whole engagement quickly turned into a fiasco. In the ensuing battle over who had the authority to do what, the results of the pen testing, including some serious vulnerabilities that had been discovered early on, were almost completely forgotten. The report itself, once it was finally delivered, was shelved for fear of further exacerbating a volatile political situation.

Vendor Bias

Vendor bias occurs when individuals or groups within the organization decide on particular products, technologies, or vendors based on political motives. I use the term "vendor" broadly here to denote any entity providing goods and services to an organization, commercially or otherwise (open source software providers, for instance, would be included as vendors even if they do not charge or are not even a formal commercial entity). Motives for vendor bias can range from a desire to protect incumbencies to back room or even nepotistic arrangements and partnerships. A cultural threat emerges when preferences for, or arrangements with, certain vendors conflict with desired security outcomes and create conflicts of interest that introduce security risk.

When an organization swears by a particular vendor, or hates another to the point where the organization refuses to buy that vendor's products (or use them freely, in the case of open source) no matter what, rational security decisions can end up held hostage by forces that may not be fully articulated or even understood within the organization. All sorts of weird behavior can emerge. An organization may end up having to devote resources and budget to workarounds to get its technology to match its security requirements. Or security teams may deny themselves the best solution because they have decided they dislike the provider on personal grounds. Risks are not limited to technology. Structurally incumbent vendors have less motivation toward efficiency and cost effectiveness. Internally, the organization may find itself behind the curve on skills and innovation by continually supporting vendors out of a sense of loyalty (or animosity to a competitor) rather than sound business analysis. There is nothing wrong with building long-standing relationships between businesses, but if a relationship develops its own political base within an organization, it can end up competing directly with security objectives and introducing uncertainty and risk.

Emotional Threats

Emotional threats challenge organizations because they are the opposite of the rational, logical decision making organizations tend to pride themselves on. In industry, emotions tend to be downplayed in favor of reason, and negative emotions like fear, jealousy, and regret are treated as less beneficial than positive ones like passion, contentment, and hope. Almost all organizations claim to have conquered, or at least controlled, emotionalism as a basis for action. Some may even have done so, as is commonly attributed to Warren Buffet's Berkshire-Hathaway, which has famously embraced a nonemotional investment style. But most organizations only pretend to be as coldly rational as they claim, giving into and even relying on "emotional intelligence" throughout their operations. Emotions can become a cultural threat when they influence decisions but the organization denies their role, making them unavailable for analysis or improvement.

Fear, Uncertainty, and Doubt

I knew a CISO who once admitted freely, if sheepishly, that the driving requirements for his security team were to address "whatever most recently scared the crap out of me in the media..." Every time a new vulnerability or threat hit the news, or even a new solution that might represent a risk if the organization did not immediately deploy it, he panicked. Weekly staff meetings were often an exercise in the troops talking the general as far off the ledge as they could, then figuring out how to respond to the fears remaining that they could not manage to dispel. The CISO knew it was a bad way to run his InfoSec program, but as much as he tried not to let his emotions guide him, he constantly worried what might happen to his company and his career if one of his fears were to actualize and he had not taken it seriously enough.

In today's digitally networked world, the number of things to be afraid of from an information security perspective approaches infinity. The past couple of years have seen cyber attacks on a massive scale against some of the largest and most well-known organizations on the planet. Emotions run high, and it is no wonder that the combination of fear, uncertainty, and doubt (FUD) has become a primary driver of security strategy. It is as though the emotional and the logical have merged. In security today, you can be labeled irrational for not being sufficiently terrified.

The problem with FUD as a basis for security strategy is that it makes crazy decisions seem perfectly justified in the heat of the moment. It is not a problem unique to security, and it can lead to responses that make less and less sense the further you get from the moment of panic. In Chapter 2 I wrote about the sense of defeatism that I think has become a dominant cultural trait in security today, and one I believe is a cultural threat that is rooted as much in FUD as it is in incidents we see happening. FUD allows us to highlight specific security events and incidents (I am deliberately not being specific here—search for "worst security incidents " in the last year if you are looking for reasons to panic) while ignoring everything that doesn't go wrong in the digital economy every day. FUD allows us to hold up the cost of cyber breaches (estimates vary widely, but several reputable attempts put it in the hefty range of $300–600 billion each year) as evidence that we need an "all hands on deck" response from industry and government.

That's certainly a big number, but elevating cyber security tends to overlook or ignore the costs of other global challenges that also warrant action. A 2014 McKinsey report, *Overcoming Obesity: An Initial Economic Analysis*, estimates the combined costs of smoking and obesity at over $4 trillion annually (twice the estimated cost of global war, violence, and terrorism), and these problems likely affect more InfoSec professionals directly than security breaches do. A rational approach based on costs and limited resources to address global problems would seem to imply that information security may not be the highest priority. But rationality is not the only force at work here, and that's the point.

Emotional Logic

Emotional logic may seem counterintuitive, but it is one of the reasons that FUD remains pervasive. It is the feeling, which we nurture and encourage, that we are making objective, rational decisions when we are really just doing what we want to do or think we need to do. Remember that covert processes happen behind the organizational facade of rationality. Since reason is prioritized in organizations, anything that is going to be accepted must be translated into the language of rationality. My CISO friend consoled himself over the fact that he was sending his team on weekly snipe hunts by couching his irrational fear in the very reasonable terms that he was being proactive. "What if we are vulnerable to this and we just don't know it yet? We're all going to be glad I made you take the time to check every single device in the infrastructure."

Psychological Threats

Psychological threats are closely related to emotional threats, maybe even contributing to some of them. But these threats are different in that they are grounded in cognitive functions and processes of the people creating them. Researchers in the fields of psychology, human development, and behavioral economics spend careers trying to understand the hidden reasons behind people's decisions. The explanations range from different types of intelligence between individuals to differing cognitive systems within each of us. The implications for security can be profound, particularly so when, like the previous examples, the covert process operates out of sight and out of mind, unavailable for analysis or even observation.

Statistical Alchemy

I see an example of emotional logic as a cultural security threat whenever I work with customers on their security metrics programs. In communicating security information, particularly information about threats and vulnerabilities, CISOs and security managers often have little more than the gut feelings of their staff to go on. No one really knows how likely or how severe an incident might be, unless of course that person has access to some level of historical data, which many organizations do not. Emotional logic can drive the process of statistical alchemy that I referenced in Chapter 3, where opinions are converted into numbers by the replacement of a mere description with a quantitative score or a scale. Statistical alchemy can magically transmute the lead of raw, emotional speculation into the much more valuable gold of scientific fact. It happens every time a security team changes a three-category ordinal risk description like high, medium, and low into an interval or ratio score that kicks out a number like "our risk score is 3.85" or "our security is 80% good." It is usually nearly impossible to retrace how they got from a risk description of "low" to a number like "3.85" given the available empirical data. In fact, the number probably makes less sense even to the security team than a straightforward "low" ever did, adding uncertainty to the risk analysis instead of removing it, but boy, it looks so much better on a graph.

Cognitive Limitations

A cultural threat resulting from cognitive limitations happens when a particular security strategy or desired outcome does not account for differences in the way people process information, interact with technology, learn, or gain new professional skills. Cognitive limitations are not as simple as differences in intelligence. They can be generational, educational, geographical, or cultural (in the larger sense as well as pertaining to organizational culture). The common trait for security is that cognitive limitations all but ensure that a rigid "one size fits all" approach to security is unlikely to succeed.

With the Audience in Mind

Consider an educational example of cognitive limitations. One measure of educational achievement is reading level. In 2002 and 2003, the U.S. government published the National Assessment of Adult Literacy (NAAL), the largest and most comprehensive study of adult literacy in the United States ever conducted by the government. Among many findings, the study estimated that the average American reads at a seventh- or eighth-grade level, with less than a fifth of the population achieving "full literacy," meaning a reading level equivalent to that of someone who has an undergraduate degree from a university. The estimate has since been used in guidelines for readability of everything from popular novels to machinery operating manuals to the labels and directions on pharmaceuticals. In information security, the creation and distribution of policies and guidelines are fundamental as a framework and basis for desired security outcomes.

Billions of dollars are spent collectively by organizations to write security policies, post them, and regularly require users to read them as evidence that they know what is expected of them when it comes to protecting corporate information assets. But how much effort is put into understanding how readable these policies are? I can tell you that the effort is not always enough, as evidenced by my readability analyses of numerous client security policies. In one case, a customer complained because they had a very expensive, very comprehensive policy creation and distribution process and yet they were still seeing continual violations of policy. "It's like no one even reads the things," the CISO said. A readability analysis showed a potentially different explanation. Using standard scales of readability, the company's policies often required the equivalent of a graduate degree to read and fully comprehend them. So everyone may have been reading the security policies, but most people likely found them impossible to understand, much less comply with. Consider just one brief snippet:

> Employees have an ethical, as well as a legal, obligation to adhere to the requirements articulated in this policy. Failure to comply with mandated security requirements results in significant enterprise risk and liability. It is incumbent upon employees to regularly review and familiarize themselves with the contents and requirements of this policy. Failure to do so can result in consequences up to and including immediate termination of employment status.

Security managers may not think it a problem that such policies are written in particular dialects of legalese and HR-speak, then disseminated through cut-and-paste templates implemented by organizations often more interested in checking a compliance box than helping people figure out what they are supposed to do. Such a policy may seem to make rational sense (you want one that functions something like a legal contract between employees and employer). But try making your security strategy actually work when the people most responsible for implementing it are also the least able to make sense of it.

Cognitive Differences

The field of behavioral economics is booming. Daniel Kahneman, Dan Ariely, and Daniel Gardner (I wonder what a behavioral economist might make of the fact that many of my favorite behavioral economy experts are named Daniel...) have all published books theorizing ways that our rational decision-making processes are often not rational at all. A general theme among their books is that human beings do not seem to process information or make decisions in the simple, linear way that we have traditionally accepted. Human decisions are a hodgepodge of cognitive activity, some deliberative and what we would recognize as rational, and others emerging from primitive intuitive pattern matching that seems to be hardwired into our evolutionary biology. The result is a set of differing cognitive functions that can grossly mislead us while providing an almost (or maybe an actual) physical sense of certainty and clarity about what we think we know.

In security, these cognitive differences manifest themselves as cultural threats most often when it comes to trying to figure out risk. People are absolutely terrible at assessing risk, or even deciding what they should really be afraid of. Doug Hubbard, the author of *The Failure of Risk Management: Why It's Broken and How to Fix It,* has gone so far as to claim that the greatest single risk most organizations face is probably the way they do their risk management, a statement that might ring sadly true for some current and former CISOs I'm aware of, not to mention a few financial institutions and a nuclear facility or two.

Logistical Threats

Logistical threats can develop whenever a security strategy is incapable of being realized due to incompatibilities with existing organizational infrastructure. Implementing a strong password policy companywide when some systems are incapable of handling complex passwords is one example. Mandating the use of certain technologies that are incompatible with legacy systems is another example. Like the other cultural threats I've described, it is when logistical issues function as a covert process affecting a perceived rational strategy that they become risky and dangerous.

Incompatible Systems

Both of the preceding examples have to do with security imposing requirements that conflict or are not compatible with existing systems. In the audit and compliance world, such situations are encountered regularly, and have produced the concept of compensating controls as a safeguard against risks that have been assessed and accepted as necessary but require additional effort to manage. In other organizations, the problem is handled by exception processes that allow people with (more or less) good reasons to opt out of certain security requirements. Whatever the case, the result is that a new system or systems must be created in order to align security strategy with security fact.

Exceptions as the Rule

I have observed organizations where over half of the systems in operation ran nonstandard configurations, ostensibly violations of the corporate equipment standards for security, but which had been granted security exceptions. One wonders how rational an organization's security strategy can be when following it properly in the deployment of technology systems actually makes you the exception. This paradox can often get lost in the fog of security, though, when the logic of what should be done according to some compliance regime or the dreaded "industry best practice" overwhelms the reality of what is actually possible within the environment.

Incompatible Outcomes

Security incompatibilities do not just occur with technology, as my previous case study of Clara, the developer in Chapter 2, demonstrated. Outcomes themselves can be at odds with one another on very basic levels. BYOD and the cloud are both current cases where business strategy can collide directly with security strategy. When the differences in strategy are managed properly, threats can be avoided. When the competing outcomes (market agility vs. security control, for example) are not properly managed, especially when logistical challenges become imbued with political, emotional, and psychological dimensions themselves, they can grow into a serious threat to security and to the organization's business.

Treating security as a strategic outcome independent of other organizational goals can create a false choice, a zero-sum game where every concession to the business is seen as a loss for security and every capitulation to security's demands is viewed as a blow to business efficiency. This is not rational, no matter what justifications and business cases are made on either side. The complexity of today's organizations and enterprises means that nothing can ever be completely secured nor ever made totally efficient. All that matters is achieving a productive balance between the various forces, including cultural forces, at work within an organization as it tries to meet its goals. This includes balancing security risk with business risk, not only the risk of having too little security, but also the business risks that can come with overly restrictive security infrastructures that hamper a company's agility and innovation.

Cultural Competition as a Source of Risk

The exercise in cultural threat modeling outlined in this chapter is never going to be as straightforward as threat-modeling-bounded technology systems. The latter are complicated systems, sometimes staggeringly so, but a complicated system has a finite set of states and possible outcomes. Theoretically, you can know them all in advance, including all the possible threats associated with the system. A complex system, however, produces emergent behaviors that cannot be known in advance but develop out of use and interaction with other system entities. The possibilities approach infinity. When a complicated smartphone or a network switch or a software program is put into someone's hands and then incorporated into a system of other technologies and, most importantly, people, it becomes a component in a complex system. It is no longer possible to predict all the ways the component will be put to use, including all the threats associated with it.

Cultural threat models show not only the risks that exist between threats in a traditional sense (an actor or natural phenomenon creating a negative outcome based on weakness in the system), but also the risks associated with legitimate interaction and competition among system components, particularly human stakeholders. A balance of forces exists within these systems, and risk to one actor or entity may equate to opportunity for another, creating scenarios where failure is both undesirable and also a natural outcome of success elsewhere. If failures or successes begin to dominate disproportionately, the whole system can begin to fall out of balance and may experience a more general systemic failure or collapse.

The lesson of cultural threat modeling specifically, and people-centric security more generally, is not about trying to enumerate every possible threat from or to the culture. This is impossible. Instead, these threat models are about trying to get a handle on the competing forces that are currently operating in any complex organizational system, to observe their origins and effects, and to attempt to bring them back into balance when they shift dangerously to one side or another. It is much harder to do when some or most of the threat entities are operating as covert processes that we cannot or choose not to observe. Risk is created by these interactions when people say they are doing one thing for a certain reason, based on logic and rational analysis, but are actually doing it for different reasons that may have nothing to do with objectivity, or are really doing another thing entirely without admitting it.

Sizing Up the Competition

People-centric risk management is not about trying to predict human behavior, at least not exactly. Instead, it is about shining an analytical light on organizational and cultural relationships to find out where covert processes, hidden behavior, and competition exist and may need to be managed and balanced. The sources of competition in organizational security programs, the pressure points where covert processes produce cultural threats, include an organization's stakeholders, priorities, and values.

Competing Security Stakeholders

Stakeholders are individual people and organized groups. A CISO is a stakeholder, as is a regulatory body that defines IT compliance and audit requirements for an industry. Information security stakeholders do not have to be directly connected to security operations. Users are stakeholders in that they depend on the confidentiality, integrity, and availability of IT assets to do their jobs. Customers are stakeholders for much the same reason. Stakeholders do not need to consciously care about information security; they need only have an explicit or implicit interest (a stake) in the results of security activities. In InfoSec, this includes just about anyone who depends on information technology.

Just because stakeholders have an interest in security does not mean they are equally supportive of security efforts or have the same goals. Stakeholders can compete against one another, even when both are dedicated to securing information systems and assets. An auditor's goals are not necessarily the same as a security manager's. The auditor wants to explore and perhaps expose as many security problems as possible, in order to force change and reduce risk in accordance with some regulatory or other requirement, irrespective of the resources required. A security manager wants to successfully complete an audit with a minimal level of time and effort. Both the auditor and the security manager want good security, but their ideas of what that means can compete fiercely when it comes to the bottom line.

When stakeholders exist outside of security altogether, competition can become even more intense. Members of an organization have many things they care about, and some of those things are more visible or more important than others. They may want agility, productivity, and innovation more than anything else. Security team members may want things to be protected and predictable. These priorities compete. A CISO is the most prominent security stakeholder in an organization, but as an executive, that CISO also has a stake in the continued growth and success of the company. If enterprise security is too restrictive, if it inhibits competitiveness or market performance too much, then the whole company may suffer, and the CISO will have failed just as badly as if a damaging security incident had caused the problem.

Organizations today are collective entities, but bureaucracy and professional specialization have created fragmentation around job roles and functions. People tend to be trained for a very specific set of capabilities that will define their careers for years or even decades. We talk about security professionals, HR professionals, and project management professionals, each with their own body of knowledge, certification requirements, and working culture. This specialization tends to result in people prioritizing the interests and assumptions of their narrow field above the desires and expectations of others. Such specialization is required to tackle complex problems in today's business environments, but it contributes to the creation of fiefdoms and silos that inhibit organizational visibility and coordination.

Competing Security Priorities

I have already devoted several pages to the ways in which security priorities can compete with non-security priorities. But it is important to call out that conflicts exist within security as well. Part of the reason is that information security has become a large discipline, with branches and subfields, in its own right. Security awareness managers and firewall administrators both operate within the larger field of InfoSec, but they are probably very different types of people. And they may not always agree on what the most important considerations for security should be. Education, experience, and interactions with technology and other people will inform their worldview in possibly very different ways.

Security professionals also have to deal with priorities that may be unwelcome to purists who wish to focus exclusively on the fundamentals of protecting information assets and enforcing security policies. Budgets and resources are as much security principles as confidentiality, integrity, and availability. Few organizations have unlimited supplies, so things that should be done are balanced against things that must be done, with the struggle being how to decide where that line is drawn. Risks and threats can often be primarily a product of how effectively a security team allocates its limited capacities, which may explain why some organizations succeed while peers that appear very similar fail hard. What is often characterized as bad luck or bad timing can often be attributed to poor handling of competing priorities.

Competing Security Values

Priorities are about choosing what is important among multiple possibilities. Values are about why we think something is important in the first place. Our security values drive our security priorities, but often for reasons that we are less consciously aware of. If our security priorities are the more or less rational rank stacking of our decisions, our security values more closely reflect the assumptions and biases at the heart of our security culture. When security values contradict one another, the effects echo across the decisions and outcomes of the whole organization.

I've worked with security teams that shared administrator passwords, with organizations that refused to allow penetration testing on certain key systems, and in places where authentication latency required 10 to 15 minutes between login and access to a business-critical system. In every case the security stakeholders responsible for the systems had balanced one value they felt was important (nonrepudiation, visibility into vulnerabilities, and productivity, respectively, in these cases) with a competing security value. Each balancing act introduced one or more risks into the environment. But none of these cases were seen as irrational or unacceptable when the organization in question described it. They might have wanted to change things, or maybe wished they could be different. But each had to deal with the fact that theirs was an imperfect world, and trade-offs were required. "Hey, it is what it is," one security manager told me, holding up his hands, when I gently pointed out one of these conflicts.

When particular security values become accepted and embedded, they can create a cultural pattern. A sort of path of least resistance develops where some ideas and proposals are more easily accepted and face less scrutiny than others because they resonate with the pattern. Patterns can develop into cultural archetypes (or stereotypes, if you prefer), like a collective personality that anticipates (but doesn't predict—these are people after all) likely outcomes. A heavily regulated organization with regular visits from auditors is likely to adopt a compliance mindset, thinking like the auditors it answers to, until most decisions are filtered through the lens of "how will this affect the audit?" An open environment that relies on the free flow of information and access to achieve success may become a security skeptic, interrogating a CISO about every proposed initiative and whether or not the control will impede people's ability to do their work.

The effect of competing cultural values has been studied outside of security, with the research into covert processes I've cited being just one example. Researchers have used the concept of competitive cultural forces as a way of measuring, managing, and transforming organizational culture, guided by the logic that if we can understand why we behave in a certain way, we stand a better chance of changing that behavior. Such theories and methods currently are utilized in management science and business consulting circles, and I am unaware of any major attempts to apply them to information security. In the next sections of the book, I will attempt to do just that.

Further Reading

- Ariely, Dan. *Predictably Irrational: The Hidden Forces that Shape Our Decisions.* New York: HarperCollins, 2008.

- Gardner, Daniel. *The Science of Fear: Why We Fear the Things We Shouldn't—and Put Ourselves in Greater Danger.* New York: Dutton, 2008.

- Hubbard, Douglas W. *The Failure of Risk Management: Why It's Broken and How to Fix It.* Hoboken, NJ: Wiley, 2009.

► Kahneman, Daniel. *Thinking Fast and Slow.* New York: Farrar, Straus and Giroux, 2011.

► Marshak, Robert. *Covert Processes at Work: Managing the Five Hidden Dimensions of Organizational Change.* San Francisco: Berrett-Koehler, 2006.

► National Center for Education Statistics. "National Assessment of Adult Literacy." Available at http://nces.ed.gov/.

► Shostack, Adam. *Threat Modeling: Designing for Security.* Hoboken, NJ: Wiley, 2014.

Measuring Your Security Culture

CHAPTER 5

The Competing Security Cultures Framework

Every organization that is concerned about protecting its information assets and systems—basically all organizations in today's networked and digital society—has an information security culture. The security culture is a facet of the overall organizational culture. Most organizations, in fact, have multiple information security cultures, reflections of local values and priorities, and not everyone inside the organization is going to share the same beliefs and assumptions about how security should and does work. What the information security team values and thinks is most important for protecting the organization will probably be different, at least in degree, from what HR (or Internal Audit, or Facilities, etc.) values and thinks is most important. In benign cases, these cultural characteristics coexist peacefully, never having cause to interfere with one another. But more often, they eventually compete. That competition may occur over resources, over money, or over simple political infighting. But the security culture that dominates, including the values and priorities that drive decisions and spending, will have profound implications for the organization's performance in regard to information security.

To ensure that organizations develop the most beneficial security culture, the most successful balance of differing priorities and motivations, we have to understand culture better. Organizations must develop techniques for translating general insights about culture into actionable intelligence. Fortunately, there are lots of theories, frameworks, and methods for accomplishing this goal, fueled by decades of research and practice in the fields of organizational performance and development. I propose my own methodology, the Competing Security Cultures Framework (CSCF), further in this chapter. But the CSCF did not develop spontaneously. I created it by adapting and extending earlier research, and it is worth spending a little time to understand those roots.

Measuring Security Culture

In Chapter 3, I described techniques for measuring culture at a high level. Particularly, I focused on qualitative data and analysis, which are commonly used in the study of culture, and differ from quantitative data and analysis methods. It is important to visit these differences directly, particularly since the information security and IT security fields often misuse the terms and concepts of measurement or suffer from a distorted understanding of what they represent. Measurement is about comparison more than about counting, and different tools are necessary for different phenomena.

The tools I have developed to measure security culture and to encourage the adoption of transformational security behaviors are primarily survey-based, with the possibility of using interviews and more interactive methods to expand on collected security culture data. These tools are used as both qualitative and quantitative approaches to measurement. Some require manual work, while others can be automated, depending on the goals and resource constraints an organization has. We will explore them in great detail in later chapters, but for now it is enough to familiarize yourself with their origins and some of the characteristics of the data they utilize.

Quantitative Data and Analysis

Quantitative data are, put simply, those that lend themselves to counting. The result of a coin toss or the result of a dice roll are simple examples. Your height and weight are two more examples. Quantitative data can be ranked in a particular order, assigned to specific categories, or expressed in standardized units. While many people associate quantitative data with math and numbers, quantitative data can be more or less mathematical depending on whether they are nominal, ordinal, interval, or ratio data. The data type in question also determines the types and sophistication of statistical analysis that can be performed. To explore these four quantitative data types further, suppose you work in a datacenter. Wandering around your datacenter, you'll see plenty of examples of all four data types, as described in the following sections.

Nominal Data

Wandering around the racks of equipment in the datacenter, you notice different computers from different vendors. You see switches, servers, and workstations, for instance. And you may notice products from Cisco, Dell, or HP. These are examples of nominal data, which means they are strictly categorical. All the devices you observe are computers, but you can differentiate between types. You also may notice that each rack has a number. These are also nominal data, as each number represents a category label, not a mathematical value. You can count the number of Cisco switches you have, but you can't do anything statistical with the categories themselves. You can't add Cisco and Dell or find the average between rack number 6 and rack number 14. Nominal data only serve to identify something as different from something else, to name it, which is where the term *nominal* comes from.

Confusingly, nominal data are sometimes called qualitative data, which I suspect is where the security industry's use of the term originated given our regular use of categorical data. Nominal data are no less empirical or scientific than other quantitative data types. But they literally don't add up. Statistical analysis of nominal data only occurs when you compare data within the categories. You might find that 90 percent of your servers come from one vendor, for example, which can tell you something. Or you might find that machines in rack number 3 fail twice as often, which might be coincidence or might imply an issue with the enclosure itself.

Ordinal Data

Suppose the datacenter team is installing some new equipment on the day you are making your observations. They are deploying and configuring three servers, and they got started first thing in the morning as you arrived. The first server is completed later that morning, the second early in the afternoon, and the third doesn't get done until late that night. The order in which the servers were finished is an example of ordinal data, which provide position and ranking but not much more. You know that the first server was set up faster than the third server, but not how much faster, at least not without gathering a different kind of data. But even the limited information about position allows you to perform more statistical analysis "out of the box" than with nominal data. You can use ordinal data to determine something about central tendency (defined in the proximate sidebar), an important aspect of quantitative analysis. The most common measure of central tendency is the average, or mean. But we can't use the mean for ordinal data, where we only have rank order (completed first, second, and last). The difference in time between completion of the first and second servers is not the same as the duration between completion of the second and third servers, so an average is impossible with just the positions.

We can, however, apply the median to ordinal data. The median is simply the middle-ranked ordinal value, the one with as many values above it as below it. In our case, the median value would be 2, representing the server that was completed between the first one and last one. We could also use the mode, meaning the value that appears most frequently in the data, although it doesn't apply as well to our server example. A clearer example would be a race where there is a three-way tie for second place, but no other ties. In this case, the mode would be 2, since more people finished second than any other ranking.

Statistical Terms

Statistics has its own language. Some terms are familiar from our everyday lives, but others are a bit more challenging. Readers who haven't taken a statistics class in a while may benefit from a quick refresher of the following terms used in this chapter:

▶ **Central tendency**   The degree to which a set of values or measurements groups or clusters around some central value in a distribution. The most well-known example of central tendency is the Gaussian distribution, or normal curve, in which values cluster uniformly around the centermost values.

▶ **Mean**   The "average" of a set of values, computed by totaling all values and then dividing that total by the number of values present.

▶ **Median**   The middle value in a set of values, where the number of values is equally distributed below and above the median value. If you have an odd number of values, the median is the one in the middle; for example, the value 2 in the sequence 1…2…3 is the median. If you have an even number of values, the median is the mean of the two middle values; for example, 2.5 in the sequence 1…2…3…4.

▶ **Mode**   The most frequent value in a set of values, the one that occurs most often. A set of values can have multiple modes, in the case of an equal number of repetitions, or none, if no value occurs more frequently than another.

Interval Data

Looking around the datacenter, you notice a digital thermometer on the wall telling you that the temperature inside is 80 degrees Fahrenheit. Now you're collecting interval data, which allows you to consider how much values differ from one another. You remember reading the outside temperature when you got out of your car that cool fall morning and noticing it was 40°F. Interval data allows you to say more than just "hotter" or "colder" in an ordinal ranking. You can now state that the difference in temperature between the inside of the datacenter and the outside world is 40°F. What you cannot do, though, is to state that it is twice as warm inside as it is outside. Ratios like this don't work with interval data, because it lacks any meaningful zero value. Zero on temperature scales like Fahrenheit and Celsius are subjective. 80°F is not twice as hot as 40°F because you can have negative temperatures. You could only make such statements about temperature if you were using the Kelvin scale, which does have an absolute zero value. But most datacenters don't sport Kelvin thermometers.

Despite not being able to bring a full range of statistical techniques to interval data, you can still do quite a lot. The mean, median, and mode all work for interval data. You can also begin using some more sophisticated statistical techniques, including the standard deviation, in your analysis. This is why your HVAC system in the datacenter tracks things like how far temperature fluctuations differ from the norm and alerts someone if things get too far away from normal. And you can make claims about the differences between interval values that you cannot make about the values themselves. If tomorrow is a warmer day and the temperature outside hits 60°F, you can state that the temperature difference on the cold day was twice the temperature difference on the warmer one (40°F difference vs. 20°F difference).

Ratio Data

Ratio data is the whole enchilada, so to speak. It possesses a true, nonarbitrary zero value, a continuous scale, and standard units. You can bring the full brunt of statistical analysis to bear on ratio data, and these data are what we are probably thinking about when we think about scientific data. For the datacenter, everything from operating costs to uptime to network traffic throughput are represented by ratio data. Ratio data are things you can count out and compare in an apples to apples way to say that A is X times bigger or Y times shorter or Z times more expensive than B or C.

One thing that may jump out at you as you're reading these descriptions is that security teams deal with a lot of different types of quantitative data, much of which is probably not ratio data. Nonetheless, given that ratio data allows more statistical analysis, some people may be tempted to "manufacture" ratio data out of other types. This desire can lead even well-meaning security professionals to fall into the trap of (thanks again, Adam Shostack) "jet engine × peanut butter = shiny!" The Shostack equation is a basic expression in statistical alchemy. Using it, you can transform nominal or ordinal data (high, medium, low) into interval and ratio data (scores like 3.85 or 80) that can then be sliced and diced statistically to derive all sorts of imaginary inferences. The problem isn't the method, it's the data. Too many security programs these days confuse "quantitative" with "empirical," and the value their metrics bring to the table are diminished as a result.

Qualitative Data and Analysis

Empirical data means that you can observe whatever it is you are measuring. *Qualitative data*, as you will recall, is most simply described as things that are difficult to count directly. But they can still be observed, so qualitative data may be every bit as empirical as quantitative data. Let's get back to our datacenter for more examples. Taking a break from your TPS reports, you notice your colleagues John and Rachel debating the quality of the marketing campaign for a new line of high-performance servers the company is considering purchasing. Rachel hates the marketing campaign, but John likes it. Rachel has a brochure on her desk from the vendor meeting they attended earlier that day.

"It looks like a kid's cartoon," she laughs. "How am I supposed to take it seriously?"

"Nah, it's kind of hip," John counters. "The vendor did a good job of not making it look like every other corporate IT advertisement. What do you think, Ken?"

Ken's sitting two cubes over, engrossed in a security awareness video that's part of the company's HR compliance program. He grunts noncommittally, without looking up.

Every one of these artifacts are examples of qualitative data. John and Rachel's conversation, the vendor brochure, Ken's security awareness video, all of them represent observable things that can be analyzed but don't lend themselves immediately to counting. You can count things about them, certainly, like the number of words spoken in John and Rachel's verbal argument or the number of pixels in the training video, but what do those numbers tell you? We are more likely to find meaningful analysis in John's comment that the brochure is trying to differentiate the vendor from its competitors, but that's a lot more difficult to directly quantify.

Qualitative Approaches Revisited

Chapter 3 listed several approaches to qualitative measures, including historical and biographical methods, ethnography, grounded theory, and action research. These are all means by which researchers can collect and analyze qualitative data. Any of the qualitative data we noticed in our datacenter example are possible targets of collection. You might make a transcript of John and Rachel's conversation or ask for copies of the brochure and awareness video. Observing such things actually makes you a data collection instrument yourself. Spend a year in the datacenter, and you might write a book about your experiences there, as some researchers have done.

The frameworks and measurement tools I present in this book draw from the experiences of qualitative researchers, but they do not depend upon or require you to be a historian, ethnographer, or social scientist. I point out the examples of qualitative data because you may come across them and want to use them in transforming your security culture. We spend a lot of time in the security field wondering about questions of who, what, where, and when. Quantitative data can help us decipher these mysteries. But we also spend a lot of time trying to figure out how and why. Often the answers to these questions are only found by observing qualitative data and interpreting the results.

Artifacts as Data

The great thing about using qualitative data to answer questions is that it allows you to greatly expand what you consider to be "data" in the first place. We don't bat an eyelash when an auditor requests copies of all of our security policies to review, but we don't usually think of those security policies as scientific data either. They totally are, or at least can be if subjected to the right analyses. The example of the readability of security policies I used in Chapter 4 is a good example. Policy documents are artifacts produced by a security program. They are also data that can reveal things about that program. When examining an organization's security culture, a huge variety of artifacts can be considered, not just the security policies of the organization. Security awareness materials, the minutes of staff meetings, source code and configuration files, even video from the CISO's offsite leadership training program can become empirical data produced by the organization, data just waiting to give up insights to the right kind of analysis.

Combining the Qualitative and Quantitative

The techniques for measuring security culture in this book will rely on two key methods of collecting data: the survey and the interview. These tools are widely used throughout industry, as anyone knows who has taken an opinion poll, worked on a marketing survey, or been part of a job interview or a focus group. What makes these tools interesting is that they allow us to observe by proxy things that are intrinsically not observable, the things that go on inside people's heads. Thoughts, opinions, and values are all real things, but observing them is hard and subject to interpretation. One of the oldest and best ways to find out what a person thinks about a topic is to ask them directly, and that is exactly what a survey instrument or an interview template does. These tools don't guarantee valid results, meaning that you may not be observing what you think you are observing. People lie, they get confused, and they contradict themselves. But unless you are psychic, there aren't many other ways to observe someone's thoughts.

It should be noted, briefly, that the advertising and marketing industries are experimenting with ever more sophisticated ways of discovering what people are thinking (or what they are doing, even when they are doing it unconsciously). Sentiment analysis, online advertising experiments, and human factors research are all contributing to making sense of human behavior. In some cases these techniques are much more precise than surveys and interviews, frighteningly so sometimes. But they remain an interpretive effort by which researchers use proxies to measure what cannot be directly counted (online ad click-throughs vs. a person's actual product preferences).

The fact that qualitative data cannot be counted in raw form does nothing to stop people from applying quantitative approaches to it. In fact, a lot of research is a combination of qualitative and quantitative approaches, sometimes referred to as *mixed methods research*. By identifying and coding specific attributes of qualitative data, it becomes possible to actually count things, to identify patterns, and to compare differences. John and Rachel's argument about the vendor marketing campaign? Well, imagine we have a written transcript of everything they said and we start looking for repetitive patterns in the text. Suppose we discover that every third or fourth sentence spoken by Rachel contains an explicit comparison between the marketing brochure and a children's cartoon. We might then code each of Rachel's statements as making either a favorable comparison or an unfavorable one. If we discover that out of 50 comparative statements made by Rachel over the course of the debate, 90 percent were unfavorable and contained words like "juvenile," "immature," and "unprofessional," we might be able to draw some inferences about Rachel's feelings both toward the advertisement and, possibly, toward cartoons in general. Someone knowing Rachel for a long time might tell you that Rachel has always thought cartoons were silly. But they might also struggle to "prove" that, and Rachel might even argue with them. Qualitative data of the sort I just described provide empirical evidence of Rachel's opinion, evidence that can be more scientifically analyzed through the lens of observable behavior.

Interviews

When comparing interviews and surveys, interviews are more qualitative than surveys because they tend to be exploratory and open-ended. When we interview someone, we just let them talk. We may structure the interview to ask specific questions or focus on a particular topic, but we don't try to completely control the interviewee's responses. What we end up with is a lot of text that must then be analyzed and coded for patterns. From these patterns we can interpret findings and insights.

If you have only a general idea about what you want to know, conducting interviews can be the best way to approach the problem. Suppose you want to know how an employee feels about working for the company and you don't want to bring any preconceived notions into the mix. An open-ended interview approach would be to simply ask that person, "How do you feel about working here?" The employee could say whatever they wanted, bring up any topics, and speak as long as they felt necessary. The downside is that you might end up with a lot of data that has very little to do with actually working at the company and much more about that person's individual life. Open-ended interviews can produce large quantities of data that must then be analyzed, and that can be a lot of work. You might want to narrow things down a bit. A semistructured or structured interview would break the open-ended question about working at the company into subtopics that encourage more specific answers. But those answers would remain open-ended, with responses varying depending on the person answering.

Surveys

Surveys are much more specific than interviews. Not only do you define the question or questions in a survey, like "how do you feel about working here?" but you also define the possible answers. You might allow the person filling in the survey to choose from three possible answers, "I love it," "I hate it," or "I'm neutral about it." Or you could go a different way and use a scale, with 1 being "I love it" and 5 being "I hate it." The point is that surveys are used when you are less interested in exploring something you don't think you know about but want to discover and more interested in more precisely defining something that you already feel like you know about.

Because survey research is specific and targeted, and because it uses preassigned classifications and categories in collecting data, it is often described as a quantitative measurement approach. In conducting surveys, you are deliberately asking questions in a way that allows you to count the number and type of answers. It is possible to generate survey questions and answers that are nominal, ordinal, interval, or even ratio values. The tricky part is that almost every survey depends on the respondent answering it based on their own knowledge, with all the messy qualitative parameters that this entails. Survey data is empirical, but what you are observing is not the phenomena you are interested in (how much money does this person make in a year?), but rather the survey taker's response to a question about that phenomenon (I actually make less than this, but I'm embarrassed to say that, so I'll pick a higher amount...). It is a subtle difference, but an important one to remember.

Other Ways of Describing Culture

Qualitative and quantitative measurements form a basis for measuring culture directly, through various tools, methods, and instruments. But it is rare to see culture expressed in terms of data, regardless of type. Organizational culture is just too complex, too rich and varied, to be reduced to a number or a single category. Instead, organizational culture tends to be described in terms of stories and metaphors that allow us to glimpse the whole by looking at a model, representation, or metaphor. People, experts and laymen alike, have been developing and using these tools to describe organizational culture for almost as long as organizations have grown big enough to have cultures of their own.

Cultural Archetypes and Stereotypes

People generalize about other people all the time (in fact, I just did it myself). When we collapse the complexity and uniqueness of an individual or a group into a catch-all set of characteristics or rules that we claim applies universally, we create a *type*. If the generalization is interpreted by others as mostly positive and accurate, or at least not negative, we call it an *archetype*, a prime example of the thing we are generalizing about. If the generalization is negative, offensive, or insulting toward those generalized, we tend to call it a *stereotype*. Describing something as an archetype implies something to aspire to or to fruitfully compare a thing against. Stereotypes are often viewed as inaccurate and biased and a thing to be avoided. In both cases, people build a predictive model based on attributes they think they understand.

Organizational cultures are subject to the same treatment. How many times have we heard a particular company being called a "culture of innovation" while another is called a "culture of dishonesty"? By applying these labels, people attempt to simplify a very complex construction of people and relationships into a single defining characteristic. The generalizations may even be accurate, but this is beside the point. By turning a culture into an archetype or a stereotype, one runs the risk of introducing more uncertainty into the analysis than one removes from it. People can surprise you, and if you base your predictions on a single data point, you introduce a single point of failure into your assessment.

Generalizing can be useful if based on rational analysis and if the inherent assumptions remain explicit. All modeling and simulation is a form of generalization. Assigning types can be useful as one of several elements in your analysis. But if it becomes a crutch that excuses you from actually analyzing things, it is a recipe for disaster. This is especially true in a multifaceted culture where the organization has several competing drives. Someone who sees only one cultural trait, perhaps because of their role in dealing with the organization, may never even see the sides of culture that would conflict with their narrow viewpoint and challenge their preconceived biases.

Cultural Frameworks and Models

When a generalization is approached more rigorously and scientifically, archetypes and stereotypes can become models and frameworks. These models and frameworks remain simplified versions of reality, subject to uncertainty and unpredictability, but the effort that goes into formulating them includes basing the generalizations on empirical evidence, and ensuring that assumptions remain clear and well articulated. Security has plenty of its own models and frameworks, so this approach should not seem alien. The classic example is the Open Systems Interconnection (OSI) reference model, with its seven layers from physical to application. The model is very simple, very generalized. It does not represent any actual existing network. But you can use it to understand the functionality of just about any modern network. This is in large part because the model does not represent how we assume networks work, but how we know they work, because they have been built in part by using the model.

There are numerous frameworks and models to choose from when exploring organizational culture. The Competing Security Cultures Framework, the model I propose and will discuss in this chapter, is adapted from one of the more well-known frameworks in the organizational culture literature. But there are others. Table 5-1 briefly lists a few of the existing models and frameworks produced over the last four decades. My point here is that, not only is culture an empirically observable phenomenon, but organizational scientists have been observing it long enough to develop models for how it works.

Visualizing Culture

Frameworks and models do not have to be visual, but they often lend themselves easily to visual representation. Most of the frameworks and models in Table 5-1 have been expressed visually at one point or another. Visualization helps us to identify patterns more easily and to make sense of relationships spatially rather than verbally. Metaphors allow us to understand one thing by relating it directly to something completely different. The visual metaphor of the iceberg in Chapter 3 demonstrates the concept of powerful forces at work below our conscious

Framework/ Model	Creator(s)	Description
Competing Values Framework	Robert E. Quinn & John Rohrbaugh	Assesses organizational culture as a set of opposing priorities and values that influence activity and decisions. Divides culture into four quadrants, each representing a "type" of culture, based on these opposing values.
Dimensions of Culture	Geert Hofstede	Assesses culture on the basis of four to six dimensions of behavior within a culture. The model proposes separate dimensions for national cultures (based on values) and for organizational cultures (based on practices).
Normative Systems Model	Robert F. Allen & Charlotte Craft	A dynamic model that assesses organizational culture on the basis of how it changes rather than how culture is structured. Proposes a four-phase approach to cultural change.
Denison Organizational Culture Model	Daniel Denison	Similar to the Competing Values Framework, assesses organizational culture as made up of four essential traits that create balance and tension.
Three Levels of Culture	Edgar H. Schein	Assesses culture on the basis of three levels of decreasing visibility, similar to the iceberg metaphor.

Table 5-1   *Frameworks and Models of Organizational Culture*

perception. In an age of increasingly complex infographics and data visualization techniques, we may be tempted to think of simpler images as less informative. But the popularity of the iceberg metaphor in describing any number of situations testifies to its success as an explanatory tool.

Many visual models of culture are relatively simple. The point is not to capture every relationship or every nuance of interaction going on inside an organization. Instead, the focus remains on primary flows of information or influence, broad patterns of behavior and internal relationships, and high-level structure. Unlike a model for a mechanism or a physical structure, where standard components exist, there is rarely a single way to accomplish something when it comes to human interactions. Culture models have to achieve a balance, reflecting not only reality, but ambiguity, to be successful. In many situations, simple is better, so long as the model does not unnecessarily oversimplify what is happening.

The Competing Security Cultures Framework

My model, the Competing Security Cultures Framework (CSCF), enables an organization to describe and interpret the different ways that security is understood and practiced by the organization's members. Specifically, the CSCF enables the organization to identify areas where competitive principles and values have emerged that may represent risk to the organization's security goals and objectives. The CSCF is based upon a venerable and well-regarded cultural model, Quinn and Rohrbaugh's Competing Values Framework, which was first described in an article in *Management Science* in 1983.

Origins of the CSCF in Competing Values Research

The original purpose of the Competing Values Framework was to understand the characteristics and organizational traits most associated with companies' enterprise performance, how well they did in their industries and markets. Using both theory and data from empirical studies of different organizations, Quinn and Rohrbaugh grouped organizational traits into related sets of core values that created specific cultures within an organization. As they discovered patterns of behavior among various subject companies, the researchers mapped them into like groups, each of which demonstrated certain areas of value and priority for a company. These patterns also revealed opposing traits, values, and priorities that were antithetical to the ones identified. Quinn and Rohrbaugh mapped these as well, using a set of axes that divided the framework into quadrants.

Quinn and Rohrbaugh found, for example, that some organizations, in certain industries, were more effective when they built hierarchies and bureaucracy to emphasize control and stability; the researchers found that other organizations achieved successful performance by staying flexible and adaptable, avoiding rigid structures of authority or function. Likewise, they found that some organizations tended to look outward, prioritizing external customers and markets to achieve their goals, whereas others benefitted from an inward gaze that valued internal cohesion and integration. The result of their findings was a visual metaphor of culture that divided organizational values into four opposing cultures, which the researchers termed clan, adhocracy, market, and hierarchy. Figure 5-1 illustrates the Competing Values Framework model.

Clan Cultures

As shown in Figure 5-1, clan culture is one of the four groupings of organizational priorities and behaviors identified in the Competing Values Framework. Clan

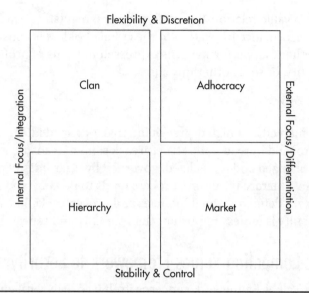

Figure 5-1 *The Competing Values Framework (adapted from Quinn and Rohrbaugh)*

cultures are community oriented, valuing a sense of belonging and inclusion. Internally focused and valuing flexibility, these organizations want all members to participate in making the organization successful. To this end, clan cultures put a great deal of emphasis on human development and the sharing of both responsibility and reward.

Adhocracies

Adhocracies, another grouping of organizational priorities and behaviors, are a riff on the idea of an ad hoc approach, one that is flexible and maybe not permanent, created as a specific response to a unique challenge. Flexibility and agility are priorities, and are made necessary because of a focus on dealing with chaotic and unpredictable external environments. Startups and entrepreneurial organizations are today's most familiar examples of adhocracies, but they also exist in larger, more traditional organizations that have a need to innovate.

Market Cultures

Market cultures contrast with clan cultures, valuing tight control over the internal workings of the organization, and focus the results of these efforts on the organization's external environment. Customers may be a key priority, but market cultures may also value relationships with partners, regulators, trade groups, and shareholders. Performance in relation to these stakeholders is considered most important, whether that performance is expressed in terms of profit, market share, productivity, or some other measure.

Hierarchies

Hierarchies are marked by a high degree of internal focus and integration, combined with tight control and bureaucratic structures designed to ensure stability. Everything is organized and formalized, governed by clear lines of authority and responsibility. In a hierarchy culture, process tends to be king, and roles and responsibilities are defined through policies and processes. Unlike an adhocracy culture, adaptability is far less important than stability and repeatability.

Adapting the Competing Values Framework to Security

The Competing Values Framework concerns itself primarily with enterprise and industry performance by companies, whether or not they are profitable, productive, or succeed in increasing their market share relative to their industry peers and competitors. The framework does not address information technology, much less information security. But the Competing Values Framework has benefitted from a great deal of empirical study and scholarly thought over the years since it was developed, and has been widely adapted and applied to other areas. This maturity and flexibility of the framework has much to offer people-centric security because it helps to explain the conflicts and competing priorities that often create security risk and failure, conflicts I have explored in previous chapters.

Adapting the Competing Values Framework to information security meant that I had to alter it and narrow it to the specific concerns of security owners and stakeholders. Instead of capturing the broad spectrum of behaviors and values that contribute to overall organizational performance, I wanted to measure and analyze those specific traits that enhance or impede information security performance in different industries and situations. But the original insights of the Competing Values Framework still apply, as does the quadrant structure of the model. The CSCF reorients and reconfigures these into a people-centric security model, which is illustrated in Figure 5-2.

The CSCF uses the same two-axes model as the Competing Values Framework but applies it to the way InfoSec thinks. The first axis represents the degree of security control valued by the organization. The second axis of the CSCF represents the continuum of focus between internal and external environments.

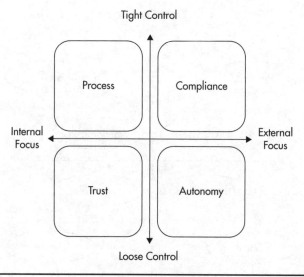

Figure 5-2   *The Competing Security Cultures Framework*

Degrees of Control

Control means the extent to which the organization attempts to direct, restrict, or influence the behavior of the people and systems it contains. The degree of control exists as a continuum ranging from tight control, representing a maximum of stability and standardization throughout the organization, to loose control, in which security may be distributed or subject to variability in terms of process and visibility across the organization. The resulting axis reflects a competing set of values that lie between the desire to make security more effective by promoting a dependable, orderly environment, and the desire to make security more effective by encouraging a flexible, situational environment.

In security programs, control is usually imposed through combinations of centralized authority, established bureaucracy, defined hierarchies, and standardized policies and procedures that define acceptable behaviors and activities. The degree of control over security is implied and operationalized by many factors, including the size of the security team and the resources available to them; executive sponsorship and support, including whether or not a CISO leads the program as part of the executive team; and the presence and enforcement of security-specific policies and standards across the organization.

You'll notice in Figure 5-2 that I altered the original spatial layout of the Competing Values Framework, inverting the control axis so that tight control

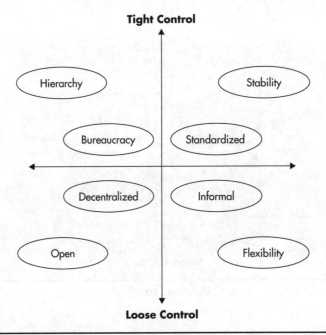

Figure 5-3 *Characteristics along the control axis*

is at the top rather than the bottom of the model. The result is that the security cultures that prioritize more control over security activities are now represented in the top two quadrants. In my experience, security in general is a control-focused culture. The change of spatial positioning reinforces this emphasis. Figure 5-3 shows various characteristics as one moves along the control axis.

Internal vs. External Focus

Internal or external focus determines whether the organization is primarily concerned with understanding and managing security as a function of the organization itself, or is primarily concerned with understanding and managing security as a function of its dealings with entities outside the organization. Outside entities may include customers, partners, regulators, the media, and even threat entities like hackers and other adversaries.

In an internally focused program, security is considered effective if the result is a cohesive and consistent program for protecting the organization's information assets. Internally focused security programs seek an enterprise-wide alignment, where security is compatible throughout the organization's operational functions.

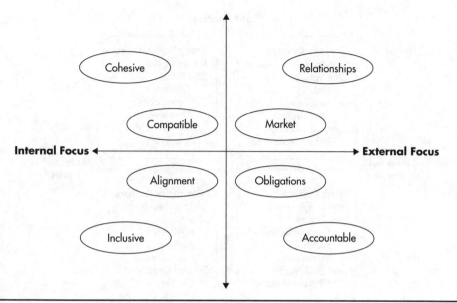

Figure 5-4 *Characteristics along the focus axis*

This may include organizations where the security team is responsible for setting direction and policy for all of the organization's information security and perhaps even its physical security, including defining standards, managing technology, and creating strategy.

Externally focused security programs consider security effective when it results in successful relations between the organization and outside entities. This external focus creates a concern for meeting contractual and regulatory obligations; for protecting protected data; and for avoiding security failures that can result in loss of reputation, market share, or the ability to conduct business. Accomplishing these goals may require a diversification of security responsibility and authority (for instance, across regulatory or technology environments) in order to meet the various needs of specific constituents and external entities. Figure 5-4 shows characteristics as one moves along the internal-external focus axis.

The CSCF Quadrants

The security-specific quadrants of the CSCF are illustrated in Figure 5-5, which also shows more detail regarding the components and values inherent in each security culture type. Each of the quadrants represents a grouping of values,

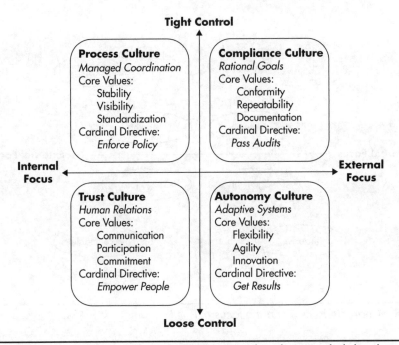

Figure 5-5   *The Competing Security Cultures Framework with expanded detail*

assumptions, and priorities that influence and shape security decisions and activities inside an organization. These security culture types include a Process Culture, a Compliance Culture, an Autonomy Culture, and a Trust Culture.

Overlapping and Competing Values

The quadrant model of the CSCF appears very orthogonal when you first look at it, with right angles creating independent cultural characteristics. This visualization tends to obscure the way that the two axes create overlapping values anchored on different perspectives on control and fields of focus. Diametrically opposed relationships like those between process and autonomy are easier to see, but there are connections and shared values throughout the four cultures as well. Figure 5-6 represents the CSCF as concentric circles that better illustrate these overlapping traits. Process and Trust Cultures, for example, may not seem to have much in common, until one realizes that they are both centrally concerned with how the organization functions internally as a coherent structure. Process and Compliance Cultures, to use another example, seem naturally congruent when thinking of information security, with their joint emphasis on control.

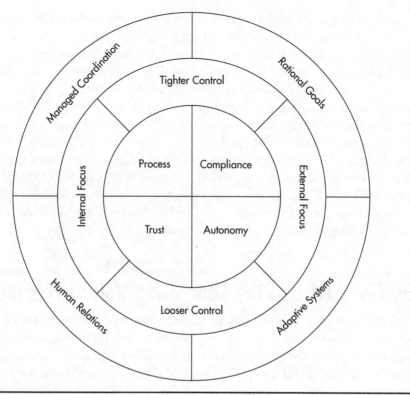

Figure 5-6   *Circular view of the Competing Security Cultures Framework*

But Compliance and Autonomy Cultures do not seem to make as much sense together, at least not until you recognize the mutual value these cultures place on addressing challenges associated with the organization's external environment, not its internal workings.

Limitations of the Framework

Noted statistician George Box once wrote, "Essentially, all models are wrong, but some are useful." My hope is that the CSCF helps organizations by serving as a useful tool for achieving people-centric security. But it is just as important to acknowledge its limits. The CSCF does not pretend to fully describe or explain every organization's security culture. Instead, the CSCF is intended to be a tool for learning and exploration, a method by which people working within the context of an organization's security culture can learn more about that culture, assign terms and concepts to it, and identify areas of risk that emerge when security priorities and values come into opposition with one another. Organizational culture researchers understand how difficult it is to measure or analyze anything as complex as the shared beliefs and relationships of a large social group. Without a place to start, without some method of simplifying the complexity of cultural transformation to achieve actionable strategies, no progress is likely to be made. Some critics complain that this simplification makes the model worthless for real-world analyses. I appreciate a reluctance to oversimplify, which is a core security behavior I will discuss later in the book, but all models are simplifications by necessity. No one expects a balsa wood model of an airplane to fly like the real thing, or an architectural model to be a real, livable building. For these purposes, the models are wrong. But they remain useful nonetheless, used by engineers and architects everywhere to understand on a smaller scale the things they build on a large one.

Why Not Just Use the Competing Values Framework?

In the decades since it was created, the Competing Values Framework has been widely adapted, and various techniques have been developed for measuring how an organization compares to the framework. Specific tools such as Daniel Denison's *Organizational Culture Survey* and Kim Cameron and Robert Quinn's *Organizational Culture Assessment Instrument* use surveys to help organizations figure out where they fit in relation to the Competing Values Framework quadrants. The data these instruments collect regarding cultural values and norms are then mapped to the various cultural attributes of the framework, producing profiles of overall organizational culture.

But why build a new, security-centric framework at all? Why would an organization not just use the Competing Values Framework directly to measure security culture, since there are already assessment tools available that are based upon it? Some of these tools, like Cameron and Quinn's OCAI, have been deployed by hundreds of organizations seeking to understand their culture and its link to business performance, market position, and industry competitiveness. It's a legitimate question to ask whether or not security teams that want to change culture should use an existing cultural framework as their starting point.

Security Culture Benefits From a Targeted Approach

The answer is about specificity and precision. Information security is a business process, just like any other. But just like other business processes, it specializes in a subset of the overall organization's functions. There are many unique aspects of security that are legitimate differentiators between our industry's activities and objectives and those of HR, Marketing, or even different parts of IT. These differences manifest themselves in the language and terms we use, the approaches we take, and the outcomes we seek. Many of these differences have a direct impact on the potential effectiveness of using a general organizational culture framework to assess security culture.

In the CSCF, I have adapted the Competing Values Framework in a way that maintains the core theoretical constructs of the model, namely the performance impacts that occur when different cultures pursue different goals in competition. But I have reshaped and reoriented the Competing Values Framework in the CSCF to specifically address areas of concern to CISOs and security stakeholders, to use language that is more aligned with the concerns of security programs, and to illuminate the behaviors and values that security teams are most often associated with. Nevertheless, many of the traits and behaviors described by the CSCF will be recognizable to other, non-InfoSec, parts of the business. This makes sense because security remains a business process that contributes business value, or at least should be considered as such.

Not Everything in the Competing Values Framework Translates Well

Targeting the traits and values that inform and shape information security practices allows a more precise picture of organizational security culture to emerge, one grounded in those elements that security owners can understand and thus better communicate to other business stakeholders. Nonsecurity people will struggle with a model of culture that requires continuous translation between performance in general terms and performance of information security. It is better to perform that translation up front, as part of the model, as the CSCF does.

Consider the adhocracy culture of the Competing Values Framework. This culture, more prevalent in startups and other companies operating in environments of intense competition and volatile markets, values aggressive independence and a greater tolerance for risk, exemplified in the Silicon Valley motto "move fast and break things." Most InfoSec professionals would never consider speed and disruption a good model for security, but adhocracy cultures feel these things are essential for their success. A direct translation of adhocracy to information security doesn't exist. But the idea of autonomy and silos of security authority, of striking a balance between control and flexibility within the enterprise, is something every CISO recognizes and must cope with.

The CSCF allows organizations to foreground the values and priorities of security and orient them into security culture types, while preserving the spirit of the model in which these cultures vie for resources, buy-in, and dominance in a competitive organizational marketplace of ideas. The CSCF illustrates these cultures at a high level. I will discuss how to diagnose and assess the strength of the CSCF cultures in Chapter 6. For now, let's explore these cultures in more detail.

Organizational Security Cultures

The four spatially opposed quadrants of the CSCF represent distinct cultural approaches to information security. Each quadrant represents a distinct security culture, although no organization will have only one of these cultures present. Some cultures may be stronger, even predominant. But all organizations are a mix of cultures, not only as a whole but in terms of different subunits within the whole. The four cultures are generalizations, models within a model, and I will explore the nuances of each in this section.

Process Culture

A Process Culture values tight control combined with an internally facing focus. Process Cultures view their success most often in terms of how well security operations are managed and coordinated, how stably and dependably operations function. From a theoretical perspective, the concept of *managed coordination* is paramount in the Process Culture. Security is seen as an organization-wide function that must be centralized and controlled to ensure that it is done right everywhere, by everyone, in the same ways.

One key feature of the Process Culture is the creation of bureaucracy to manage information security activities. *Bureaucracy*, briefly, is a system of management in which specialized professionals act according to accepted rules to accomplish goals. The word "bureaucracy" has changed meanings over the two centuries since it was coined, but negative connotations have always accompanied its use. Not until German sociologist Max Weber began studying bureaucracy scientifically in the early twentieth century was the idea rehabilitated somewhat. In Weber's view, bureaucracy was necessary for society to function effectively in a modern world grown too complex to achieve its goals through the efforts of individuals and small groups without unique skills and training.

Security, along with most other organizational functions, has also grown too large and complex for any one person to do the job. Specialization has led to a variety of security-related roles, including the technical, the operational, and the managerial. In order to coordinate and optimize these disparate resources, organizations create hierarchical structures, including job families and organizational charts, to segment activities and areas of responsibility. These roles and specialties develop their own bodies of knowledge and paths for advancement, all governed by defined processes and standards of behavior.

Core Values of the Process Culture

Core values within a Process Culture develop out of a desire to keep things running smoothly and predictably, and include

▶ **Stability**   Ensure that the organization maintains its existing functions and structures over time. Change, especially unplanned change, is disruptive and is to be avoided or managed very carefully.

▶ **Visibility**   Ensure that the organization understands how it functions and can trace or predict outcomes easily. Blindness and blind spots not governed by established process represent uncertainty and risk.

▶ **Standardization**   Ensure that all operations are managed according to formally established rules, well understood by all members. Individual freedom creates exceptions and discrepancies that must be managed, degrading operational efficiency.

A cardinal directive of the Process Culture might be stated as *enforce the policy*. In my experiences consulting, "security policy" has become something of a metaphor for the collected body of rules governing the organization's security activities, from the highest-level acceptable use policy down through the intricacies of firewall rules and intrusion detection system (IDS) tuning. *Enforce the policy* implies doing things the organization's way, submitting to controls and restrictions, and thereby ensuring that the goals of the organization are met.

Examples of Process Cultures

In over 25 years of working in InfoSec, I have encountered many organizations where the Process Culture dominates, beginning with my first job as an operations officer in the Central Intelligence Agency. The U.S. government is perhaps an epitome of the Process Culture. The U.S. intelligence community is even more intense, especially when it comes to security. Classification, compartmentalization, and deeply embedded organizational hierarchies were not just the norm, they were my life. In my career since, I have seen similar cultures in other government agencies I have worked with, whether at the federal, state, or local level. This makes a great deal of sense when you consider that Max Weber's work was based in large part on the growth of civil administrations as nation-states modernized. Government was, if you will, a key early adopter of bureaucracy, an innovation that was sorely needed as states were expected to better manage, provide services for, and control their citizens.

One of the most dominant Process Cultures I have encountered since joining the private sector was in the retail industry. This company had a procedure for everything security related, all run as part of a highly centralized program under a powerful and aggressive CISO who was considered an equal member of the company's executive staff. The security culture mirrored the corporate culture, where everything was done, literally, by the "book" of policies and standards that existed to manage the stores, corporate offices, and even contractors and partners who worked with the firm. The strong Process Culture of the security program was neither good nor bad in general, but it worked in the larger context of the company. People understood rules and standards, and expected the security program to work the same way.

Financial firms, manufacturing companies, and utilities also tend to exhibit strong characteristics of a Process Culture.

Compliance Culture

Compliance Cultures, like Process Cultures, value tight control over the organization's security activities. But where a Process Culture applies that control for internal purposes, the Compliance Culture is externally facing and views security success most often in terms of how well it supports relations between the organization and outside entities. In the Compliance Culture, security benefits the organization to the extent that it addresses the concerns of other stakeholders, whether those are customers whose data the organization manages, regulators seeking to control the conduct of certain types of business, or even hackers looking for a target. The theoretical perspective that best describes this approach is *rational goals*. Security is a goal because it helps or impedes the ability of others to meet their goals, not because the organization values it independently.

A Compliance Culture is driven by demands outside the organization. In recent years, security regulations and frameworks—including ISO 27001, the Payment Card Industry Data Security Standard (PCI DSS), the Health Insurance Portability and Accountability Act (HIPAA), the Health Information Technology for Economic and Clinical Health (HITECH) Act, the Federal Information Security Management Act (FISMA), and a host of other global regimes—have played an increasingly important role to information security programs and CISOs. The increasing number and severity of security incidents, and the media coverage and public scrutiny they produce, will do little to abate this trend. If anything, organizations can expect an increase in regulatory focus in the coming years, along with the potential for loss of markets and customers in the event of a major breach. Compliance Cultures are deeply concerned with ensuring that their organizations navigate these turbulent waters safely.

Core Values of the Compliance Culture

Core values within a Compliance Culture reflect the insecurity and perceived need that surrounds accountability to the organization's external stakeholders, including

▶ **Conformity**   Ensure that the organization adheres to expectations and requirements set by others, often through mirroring these requirements internally. Uniformity within the organization may not be a priority, but the organization must be able to meet all demands of specific outside stakeholders.

▶ **Repeatability**   Ensure that the organization can reproduce processes and results on demand. Situations in which operations do not produce the expected results are dangerous failures.

▶ **Documentation**   Ensure that the organization maintains evidence that it is meeting its obligations and the expectations of others. Operational processes that cannot be proven to function as required risk sanctions from anyone in a position to hold the organization accountable.

A cardinal directive of the Compliance Culture can be expressed as *pass audits*. Audits are not only planned, structured assessments performed or demanded by an interested third party. Several organizational theorists consider unplanned system failures to be, in the words of Karl Weick, "brutal audits." A security breach reveals weakness and poor security controls in exactly the same way that an audit does, only with much more stress and more serious consequences. Penetration testing and red teaming evolved out of this understanding that it was better to subject the organization to a controlled attack than to wait for the uncontrolled one. So *pass audits* is as much about the successful response to a real security attack as it is about appeasing your QSA during a PCI audit.

Examples of Compliance Cultures

Compliance Cultures are most prevalent, as you might imagine, in highly regulated industries. I have seen strong Compliance Cultures in the insurance industry and in healthcare organizations. But from an information security perspective, PCI DSS has been the most influential driver of Compliance Culture, for several reasons. First, PCI DSS has real reach and unambiguous teeth. Organizations that want to process credit card data, and a great many do, have to comply with PCI DSS or else they don't get the privilege. Second, PCI DSS tends to be highly prescriptive, meaning that the standard actually tells you specifically what you have to do. Many regulatory regimes outline high-level principles of security and generalized actions that must be performed, but remain open to a lot of interpretation. HIPAA/HITECH is a great example here, as the healthcare security and privacy regulation is meant to be applied to a huge number of very different organizations and must be more flexible than the laser-beam focus of PCI DSS. Finally, the business nature of PCI DSS—a regulatory framework designed by companies, primarily for companies, with an ecosystem of other companies supporting it—makes compliance seem easier for corporate organizations to understand and implement.

But PCI DSS is interesting in that the very things that make it influential can work together to form a sort of trap that many organizations fall into, one that says something about the Compliance Culture in general. PCI DSS lends itself to what some in the security industry, myself included, call "checkbox compliance." While good security almost always equates to good compliance, becoming a matter of translating a security program into the language of whichever auditor is reviewing it, good compliance does not necessarily equal good security. Several of the largest breaches in recent years have involved companies, and even systems, that were certified as PCI DSS compliant. Just because an organization can pass a traditional audit, in which a (mostly) friendly entity asks the organization if it has done what it was supposed to do, adversaries conducting a brutal audit in the form of an attack don't give a damn if you have checked all the right boxes.

Compliance Cultures often overlap with Process Cultures, as many of the benefits of one apply to the other. But the difference between the cultures is that area of focus, which can be a source of cultural conflict and risk. If Process Cultures run the danger of bureaucratic inefficiencies in the name of coherent security operations, Compliance Cultures risk losing sight of the big picture of security by focusing on the individual mandates forced on them from the outside.

Autonomy Culture

At first glance, the Autonomy Culture might not seem very compatible with information security. And if you were to conduct a study that expected to find fewer security cultures where autonomy is the dominant culture, at least on paper, you would not be disappointed. Most security professionals find the idea of letting everyone in the organization decide for themselves what level of security works best to be irrational and dangerous. But look closer and you begin to see that the question is more complex. Security is often at odds with other parts of the business, sometimes even at odds with itself. The criticism of security programs as "the 'no' team, not the 'go' team" reflects the suspicion some people have that security can do at least as much harm as good, protecting the organization at the cost of speed, efficiency, and progress.

Autonomy Cultures exhibit less centralized control while also facing outward from the organization. The theoretical basis of the culture is that of *adaptive systems*, in which people, process, and technology can reshape and reorient themselves as necessary to meet changes in their environment. The idea is that those closest to a situation have a better awareness of what is happening and what is required. Logic dictates that they should also have the power to act on that unique situational insight. The result is an organization that can respond in part without requiring similar changes, or even involvement at times, by the whole.

Autonomy Cultures in security, it should be said, are not "anything goes" environments. I have never, at least in the last decade or so, encountered an organization that believed security was completely unimportant. But I have worked with a lot of organizations for whom security is a compromise, a more or less balanced trade-off not only between locking things down and opening them up, but between the need for centralized control and local situational awareness. Many reasons exist to push security authority and responsibility out, to distribute it throughout an organization. Sometimes this is a reflection of a corporate structure that has many autonomous or semiautonomous divisions. At other times, federation occurs because of more operational or market needs.

Core Values of the Autonomy Security Culture

Core values within an Autonomy Culture emerge from the need to manage different levels of security, for different reasons, in different places, and include

▶ **Flexibility**   Ensure that the organization responds to changing events and environments. Unexpected change is unavoidable and actually represents an opportunity for those who can adapt.

▶ **Agility** Ensure that the organization moves quickly and efficiently to take advantage of opportunities. Wasting time debating options or dealing with bureaucracy risks sacrificing first-mover advantages.

▶ **Innovation** Ensure the organization not only reacts to change, but creates it, discovering new ways to improve before competitors do. The best ideas come from unexpected places, from individual forward-thinkers, and to forbid experimentation is to court obsolescence.

A cardinal directive of the Autonomy Culture could be summed up as *get results*. An organization in a highly volatile and competitive environment can literally face extinction if it fails to be innovative, adaptable, and agile, all characteristics that a risk-averse security program can impede. A failure from overly cautious approaches to security can be as deadly as a failure that occurs as a result of a major breach. Many social media companies and technology startups today face exactly this paradox. The information they manage is the raw material of their business. Locking information down, protecting it, takes resources and may diminish the value of the data. A scrupulous company, doing right by its customers or users on security and privacy, may find itself outmaneuvered by a competitor that put those extra resources into marketing and user interface design instead of data protection.

Freewheeling startups are not the only organizations that find value in some form of Autonomy Culture, though. Lots of organizations divide authority and responsibility for IT and security among different groups, or embed them into lines of business or geographical regions. The main feature of an Autonomy Culture is simply that the organization has concluded that centralized, standardized security does not work as well as individually or locally managed security, and has delegated the authority for it among different entities.

Examples of Autonomy Cultures

I haven't found an industry that explicitly advocates for a security culture of Autonomy, at least not out loud. In today's environment, stating that security should be left up to individuals, allowing them to decide for themselves what needs to be protected and how, might be seen as reckless. But plenty of organizations function this way, even if they don't print it on the brochure. Startups, especially technology startups, are often forced to move so fast that security (along with everything else) is handled by individuals. Similarly, some parts of academic institutions are more autonomous because they are meant to be open systems for the free exchange of information. Security people, in my experience, tend to see the values and traits of an Autonomy Culture as a necessary evil, at best.

Where Autonomy Cultures do exist, they look at the idea of freedom differently. Autonomy in security is different from the adhocracy culture in the original Competing Values Framework, where it represents a deliberate rejection of rules, standards, and bureaucracy in favor of being a nimble competitor. Few in security, even proponents of more autonomy, would make the claim that security policies, processes, and other mechanisms of control are actually harmful to the business and should be avoided. Instead, Autonomy Cultures prioritize the idea that centralized control and standard security process are not the only way to go and must be balanced with other concerns. I've usually found evidence of Autonomy Culture by looking between the lines, examining the conflicting priorities of the security team and the rest of the organization.

One of the best examples of Autonomy Culture's influence on security is the "bring your own device" movement, or BYOD. The consumerization of technology, which has integrated powerful and sophisticated networked computing devices into the lives of everyday users, combined with a profusion of social and information services that integrate with those devices, has made almost everyone an advanced IT user. Companies have, sometimes inadvertently, encouraged consumerization through the growing erosion of the boundaries between work life and personal life. Many people expect and are expected to be quickly available at all time by friends, coworkers, and bosses alike. As both opportunities and demand for connectivity and availability grow, unique ecosystems have developed. Big players, like Apple and Google, as well as many other large and small competitors produce phones, tablets, and personal computers with disparate user bases. The resulting platform diversity has strained the ability of corporate IT to keep up, and personal preferences driven in part by younger generations who want "cool" rather than "company approved" tech has made BYOD as much about reputation and retaining talent as it is about managing IT infrastructures.

I once heard a CISO say, "I question the sanity, not to mention the judgment, of anyone who wants to bring their iPhone to use at work." This executive was less concerned with Apple in particular; he mentioned that he had an iPhone for personal use. But he was adamant that the freedom to access the corporate network with any device was an unacceptable security risk. Contrast that with companies like Cisco, where carefully managed BYOD is part of the fabric of company life, and you can see the difference between the values of the Process Culture and those of the Autonomy Culture.

Trust Culture

Cultures of trust tend to insist that security must be a shared, collaborative process. Trust Cultures achieve success when everyone is a stakeholder in security, with the right skills, knowledge, and awareness to make good decisions. The theoretical perspective of a Trust Culture is *human relations*, the recognition that, as I said in Chapter 1, security is people!

Trust Cultures embody an approach that favors looser control (since the organization's members are dependable participants who don't require constant supervision) and looks inward to the people who embody the organization. This can only be accomplished through educated, engaged members who remain committed to organizational success at a very personal level.

Many people work in organizations that see themselves as communities or even families, and some people invest a great deal of their own sense of self-worth into their profession and their employer. In security, this cohesion can function a bit differently, but it is still very much there. For security programs, the place you are most likely to find proponents of the Trust Culture is inside the security awareness team. Every security awareness professional I've talked to or heard speak—and thanks to Lance Spitzner and the SANS Securing the Human Project there have been quite a few—has been absolutely passionate about making nonsecurity folks understand why security is important, and then giving them the tools to make the best security decisions. They view people not as a threat to be managed, but as a resource to be valued.

Core Values of the Trust Culture

Core values within a Trust Culture emphasize the need to interact and cooperate as a team, and include

- ▶ **Communication**   Ensure that the organization shares information clearly and efficiently with all members. If people cannot understand what they are supposed to do, and why, they will fail.

- ▶ **Participation**   Ensure that the organization encourages everyone to take ownership and become a stakeholder, rather than foisting responsibility onto other parties. "Passing the buck" is seen as irresponsible and risky, as well as a violation of the social contract.

- ▶ **Commitment**   Ensure that people want to make the organization great by ensuring that the organization does all it can to make people great. Wasting good people is bad business.

A cardinal directive of the Trust Culture might be stated as *empower people*. In security environments this means not treating people like the enemy, but rather giving them what they need to be allies to the security team. I've seen more than one security program obsess about insider threats, viewing almost everyone outside of InfoSec as time bombs just waiting to go off in explosions of ignorance, incompetence, or active malicious intent. A Trust Culture does not ignore the possibility that people can become problems; but it believes that these problems, more often than not, can be avoided by simply understanding what a person really needs in order to do the right thing, and then giving that to them.

Examples of Trust Cultures

As with Autonomy Cultures, I have not found Trust Cultures to be unique to a specific industry. Most organizations beyond a certain size have a security awareness program, often driven by a compliance requirement. Whether the awareness program is evidence of a Trust Culture, devoted to empowering the members of the organization so that they can make better choices, or evidence of a Compliance Culture, in which awareness is only important to the extent that it serves other interests, can be hard to decipher. But I have yet to find a security awareness officer who was only interested in checking a box on an audit form. They all want to appeal to hearts and minds.

The real challenge for Trust Cultures is that, of all the cultural traits in the CSCF, trust tends to come hardest to security professionals. We are not, by nature, a trusting lot. People in InfoSec tend to focus on what can go wrong more than what can go right, and we never have to look very far or hard to have our worst suspicions of danger confirmed. Security is about locking things down and restricting access to them. We tend to want to control people's behavior. Empowering them can feel like something best left to HR. But for many others in an organization, trust and a sense of community are quite important, even taken for granted. This tends to limit the influence of Trust Cultures in information security programs and to foster more competition between them and other quadrants of the CSCF.

As the first section of this book argues, however, it is exactly this competitive tension between different priorities and requirements that fuels security risk. A Trust Culture does not imply a naive assumption that everyone is nice and fair and puts the interests of the organization first. A Trust Culture rests on a foundation of cooperation and shared responsibility. This means that people know what the right choice is. But it also means that people recognize that some choices are harder than others, and that compromises and trade-offs must be made. Trust is about communicating conflicts of interest as much as it is about posting awareness posters reminding everyone of a policy, and having faith that the organization will listen.

Further Reading

► Cameron, Kim S., and Robert E. Quinn. *Diagnosing and Changing Organizational Culture: Based on the Competing Values Framework.* 3rd Ed. San Francisco: Jossey-Bass, 2011.

► Quinn, Robert E., and John Rohrbaugh. "A Spatial Model of Effectiveness Criteria: Towards a Competing Values Approach to Organizational Analysis." *Management Science* 29, no 3 (1983): 363–377.

► SANS Institute. "Securing the Human." Available at www.securingthehuman.org.

CHAPTER 6

The Security Culture
Diagnostic Survey (SCDS)

The Competing Security Cultures Framework, introduced in Chapter 5, is a cornerstone of this book's people-centric security approach. It provides a means of visualizing the tensions between information security stakeholders, priorities, and values that exist in every organization. There will always be differences between organizational cultures, and every company and enterprise will have its own unique approach to InfoSec, a mix of cultures, beliefs, and assumptions that will drive everyday decisions and behaviors across all people involved. The CSCF encourages observation and identification of these unique traits, placing them in a spatially oriented framework that allows the organization to understand itself and to chart pathways to cultural improvement and transformation.

No organization is likely to be of just one cultural type. Take a moment and consider your own organization's culture. Would you say you have a Compliance Culture, where audits are top of mind for the security team? Compliance tends to be a key driver of InfoSec these days. But at the same time, do you also have a security awareness program in place? Do you emphasize security awareness more generally, or only for those specific areas that you are audited against? You probably have a number of security policies and standards, but are there also areas where people and groups are given more discretion in how they use or manage technology, such as with BYOD?

Chances are that all of the CSCF traits will be familiar to you in some way, representing some aspect of security that your organization values and promotes. Security culture, like organizational culture in general, is multifaceted and flexible. The interesting question is, if you really got down to it and were forced to choose, which values would come out on top? If, like Clara the developer from Chapter 2, you needed to make hard choices between what was right for security, what was right for the business, and what was right for yourself, which would you give highest priority? For which decisions would you be rewarded and for which would you be punished, no matter what the "party line" says about the importance of security? That balance is the true face of your security culture.

The CSCF is useful to help conceptualize security culture, but it doesn't tell you much about your own organization or the balance between competing information security values in your particular case. To determine that, you need a measurement instrument of some sort. I designed the Security Culture Diagnostic Survey (SCDS) to be that instrument. Using the SCDS, InfoSec teams can collect empirical evidence about the cultural and behavioral norms that exist regarding security within their organization. The result is a profile that describes the balance an organization exhibits between the four different security cultures of the CSCF and their associated values and behaviors. The SCDS builds upon the research and operational development of the Competing Values Framework, discussed in Chapter 5, as well as my own adaptation in the CSCF.

SCDS Format and Structure

The SCDS is designed to elicit data regarding cultural traits and information security values that exist within an organizational environment. The SCDS is accompanied by a scoring process for using the responses to survey questions to compute the level of a particular cultural attribute against a scale, as well as a visualization process by which these scores are oriented spatially against the CSCF quadrants to create a security culture map or profile. These culture maps, described in Chapter 7, can be used to drive discussion, brainstorm transformation strategies, and communicate to InfoSec and organizational leadership.

How Surveys Work

Most people are familiar with surveys. We've all taken them in one form or another, whether it was filling out a form describing our satisfaction with a particular product or service; being asked structured questions about what we might buy, who we might vote for, or what personality types we are looking for in a romantic partner; or taking an employee survey asking us how we feel about our company, leadership, or individual job. The Internet has improved networking and communication in general, and several companies offer specialized online survey tools that make it easy for just about anyone to set up a survey and start asking questions of respondents.

Surveys have become so commonplace that people tend to take them for granted, forgetting that they can be sophisticated research tools in the right hands. Like a chromatograph, a network protocol analyzer, or a video camera, surveys collect data as inputs that can then be analyzed. But instead of chemicals, packets, and photons, surveys collect human verbal or written responses. Most of us understand how to ask questions and get answers, a skill we have to learn early as language users. So surveys can seem easier and less specialized than some of those more technical instruments. But like them, survey research is built on a body of theory and empirical research that enables social scientists to collect data in valid and repeatable ways. Unlike the more technical instruments, however, distinguishing between a "good" survey, one that produces scientifically valid data, and a "bad" survey, where someone is just asking questions of someone else, can be difficult.

A detailed overview of survey theory and practice is outside the scope of this book, but there are some general aspects of surveys that tend to differentiate those that are more scientifically rigorous from those that are less so. These traits include

▶ Clearly understood objectives for the survey
▶ Pre-established research questions the survey should answer

▶ An explicit conceptual and analytical framework in which to evaluate the responses
▶ Well-designed survey questions and variables

The SCDS attempts to meet the first three criteria by grounding itself in the Competing Security Cultures Framework itself. The CSCF defines what needs to be understood and how to evaluate the results of security culture measurement. What is left is the fourth criteria, the need for the specific questions and scores by which that measurement is achieved.

Questions in the SCDS

The SCDS is made up of ten questions, each with four responses that align to the four quadrants of the CSCF. The questions correspond to key organizational activities that influence and are influenced by norms and behaviors central to information security culture. You may notice at first glance that many of the questions do not specifically mention security. This is deliberate. Security is, as I have emphasized, a business process just like any other. Security culture does not grow out of how the InfoSec team looks at information security. That's just navel gazing by everyone sitting on top of the iceberg. Security culture is about how the hidden assumptions under the surface influence how security gets done. These hidden assumptions influence things like how the organization is run and the InfoSec team within it, things like the management of core operations or technologies, or about how we judge people's performance and hold them accountable for outcomes. Security doesn't drive any of these things inside an organization, but they drive everything the security organization accomplishes.

Table 6-1 provides the questions and responses that comprise the SCDS. The sections following Table 6-1 explain the questions and responses in more depth, and a subsequent section explains how to score the SCDS results. Editable versions

of the SCDS are available for download from http://lancehayden.net/culture. These versions include templates for assessing a single InfoSec culture or comparing multiple security cultures within the organization or across time. Instructions for completing each of these surveys are generally described later in this chapter, and specific instructions for each template are included in the downloadable versions.

1. What's Valued Most?

Question 1 asks respondents to think of the key values affecting their organization's security culture and to identify the top-of-mind priorities that best describe

1.   What's valued most?

A. Stability and reliability are valued most by the organization. It is critical that everyone knows the rules and follows them. The organization cannot succeed if people are all doing things different ways without centralized visibility.

B. Successfully meeting external requirements is valued most by the organization. The organization is under a lot of scrutiny. It cannot succeed if people fail audits or do not live up to the expectations of those watching.

C. Adapting quickly and competing aggressively are valued most by the organization. Results are what matters. The organization cannot succeed if bureaucracy and red tape impair people's ability to be agile.

D. People and a sense of community are valued most by the organization. Everyone is in it together. The organization cannot succeed unless people are given the opportunities and skills to succeed on their own.

2.   How does the organization work?

A. The organization works on authority, policy, and standard ways of doing things. Organizational charts are formal and important. The organization is designed to ensure control and efficiency.

B. The organization works on outside requirements and regular reviews. Audits are a central feature of life. The organization is designed to ensure everyone meets their obligations.

C. The organization works on independent action and giving people decision authority. There's no one right way to do things. The organization is designed to ensure that the right things get done in the right situations.

D. The organization works on teamwork and cooperation. It is a community. The organization is designed to ensure everyone is constantly learning, growing, and supporting one another.

3.   What does security mean?

A. Security means policies, procedures, and standards, automated wherever possible using technology. When people talk about security they are talking about the infrastructures in place to protect the organization's information assets.

B. Security means showing evidence of visibility and control, particularly to external parties. When people talk about security they are talking about passing an audit or meeting a regulatory requirement.

C. Security means enabling the organization to adapt and compete, not hindering it or saying "no" to everything. When people talk about security they are talking about balancing risks and rewards.

D. Security means awareness and shared responsibility. When people talk about security they are talking about the need for everyone to be an active participant in protecting the organization.

Table 6-1   *The Security Culture Diagnostic Survey*

4.   How is information managed and controlled?

A. Information is seen as a direct source of business value, accounted for, managed, and controlled like any other business asset. Formal rules and policies govern information use and control.

B. Information is seen as a sensitive and protected resource, entrusted to the organization by others and subject to review and audit. Information use and control must always be documented and verified.

C. Information is seen as a flexible tool that is the key to agility and adaptability in the organization's environment. Information must be available where and when it is needed by the business, with a minimum of restrictive control.

D. Information is seen as the key to people's productivity, collaboration, and success. Information must be a shared resource, minimally restricted, and available throughout the community to empower people and make them more successful.

5.   How are operations managed?

A. Operations are controlled and predictable, managed according to the same standards throughout the organization.

B. Operations are visible and verifiable, managed and documented in order to support audits and outside reviews.

C. Operations are agile and adaptable, managed with minimal bureaucracy and capable of fast adaptation and flexible execution to respond to changes in the environment.

D. Operations are inclusive and supportive, allowing people to master new skills and responsibilities and to grow within the organization.

6.   How is technology managed?

A. Technology is centrally managed. Standards and formal policies exist to ensure uniform performance internally.

B. Technology is regularly reviewed. Audits and evaluations exist to ensure the organization meets its obligations to others.

C. Technology is locally managed. Freedom exists to ensure innovation, adaptation, and results.

D. Technology is accessible to everyone. Training and support exists to empower users and maximize productivity.

7.   How are people managed?

A. People must conform to the needs of the organization. They must adhere to policies and standards of behavior. The success of the organization is built on everyone following the rules.

Table 6-1   *The Security Culture Diagnostic Survey*

B. People must demonstrate that they are doing things correctly. They must ensure the organization meets its obligations. The success of the organization is built on everyone regularly proving that they are doing things properly.

C. People must take risks and make quick decisions. They must not wait for someone else to tell them what's best. The success of the organization is built on everyone experimenting and innovating in the face of change.

D. People must work as a team and support one other. They must know that everyone is doing their part. The success of the organization is built on everyone learning and growing together.

8. How is risk managed?

A. Risk is best managed by getting rid of deviations in the way things are done. Increased visibility and control reduce uncertainty and negative outcomes. The point is to create a reliable standard.

B. Risk is best managed by documentation and regular review. Frameworks and evaluations reduce uncertainty and negative outcomes. The point is to keep everyone on their toes.

C. Risk is best managed by decentralizing authority. Negative outcomes are always balanced by potential opportunities. The point is to let those closest to the decision make the call.

D. Risk is best managed by sharing information and knowledge. Education and support reduce uncertainty and negative outcomes. The point is to foster a sense of shared responsibility.

9. How is accountability achieved?

A. Accountability is stable and formalized. People know what to expect and what is expected of them. The same rewards and consequences are found throughout the organization.

B. Accountability is enabled through review and audit. People know that they will be asked to justify their actions. Rewards and consequences are contingent upon external expectations and judgments.

C. Accountability is results-driven. People know there are no excuses for failing. Rewards and consequences are a product of successful execution on the organization's business.

D. Accountability is shared among the group. People know there are no rock stars or scapegoats. Rewards and consequences apply to everyone because everyone is a stakeholder in the organization.

Table 6-1 *The Security Culture Diagnostic Survey*

10.	**How is performance evaluated?**
A.	Performance is evaluated against formal strategies and goals. Success criteria are unambiguous.
B.	Performance is evaluated against the organization's ability to meet external requirements. Audits define success.
C.	Performance is evaluated on the basis of specific decisions and outcomes. Business success is the primary criteria.
D.	Performance is evaluated by the organizational community. Success is defined through shared values, commitment, and mutual respect.

Table 6-1 *The Security Culture Diagnostic Survey*

daily decision making. The response choices allow the respondent to differentiate between the relative importance of stability and standardization, external validation and review, adaptability and freedom of choice, and a sense of shared community and responsibility. These response choices begin the descriptive differentiation of the organization's security culture into the four quadrants of the CSCF.

2. How Does the Organization Work?

Question 2 focuses on how the organization gets things done, how it divides responsibility and authority, and how it embeds those values into hierarchies and organizational divisions. Organizational work habits define most aspects of organizational behavior by creating and encouraging some forms of communication and interaction among members, while limiting and discouraging others. Over time, these behaviors become ingrained and instinctual, as the "shape" of the organization becomes part of the culture. Responses to this question allow respondents to define whether the organization looks inward or outward for its marching orders, whether the primary stakeholders are internal or external, and whether the division of labor and management is designed to promote individual and group initiatives or to place and preserve control in more centralized hands.

3. What Does Security Mean?

Question 3 is the most security specific in the SCDS, asking the respondent to explicitly define how he or she or the organization conceptualizes information security. The responses encourage respondents to think of security in terms of how it is perceived and implemented within the organization. In some organizations, security is synonymous with the infrastructure of security, whether those systems are technological or process based. Other organizations see security in terms of effects and results, the outcomes of the process rather than the means of its achievement. Of course, a balance must exist between the different conceptualizations, but the question allows respondents to weight what the typical member of the organization is referring to when he or she talks about security.

4. How Is Information Managed and Controlled?

Information is the lifeblood of most organizations today, central both to the general business activities of the enterprise and to information security. Question 4 asks respondents to describe the management and control of information as a shared resource. The flows of information, its owners and uses, and the beliefs about how it should be disseminated and shared are defined within the responses. Information control is not necessarily security specific, but the way in which an organization views information as a tool and a commodity has a direct bearing on how the organization feels about restricting access to it and otherwise controlling information uses for security purposes.

5. How Are Operations Managed?

Question 5 asks respondents to select and prioritize the organization's everyday functional activities, including tasks, interactions, decisions, and evaluations. Organizational operations, like organizational structure, tend to become "formal and normal" over time. Even a chaotic operational environment, subject to individual decisions and little oversight, can become a "normal" way of doing things. Just ask anyone who has been responsible for changing such an environment. As operational realities give way to habits, the habits encourage particular ways of looking at how new operations are conducted. This question elicits data about where the operational environment, including the habits and norms that it represents, is situated within the four cultural categories described in the CSCF.

6. How Is Technology Managed?

Question 6 examines the management of technology as an organizational resource. Like other resource-centric questions in the SCDS, it asks survey respondents to describe whether technology is subject to more or less control, and whether it is put to use to increase the success of internal stakeholders or external stakeholders. Technology management can have profound implications for security culture, adding both freedoms and constraints to members throughout the organization. These implications may or may not make the job of the CISO or InfoSec manager easier.

7. How Are People Managed?

Although a people-centric approach to security is the central theme of this book, not every organization manages people in the same way, for the same reasons. Question 7 asks respondents to describe how people are treated and utilized as a resource within the organization. Is that management style formal and centralized, as with a traditional human resources department that may treat people much like any other organizational asset? Or is the environment more like a family, a community, or a social movement, where people are elevated above other components of the organization and given special focus and privilege?

8. How Is Risk Managed?

Question 8 gathers data from respondents about the understanding and management of risk within the organization. Risk is often subject to different interpretations and definitions within an enterprise, as I have described in previous chapters. How risk is understood, whether it represents a negative or a positive, and what should be done to reduce, accept, or even encourage it become key considerations for security. This question explores how risk management may differ between cultural categories within the CSCF and documents the means by which the organization addresses risks and opportunities in the conduct of its business.

9. How Is Accountability Achieved?

The means by which organizations hold members accountable for their actions can be deeply influenced by the culture of the organization, and can serve as a reflection of those core cultural traits. Question 9 asks survey respondents to explain the ways in which their organization understands and undertakes accountability. Depending on the culture, accountability may be mechanistic and the product of strict measures, or it may prove more situational and subjective. How accountability is perceived can play a part in how people within the organization make decisions, how they view their jobs and responsibilities, or even how they interact with and support (or fail to support) other members.

10. How Is Performance Evaluated?

Performance evaluation, like accountability, is a core requirement for organizational success. It is also, like other traits, culturally situated and influenced by norms and beliefs. While related to accountability, Question 10 focuses more directly on the measurement of success or failure than on the designation of who is responsible for those successes or failures. The question asks respondents to define the methods by which evaluation is conducted, whether success criteria are formalized or ad hoc, internally driven or influenced by outsiders, and whether performance is a shared or more individualized organizational activity.

SCDS Scoring Methodology

The SCDS uses an ipsative scale for measuring responses. Ipsative scales may be less familiar to you than the Likert scales typically seen in many surveys. Likert, or normative, scales use responses that force a survey respondent to answer in the form of a rating. Ratings may be numeric, such as asking a respondent to rate a preference on a scale of 1 to 5. Or they may be descriptive, asking the respondent to rate their agreement with a particular statement from "strongly agree" through to "strongly disagree." With Likert scales, each response is independent of other responses. If a survey asks a respondent to rate how they feel about different aspects of their job using a Likert scale, it is perfectly acceptable for the respondent to rate everything "strongly agree" or at a "5" level, depending on the scale. There is typically no ranking involved, where a "1" rating on one item would necessitate a "5" ranking on another, related item.

Ipsative scales force a respondent to choose between a series of two or more options. For each question in the SCDS, survey respondents are asked to weight the four responses by indicating the extent to which each accurately answers the question. There are pros and cons to using both the Likert and ipsative response systems, but ipsative scales work best when responses are not intended to be independent and should reflect differing but related degrees of preference between response items.

The CSCF describes organizational cultural environments, where opposing norms and values are present. An organization may exhibit a balance between cultural traits, but it cannot be completely one type of culture while also being completely another type of culture. Consider an enterprise, for instance, that has a very strong, deeply ingrained control culture, formal and strict hierarchies and bureaucratic command structures, and a process-driven infrastructure of policies and controls. It is extremely unlikely that this same organization will also allow individuals to make independent decisions, follow nonstandard processes, and regularly flout policies or circumvent established controls. The incompatibility of the cultures will create friction and failure until they are normalized, either with one culture attaining predominance and the other being marginalized, or by a mixing of the cultures that forms a compromise balance between the two.

An ipsative response scale for the SCDS reflects these trade-offs between cultural attributes within the SCDS and the CSCF. Each SCDS question has four possible responses that reflect differing and competing values. Respondents must assign a total score of 10 points across all four responses, dividing the points among the responses based on how strongly or weakly each of the statements reflects their own organization. For instance, if response A reflects the organization's values perfectly and no other response is applicable, the survey respondent might assign a score of 10 points to that response. But the respondent would then have to assign all other responses a 0 score, indicating those values are not present to any degree. Similarly, if a response is in no way reflective of the organization's values and assumptions and never influences behavior, the respondent might score it a 0, leaving the remainder of the weighting to be divided between the other three responses.

No organization is likely to exhibit a single cultural attribute or single set of values to the exclusion of all others. SCDS scores will usually reflect a balance between responses, which correlates to a balance between the four quadrants of the CSCF and the cultures each represents. It is possible in some cases that a particular set of values will be perceived as absent from the organizational environment and be assigned a 0 weighting. A respondent may decide, for instance, that some values associated with the Autonomy Culture are not present and therefore score several of the "C" responses as a 0. But there will likely be other areas where some delegation of control or decision making is allowed, even if those values remain small.

Scoring the SCDS Results

Scoring the SCDS is relatively straightforward, as I described in the last section. Respondents divide 10 points between each of the four possible responses, assessing the degree to which the statement reflects the values within their organizational environment. It is unnecessary for survey respondents to understand or even be aware of the CSCF, or divisions of organizational culture in general. They only need to decide to what degree each response statement describes the values of their own organization for the SCDS question under consideration.

Those tasked with interpreting the SCDS results will require a bit more insight into how the questions and responses are designed. If you have familiarized yourself with the CSCF presented in Chapter 5, you will quickly recognize patterns when you examine the survey response choices. Each response describes traits, values, and activities that are associated with one of the CSCF cultural quadrants:

▶ "**A**" responses reflect values and traits that are internally facing and prioritize tighter control. These attributes, including concerns over stability, the existence of standards and bureaucratic lines of control, and a desire for centralization, are priorities that tend to exist more strongly in Process Security Cultures.

▶ "**B**" responses reflect values and traits that still prioritize tight control, but are aimed at external stakeholders. Attributes include regular review, the need for justification and documentation of activities, and an audit-driven approach to the business, all of which are priorities more often found prevalent in Compliance Security Cultures.

▶ "**C**" responses reflect values and traits that are externally facing, but prioritize less control over decisions and activities. Flexibility, adaptability, and the need to be agile and unhampered by rigid bureaucracy and lines of authority are the dominant attributes, which are most often found in Autonomy Security Cultures.

▶ "**D**" responses reflect values and traits that are internally facing and more loosely controlled. Attributes include cooperation and transparency, shared responsibility and empowerment, and a sense of individual ownership and mutual support, all of which are indicative of the priorities existing in Trust Security Cultures.

Once the SCDS is completed and the survey owners have a set of responses, data analysis can begin. Analyzing SCDS data can be as simple as aggregating and averaging an organization's SCDS scores to show overall cultural traits. Or the survey owners can take more sophisticated paths: comparing scores, visualizing data, and using insights from the SCDS to plan InfoSec culture transformation strategies. The case studies in the next section serve to illustrate several ways that SCDS scores can help an organization understand and improve information security. I will discuss visualizing and mapping information security culture and the relationship between SCDS scores and the CSCF in the following chapter.

Security Culture Diagnostic Strategies: Case Studies

There are several strategies for using the SCDS to diagnose and assess security culture within an organization or between organizations. The most obvious strategy is to take a general measurement of overall security culture across the entire organization. Another strategy is to administer the SCDS separately to organizational divisions, allowing for comparisons, for instance, between the core information security program team and a group that has nothing to do directly with security. This can reveal cultural gaps between those who are responsible for managing security and those who are responsible for other business functions that may compete with security. A third strategy is to administer the SCDS to two different organizations prior to a merger or acquisition to determine the compatibility of their security cultures. A final strategy is to use the SCDS to assess how to improve people-centric security through cultural transformation. By measuring an existing security culture and then imagining what a future, improved culture would look like, an organization can map out desired changes. The following case studies of representative, but fictitious, organizations will cover each of these strategies.

ABLE Manufacturing: Measuring an Existing Security Culture

ABLE Manufacturing Corporation is a midsized company, producing both consumer goods that it sells directly and industrial products that it sells to other companies. Family owned and privately held, the company has always tried to foster a close-knit workplace environment. Many employees of ABLE Corp. have worked there for over a decade. ABLE considers itself above average in its use of information technology for its size and industry. Information security has been driven over the years primarily by requirements for PCI DSS compliance, as ABLE processes credit cards directly. The existing InfoSec team is cross-functional, with people from IT and from Internal Audit.

In the wake of recent information security breaches elsewhere, the CIO had become concerned about ABLE's security posture and thus hired a Director of Information Security (DIS), reporting directly to her. The new DIS previously worked for several companies and had seen firsthand how cultural differences can exacerbate security risks. He persuaded the CIO that many of the incidents that she was concerned about were the result of people-centric failures and not simply technology or process deficiencies. The CIO gave the DIS approval to launch a cultural baseline project to identify potential areas of conflict, and the DIS engaged an SCDS-based assessment of ABLE's existing security culture.

Respondents were a small mix of managers within the CIO's organization. Figure 6-1 shows a sample of the average scores for the first three survey questions and their associated response rankings.

ABLE's SCDS responses revealed several things. First, consistently high scores were associated with "A" responses, which are linked to the Process Culture in the CSCF. These scores indicated that centralized management and standard

1.	What's valued most?	Score
A.	Stability and reliability are valued most by the organization. It is critical that everyone knows the rules and follows them. The organization cannot succeed if people are all doing things different ways without centralized visibility.	4
B.	Successfully meeting external requirements is valued most by the organization. The organization is under a lot of scrutiny. It cannot succeed if people fail audits or do not live up to the expectations of those watching.	2.5
C.	Adapting quickly and competing aggressively are valued most by the organization. Results are what matters. The organization cannot succeed if bureaucracy and red tape impair people's ability to be agile.	1
D.	People and a sense of community are valued most by the organization. Everyone is in it together. The organization cannot succeed unless people are given the opportunities and skills to succeed on their own.	2.5
	Total Score	10
2.	How does the organization work?	Score
A.	The organization works on authority, policy, and standard ways of doing things. Organizational charts are formal and important. The organization is designed to ensure control and efficiency.	5
B.	The organization works on outside requirements and regular reviews. Audits are a central feature of life. The organization is designed to ensure everyone meets their obligations.	1
C.	The organization works on independent action and giving people decision authority. There's no one right way to do things. The organization is designed to ensure that the right things get done in the right situations.	1
D.	The organization works on teamwork and cooperation. It is a community. The organization is designed to ensure everyone is constantly learning, growing, and supporting one another.	3
	Total Score	10
3.	What does security mean?	Score
A.	Security means policies, procedures, and standards, automated wherever possible using technology. When people talk about security they are talking about the infrastructures in place to protect the organization's information assets.	3
B.	Security means showing evidence of visibility and control, particularly to external parties. When people talk about security they are talking about passing an audit or meeting a regulatory requirement.	4
C.	Security means enabling the organization to adapt and compete, not hindering it or saying "no" to everything. When people talk about security they are talking about balancing risks and rewards.	2.5
D.	Security means awareness and shared responsibility. When people talk about security they are talking about the need for everyone to be an active participant in protecting the organization.	0.5
	Total Score	10

Figure 6-1   *Sample SCDS scores for ABLE Manufacturing Corp.*

policies and procedures were priority values for ABLE. This came as no surprise to the CIO. ABLE is family owned, with several family members in key leadership positions and on the board. Authority flows from them through a strong chain of command to the entire firm. And being a manufacturing company, ABLE is all about stable, repeatable processes.

It was also unsurprising to those reviewing the results of the SCDS assessment that "D" responses were rated so highly. These responses are tied to the Trust Culture in the CSCF, which emphasizes human development and a sense of community. ABLE employees are encouraged to think of themselves as an extension of the owning family and to expect to share in both success and failure. Mutual respect and support are key company values.

Discrepancies were discovered as well. The "B" response scores, which are aligned with the Compliance Culture, exhibited quite a bit of variance. These responses indicated that ABLE cared about meeting external stakeholder requirements, whether from customers or regulators or both, but was not structured around compliance. Further investigation revealed that audits, particularly PCI DSS audits in the context of security, were the responsibility of specific teams. Generally, ABLE employees were not directly or regularly involved in these compliance activities. The existing security team, however, considered PCI DSS compliance one of its most important responsibilities and had structured itself accordingly.

Another interesting data point involved the perception of security as a hindrance to business operations. Although the "C" response scores, which are aligned with the Autonomy Culture in the CSCF, tended to be low for these SCDS results, the response to Question 3 about security's meaning and purpose revealed a score over twice as high as the other questions' "C" response scores. This might indicate a conflict in which people perceive security as less an enabler of the business than a blocker. More exploration was needed to confirm whether such a perception was at the root of that particular score, but it pointed the reviewers in an interesting direction for considering security's role in the company.

Comparing Different Security Cultures Within ABLE Manufacturing Corp.

As an outcome of the initial pilot SCDS assessment, the Director of Information Security was given permission to expand the project and focus on comparing results from ABLE's security team members to results from other parts of the company. This would enable the CIO and the DIS to gauge whether there were significant differences in security cultures between those owning and using IT resources and those tasked with protecting them, and then assess whether those differences might result in competing values and create risks for the organization. A sample of these results is shown in Figure 6-2.

1.	What's valued most?	ABLE InfoSec	ABLE Corp
A.	Stability and reliability are valued most by the organization. It is critical that everyone knows the rules and follows them. The organization cannot succeed if people are all doing things different ways without centralized visibility.	4	4
B.	Successfully meeting external requirements is valued most by the organization. The organization is under a lot of scrutiny. It cannot succeed if people fail audits or do not live up to the expectations of those watching.	4	0.5
C.	Adapting quickly and competing aggressively are valued most by the organization. Results are what matters. The organization cannot succeed if bureaucracy and red tape impair people's ability to be agile.	0.5	2.5
D.	People and a sense of community are valued most by the organization. Everyone is in it together. The organization cannot succeed unless people are given the opportunities and skills to succeed on their own.	1.5	3
	Total Score	10	10

2.	How does the organization work?	ABLE InfoSec	ABLE Corp
A.	The organization works on authority, policy, and standard ways of doing things. Organizational charts are formal and important. The organization is designed to ensure control and efficiency.	4	5
B.	The organization works on outside requirements and regular reviews. Audits are a central feature of life. The organization is designed to ensure everyone meets their obligations.	5	1
C.	The organization works on independent action and giving people decision authority. There's no one right way to do things. The organization is designed to ensure that the right things get done in the right situations.	0	1
D.	The organization works on teamwork and cooperation. It is a community. The organization is designed to ensure everyone is constantly learning, growing, and supporting one another.	1	3
	Total Score	10	10

3.	What does security mean?	ABLE InfoSec	ABLE Corp
A.	Security means policies, procedures, and standards, automated wherever possible using technology. When people talk about security they are talking about the infrastructures in place to protect the organization's information assets.	3	6
B.	Security means showing evidence of visibility and control, particularly to external parties. When people talk about security they are talking about passing an audit or meeting a regulatory requirement.	5	1
C.	Security means enabling the organization to adapt and compete, not hindering it or saying "no" to everything. When people talk about security they are talking about balancing risks and rewards.	0.5	2.5
D.	Security means awareness and shared responsibility. When people talk about security they are talking about the need for everyone to be an active participant in protecting the organization.	1.5	0.5
	Total Score	10	10

Figure 6-2 *Comparison of sample SCDS scores for ABLE InfoSec and Corporate*

Comparing the results of the SCDS for the ABLE InfoSec team with the results for the rest of the organization showed some immediate value discrepancies that could be indicative of competing cultures within the company. Once again, scores associated with a Process Culture were high for both the information security team and for the corporation as a whole. But interestingly, respondents outside of the security team defined security in terms of processes and policies to a greater extent than the security team did. For your average ABLE corporate employee, when you talked about security, you were talking about security policies and standards, which were the things they were most familiar with. Everyone at ABLE had to go through annual security training, which emphasized the corporate security policies. The results demonstrated the security team had a more nuanced view, one in which security policies and standards are important, but not the totality of ABLE's InfoSec infrastructure.

Divergent values and cultures were very apparent when it came to compliance and audits. For the security team, if any one thing defined security, it was a successful PCI DSS audit. Much of the InfoSec infrastructure had come about in response to PCI DSS audit requirements. But outside of the security team, compliance with PCI DSS was far removed from the average employee's mind. Many did not even know what PCI DSS is, other than some sort of audit the organization has to go through and something the information security team is responsible for. The survey results showed that ABLE employees tended not to worry about compliance issues in general, and that the company was not structured in a way that encouraged them to do so. As it turned out, the higher ratings on the initial pilot SCDS assessment were more a reflection of the fact that IT managers were the primary respondents than evidence that a Compliance Culture existed within the company.

Differences in cultural values were reinforced again when the CIO and DIS reviewed the scores for Autonomy and Trust Cultures. The security team often expressed frustration that, even in a process-driven company like ABLE, security often got a lot of pushback over rules and standards. ABLE's security team tended to be risk averse and viewed exceptions to and deviations from the security rules and standards as creating risk. Although the rest of ABLE's employees were hardly advocating an "anything goes" culture, given their SCDS responses, nevertheless the corporate culture was much more permissive in the name of business agility than was the security team culture.

The competing values in play within ABLE's organizational security culture both explained a lot to the CIO and concerned her. It became apparent that the security team culture was different, in some cases markedly so, from that of the rest of the company. In addition to creating political friction, these differing values meant that people responsible for protecting company assets were motivated by very different ideas about what was required to do business successfully. A complete cultural transformation project was not something that ABLE was prepared to dive into immediately, but the results of the assessment convinced the CIO to grant the DIS's request to significantly increase ABLE's training and awareness budget so that he could "get the word out" about security and start normalizing relations between his information security team and other ABLE corporate stakeholders.

CHARLIE Systems, Inc.: Comparing Security Cultures of Two Organizations

CHARLIE Systems, Inc., is a technology firm that makes several acquisitions each year. CHARLIE feels strongly about ensuring a cultural fit between the firm and any company that it buys. Corporate culture has traditionally been the primary focus for CHARLIE, but a couple of recent acquisitions have forced CHARLIE to consider how information technology cultures in general, and InfoSec cultures in particular, align as well. The company found out the hard way that an incompatible information security culture in an acquired company can create problems that, had they been foreseen, might have changed CHARLIE's decision about the deal.

CHARLIE Systems has a CISO who reports to the CIO, and a centralized security infrastructure. The CISO enjoys quite a bit of influence within the company and, after pushing to add security to the cultural assessments that CHARLIE performs as part of its due diligence, she was able to institute an SCDS-based program to collect security culture data on any potential acquisition. The first company against whom the assessment was performed was EZ Company, a small software startup with an innovative online workflow and collaboration product. Sample SCDS results comparing the companies are shown in Figure 6-3.

As you can see, major cultural differences exist between CHARLIE and EZ. The former is a large, established company that has been around for more than 15 years. The latter is a startup of two dozen people that was founded 18 months before the acquisition. Although it has received some venture funding, EZ has always been a close-knit, highly motivated group, most of whom have known each other since college. "Kick ass, take names, have fun" is the company's informal motto.

1. What's valued most?	CHARLIE	EZ
A. Stability and reliability are valued most by the organization. It is critical that everyone knows the rules and follows them. The organization cannot succeed if people are all doing things different ways without centralized visibility.	3	1
B. Successfully meeting external requirements is valued most by the organization. The organization is under a lot of scrutiny. It cannot succeed if people fail audits or do not live up to the expectations of those watching.	3	1.5
C. Adapting quickly and competing aggressively are valued most by the organization. Results are what matters. The organization cannot succeed if bureaucracy and red tape impair people's ability to be agile.	2.5	5
D. People and a sense of community are valued most by the organization. Everyone is in it together. The organization cannot succeed unless people are given the opportunities and skills to succeed on their own.	1.5	2.5
Total Score	10	10

2. How does the organization work?	CHARLIE	EZ
A. The organization works on authority, policy, and standard ways of doing things. Organizational charts are formal and important. The organization is designed to ensure control and efficiency.	3.5	0.5
B. The organization works on outside requirements and regular reviews. Audits are a central feature of life. The organization is designed to ensure everyone meets their obligations.	2.5	0
C. The organization works on independent action and giving people decision authority. There's no one right way to do things. The organization is designed to ensure that the right things get done in the right situations.	2	6
D. The organization works on teamwork and cooperation. It is a community. The organization is designed to ensure everyone is constantly learning, growing, and supporting one another.	2	3.5
Total Score	10	10

3. What does security mean?	CHARLIE	EZ
A. Security means policies, procedures, and standards, automated wherever possible using technology. When people talk about security they are talking about the infrastructures in place to protect the organization's information assets.	4	2
B. Security means showing evidence of visibility and control, particularly to external parties. When people talk about security they are talking about passing an audit or meeting a regulatory requirement.	3.5	0
C. Security means enabling the organization to adapt and compete, not hindering it or saying "no" to everything. When people talk about security they are talking about balancing risks and rewards.	1	5
D. Security means awareness and shared responsibility. When people talk about security they are talking about the need for everyone to be an active participant in protecting the organization.	1.5	3
Total Score	10	10

Figure 6-3   *Sample SCDS scores for CHARLIE Systems, Inc., and EZ Company*

Looking at the scores, the CISO is concerned about the cultural differences. Structure and stability are not key values at EZ. Quite the opposite, in fact. Many of the employees wear multiple hats, jumping in and out of each other's roles as the situation demands. As a result, decision authority has been widely decentralized, and EZ employees have a lot of faith that everyone will do the right thing for the company...and the right thing is building and selling very cool software that people enjoy using.

For the CISO and the executive team at CHARLIE Systems, what is considered the "right thing" is more nuanced. Being publicly traded, CHARLIE has shareholder and regulatory obligations, including SOX compliance. The company is PCI DSS certified and must comply with a broad range of privacy regulations given the business it does in Europe. EZ Company has almost no experience with auditors or compliance, and the SCDS scores reinforce some concerns the CISO has about the way EZ manages its own software development and IT processes. She wonders whether EZ's developers are going to fit easily into the more formal, centralized development process at CHARLIE, which has multiple controls in place around secure software engineering.

The SCDS scores and the competing values and security cultures that exist between CHARLIE Systems and EZ Company are not necessarily show-stoppers for the acquisition. But the SCDS results do allow CHARLIE's executives to weigh very real, but much less visible, risks and costs of the deal. Would CHARLIE still think the deal was good if 80–90 percent of EZ's developers were to quit after finding their new environment too restrictive? And what is the risk that EZ's prioritizing of cool features over security and privacy implications could lead to a security incident in the product, the company, or for a customer down the road?

DOG: Comparing Existing to Desired Security Culture

The Department of Governance (DOG) is a state agency responsible for overseeing aspects of business operations at other state agencies, particularly concerning contracts management, public-private partnerships, and legal and ethical issues. Like many state agencies, the DOG is bureaucratic, centralized, and risk averse. In an effort to improve communication and efficiency, as well as to attract better employee candidates to the agency, the CIO proposed implementing an IT transformation project, including such innovations as bring your own device (BYOD) and e-government initiatives. To his frustration, the CIO discovered this was easier said than done, as a minor rebellion, led in part by his own information security manager, attempted to block the initiative on the grounds of unacceptable security risks. "No one will be connecting devices we don't control to this network while I'm here," the security manager stated pointedly during one of the CIO's staff meetings. Not long afterward, the CIO and the InfoSec manager mutually agreed that the InfoSec manager's transfer to another agency was in everyone's best interests.

The CIO recruited a new information security manager from a local university. The new manager was younger and more supportive of a flexible security environment that balanced security risks with business opportunities. A cornerstone of the effort, the CIO and security manager agreed, would be a two-year cultural transformation initiative. An SCDS assessment was conducted to baseline the existing cultural values held by the security team and to articulate where the organization needed to be in terms of security culture to make the CIO's desired initiatives, including the BYOD rollout, more likely to be successful. A sample of these current and desired scores are shown in Figure 6-4.

The CIO and security manager both promoted the case for a more balanced set of security values. Neither had any illusions about the bureaucratic and structured environment in which they worked, and they did not want to turn it into a startup culture. But many DOG staff members had expressed a desire for a BYOD program. The goal was to gradually change the way that employees, and particularly those in both information technology and InfoSec, looked at their world. Instead of thinking about risk in a way that made some in the department afraid to embrace change, the DOG culture had to start at least balancing that apprehension with a healthy concern for the risk of not changing at all.

One key area of change would be to move from a security culture that values not giving anyone the ability to make their own decisions to a stronger Autonomy Culture. But loosening the control over individuals in terms of their IT use would require giving them the skills necessary to make better decisions on their own. For this reason, a boosting of the Trust Culture would be necessary as well, which would mean involvement and awareness programs to help everyone become their own quasi-security managers.

By the same token, structure and stability would continue to be a core value for DOG. But the organization would no longer be so heavily weighted toward a Process Culture. Exploring the SCDS results and developing the desired culture revealed that policies and standards were often used simply to enforce the status quo, rather than to enable performance. The CIO wanted to keep the bureaucracy that worked, adapt to the bureaucracy that would prove to be required no matter what he did, and strip away the bureaucracy that was stifling his organization and slowing it down.

1.	What's valued most?	Score Current	Score Future
A.	Stability and reliability are valued most by the organization. It is critical that everyone knows the rules and follows them. The organization cannot succeed if people are all doing things different ways without centralized visibility.	5.5	3
B.	Successfully meeting external requirements is valued most by the organization. The organization is under a lot of scrutiny. It cannot succeed if people fail audits or do not live up to the expectations of those watching.	2.5	2
C.	Adapting quickly and competing aggressively are valued most by the organization. Results are what matters. The organization cannot succeed if bureaucracy and red tape impair people's ability to be agile.	0.5	2.5
D.	People and a sense of community are valued most by the organization. Everyone is in it together. The organization cannot succeed unless people are given the opportunities and skills to succeed on their own.	1.5	2.5
	Total Score	10	10
2.	How does the organization work?	Score Current	Score Future
A.	The organization works on authority, policy, and standard ways of doing things. Organizational charts are formal and important. The organization is designed to ensure control and efficiency.	7	4
B.	The organization works on outside requirements and regular reviews. Audits are a central feature of life. The organization is designed to ensure everyone meets their obligations.	1	2
C.	The organization works on independent action and giving people decision authority. There's no one right way to do things. The organization is designed to ensure that the right things get done in the right situations.	0	1.5
D.	The organization works on teamwork and cooperation. It is a community. The organization is designed to ensure everyone is constantly learning, growing, and supporting one another.	2	2.5
	Total Score	10	10
3.	What does security mean?	Score Current	Score Future
A.	Security means policies, procedures, and standards, automated wherever possible using technology. When people talk about security they are talking about the infrastructures in place to protect the organization's information assets.	5.5	2.5
B.	Security means showing evidence of visibility and control, particularly to external parties. When people talk about security they are talking about passing an audit or meeting a regulatory requirement.	4	2.5
C.	Security means enabling the organization to adapt and compete, not hindering it or saying "no" to everything. When people talk about security they are talking about balancing risks and rewards.	0	2.5
D.	Security means awareness and shared responsibility. When people talk about security they are talking about the need for everyone to be an active participant in protecting the organization.	0.5	2.5
	Total Score	10	10

Figure 6-4   *Sample of current and desired SCDS scores for Department of Governance*

The security culture and values work that the CIO and new InfoSec manager performed was not an easy fix that automagically transformed the culture. But by measuring the current state and setting defined goals for a future state of IT and information security values and culture, they were able to articulate a strategy and a plan to DOG leadership that aligned with the goals of making government work more efficiently, more transparently, and in a way that would continue to attract the best candidates to public service in the state.

Creating Culture Maps with the Security Culture Diagnostic Survey

The Security Culture Diagnostic Survey (SCDS) described in Chapter 6 enables an organization to define and measure its information security culture by having respondents assign scores to specific values, assumptions, and norms that align with the four general security culture types of the Competing Security Cultures Framework. The inherently visual nature of the CSCF, with its quadrants and competing value axes, also enables and encourages users of the SCDS to visualize the insights that the SCDS scores provide. The resulting graphical representation makes the insights regarding cultural conflicts and interrelationships generated by the SCDS more intuitive and powerful and provides a great visual tool for exploring and transforming the organization's information security culture.

This chapter will describe how to use SCDS results to create visual "maps" of InfoSec culture, as well as how to interpret those maps once they are built. Expanding upon several of the case studies from Chapter 6, I will describe how each organization incorporates CSCF visualizations into their SCDS analyses. Mapping security culture against the CSCF is an important component of any effort to facilitate culture change and promote people-centric security within an organization.

Mapping and Visualization Tools

I am not a visualization guru, nor do you have to be to take advantage of the CSCF and the security culture maps you can produce using the SCDS. All culture maps created in this chapter were done using standard office productivity software, specifically spreadsheet and presentation programs. You probably already have access to standard office productivity software, but if you need tools, you have a lot of choices, including open source software from Apache OpenOffice (as well as LibreOffice and NeoOffice) and commercial software from Apple and Microsoft. Of course, for those readers skilled in the visual arts, I have no doubt you can improve upon my humble examples.

Security Culture Maps

I refer to the visualizations of culture created using the SCDS as maps intentionally. Maps are metaphors. Conventional maps help us to navigate physical geography in the "real" world, such as when we search for directions to a recommended restaurant or plan a trip across the country. Other maps enable us to navigate conceptual geographies, such as a mind map to help us navigate our own ideas, or a topic map to formally explore the linkages between bodies or instances of knowledge. Like all metaphors, maps are about describing one thing in terms of something else. The map is not the reality, but it can help us understand that reality better, as long as we keep in mind the assumptions and limitations that go into it. The dot on a map of the United States that has "Austin" written next to it is, of course, not the city I live in. It has absolutely no similarity to the actual city of Austin other than the suspension of disbelief that everyone using the map agrees to practice in order to get something useful out of the shared experience.

The concept of a culture map is about more than just a shared visual metaphor that describes your organization's security culture. The purpose of a culture map is not only to measure or visualize security culture, but also to change it. Maps imply a journey and a destination, starting in one place and ending in another. Maps help you orient yourself and find the best route to where you want to go. Transforming culture and making your way to a more people-centric security infrastructure is a journey. It will take time and effort, and it cannot be achieved by putting a vendor's product into your datacenter any more than you can instantly teleport from New York to San Francisco. But to get from here to there, you're going to need a guide, a compass, and a map.

Mapping Security Culture Using the CSCF

The CSCF is the starting point for mapping your organization's unique security culture because it visually represents a general cultural landscape for InfoSec. Unlike a street atlas or a geographical map, though, you don't point to one place on the CSCF and say "here we are." Culture in the CSCF is determined by the relative strength of each of the four cultural types within your organization. The closest physical analogy is a bit like standing in Four Corners, the spot in the United States where New Mexico, Colorado, Utah, and Arizona meet. Depending on how you lean, there may be more of you in one state than in another. With the CSCF your organization's values and assumptions do the "leaning," and your culture is where you end up, driving the decisions and behaviors you can expect from people. If you are a CISO and you are leaning heavily in one direction while others in the organization are bent over backwards the opposite way, you may find yourself in a different state of mind, if not actual geography. That can be a problem because security risks are often created in the space between cultural priorities. But you may not even notice that everyone thinks differently about InfoSec until you can locate different people, and the direction they are leaning, on the culture map.

Figure 7-1 shows a narrative representation of the CSCF, using the idea of "You are here" that you see on maps located everywhere from malls to national parks. Just like a map that tells you what reference points to look around for to triangulate your own location, the CSCF gives you behavioral reference points

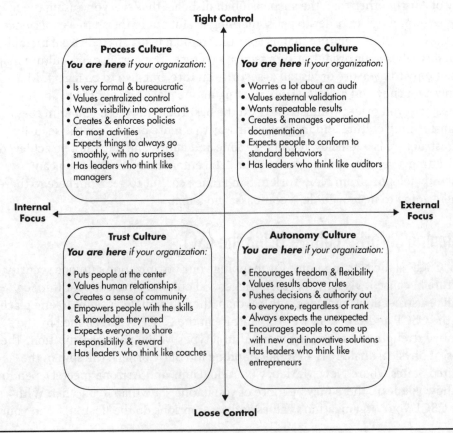

Figure 7-1 *Narrative cultural reference points in the CSCF*

that can indicate where your organization is located in terms of control (tighter or looser) and perspective (inward or outward focus).

While the CSCF can function as a map to orient yourself generally in terms of your security culture, it lacks the specificity of the SCDS as a measurement instrument. If, however, you use the SCDS results to provide coordinates on that map, you can literally draw a better picture of your InfoSec culture, one that gives more insight into improving people-centric security. Culture maps that combine the CSCF and SCDS results accomplish just this goal.

Composition of a SCDS-based Culture Map

Security culture maps are created by superimposing an organization's SCDS responses on the CSCF visual model. The example security culture maps presented in this chapter are based on the case studies from Chapter 6. Recall that the SCDS gives us a scoring system by which we can associate different responses about the ten organizational characteristics and activities with cultural types in the CSCF. Using these scores, we can judge the relative strength of a Process Culture, for example, against an Autonomy Culture, Compliance Culture, or Trust Culture. By graphing these scores in the context of the CSCF, we can make those comparisons more intuitive and visual to help security teams better articulate cultural risks and help consumers of SCDS findings absorb the results.

Superimposing SCDS Responses on the CSCF Visual Model

While there are many different data visualization techniques, I prefer three basic types for my security culture maps, but data are data and you should feel free to experiment with whatever works best in your organization. Each of the preferred methods I use has its strengths and weaknesses, which I will describe as we move through the following examples. All of the maps are created from the same organizations and results that I profiled in Chapter 6.

The first example of a security culture map is the most complicated, imposing specific SCDS scores as a bar chart onto the general visual model of the CSCF. Figure 7-2 shows a map for the general culture of ABLE Manufacturing Corporation, as defined by the average of all SCDS scores. Responses to each of the ten questions are indexed to align with specific CSCF quadrants. "A" responses indicate characteristics of a Process Culture, "B" responses align with a Compliance Culture, "C" responses imply an Autonomy Culture, and "D" responses correspond to a Trust Culture. By dividing and averaging the four response categories, we can derive an

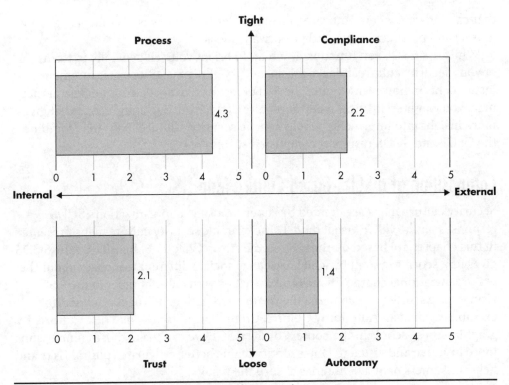

Figure 7-2 *General culture of ABLE Manufacturing by SCDS scores*

overall score for the organization's cultural values and the relative strength of each cultural type in the CSCF.

Looking at the culture map in Figure 7-2, you can immediately notice some big differences across cultural values inside of ABLE Manufacturing. The map is top-heavy, indicating that tighter control is an important organizational value. Similarly, the map is heavily weighted in the two left quadrants, which implies more of a focus internally than externally. But the anchor point for both of these observations is the dominance of the Process Culture quadrant. Adding actual SCDS score averages to the map helps a reader understand that the Process Culture scores, on average, are nearly twice that of the next nearest cultural type.

ABLE Manufacturing is obviously, according to its SCDS scores, an organization that values stability, centralized control, and standard ways of getting things done. The general scores do not differentiate between how security teams see things versus how the rest of the organization may look at the world. It simply represents the overall culture as determined by the average results of the SCDS.

Suppose we wanted to drill a little more deeply and see just how those averages were attained. We could expand the culture map as shown in Figure 7-3, which provides a representative example of all the responses to the SCDS questions.

Breaking out the scores by individual responses makes the results more interesting, and the variance shows that no single CSCF quadrant is as monolithic as it might appear judging only by averages. Instead, each quadrant has at least one score that is at odds with the overall result. Process may be the strongest cultural type within the organization, but at least one score is less than half of the average, implying that not every business activity prioritizes centralized, stable operations as a cultural value. Conversely, even the lower-scoring quadrants demonstrate values that are at odds with the dominant trend. Most of the organization's value scores do not reflect a culture that values nonconformity and flexibility. But in at least one case, the management of technology, the organization is equally balanced between a Process Culture and an Autonomy

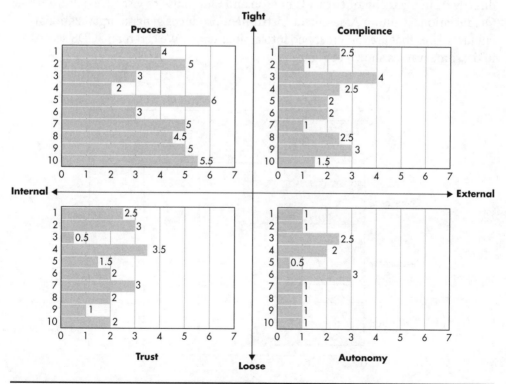

Figure 7-3 *Total SCDS responses for ABLE Manufacturing*

Culture. Think about the impact on security of an organization that centralizes everything except the ability to control corporate IT systems, which is decided by individual divisions or geographic locations. The competing values between those two cultures could easily create headaches and risks for any security team.

Other Techniques for Mapping Security Culture

Using bar charts in each of the four quadrants is not the only way that we can visualize SCDS results. A more traditional bar chart can quickly show us the scores as a list rather than an overlay of the CSCF. An example of this simplified culture map is shown in Figure 7-4. The simplified chart makes it easy to compare SCDS scores directly, but it loses the visual connection to the CSCF. I often find it useful to combine the two maps, using the simplified chart as a legend to quickly compare scores while showing the quadrant-based map to visualize relative strengths within the cultural types.

One more visualization technique that I find useful for culture maps is pulled directly from the techniques that Cameron and Quinn use to visualize culture. Their Organizational Culture Assessment Instrument produces general organizational culture scores that are then mapped into a radar chart. We can map SCDS scores in the same way, as shown in Figure 7-5.

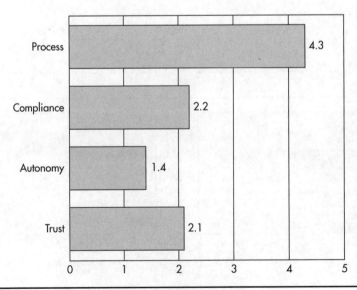

Figure 7-4   *Basic bar chart for ABLE Manufacturing SCDS scores*

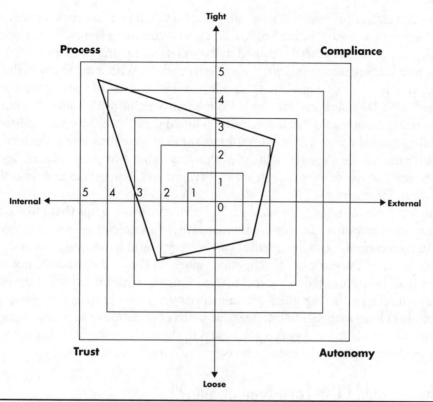

Figure 7-5   *ABLE Manufacturing general culture using radar chart*

The radar chart map has the advantage of giving the culture a definite shape, one that is visually intuitive and recognizable. The radar charts look like what we would expect from a map, assigning cultural scores in a way that implies territory within the CSCF model. But radar charts have also been subject to critique over recent years. Some graphing programs and online services do not even offer them anymore as a visualization option. The critiques vary, but mainly revolve around the idea that, while a radar chart can create a powerful visual first impression, it actually tends to make analysis of results more difficult. People tend to be more adept at straight-line comparisons, like the one in the basic bar chart example in Figure 7-4. In a radar chart your eye has to travel around the chart, mapping each data point to the one before it in a way that can be more difficult than when those scores are placed side by side.

Another difficulty I have with the radar chart is that it can take the map metaphor a bit further than I like. The map of ABLE's general culture in Figure 7-2 is quite clearly a set of survey scores, mapped to the different quadrants of the CSCF. You never lose touch completely with the underlying data. With a radar chart, the temptation is to see a "shape" that the culture takes, instead of a set of answers to specific SCDS questions. Divorced from an association with a survey, a radar-based culture map can try to force-feed too much complexity into a simplistic two-dimensional image. An organization may decide "we look like a diamond, when we need to be a square" instead of thinking about why particular SCDS scores, and the values they reflect, are higher or lower than others and what that may mean for security.

But for all the critique, it is often the radar chart culture maps that I find elicit the strongest response, that *ah-ha!* moment where an executive or a stakeholder gets it. As a communication tool they can be very useful in pointing out and communicating the essence of competing values. In Figure 7-4, it's hard not to notice that the culture skews sharply toward Process, with the values of the other three cultural types having much less influence over the enterprise. A more specific or precise culture map that fails to make as much of an intuitive impression may end up failing in its central purpose, which is to show where the organization is (You are here!) and give it a better idea of where it might want to be.

"When Should I Use Each Type of Map?"

There is no one right way to present the results of a cultural measurement exercise. The best way to do it is the way that works the best to stimulate thought and action. What is most important is to realize the key strengths and weaknesses of each technique and to pick the right tool for the right job. If you are the Security Awareness Manager and you've got five minutes out of a two-hour meeting to get senior management's attention, you might very well decide that a radar-based culture map is the way to go. If you are the CISO tasked with transforming security culture, the idea that you're going to make your culture "more symmetrical" is probably less useful than figuring out how to influence specific SCDS responses by changing values within the organization.

Given the introductory nature of this book, I will rely heavily on radar charts throughout this chapter and others. They are the easiest way to quickly convey a cultural "shape" that gets the point across. But when it comes time to operationalize culture into measurable activities, it will always be necessary to fall back on

SCDS scores. The "shape" of your culture only changes when people give different responses to the SCDS, reflecting different opinions about the organization. The only way to accomplish that is to transform the values that people hold about how your organization should manage itself, its behaviors, and its InfoSec strategies and activities.

Data visualization is a science and an art unto itself, and you should always keep in mind that the specific techniques I present in this book or that other researchers or practitioners have developed are just a few of the options available to you. You may develop a completely novel (and maybe even strange) way of mapping security and organizational culture using the SCDS data, and I encourage that if it works within your unique context and environment. How an organization visualizes the existing culture can itself be dependent on that very culture. Feel free to experiment, and let me know if you come up with something especially good!

Mapping Specific Values and Activities

All the preceding examples have focused on the general information security culture of ABLE Manufacturing, as defined by the aggregate scores resulting from a company-wide SCDS assessment. But we got a hint in Figure 7-3 that we have uncovered some interesting patterns and discrepancies in the results. An organization's culture, including its security culture, is the product of many different values and activities. These are reflected in the ten questions of the SCDS. How an organization views information and how that same organization views risk, to use two examples, are probably separate sets of values and assumptions about what is important. Both contribute to the overall organizational culture, and both drive activities and decisions that impact security. But they often function as conceptual silos, except in the minds of people who like, or are paid, to think about the intersection between information use and business risk.

It can be very useful to visualize not just general culture, but specific cultural values. These values can then be compared directly. Building a culture map around specific SCDS results is no more difficult than building one for general culture. Figure 7-6 shows all three maps for the average score resulting from responses to SCDS Question 3, "What does security mean?"

Mapping single responses is useful when analyzing and interpreting specific traits in the context of the overall culture. It can help identify competing values that may lead to risk. It is also useful in fine-tuning a cultural transformation program by allowing the organization more precision in terms of identifying behaviors, norms, and assumptions to target, and the measurement of the resulting changes.

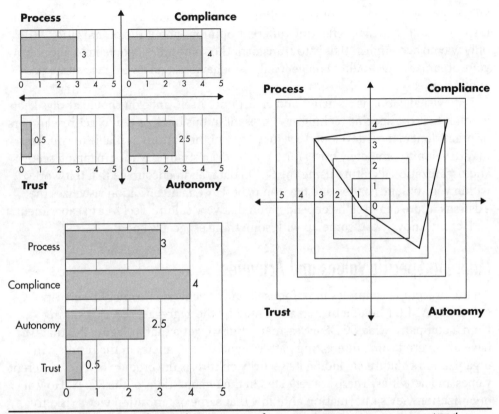

Figure 7-6 *Culture maps for single ABLE Manufacturing SCDS response score ("What does security mean?")*

Interpreting and Comparing Culture

People who make or use maps and visualizations have concerns that may be aesthetic (ugly maps are less useful) as well as functional (less useful maps are less useful). You create a map to help you accomplish something, to get somewhere you want to go. Creating the map is the first step of this process. Reading it, interpreting it, and using it to figure out where you are, where others might be, or to plot a course from here to there comes next. Culture maps serve these orientation and navigational purposes, too. Once you have visualized the SCDS data to graphically represent your organization's cultural attributes and values, it's time to put those visualizations to use in improving and transforming your security culture.

Interpreting SCDS Results

Looking at the culture map in Figure 7-2, we see the general culture as defined by ABLE Manufacturing's SCDS responses. What do the scores and their associated visualizations tell us? How do we use the maps to craft a story about ABLE's cultural values and to decide what, if anything, needs to be done to change them?

Dominant Culture: The Way Things Get Done

ABLE Manufacturing cares a lot about stability and standards. That much is obvious from the SCDS scores, which consistently rate organizational behaviors associated with a Process Culture more highly than any other cultural attributes. ABLE does, of course, exhibit other cultural traits. Compliance-related behaviors are important, as are behaviors and values associated with community and fostering a people-friendly workplace. ABLE even exhibits a bit of an Autonomy Culture, in some cases allowing freedom and independence rather than requiring adherence to strict rules. But if we were asked what is the dominant culture within ABLE, the answer would have to be Process.

A Process Culture makes sense for ABLE, a private manufacturing company, where consistency of production and standard levels of product quality are highly valued by the business. ABLE manufactures a relatively few number of things and believes that it does so very well. The ownership structure of ABLE keeps the hierarchy and organizational chart stable over time, with clear lines of power back up to the family members at senior levels of management and the board.

When performing a cultural diagnostic exercise, identifying one or more dominant cultures is a good first step. The dominant culture tends to drive behavior, to define the organization's core beliefs, and to provide an anchor point against which divergence from that culture can be compared. If organizational culture can be defined as "the way we do things around here," then the dominant culture represents the most likely way that things will get done. There will always be exceptions, but the more dominant a particular cultural type is within the organization, the more glaring are the deviations from it when they do occur. We have explored in previous chapters how organizational culture becomes invisible, functioning below the surface of our observable behaviors. When things seem to be going right, when everything is moving smoothly and as expected around us, we seldom think to ask "why did you do that?" Decisions seem natural, in accordance with our assumptions about how the world works. It's only when something or someone challenges those assumptions that we find ourselves conscious of them.

Cultural Conflict: "You Can't Do That Here..."

Consider the case in which a new marketing manager is hired into ABLE, tasked with updating the company brand and making ABLE's products more attractive to younger consumers. Arriving her first week to go through company orientation, the manager is surprised to find that she will be issued a corporate standard laptop computer running Microsoft Windows.

"But I'm an Apple user," the new manager says. "I'd like to have a Mac as my work computer."

"Sorry," the IT representative tasked with getting her set up replies, "we standardize on Microsoft products. You can't have a Mac."

"Well, I'll need to use my personal Mac for some work things," the manager replies. "How can I get it connected to the corporate network?"

"You can't," the IT technician repeats, a bit horrified. "That would be an enormous security violation."

"Well, I need an exception," the manager says, now annoyed. "I can't do my job using only a Windows machine."

"You better figure out how," the tech tells her, sort of amazed at how arrogant this new employee is proving to be. "You can't just connect anything you want to our network because you decide you need it."

ABLE's technician and newly hired manager have both just been given a lesson in cultural conflict, one that was disconcerting to both of them. The differences between their assumptions and values may even result in negative impacts on ABLE. If the marketing manager is not just exaggerating and really does need to use a Mac to be fully productive, then the company will suffer when she is not able to do the job ABLE hired her to do because of a bureaucratic requirement. She may even decide to quit altogether, or may be tempted to use her personal technology devices in violation of the company security policy. ABLE's processes may actually get in the way of the company's ability to execute on its own goals and objectives.

This sort of conflict happens every day in organizations around the world. People realize the world doesn't quite work the way they assumed it does and are surprised when behaviors they consider strange and bizarre prove to be routine and normal to others. The experience can be awkward and uncomfortable, but shaking ourselves out of our own complacency is often the only way to grow and improve, both individually and as organizations. Using cultural measurement and evaluation tools like the CSCF and the SCDS can help shine a spotlight on these differences in a methodological and controlled way, giving the organization better visibility into its own nature.

Cultural Intensity

Cultural intensity is the degree to which a particular cultural type operates within the organization. When one cultural type is significantly more intense than the others, as in the case of Process Culture in ABLE Manufacturing, that culture is dominant. But not every organization has a dominant culture as intense as Process is at ABLE. The case study of CHARLIE Systems, Inc., from Chapter 6 is an example. Looking at the radar chart in Figure 7-7, CHARLIE's organizational culture is less weighted in any particular quadrant, with no single average score more than twice the intensity of any others.

Cultural intensity provides clues as to how the organization will behave in everyday operations, as well as when facing particular situations or events. The strength of feeling that goes into individual SCDS responses can be a proxy for the intensity of the underlying values that will drive people's decisions and influence how they make choices. Where a cultural type is more intense, you can expect to see the organization adopting strategies that prioritize those shared values and assumptions. In ABLE Manufacturing, one would expect to see people falling back on policies and processes when making decisions, asking themselves, "What do the rules say I should do?" When decisions to bend or break the rules are made, they are likely to be seen as exceptional behaviors, maybe even defined through formal exception processes and procedures.

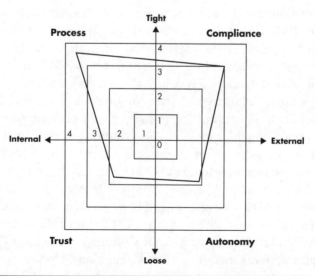

Figure 7-7   *General culture for CHARLIE Systems, Inc.*

In CHARLIE Systems, we would expect to see more influences on behavior than just the processes in place within the company. For CHARLIE, Compliance is a cultural trait nearly as strong as Process. Recall that CHARLIE is a publicly traded tech company that must also undergo regular PCI DSS audits. This means that CHARLIE must look outward as much as it looks inward. Policies and processes are important to the company, particularly in that they support audits and compliance efforts. But company standards do not drive external verification. Quite the opposite. If external audit requirements change—for instance, a new law requires additional regulatory oversight over publicly traded companies or PCI DSS is updated—CHARLIE's internal policies will follow suit, even if it means changes to internal behaviors that affect the existing bureaucracy.

Cultural Anomalies and Disconnects

Mapping also allows us to quickly explore cultural differences that may need to be harmonized to improve people-centric security. The engine of the Competing Security Cultures Framework is the idea that conflicting organizational values tend to produce security and performance risks. Only by identifying and deconflicting these competitive values will we eliminate those risks. Culture maps can help pinpoint such discordant cultural traits in a way that is easily understood by the stakeholders who will be responsible for making cultural transformation happen.

Looking at another example from ABLE Manufacturing, Figure 7-8 shows the culture maps for three different organizational activities: management of operations, control of information, and the way that security is understood within the company.

Looking at the three activities, we can see that each is more or less dominated by a different cultural type within the organization. Operations are managed according to the highly process-oriented culture that is inherent to ABLE. Information, however, is controlled most intensely using values and assumptions that are associated with a Trust Culture, where user empowerment, collaborative sharing, and transparency are the key priorities. In such an environment, we would expect to see behaviors regarding information to be governed less by formal rules and standards and more by notions that information is a resource to be shared among people who rely on one another to do the right thing with it. So immediately, we have two sets of values that could create opportunities for competition and conflict.

Compare the control of information and the management of operations with the meaning of security inside the company. ABLE thinks about information security primarily in terms of a Compliance Culture, even though Compliance is not a core cultural trait generally within the company. On inspection, this is not as surprising as it may first seem. ABLE's introduction to IT and information security came primarily through PCI DSS requirements, and meeting those audit

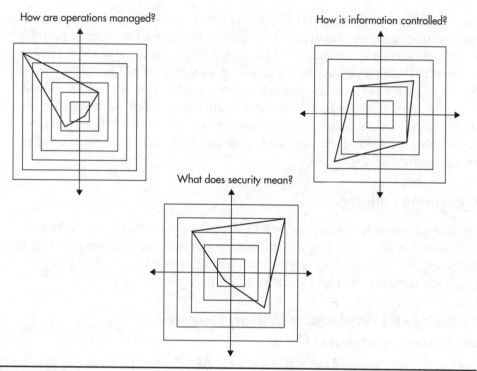

Figure 7-8   *Competing cultures inside ABLE Manufacturing*

requirements has been part of the security team's DNA since inception. In many ways, ABLE associates security with audit and PCI DSS, both within the security team and outside of it. As long as PCI DSS certification is maintained, the company feels successful and secure.

Now consider the ramifications of an organization where managing operations, controlling information, and information security all mean different things to different people, some of whom may not consider those functions directly related. Depending on your own organization, this scenario may not be difficult to envision. We tend to treat different things differently, and it takes an effort to deliberately link them. ABLE Manufacturing certainly thinks about information management in the context of PCI DSS. However, managing information is not the same thing as managing PCI DSS certification. Different assumptions and values govern both activities. It is through these differences that risk can develop.

Think of the example of information classification. PCI DSS requires a basic level of data classification, meaning ABLE must at least be able to identify cardholder data. But even assuming that cardholder data is identified and protected, how can

ABLE be sure that other types of data are protected? How can the company know for sure that, in certain situations, Compliance Culture values around protecting information will not be superseded by Trust Culture values? The short answer is, it can't. There will always be scenarios where the value of Trust goes head to head against the value of Compliance, and given that both cultures are almost identical in intensity, it's hard to say which will win out. But we can predict that if cardholder data is compromised somehow, that it is quite likely the person responsible will believe that they had made the right decision at the time, given the company's culture.

Comparing Cultures

Beyond interpreting the culture map to identify how organizational values and behaviors can affect security, we can also use our maps to help compare cultures. Extending the case studies discussed in Chapter 6, we will use culture maps to make our comparisons more visual and intuitive.

Comparing ABLE Manufacturing's Security Employee and Nonsecurity Employee Cultures

Previously, we compared the SCDS scores of ABLE's security team and the scores of the company as a whole. These scores reflected that members of the security team viewed ABLE's security culture differently than the rest of the company viewed it. If we take the responses to the first SCDS question, "What's valued most?" and create a culture map from the scores, we get the map shown in Figure 7-9. The solid line represents the responses from the security team, while the dashed line shows those from outside the security team.

This map illustrates an agreement between security and nonsecurity members of the organization regarding the importance of Process-related values. But it also shows that in other cases, the security team subscribes to different values than employees elsewhere in the company subscribe to. For security team members, Compliance-related values are every bit as important as standardized, stable policies and central control. For the rest of the organization, these values are not prioritized at all in comparison. Instead, ABLE employees outside of security see Trust-related values as key priorities, while the security team rates these values much less intensely.

So how can ABLE Manufacturing interpret these results? Knowing, as we do now, a bit more about the company, the scores make sense. ABLE grew as a community, a close-knit firm that valued people as an extension of the owners' family. That feeling is baked into the corporate fabric. Only later, in the face of a regulatory requirement, did security become important. As employees were hired

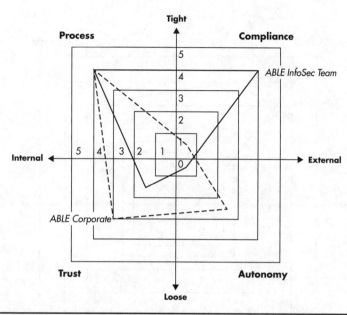

Figure 7-9   *"What's valued most?" responses of ABLE security employees compared with those of nonsecurity employees*

in or trained to manage PCI DSS compliance, security evolved into a specialized function with a specific mission. Values changed, at least in the context of what different cultures within ABLE considered most important on a daily basis.

Knowing these differences makes it easier to spot trends and formulate plans of action to improve people-centric security. The silo in which the security team functions begins to make a bit more sense, as does the frustration that team feels when the rest of the company pushes back on initiatives or requirements the team feels is necessary for successful security and compliance. By comparing these competing values, it becomes possible to formulate plans of action to increase awareness, promote specific values, and transform ABLE's security culture.

Comparing DOG's Current Security Culture to Its Desired Security Culture

The next example compares the current culture of an organization to the culture it wants or needs to cultivate. The Department of Governance profiled in Chapter 6 had decided cultural transformation was necessary to achieve the agency's long-term strategic goals. The CIO and his security manager wanted to transform an overly bureaucratic and risk-averse culture into something more balanced. Figure 7-10 translates this strategy into a culture map.

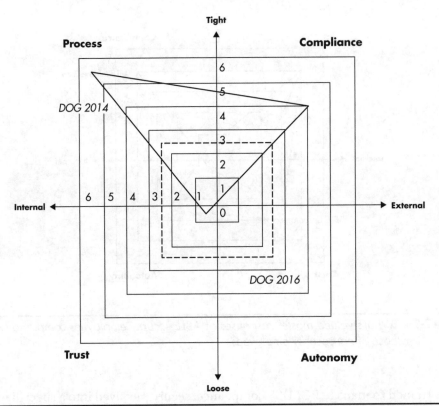

Figure 7-10 *Department of Governance security culture transformation strategy*

Using culture maps to express SCDS results visually can help stakeholders in a cultural transformation effort to more easily express concepts, comparisons between values and cultures, and strategies for change and improvement. It is important to always keep in mind that these maps are metaphors, necessary simplifications that make it easier to compare very complex organizational behaviors and interactions. The pictures they provide mean nothing without solid underlying data, in this case, the responses and scores collected through the SCDS.

CISOs, security awareness managers, and any member of an organization concerned with or responsible for managing and changing human security behaviors must strike a balance between oversimplification and scientific rigor. A picture can be worth a thousand words, but a rhombus alone is not going to enable you to do much to create functional, people-centric security. The next chapter will discuss methods for giving your cultural assessment projects the best chance for success.

Implementing a Successful Security Culture Diagnostic Project

We've covered a lot of territory in this part of the book, including a framework (Chapter 5) and a survey (Chapter 6) for measuring an organization's information security culture, and security culture maps for visualizing and communicating the survey results (Chapter 7). As you've read, you can interpret the data collected from such measurement projects not only to understand where your security culture is today, but also to determine where you want your security culture to be in the future. But one question still remains: how does an organization actually perform a security culture assessment? This chapter tackles that question, discussing how you can get support for diagnosing your organization's security culture, how to execute a security culture diagnostic project, and where to go next with your results.

Getting Buy-in for the Security Culture Diagnostic Project

Recall the Chapter 3 discussion of the correlation between organizational culture and organizational performance. The research evidence is pretty strong that an organization's culture impacts its performance. If we accept that evidence, then we accept that the performance of an organization's security culture, its relative strength or weakness in certain areas, has some effect on the organization's security performance. Most security professionals I know find this notion intuitive, even if they don't know exactly how to measure or articulate culture's effect on security.

Direct Benefits of Security Culture Improvement

When I talk about improving InfoSec culture, I mean a couple of specific things. First, improving security culture necessarily includes increasing the organization's understanding of, and visibility into, how its culture works. You cannot improve something that you have no ability to measure in the first place. No matter what your culture is today or how you define improvement, making the culture that exists below the surface visible to those above is a first requirement. Sales cultures, ethical cultures, even the cultural aspects of language and social communication, can vary between enterprises and within them, and security is just one of these many variations. When I talk about increasing cultural visibility, I mean learning to measure and analyze the security culture to a level where you know enough about it and how it works to make changes that will stick, and that you can demonstrate have stuck.

Second, improving security culture means improving the way that information security competes with other values existing inside the organization. That doesn't always translate into security being the most important consideration in every decision. But the reality today is that security often loses out in decisions when the decision makers are far removed from the people who are directly responsible for security. When making decisions, top of the mind tends to be top of the list, and security can find itself drowned out when many different stakeholders are involved. Improving security culture is about raising security awareness and not just about specific decisions like whether or not to click a link in a fishy (phishy?) e-mail. The end goal of security awareness programs is more than just rote behavior. It's really mindful security, a state of which security awareness is so much a part of the flow of organizational activity that people think about security even when making decisions that they have not been specifically told are security related.

Increased Security and Efficiency

When security is part of everyday decision making across an organization, then good security practices have a much better chance of permeating more of the organization's activities. And as more activities are performed in a secure way, or at least in less insecure ways, overall security within the organization will increase. This is nothing more than a fancy way of talking about habit. Security works better when it is performed as habitual behavior, rather than as something that requires forced, conscious consideration. And culture is, at the core, the sum total of more-or-less habitual thoughts and behaviors existing within and among the organization's members. Improve the culture, improve your habits, and you cannot fail to improve information security.

Efficiency is increased in regard to security when cultural improvements remove friction and conflict resulting from cultural competitiveness. Think of how much time and effort have been expended within your organization while security stakeholders fight, negotiate, and compromise with other business stakeholders to balance their mutual interests. Some of this tension is the result of legitimate differences in opinion over the risks and opportunities presented by differing strategies and operational necessities. But a lot of it, in my experience over the years, boils down to competing cultures and the competing values and priorities that they spawn. We do things this way, you do things that way, and never the twain shall meet. Cultural improvement means cultural outreach, the ability to explain not only what you do, but why you do it. And when stakeholders have that level of visibility, the potential for more evidence-based management opens up huge opportunities to eliminate waste. Even in a worst-case scenario, where there are legitimate cultural impasses, at least the organization will know what it's dealing with and can appeal to a more powerful arbiter for resolution, saving everyone time and heartburn.

Reduced Risk and Costs from Incidents

The most enticing potential outcome for security culture improvement, particularly in today's environment of highly publicized security breaches, is for transformation to actually prevent or reduce the number and severity of security breaches. CISOs, and lately all of the leadership, are looking for any solutions that can help them to curtail security breaches. Process and technology will always be crucial components of any security solution, but people and culture represent perhaps the greatest heretofore untapped source of information security value left. Information security professionals have done so little historically with respect to the people aspect of security that it doesn't take much effort to start seeing returns.

The growing visibility and clout of security training and awareness programs is evidence of more progressive organizations' attempts to leverage cultural resources to improve security and reduce risk. I have devoted much ink earlier in the book to emphasize the role of security awareness professionals as the "tip of the spear" when it comes to security cultural transformation. But we still have a long way to go. Quality of security awareness programs varies a great deal. I have seen phenomenal programs that actually "move the needle," as Lance Spitzner likes to say, and I have seen programs that do little more than pay slide-based lip service to awareness as a means of meeting a compliance requirement. The former represent true improvement strategies. The latter do not, plain and simple; they may check a box, but they don't move any needles.

Organizations that really want to leverage security culture and awareness as a means to reduce risk and costs need to do much more … impact more decisions and win more hearts and minds to the cause of security. But CISOs and security professionals still struggle with the question: How do I show that linkage between security culture and security performance? How do I demonstrate that directly addressing our organization's security culture is worth the money and time for a diagnostic project?

Estimating the Financial Impact of Security Culture

The best way to make a case that a security culture diagnostic project is worth the cost is to show how much impact cultural improvement can have on the organization's bottom line. We can begin to show the value that stronger InfoSec cultures bring by creating a basic model of security culture impact on the likelihood and cost of security incidents. In other words, we can show senior management just how much a weak security culture might cost them.

The case study presented in the following section uses a basic probabilistic model, called a Monte Carlo simulation, to estimate the financial impact of different security cultures within an organization. Monte Carlo simulations are used widely in industry for estimating all kinds of risk, from financial performance to the likelihood of project failures. They are less commonly used in information security in my experience, although I've introduced a few companies to them during my professional travels. At a high level, I will make some assumptions about security culture and the likelihood of security incidents, build a set of scenarios that incorporate those assumptions, and then test those scenarios statistically by simulating them repeatedly. The outcome of the simulation will show the expected results of a security culture's impact on an organization's losses from security incidents.

Monte Carlo Simulations

Monte Carlo techniques emerged out of World War II and the efforts to create the first atomic bomb. The scientists working on the Manhattan Project named their models after the famous European casino in Monaco, and used them to estimate the probabilities of the random behaviors of sub-atomic particles in the weapons they were building. Monte Carlo techniques took advantage of statistical analyses and the availability of electronic computers capable of doing more sophisticated calculations more quickly than the existing manual methods.

Put simply, Monte Carlo models function by allowing people to repeatedly simulate events about which they know certain things, such as a set of possible outcomes and the likelihood of each of those outcomes. A good example is the outcomes from rolling two six-sided dice. Assuming the dice are fair, the probability of rolling a 7 is known (1/6 or about 17 percent). But how could we test whether 7 really comes up once out of every six rolls? One way would be to roll two dice 100 or 1000 or 10,000 times and record the result of each scenario (the rolling of two dice). After all those repeated scenarios, we would expect the number of 7s we rolled to approach 17 percent of our total rolls. Rolling dice thousands of times, however, is not something most people have time to do outside of Las Vegas. But, those parameters can be plugged into a computer to have it randomly simulate rolling dice, which would be much faster and achieve the same result. That's a Monte Carlo simulation.

(continues)

Monte Carlo Simulations (continued)

There are many tools available for doing Monte Carlo simulations, and a full discussion is beyond the scope of this book. You can build simulations directly using spreadsheet programs like Microsoft Excel or Open Office Calc, although this can take some manual effort. There are also plenty of free and commercial add-ins and applications for doing simulations. An Internet search for Monte Carlo tools will return many options you can explore to get started. I tend to use a variety of these tools, depending on what I want or need to accomplish.

Before we begin our case study, we need to say a word about *assumptions*. In any good model, including our Monte Carlo simulation, assumptions are made explicit. You should state your assumptions up front, the same way a researcher should define her hypothesis before she conducts an experiment. Models are simplifications that contain uncertainty, and only by acknowledging what assumptions we have made in building the model can we expect others to take the outcomes we predict seriously. Stating our assumptions openly and transparently gives everyone a chance to understand the uncertainty involved in our estimates, to identify things we might have missed or gotten wrong, and to suggest new data or changed assumptions that can make the model better.

Case Study: FOXTROT Integrators, Inc.

This case study simulates how a weaker or stronger security culture affects the potential financial losses from security incidents at a hypothetical company, FOXTROT Integrators, Inc. Like all the other example organizations discussed in this book, FOXTROT's security culture and values compete with the cultures and values of other stakeholders and other business imperatives. What we want to know is, if FOXTROT's information security culture were to compete more effectively within the organization, would FOXTROT's security improve?

Assumptions

To build the probabilistic model for this case study, I need to make a few assumptions. They are not blind guesses, or tricks, but rather just the ground rules that describe how I think the real FOXTROT operates. If I had empirical, historical evidence, then I could use it to fill in some of these blanks. Otherwise, I must make a best judgment estimate. In this case, that doesn't necessarily limit me. I'm not trying to convince anyone exactly to what extent cultural change specifically impacts security performance. I'm simply trying to make the logical case that the strength or weakness of a security culture does impact security performance.

My first assumption has to do with the outcome of the model, namely that the amount of money that security incidents are costing FOXTROT is a good proxy for how well information security works within the company. If the simulation shows that a stronger security culture reduces security incident–related financial losses, that is the same thing as saying information security is improved in the context of the case study. Someone might debate that assumption, but that's the power of making your assumptions explicit. The argument becomes more concrete, focused on the merits of the model and how it can be made more accurate.

My second assumption is about information security–related decisions. I assume that FOXTROT, as an organization, makes a decision with potential security impact about once a week. I don't specify what this decision is. It could be a team decision about which new software to implement or a decision by an individual developer, like Clara from Chapter 2, about whether to complete a security review. It might be an employee deciding whether or not to open an unfamiliar e-mail link or attachment. The point is that any of these decisions has the potential to cause a security incident. Whether or not an average of 52 decisions per year is realistic is immaterial here. Remember, I'm trying to establish a correlation, not a specific number. I only need to be specific about the nature of the decisions—that each one has the potential to cause a security incident. It's unlikely that the number will stay static, year in and year out. So in addition to the average of 52 decisions, I will assume that the number of decisions each year follows a normal, or bell-shaped, curve. And I will assume that the number of events each year exhibits a standard deviation of 5 decisions, which simply means I can be pretty confident that FOXTROT will make somewhere between 42 and 62 security-impactful decisions in any given 12-month period.

My third assumption is that the strength of an organization's information security culture influences how security-related decisions are made. When security culture and priorities are forced to compete with other organizational cultures and priorities, security may or may not prevail depending on how weak or strong the security culture is within the organization. If the security culture is weak, security will lose out in these contests more often. When security fails to overcome competing priorities, decisions will be made that are bad for security, although they may be good for other stakeholders. In the case of Clara the developer from Chapter 2, her decision to prioritize project completion over

Assumption	Value
Reduced financial losses from security incidents reflect better information security at FOXTROT	Financial loss from information security incidents
Annual number of security-related decisions FOXTROT makes	Average: 52; Range: 42–62
Information security culture influences whether security is prioritized in security-related decisions	Number of bad security decisions FOXTROT makes

Table 8-1 *FOXTROT Security Decision Model and Assumptions*

security review completion represented a bad security decision, one that could lead to an incident. If security culture is strong, decisions that favor security over other priorities will be made more frequently, and other stakeholders may have to compromise. These good security decisions reduce the chances of an incident.

Table 8-1 lays out the assumptions I have made so far for this case study.

Scenarios

The next step in the case study is to consider how the strength of the security culture influences whether bad security decisions get made. To accomplish this within the model, I have hypothesized three levels of security culture: weak, moderate, and strong, each with its own set of assumptions. Strength of the security culture may be a function of the organization's training and awareness program, or it may be because the organization operates in a highly regulated or highly sensitive industry. Whatever the root cause, the strength of the security culture is defined as how often a member of the organization will prioritize security when making a decision, even when faced with a competing cultural value. This strength is a measure of how well security competes with other cultures in the environment. When security is put first in the decision, security wins in the model. Table 8-2 lists the three levels of security culture strength based on this definition.

Security Culture Strength	Chance That a Bad Security Decision Is Made
Weak	80% chance of a bad security decision
Moderate	50% chance of a bad security decision
Strong	20% chance of a bad security decision

Table 8-2 *Levels of Security Culture Strength*

The "68-95-99.7 Rule"

In the FOXTROT example, I am confident that the actual number of security-impactful decisions in a given year is somewhere between 42 and 62. I have this confidence because of a statistical guideline known as the "68-95-99.7 Rule," also sometimes called the "three sigma" rule. In statistics, standard deviation is a measure of dispersion of data, symbolized by the Greek letter sigma, σ. Assuming a normal distribution, data values are distributed equally around the mean, decreasing as one moves away from that value, and measured in terms of standard deviations. A general rule of thumb is that 68 percent of values will lie within one standard deviation of the mean, 95 percent of values will be within two standard deviations, and 99.7 percent within three standard deviations. In the case of FOXTROT, because the standard deviation is five decisions impacting security, I can be reasonably confident that an assumed range of 42 to 62 decisions will be accurate 95 percent of the time. The following illustration depicts the 68-95-99.7 rule in a normal distribution.

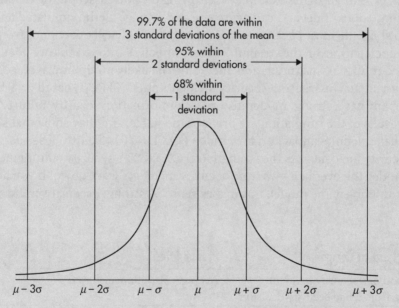

(Courtesy of Dan Kernler with permission granted under the terms of the Creative Commons Attribution-Share Alike 4.0 International license, http://creativecommons.org/licenses/by-sa/4.0/legalcode)

The case study scenarios are almost complete. All I need now is to define my assumptions about how often security incidents will take place and how severe they will be. I assume the chance of security incidents resulting from bad choices will be similar to chances in a coin toss. Without hard data either way I assume that, on average, FOXTROT will see a security incident result from 50 percent of their bad security choices, give or take a bit. For any single information security incident, I estimate that FOXTROT's minimum loss will be $10,000. I also assume the company will lose no more than $5 million on any one security incident. These are both extreme values, however, and I assume that the most likely cost per incident will be a quarter of a million dollars.

Table 8-3 lists these assumptions.

Testing the Scenarios

I now have all the components of a model that I can simulate using a Monte Carlo analysis. I can plug all these assumptions into my simulation and then "run" the scenario a couple hundred times, each run simulating a hypothetical year of total financial losses from all information security incidents FOXTROT experiences. Similar to the example of throwing dice discussed in the "Monte Carlo Simulations" sidebar, I can aggregate and average all the simulated annual losses to show the most likely annual losses FOXTROT will experience from security incidents given the strength of the company's InfoSec culture. Figure 8-1 shows the results of this simulation, including the likely minimum, average, and maximum annual losses from security incidents at FOXTROT, based on whether the company has a strong, moderate, or weak information security culture.

The results of the simulation are pretty remarkable, and they show that security culture has a definite impact on how much FOXTROT is likely to lose each year from security incidents. As the strength of FOXTROT's security culture increased in the model, the overall losses from security incidents went down. If you accept the assumptions of the model, this makes sense. A stronger security culture

Security Incident Component	Probabilities
Likelihood of a security incident resulting from a bad security decision	Average: 50%; Range: 40–60%
Severity of security incident (total financial loss)	Min: $10,000; Most likely: $250K; Max: $5M

Table 8-3 *Likelihood and Severity of Security Incidents Resulting from a Bad Security Decision*

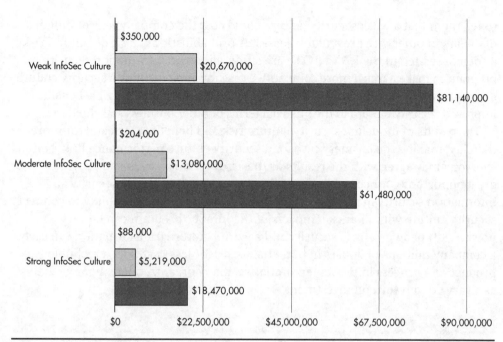

Figure 8-1   *Monte Carlo simulation results of FOXTROT annual security incident losses by security culture strength*

means that every security-related decision is more likely to favor security over a competing cultural value, resulting in a good security decision instead of a bad one. The fewer the bad security decisions being made, the lower the likelihood that a decision will contribute to a security incident and cause losses for the organization.

The model allows for a wide range of possible outcomes. Not every year will bring catastrophic security incidents and huge losses. Even assuming a weak security culture, sometimes FOXTROT will get lucky and may not lose much more than it would have if a stronger culture had been present. But as bad security decisions pile up, so do the costs of a weaker security culture. The effect of security culture on average losses amounted to multimillion dollar differences. And in the case of a strong InfoSec culture, the model estimated that the *maximum* annual losses incurred by a strong security culture were millions of dollars less than the *average* losses experienced by a weak security culture.

Using the Results of the Model

It is one thing to tell senior management that information security is a cultural problem and that resources are needed to improve it. It is something else entirely to tell them that a weak security culture could cost the company tens of millions of dollars in otherwise preventable losses. A probabilistic analysis of cultural risk, as demonstrated in the FOXTROT case study, allows an information security program to make a much more competitive case for implementing a security culture diagnostic project within an organization. The results reveal the tangible benefits of improved security culture in the financial terms of other business stakeholders.

The results of modeling security culture risk and benefits are useful for more than just making the business case for a security culture performance link. Not everyone may agree with the results or the assumptions, which can provide a great opportunity for concrete discussions about people-centric security and information security in general within the organization. And the ability to connect security culture with financial impacts of the InfoSec program can be very powerful. If people-centric security and security culture transformation can save a company millions of dollars in potential losses for less cost than a technology product or a process improvement initiative, many organizations might view this as a very good return on investment.

Executing a Security Culture Diagnostic Project

The FOXTROT case study made the case for a link between security culture and security performance, but no improvement in security culture is possible if an organization cannot effectively assess the culture they have. Even the most plausible hypotheses and the most intuitive frameworks are only part of the solution. The Competing Security Cultures Framework and the Security Culture Diagnostic Survey provide a viable basis for creating a map of security culture. But they don't create that map themselves, and they don't take you from point A to point B. People still have to do that.

Diagnosing security culture must be done in the context of a project and, like any project, it can be done well or it can be done poorly. The remainder of this chapter focuses on how to successfully design and execute your security culture diagnostic project. The time and care you put into assessing your culture will determine how much insight and value you get out of it, so it is important that you address and plan for the following project phases:

1. Project setup
2. Collection of data
3. Analyses of responses
4. Interpretation of culture and communication of results

1. Setting Up the Project

Culture, although measurable to a certain degree, is also naturally amorphous and hard to pin down. Measuring a collective set of human interactions is never going to be as easy as measuring packet throughput in your network or the money you spent last year on vendor security products and services. So the worst thing an organization can do when embarking upon an assessment of security culture is to conduct a project that is ill considered, vaguely conceptualized, and poorly designed. Planning for the security culture diagnostic project is the most important stage, as it will determine how well everything else goes afterwards.

Defining the Project Strategy

As obvious as the goals and objectives of the security culture diagnostic project may seem at first glance, they probably aren't. And in any event, like assumptions in any model, project strategies should be laid out explicitly in advance and documented. That way everyone is on board, or at least should be, from the beginning in terms of what is hoped for and what is expected out of the project.

A key strategic consideration is which culture or cultures the project intends to measure and describe. Is the project goal to ascertain the existing security culture across the entire company? Or does the organization only want to discover the security culture for a specific group, such as the security team itself?

Most SCDS-based projects, and the linkages to the CSCF cultural quadrants they create, are going to have some sort of comparative function. The whole idea of linking security risk to cultural competition implies that more than one culture is striving for predominance. Cultural diagnostics help identify these discrepancies and conflicts and make them visible to the organization. So what is the project's comparative strategy? The culture of the security team is an obvious choice, but given that any organization may have a large number of subcultures, which are the most important for comparison? The easiest comparison to be made is that of the entire corporate culture. But there may be other cultural values that need exploring, particularly in the wake of a security incident.

A third aspect to consider is whether and how the SCDS results will be fed into a follow-on transformation project. Do you want to change particular aspects of the security culture, such as making it more process or people oriented? Or do you hope to make competing cultures more closely aligned? These decisions will drive analysis and the communication of results down the line.

These are only a few of the possibilities an organization should consider before embarking on a cultural measurement initiative. Strategy is critical. If you are running a security culture diagnostic project, you should be able to easily explain why you are doing it, how you are doing it, and what you expect to get out of doing it, all in as much detail as possible.

Defining the Context of the Assessment

Beyond the "why?" of strategy lies the "why?" of context. Understanding the context in which the cultural assessment is performed can be as important as understanding its goals. For example, is the SCDS being administered because the company has been rocked by several information security incidents in recent years and senior management is demanding to know why all the expensive products and services they purchased don't seem to work? Or is the diagnostic project necessary because the company is making an acquisition and needs to understand possible security implications?

Context can also refer to environmental factors such as time pressures, the attitudes of senior leadership, legal and regulatory requirements, or a passion for innovation. Each of these motivations will shape and steer the security culture diagnostic project more or less subtly. Issues of duration, cost, and desired outcomes are often revealed when an organization takes the time to formally identify the context in which the project is being attempted.

Performing a Cost/Benefit Analysis

There's no way around it: assessing and analyzing your security culture is going to cost time and money. The ability to articulate to those who hold the purse strings how spending that time and money will produce a positive return is invaluable. Equally valuable is a realistic expectation of how much bang the organization can expect for each buck spent on understanding itself better. In the FOXTROT case study, financial simulation projected potential savings of millions of dollars resulting from fewer security incidents occurring in a strong security culture. Estimates like these can help make the case that money is not being wasted on mere navel gazing. At the same time, it would be unrealistic to undertake a multimillion-dollar cultural transformation project in the hopes of reducing losses that are far less than the cost of transformation.

Engaging Senior Management

Nothing says "we're serious" like direct executive involvement. By this, I don't mean an e-mail from the CIO saying information security culture is important and everyone is expected to cooperate with the security team on this project they are doing. I mean direct, active, and interested involvement. No security culture diagnosis is going to get that level of involvement if project owners fail to engage with executive sponsors.

CISO or senior InfoSec program leadership support is the first rung on this ladder. If the CISO does not believe in cultural change, the project is likely dead on arrival. But in my experience, most CISOs are interested in anything that can give them a leg up both in protecting the organization's information assets and in helping the security team compete directly with other stakeholder groups. The ability to identify and explain cultural risks to security gives senior security leaders an opportunity to talk about something other than hackers, system vulnerabilities, and the network segmentation requirements of PCI DSS.

Organizational culture is a field more familiar to MBAs and management consulting than to engineers and system administrators. Engaging the organizational leadership on a security culture diagnostic project can provide a security team with the opportunity to speak another language, a language that links security directly with organizational performance. Once one or more senior leaders are on board, the folks conducting the security culture assessment can hope for better access to resources and data.

It is also important to remember to keep senior sponsors involved and informed throughout the security culture diagnostic project. The project is likely to run into obstacles over the course of its life. The ability for a project team or a CISO to quickly call on a senior sponsor outside of security to remind everyone of why the organization is committed to people-centric security and cultural improvement can mean the difference between success and failure of the initiative.

At the very least, an organization's leadership should define minimum expectations for participation in the project. They should actively promote and share the project's goals and their expectations for its outcome with their teams and the executive staff. The tone should be positive and encouraging, an extension of the project team's outreach. Additional expectations to be communicated throughout the organization include the need for honest feedback from members of the organization about the project, information about how data will be collected and used (and not used) during the project, and a promise to share the results with everyone.

Engaging Other Stakeholders

Senior management's support and interest are not the only ingredients for success in a security culture diagnostic project. Successful execution will demand cooperation and active involvement from many corners of the organization, including users, front-line managers, and area specialists who can help interpret results and discrepancies in the collected data. Even when the organization's top leaders lay out minimum expectations, if participants in the security culture diagnostic project aren't engaged properly, they may feel like they are being forced to do something they don't really understand rather than something they feel is important and worth taking seriously because they know it will benefit them directly.

Most often, it will be the InfoSec program that initiates a security culture diagnostic project. It may even be specialists within the security team, like the training and awareness owners. For the owner of the project, the most important thing to remember is to keep your eyes on the prize. People-centric security will benefit everyone, but you will have to sell that concept to just about everyone, likely starting within the InfoSec program itself.

It may be challenging for members of a security program to recognize or accept the inherent value of other cultures and priorities within the organization. As I have discussed previously, information security professionals can take themselves and their duties very seriously, to the point of feeling like security trumps all other organizational considerations, or even the people in the organization. Cultural intolerance is what drives some security techno-utopians (just to take an example) to make ridiculous statements like "this job would be so much easier if I didn't have to deal with the users…" Well, of course it would. It is always easier when you only have to deal with people who think the same thoughts and value the same things as you. But engaging other stakeholders means taking a more accommodating and diplomatic approach to improving information security culture.

A savvy culture hacker will move slowly and deliberately to take the message of cultural improvement to others, to align the goals of the project with their goals. Once the security team understands that tolerating other cultural imperatives might make their own jobs easier, the security culture diagnostic project owner can move on to helping others outside of security realize how a better security culture could solve problems for them, including problems they may not have even realized they had.

Building the Project Team and Plan

Formalization is a key driver of success for any organized activity. It's the reason the Process Culture in the CSCF can be so predominant in many organizations. Everyone has plans. We think about ways to make our world and our lives better all the time. But there's a difference between sitting in your cubicle and fantasizing about that Internet business that will enable you to enjoy a four-hour workweek and actually creating a startup company. The former can be accomplished with nothing more than imagination and time. The latter is going to require you to stop imagining and start actually building something.

Any organizational project that hopes to achieve results will be assigned a formal team, and that team will develop an equally formal plan. Team and plan both will be documented and officially signed off on by the senior leaders and sponsors who have been engaged for support in the first place. The size of the team and the resources provided to it will be developed out of the cost/benefit analysis described earlier. The team must be sufficiently capable of meeting the goals the organization has laid out for itself. That means the team must include skilled personnel, internal to the organization where available and supplemented by outside consultants where necessary. The project plan will be very clear about who is involved, what they must do, and what the organization will get out of those activities.

Incentives are also critical to project success. Many of the examples of cultural risk I've described come from situations where people are given multiple responsibilities but are then rewarded or punished disproportionately for only some of those responsibilities. It would be ironic, although probably not shocking, to find that your measurement of competing security values failed due to competing organizational priorities.

Not every security culture diagnostic project has to be huge or enterprise-wide. Security culture assessment is a great place for small experiments, pilot projects, and exploratory initiatives. These can often be accomplished and value achieved for a small investment of time and money. But even when ambitions are small, everything should be formal, with a paper trail that allows everyone to see at the end of the project just how well the organization executed on its strategy.

2. Collecting Data

With the SCDS project design in place, it is time for the organization to collect actual data. As part of the strategy and planning process, decisions will already have been made about which cultures to target for assessment and for what purpose. The most important outcome of these decisions is the determination of who will actually complete the SCDS.

Using the Security Culture Diagnostic Survey

The SCDS is freely available, under a Creative Commons license, for use in measuring your organization's security culture. You can find it available for download at http://lancehayden.net/culture, along with instructions for administering the survey to your own organization.

There are multiple ways of administering organizational surveys like the SCDS, including automated tools and websites that can help you set up and administer online surveys for your organization. A quick web search on survey tools will give you many options to choose from, but to use any of these tools you will end up having to translate the SCDS questions and responses into a survey instrument you can post and disseminate to respondents. PollDaddy, SurveyMonkey, and SurveyGizmo are a few online companies that provide easy and affordable tools for preparing and conducting surveys within your organization.

You should also decide up front, even during the planning process, how many people you want to take the survey. The more respondents you have, the larger the data set you can analyze. The downside is that these large, automated surveys are more difficult to explain and promote across different groups of stakeholders. Running the survey as a smaller exercise, with a select group of respondents, enables you to more effectively engage and train them on how the CSCF and SCDS work. However, working with smaller respondent groups may cause concerns about not getting enough representative data about the entire organization or group, particularly in large corporations. These concerns can be mitigated through the use of random sampling techniques that allow you to generalize your survey responses across an entire organization while asking only a small subset of the total members to respond. SurveyMonkey, one of the online survey companies I mentioned previously, has a good blog post on choosing random sample recipients for surveys like the SCDS. You can find it on the SurveyMonkey blog at www.surveymonkey.com.

Organizing Respondents

Respondents for the SCDS must be treated carefully and respectfully if the organization wants to get valuable insights from their participation. Transparency is always the best policy, and the organization should share as much information as possible about the survey, which is another reason to limit participation in the beginning and build mindshare within the organization. Who you want to include depends on what you are trying to accomplish. If you want to measure the security culture of the entire organization, you need a representative sample from across the organization. If your focus is the security team, you can limit your respondents. When comparing different groups or functions within the enterprise, you need to identify respondents from the targets of comparison. You would make similar adjustments for whatever cultural measurements you want to accomplish. Some things to consider regarding survey participation include how you plan to market the survey to potential respondents, what kind of identifiable information you will collect about respondents and how you will protect that data, and how you intend to encourage honest answers to your survey questions.

Marketing and Positioning the Project   The organization should consider ways to make participation in the SCDS project attractive to respondents. If participation in the survey is mandatory, the organization should think about how to at least make it as pleasant an experience as possible. If survey participation is voluntary, then getting people to want to participate is important. The worst outcome for a survey-based initiative is to decide to go wide with participation, allowing everyone to take the survey, only to find that response rates are very low. If the end result is survey data from a quarter of the organization or less, that gives the appearance of failure. Worse, even if 25 percent of the organization is still a lot of people, the data is likely to be less reliable in terms of describing the entire organization's security culture than a smaller, truly random sample would have been.

Conducting the survey should be marketed as a privilege, a chance to be part of something special and important to the organization. Consider formal invitations from senior management to participate or rewards for doing so, such as gift cards, or company-wide recognition as being part of the project. Respondents should be made to feel special, that their opinions are important to the success of the company, rather than feel like they just got robo-called by a professional polling firm during dinner. Another useful way to motivate participants is by allowing them to claim their involvement in the project for credit and recognition in performance reviews or training plans.

Selected participants should be provided training in the CSCF and SCDS, either in person or via teleconference. Where neither of these options is possible, the organization should provide a detailed documentation package that shows how the project will work. The instructions I provide as part of the SCDS, as well as examples and material from this book, can all be used to support the creation of such a package.

Collecting Demographic Data   The organization must consider which, if any, demographic data to collect as part of the security culture diagnostic project. The SCDS templates that I provide do not specify demographic information. In reality, the only required demographic data you may need to collect along with the SCDS is the group or division to which a respondent belongs. You would need that to be able to compare results between cultures. But in an SCDS project where the organization wants to map the general culture without comparisons between subcultures, even that data is not required. Realistically, though, you will want to collect at least basic information about who a respondent is and where in the organization they work. This may or may not include personally identifiable information about individual participants, which I cover further in the next section. But information about roles, how long an individual has worked for the organization, and whether or not they are a manager; if they possess technical skills; or are associated with security in any way are all useful data points.

Beyond basic demographics, the organization can consider collecting additional data that may prove useful in diagnosing competing values and cultural risks regarding security. Lots of things influence a person's worldview, their assumptions about how things work. Age, gender, educational background, even where you sit on the organizational chart can all influence how you look at things. Capturing this information as part of the SCDS responses gives the organization an opportunity to slice and dice cultural data along many potential axes. Sure, the finance team is heavily Process-centric, but maybe the higher you go up the chain of command, the more Autonomy begins to emerge as a desirable value. Or the majority of your security team may eat, drink, and breathe Compliance, except for your security awareness managers, who may see Trust as equally important.

Ensuring Privacy and Anonymity   The challenge with collecting detailed demographic information is the balance between collecting too much information and not enough. In today's environment, where protecting your personal data and dealing with threats of surveillance and privacy erosion are top of mind, people are often much more wary of sharing too much information about themselves. This reaction may seem counterintuitive in a world of social networking and blogging, but viewpoints tend to change when it's your boss or another authority figure asking you to share what you think of them, specifically or generally. This is why many 360-degree reviews and other employee surveys are conducted anonymously.

Respondents must be reassured that the opinions they give about the organization's culture will not get them into trouble or be used against them in some other way. Project owners should be very specific about why they are collecting any particular demographic data and tie those reasons back to the strategy of the security culture diagnostic project. Collecting names and personally identifiable information can make respondents the most nervous, but if the organization wishes to follow up SCDS responses with more detailed interviews or focus groups, this information may be necessary. One compromise is to offer an "opt in" feature, allowing people to volunteer such information and give permission to contact them for follow-on discussions if necessary.

In some cases you may actually run into regulatory and legal issues that preclude you from collecting personally identifiable information, particularly in countries with strong privacy laws. Most organizations, at least in the United States, have significant leeway when conducting internal employee surveys, since demographic information such as job role, location, and which part of the organization an individual works for is all part of the company record and unlikely to be considered private. This may not be the case in other countries, with different privacy laws, so the organization should check before collecting such data. Similarly, any questions asking for demographic information regarding race, gender, or religious preferences should be cleared with HR and even the corporate legal department before going into a survey, just to be sure.

Collecting Honest Responses   Reassuring respondents that the information they provide will be used objectively, to achieve predetermined goals, improves the chances for honest feedback. Senior management should make clear at the beginning, and project owners should reiterate throughout the duration of the project, that participating in the SCDS will not negatively impact the respondent, their relationship with their manager or peers, or their performance appraisal.

Beyond just assuring that honest responses will not have negative consequences, the project sponsors and teams should reiterate how important such honesty is to the success of the project. There are no right answers when measuring culture, and respondents should be educated against perceiving the project as an attempt by management to confirm that the culture is a certain way rather than an exploration of what the culture actually is. "Tell us what you think, not what you think we want you to tell us" could be a good motto for any cultural feedback initiative.

Data Management and Storage

As part of project design and planning, make sure to give sufficient thought to how data from the SCDS will be managed and stored. Project data and responses from participants, especially when they contain personal or sensitive demographic data, should be kept secure in accordance with the organization's data classification and information protection policies. Communicating that this information will be handled responsibly and securely is also important for reassuring participants in the project that their personal information will remain private and protected. This may influence how they complete the survey. Details about the mechanisms for doing so should be made available and transparent to participants. Many of us have taken internal surveys or training where vague assurances of anonymity are made, but I tend to find that less than reassuring when I have to use my employee credentials to log into the system before I can participate.

3. Analyzing Responses

Whether you are collating scores into a spreadsheet or building them out from a tool, the first step after collecting raw SCDS data is to analyze those responses and turn them into something coherent. Detailed instructions for scoring the SCDS were covered in Chapter 6, and can be found in the documentation of the survey online. But there are some tips and suggestions that I can provide by way of guidance to help you make your security culture diagnostic exercise as fruitful as possible.

Generating Security Culture Scores

Security culture scores are generated by aligning specific SCDS responses with quadrants of the CSCF. Recall from Chapter 6 that the responses in the SCDS instrument are organized into four alphabetical categories and that each category is mapped to a specific CSCF cultural trait. Table 8-4 reviews this alignment.

General security culture scores for each CSCF quadrant are generated by averaging the sum of the scores for each SCDS response category across all ten SCDS questions. For more granular inquiries—for instance, on the specific values and alignments related to the management of technology, security, or risk—the scores are taken from each of the key organizational activities and traits. For ease

of use, a worksheet is available for download at http://lancehayden.net/culture to help you calculate your SCDS culture scores.

Creating Culture Maps

Visually mapping your culture scores, as I demonstrated in Chapter 7, takes a bit more effort than simply calculating them, but it does not require anything more than standard office software. Microsoft Excel and Apache OpenOffice both allow the creation of radar-style charts from a set of data. Some spreadsheet and

SCDS Response Category	CSCF Alignment
"A" responses	Process Security Culture
"B" responses	Compliance Security Culture
"C" responses	Autonomy Security Culture
"D" responses	Trust Security Culture

Table 8-4   *SCDS Scores Aligned with CSCF Quadrants*

charting tools do not offer radar charts, for reasons I touched on in Chapter 7, so if you wish to employ that visualization you will have to use a tool that supports it. The rest of my charts I tend to do relatively manually, building them individually and then manipulating them into the quadrants of the CSCF as images. I like the control of this process enough to make the extra time it takes worthwhile. But the list of charting and visualization tools, including freely available options, is growing all the time. I encourage readers to explore them, as I am doing, and to put them to use where they work.

4. Interpreting Culture and Communicating Results

After the numerical dust has settled and you have a formal set of scores and visual maps to represent your security culture(s), the process of interpretation and communication begins. Having done all this great work to put boundaries around your security culture and identify areas of competing values and possible cultural risks to your security posture, it's time to use those results to interpret culture, support people-centric security goals, and communicate progress to other stakeholders.

Aligning Data with Project Goals

Interpreting your security culture diagnostic results is, primarily, a process of aligning what you have found with what you set out to do. Aligning the collected data and resulting scores to your strategic objectives creates the value inherent to improving people-centric security. It is also the big reason that it is so important to identify and document those goals ahead of time, to get buy-in for them, and to properly set expectations about outcomes. Many attempts to measure culture end up falling into a trap of amorphous ambitions, with insights and fascinating anecdotes that entertain but are difficult to turn into actions. Culture is a forest of human interactions and social behavior. Your strategy is the trail of breadcrumbs you leave to help you find your way back out again.

Descriptive Goals   If your main objective was to measure one or more aspects of security culture within the organization, to get a picture of what it looks like as a way of understanding how it works, then your diagnostic strategy was primarily descriptive. Every cultural assessment project is a descriptive effort, in that it attempts to make visible the values and assumptions operating below the surface of organizational behavior.

Comparative Goals   When you begin to put your descriptions of culture side by side, to notice differences between them and consider why those differences exist, you've moved from descriptive to comparative goals for the diagnostic project. Mapping the security culture against the organizational culture, or the security culture that exists against the security culture you would like to have, requires comparative analysis. When the SCDS project strategy includes these comparisons, you can now use your results to get more insight into the questions you hoped to answer. Sometimes those answers may surprise you and may generate new questions.

SCDS results should be analyzed in the light of the comparative objectives defined as part of the strategy. Do the SCDS results line up with people's expectations or perceptions about the nature of the organizational security culture? If discrepancies exist, where? And what might have caused them? In Chapters 6 and 7, we saw several examples where a small set of organizational activities can skew a cultural quadrant, making that culture seem more predominant when, in fact, just a few outliers in key behaviors are skewing the results. Discoveries like this can point to fruitful areas of exploration, and can directly drive changes to training, awareness, and policy that become more targeted approaches to security behavior.

Transformative Goals   Transformative goals are those that involve changing existing culture. If you are comparing existing security culture to desired security culture, for example, knowing how the two cultures differ is just the start. Security culture maps show where specific changes are necessary and to what degree. Often, even in cases where an organization knows that change and cultural transformation are necessary, completion of a diagnostic project is a necessary prerequisite to knowing how that change might take place.

SCDS scores and security culture maps allow an organization to plan specific, measurable actions directed at cultural change. This is an important point, especially for countering critics of cultural measurement who argue that culture is too vague to pin down. By focusing on ten core activities, the SCDS identifies behavioral components that directly impact security, names them, and provides a way to analyze them. Changing culture means changing the ways that these activities are undertaken within the organization. If, for example, a company discovers from the SCDS that people do not take policies and procedures seriously, that represents a direct path to action—promoting the behaviors inherent in a more Process-driven enterprise. Those values can be instilled by including them in training programs, building them into performance reviews, and measuring how often violations occur. Changing things is no longer as vague or fuzzy as it might have been, although this does not minimize the work necessary to alter people's beliefs and habits. But at least you know what those beliefs and habits are.

Communicating Security Culture

Getting the security culture message to the right people in the right way means the difference between a successful, well-received diagnostic project and one that misses the mark. Failed projects, at the very least, make it unlikely that the organization will be willing to invest time or money into future efforts, creating a self-fulfilling prophecy about how hard it is to measure culture. But the bigger loss will be the inability of the project to support increased cultural maturity and improved security throughout the enterprise. Measuring culture is only ever the first step, leading to action and change. Convincing people that the effort necessary to change is worth it depends on how well you communicate the benefits of transformation.

Knowing the Audience   Knowing the audience is key in any cultural diagnostic project, both in terms of understanding your audience and shaping your message to meet its unique needs. Project leaders should carefully consider SCDS results in shaping the perceptions of all the stakeholders involved in the project, from senior management down to individual contributors and respondents across different groups. If care has been taken to position and market the CSCF and SCDS, the audience will already understand why they were asked to participate. Now the project team must shape the message about results and insights for that audience.

Our own culture will invariably be more familiar to us than someone else's, which may make the things they prioritize or care about seem strange or even wrong. In a security culture diagnostic project, you are likely to see people with strong cultural biases one way or the other struggling to understand why everyone doesn't see security priorities they way they do. When communicating cultural diagnostics and risks to respondent and stakeholder audiences, it can help to begin by reviewing the results in the context of the culture they most closely identify with, exploring those results and bringing the message back to familiar values and assumptions. Leading the discussion of transforming security culture by always starting with the security team's perspective of the world can give the impression that the security team's vision is the preferred one. You can lose your audience quickly with this approach, which tends to make people feel like they are being told that they believe the wrong things. Instead, the project team should start with more familiar territory, then use examples of competing security cultures and values to explain why misunderstandings can happen and the risks that such conflicts carry.

Another benefit of thinking about culture locally at first, through the eyes of the stakeholders living it, is the chance for the project team to challenge their own assumptions. Most of the time, security culture diagnostic initiatives will be run by the security team. Understanding empirically that not everyone shares their worldview, and having to communicate and defend that worldview by first empathizing with other ways of seeing things, can give security professionals a new perspective on the marketplace of ideas in which they have to compete.

Choosing a Medium   There is no one best way to communicate, no single medium by which insight can be transferred more effectively than through other mediums. The intended audience will often drive the choice of medium, according to both convention and experience. Slide-based presentations have become so ingrained in the corporate world that even though they may not be the best medium for certain ways of communicating, you can alienate your audience if you don't use them. But you should always try to pick the best tool for the job.

Scores, charts, and maps notwithstanding, the strength of the CSCF is that it allows you to tell a story about culture. Your story will have protagonists and antagonists, plot points and conflicts. The SCDS does not create that story. It simply organizes the themes in a way that allows you to put structure where it hasn't existed before. Motivations that have previously seemed mysterious and irrational now make more sense. Visuals can help, but don't expect a culture map to be immediately and obviously intuitive to your audience. You have to walk them through it, interpret for them, be a storyteller.

Many presenters today have mastered slide-based presentations as a storytelling technique. Many others have not. But technology has set us free from an overdependence on slides. I encourage you to explore alternate presentation tools such as Prezi (http://prezi.com), Haiku Deck (www.haikudeck.com), or any of the numerous free and commercial mind-mapping tools that also support graphical presentations.

Looking to New Horizons   As part of your security culture diagnostics presentation, you will also want to get your audience excited about future opportunities for people-centric security. Looking out to the horizon of what comes next can give your organization a powerful incentive to keep going with better and more sophisticated cultural assessments. Remember that the culture–performance link has no natural limits. The more mature and effective the security culture or the larger organizational culture is, the better the results will be of every activity and decision the organization undertakes. Cultural measurement, it should be emphasized, starts with orientation, the act of finding out where you are right now. The map metaphor emphasizes this need for location and situation as the first step of a longer journey.

From Measurement to Transformation

The first two parts of this book have focused on measuring and diagnosing organizational security culture. They have presented ways to describe it, analyze its relative intensity, and identify areas of cultural conflict and risk that may result in security failures. Throughout, the goal has been to transform organizational security culture into a more people-centric security environment.

But understanding security culture is not the same as transforming it. Diagnosis is an improvement over uncertainty, but it does not do anything to make a system better. Initiating change and driving new behaviors require their own structures and efforts. Using the CSCF and the SCDS can show exactly where your organization stands culturally and can help your organization formulate where it thinks it should be. But what is the path to realize that change? It's great to say "we want security to be less bureaucratic and more flexible," but where is the framework and what is the initiative to define what "more flexible" means and how to achieve that goal?

The third part of the book will look to the more tactical challenge of developing behavioral change that is the engine of cultural transformation. As with my adaptations of previous research into cultural measurement, I have grounded security behavioral change in research from other disciplines. And in the case of the Security FORCE Behavioral Model that I will describe, I have traced these behavioral strategies back to the CSCF to create a structure by which the groundwork laid in understanding your security cultures can be used to build a powerful transformation strategy.

Further Reading

Although neither of the following books are Monte Carlo textbooks, both discuss the use of Monte Carlo simulations in risk analysis.

- ▶ Hubbard, Douglas W. *How to Measure Anything: Finding the Value of Intangibles in Business.* Hoboken, NJ: John Wiley & Sons, 2007.

- ▶ Savage, Sam L. *The Flaw of Averages: Why We Underestimate Risk in the Face of Uncertainty.* Hoboken, NJ: John Wiley & Sons, 2009.

Transforming Your Security Culture

From Diagnosis to Transformation: Implementing People-Centric Security

The first two parts of this book have addressed culture generally, security culture in particular, and ways to articulate, diagnose, and analyze the security culture in your organization. Culture, however, remains a huge and inclusive phenomenon in any enterprise, the sum total of the assumptions, beliefs, and values mixing and interacting below the surface of easily observable behavior. Culture can be transformed, but transforming it is like changing the flow of a river. It isn't easy when the river is constantly trying to revert back to its previous course. It is an exercise in organizational engineering. Your strategy has to be very specific and well understood or you will fail. The third part of this book is about developing a structured, measurable strategy to implement people-centric security, to transform security culture, by coming full circle and dealing directly with human and organizational behavior.

Diagnosis and Transformation: One Coin, Two Sides

Understanding culture and changing culture, diagnosing and transforming it, are deeply intertwined ideas, which I illustrate in Figure 9-1. We don't need to understand culture if we are content with continuing to operate on instinct organizationally, more or less unaware of why people make certain decisions and not concerned with whether or not they were the best ones. Our assumptions and values are embedded in everyday enterprise activity. They are reflexes we don't have to think about, habits and rituals we fall back on whenever necessary. Culture takes care of itself. But for those times when we wonder why we keep making the same bad decisions over and over again, when we have this nagging feeling that we could be doing so much better if we could just get out of our own way, we start the process of increasing cultural awareness and visibility, eventually to the point where we can shape it to our own desires and purposes.

The CSCF as a Framework for Understanding

You can't change something you don't understand. Your organizational security culture, left unanalyzed and unexplored, will always remain something of a mystery. People follow the rules and live up to expectations…until they don't. Everyone behaves rationally and does the right thing…until they don't. And when the iceberg keeps drifting south no matter how much people lean to the north, it's very tempting to just give up and blame everything on fate or on the stars that are aligned against us.

The Competing Security Cultures Framework is one attempt to exert more control over your organizational security culture. No framework can precisely

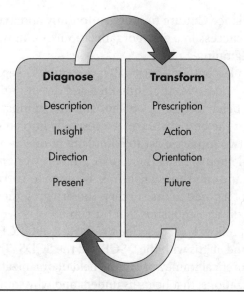

Diagnose	Transform
Description	Prescription
Insight	Action
Direction	Orientation
Present	Future

Figure 9-1   *Diagnosis and transformation of culture*

model every variable in a culture, any more than a computer simulation can precisely model the weather, but the CSCF allows us to understand more about how our security culture operates, in the same way that a weather model helps us reduce uncertainty about the chance of rain tomorrow. It helps identify patterns and tendencies that give insight into what drives activity.

Using the CSCF gives us a picture, sometimes figuratively and sometimes more literally, of how our security cultures and subcultures operate and where they come into conflict with one another in ways that can create risks. This situational awareness not only shows what really matters inside the organization, but can point to the unconscious, and usually well-intended, motivations that underlie habitual security problems.

What Is the Framework for Transformation?

Simply understanding your organization's security culture won't change it, of course. Security culture transformation is certainly possible using the CSCF and Security Culture Diagnostic Survey. Both tools provide a means for creating a map, a navigational aid showing where the organization is and helping it decide where it desires to be. But the mechanics of getting there is not something that a fundamentally diagnostic model is best equipped to explain. "Move from an overweighted Compliance Culture to more Autonomy and Trust" may be the best prescription for success in a given organization, but knowing that is what is needed is only the beginning.

Implementing people-centric security always requires keeping one eye on culture, on the values and drives that influence and direct our behavior, while keeping the other on behavior itself. A diagnostic model must be balanced by a behavioral model for the best chance of successfully implementing people-centric security. The two models exist to complement one another, like a medical diagnostic tool complements a treatment plan. An X-ray or an MRI scan can produce a diagnosis, and can show what must be done to correct the problem or pathology, but it is not a guide to the surgery, the drug regimen, or the diet and exercise that specifically accomplishes that outcome.

In the chapters that follow I will describe the Security FORCE Behavioral Model, which complements and aligns with the CSCF and the SCDS. The model is based on a well-researched theoretical framework in the field of organizational behavior, called high-reliability organizations, that helps us understand why some organizations fail less often and less spectacularly than others. The Security FORCE Model represents my specific application of high-reliability organizations to InfoSec. My model is just one approach, and understanding a bit about alternative approaches may help you see why I favor it. The rest of this chapter discusses some of those alternatives.

Behavioral Models for Security Culture Transformation

Information security today is undergoing a series of experiments in behavioral engineering and cultural transformation, although we do not tend to use those terms directly. But the entire compliance approach to security, including the development and enforcement of new compliance regimes, demonstrates attempts by those inside and outside the security industry to impose change. The compliance approach may be the most visible of these attempts, but even it is just one set of interventions that you can find in the industry today.

Compliance and Control Regimes

I've mentioned it in previous chapters, but it bears repeating that compliance is probably the biggest driver of activity today in information security. Many companies that have neglected or been less than aggressive in their information security activities have significantly increased those efforts in the past decade or so, as a direct result of compliance requirements like PCI DSS, HIPAA, SOX, and privacy and data protection laws passed by governments around the globe.

Compliance is perhaps the most directly behavioral approach to transformation and people-centric security, since it is all about forcing people to make new or different choices. These decisions may include enterprise management being forced to add budget for security, IT operations being forced to create and implement new processes and technologies to support security, and information and IT users and owners being forced into accountability for their actions. Behind all of this are the direct or indirect fears of enforcement and the consequences of failed audits. Organizations that do not implement externally mandated behaviors or controls on behavior, or agree to be bound by third-party assessments of their due diligence, may find themselves subject to investigation, legal action, fines, and being cut off from their ability to run critical business functions, such as processing credit card transactions.

As powerful as compliance is as a motivation for security, its weakness lies in the reliance on sanctions and punishments for failing to comply. Most organizations that adopt a compliance standard like PCI DSS do so because they have to, not necessarily because they believe it is the best way to secure their information. By mandating a minimum level of security required for compliance, regulators and industry groups can even create a perverse incentive to "dumb down" the complexity of security to include only what is mandated by the framework or standard in question. This may lead to "checkbox" InfoSec programs, where security becomes synonymous with a finite set of specific controls imposed by an outside party that may not have much idea about how an organization actually works.

"Let's Sue the Auditors..."

In the wake of high-profile breaches of several large corporations, like that of Target in 2013, at least one PCI DSS Qualified Security Assessor (QSA) has found itself on the receiving end of a lawsuit. Trustwave, the QSA for Target, was sued for negligence in its support of Target's information security. The lawsuit spawned a number of responses about whether or not a QSA should be held liable for a client's security failure, but it also prompted a lot of discussion about whether or not the incident called into question the viability of PCI DSS as a security standard, and even the idea of security assessments in general (a simple Internet search on "PCI DSS lawsuits" will uncover several such analyses).

(continues)

"Let's Sue the Auditors..." *(continued)*

A number of the critiques of PCI DSS in particular go beyond that one standard to more generally address the shortcomings of using compliance and control regimes as a security behavioral framework. These include conflicts of interest between paid auditors and the companies who employ them to do audits, the nature of a relatively static and prescriptive set of controls to address a dynamic and mutable security environment, and the favoring of simpler, easier checklists over the hard challenges of securing complex information systems.

Security Process Improvement

At the opposite end of the transformation continuum from compliance and control regimes are security process improvement methodologies, which take a more systematic and holistic approach to security transformation. Instead of the narrow perspective of compliance, which defines what an organization must do, security process improvement takes the perspective of how an organization should do things and lets the resulting process drive appropriate controls and compliance efforts. ISO 27001, an international standard for information security management, is probably the most widely adopted of these approaches, with thousands of implementations worldwide. But other frameworks, most notably the U.S. Federal Information Security Management Act (FISMA) and the supporting guidance created by the National Institute of Standards and Technology (NIST), also enjoy a great deal of support.

Security process improvement frameworks like ISO 27001 and the NIST Special Publications do not attempt to force a prescriptive, controls-centric security framework on every organization, subject to standardized, recurring audits. Both ISO 27001 and FISMA do have an audit component, but the fact that many enterprises voluntarily implement the international standard or the NIST guidelines best practice architectures for their InfoSec program is telling. These organizations may never undergo a formal audit of their program, but they recognize ISO and NIST as good ways to "do security" nonetheless.

I am a proponent of ISO 27001 and of the process improvement approach it and NIST promulgate. When implemented properly, they offer a comprehensive blueprint for security that demands leadership buy-in, thoughtful analysis of what the organization actually needs in terms of security, and a risk-based selection of controls that work best for the enterprise, rather than satisfying an external party imposing a one-size-fits-most list of "necessary controls" with little associated context or nuance. An unfortunate problem is that many organizations don't implement security process improvement frameworks correctly and manage to turn them into just another checklist of controls. This is especially frustrating to me as a certified ISO 27001 auditor when I see an organization take the standard and skim over the main body before latching on to Annex A, a list of possible controls the organization may select from. We're so used to thinking of security in terms of controls that we're sometimes conditioned to ignore everything else.

Another limitation of the security process improvement approach is that it can be difficult to implement incrementally. Whether you are facing an audit or not, both ISO and NIST tend to assume a static InfoSec program, a complete system that must be either augmented or created. This tends to require a top-down implementation directive, usually mandated within a finite time frame, rather than a process that is gradual and organic. In the case of ISO 27001, the result is that organizations regularly choose to limit the scope of their information security management system (ISMS), perhaps to a single data center or enterprise application. Making the ISMS apply to the entire organization at once is perceived as being too difficult.

"But We Don't Do E-Commerce Here..."

I once did a global tour of a multinational company's regional offices and divisions, ostensibly to assess the company's information security program against the requirements of ISO 27001. With offices and divisions in many different nations, some operating as directly managed subsidiaries and others as quasi-independent partnerships and joint ventures, wide differences soon became apparent. As the challenges of diving into the specific and nuanced ways that different regional offices ran their security programs threatened to overwhelm the resources devoted to the project, the company decided instead to simply fall back on assessing the percentage of implemented controls listed in Annex A of the standard. This would provide, it was thought, an "apples to apples" comparison of InfoSec program efforts.

(continues)

"But We Don't Do E-Commerce Here..." *(continued)*

The controls assessment proved unsatisfactory, with the quantitative scoring of controls only doing a limited job of alleviating the company's uncertainty about how security was managed across different geographies and cultures. And it proved frustrating for both the regional offices and the assessment team. Saddled with a prescriptive and inflexible list of controls that had to be assessed and scored in the same way for each company, it became difficult to explain discrepancies in the final grades. E-commerce, for example, is the subject of several controls under Annex A, and the assessment team was required to note whether the office had those controls in place. Without leeway to alter the scoring, many offices were less than happy to find out that we were taking points off for the failure to implement the "required" controls. I could only nod sympathetically every time one of the local security employees complained, "But we don't do e-commerce here..."

Technology and Automation Approaches

I would be remiss not to include technology approaches to the list of potential behavioral models, approaches that believe it is possible to automate people's behaviors within the organization, usually by limiting what they can do, but also by predicting what they might do. At the center of much of this effort lies the promise of big data and advanced analytics, which many believe will completely revolutionize the practice and industry of information security, in part by letting machines do the learning and deciding instead of people. These systems operate at the intersection of surveillance and security, gathering data about a bewildering variety of activities and processing it to find patterns and support organizational decisions, which may themselves be automated.

In the post–Edward Snowden world, many people find the idea of increasing levels of analytically driven personal and professional surveillance creepy and disturbing, regardless of whether those techniques are being used by social networks, advertisers, rental car companies, our employers, or intelligence agencies. Although I share some of these concerns, I find my bigger problem with the big data movement in information security to be the hype around capabilities.

I don't have any doubts about the power of analytics, but I also have an abiding faith in people and their ability to circumvent, intentionally or through sheer (good, bad, or dumb) luck, just about any technology system designed or intended to control their behavior. Of course the technology will win some of the time. But I'm always skeptical of claims like the one I heard a data scientist make during a talk at a security conference not too long ago. "In five years," the speaker said confidently, "there won't be anyone in security besides data scientists, because we won't need them."

Making It Personal...

Wouldn't it be great if our security systems could tell what users were thinking and decide who was a potential threat? Well, Fujitsu is working on doing just that. In early 2015, the company announced the development of innovative technology that can pick out vulnerable users by profiling them psychologically and behaviorally. The system, according to Fujitsu and industry write-ups, analyzes everything from e-mails and visited websites to mouse clicks and keyboard actions, and produces a profile of each user designed to predict the likelihood that person might succumb to a cyber attack. The company figured at the time that the technology was a year out from production.

Maybe it wouldn't be so great after all. Fujitsu's technology sounds a bit like information security's version of the film *Minority Report.* And there is no question that advancement in behavioral analytics makes such human monitoring capabilities seem less like science fiction every day. The question is to what extent technology like Fujitsu's automated psychological profiling is likely to impact organizational security culture and practice. Will organizations accept the potential surveillance and privacy trade-offs that such technologies bring, in the name of improved security? And will people accept such intrusive activities into their lives? Perhaps most importantly, one has to wonder if a panoptic culture of security, one driven by knowing you are being watched all the time, is as desirable or effective a culture as one where people value good security behaviors so much, and practice them so conscientiously, that they don't need to be under constant surveillance.

Security Needs More Options

To summarize my points, I think that the behavioral models currently available to people-centric security, while useful in many ways, often come up short in terms of their ability to successfully transform security culture:

▶ **Control and compliance regimes**   Often too prescriptive, too specific and standardized, creating a least common denominator state of security prioritizing "checking the box" over addressing problems

▶ **Security process improvement frameworks**   Often not prescriptive enough, embracing context and uncertainty when people just want to be told what to do, making implementation stressful and hard

▶ **Technology and automation approaches**   Offer solid data and evidence, but risk the trap of thinking human beings can be managed like machines, deterministically, when history proves otherwise

If the bad news is that none of these approaches are fully aligned with developing a people-centric security culture, then the good news is that there is opportunity for new behavioral frameworks to be explored and implemented. Comparing the three I've called out is a classic opportunity for a Venn diagram, like the one shown in Figure 9-2. Opportunity lies in developing new behavioral models that

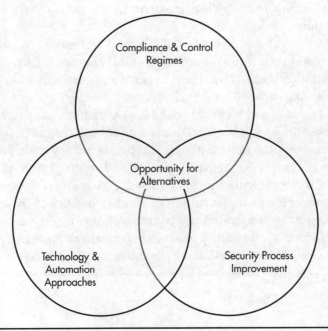

Figure 9-2   *Opportunities for new security behavioral models*

complement security culture models like the CSCF and provide the best elements of the various existing models.

In the following chapters, I propose and describe a new framework, the Security FORCE Behavioral Model, which is designed to address these shortcomings and add value to an organization's transformation to people-centric security.

Further Reading

▶ Fujitsu. "Fujitsu Develops Industry's First Technology That Identifies Users Vulnerable to Cyber Attack Based on Behavioral and Psychological Characteristics." January 19, 2015. Available at www.fujitsu.com.

▶ Hornyak, Tim. "Fujitsu Psychology Tool Profiles Users at Risk of Cyberattacks." *NetworkWorld*, January 21, 2015. Available at www.networkworld.com.

▶ ISO/IEC. 27000:2014, *Information technology – Security techniques – Information security management systems – Overview and vocabulary* (third edition). January 15, 2014. Available at http://standards.iso.org.

▶ NIST Computer Security Division (CSD). Federal Information Security Management Act (FISMA) Implementation Project. Available at www.nist.gov.

10

Security FORCE:
A Behavioral Model for
People-Centric Security

I nformation security professionals need new ways of thinking about the problems we face and how to confront them. In the industry, we talk a lot about how much the world has changed over the years. Our current technology environments would be stunningly complex to early security professionals, and our threat environments would be terrifying. I remember when firewalls were all we needed to protect our networks, intrusion detection systems were a new-fangled technology, VPNs didn't exist (at least not for the common person), and cell phones could only be used as phones. It's like the opposite of the old man telling tales of walking to school barefoot, in the snow, uphill both ways. Looking back, it all seems so idyllic, the good old days when almost no one wanted to steal your information, those who did want to steal it usually couldn't, and the really bad ones who could steal it often were caught before they were able to do too much permanent damage.

Perhaps security professionals today can be forgiven for taking a glum view of the world. But for an industry that has seen so much transformation, it's surprising how poorly our frameworks and models have kept pace. To be sure, our technology has come a long way. But our basic concepts have not evolved all that much. We still act as though confidentiality, integrity, and availability (CIA) mean the same things they did 30 years ago, that risk can be measured in three colors, and that controls are the essential building blocks of security life. Information security is a remarkably conservative discipline to be living and working so close to the bleeding edge of information age disruption.

The purpose of this book, and the frameworks I propose in it, is not to say that what we've done in the past doesn't work, or to advocate abandoning the CIA triad, heat maps, or control frameworks. That would be silly and disingenuous. But I do believe that the tools in our toolbox are no longer enough to get us where we need and want to be. There are many directions security can take, and is taking, to innovate. Some of these directions are extensions of technology, like big data. Some, like increasingly aggressive regulation, focus on controls. I am an advocate for improving culture and behavior, for developing more people-centric solutions to security challenges. I believe they offer the best opportunity to change things, to right ourselves before we start seeing disruption that makes today's world look as idyllic as the one I remember from my early days in the field.

The Security FORCE Behavioral Model, hereafter referred to more simply as Security FORCE, offers another tool for organizations to utilize in securing their information and enterprise assets. It won't replace all the other tools or be useful in every situation, but it can help provide another angle of assessment and insight that may just be the perspective an organization needs to make real headway against security problems that have seemed unsolvable up to now.

Origins of Security FORCE

My experiences working with organization after organization over the years have gradually coalesced into a form of pattern recognition that causes me to see information security as a behavioral and cultural problem, one perpetuated as much by security itself as anyone outside the discipline. What I have observed over and over are security cultures that exhibit irrational attitudes toward risk and failure, struggle to reconcile expectations with actual operations, don't bounce back from problems very gracefully, tend toward oversimplification, and make a habit of ignoring or marginalizing the people closest to the problems. It only takes a few of these traits to destabilize even a good organization's information security posture.

A lot of research and work has gone into understanding why some organizations fail more often or less often than others, and it turns out that the patterns I just described are not unique to security, but can be found across industry, organizational, and geographic lines. Among the most prominent researchers into the traits and characteristics of organizations that fail versus those that don't is Karl Weick.

Karl Weick has been exploring organizational culture and behavior, and their effects on performance and failure, for half a century. *The Social Psychology of Organizing*, a book Weick originally published in 1969, is considered a classic and has been translated into multiple languages. I've personally followed Weick's work for well over a decade, ever since I was first introduced to it in graduate school, and I've talked about other areas of his work earlier in this book. But the most important application of Weick's work for security is his research, along with colleague Kathleen Sutcliffe, into the concept of high-reliability organizations, or HROs, summarized in their book *Managing the Unexpected*. Weick's research, especially his work with Sutcliffe, is a central driver of Security FORCE.

In essence, high-reliability organizations fail less often and prove more robust when failure does happen because of several cultural traits that define how HROs work and think collectively. Security FORCE captures these traits and adapts them specifically to people-centric security.

The concepts and tools I introduce in this book—the Competing Security Cultures Framework and Security FORCE—are both adaptations of research efforts that began and were developed elsewhere. More importantly, these frameworks and models have the benefit of years of empirical study behind them. They have worked where people have applied them in other industries, and information security can benefit by mapping and applying them to our own challenges. Culture and behavior are phenomena that apply as much to security as to any other organized activity. Before we discuss Security FORCE further, it's important to understand not only what defines a high reliability organization but also the common traits and principles these organizations share.

HRO Research

Weick and Sutcliffe describe high reliability organizations as those enterprises and organizations that have learned to adapt to dangerous and hostile environments, where many more things can go wrong than in "normal" environments, and where things that do go wrong tend to go wrong in a much worse way, up to and including people dying. In an organization where the chances of mistakes and problems occurring are higher than usual, you would expect more things to "break" more often. And when things breaking brings worse-than-average consequences, possibly disastrous ones, then you would expect really bad things to happen.

But HRO researchers have found that things work differently in these organizations from what might be expected. HROs often exhibit fewer problems, with less severe consequences, than the average organization. Why would that be? Well, it makes sense if you think about it. An organization that operates in a low-risk, low-impact environment may be able to muddle along indefinitely, even while making mistakes and failing on a regular basis, never managing to fundamentally change its ways even when that means never realizing its full potential. But an organization that faces catastrophe at every turn must learn to survive by skill and constant vigilance. Otherwise, it won't survive at all.

Weick and Sutcliffe identified specific examples of organizations that operate as HROs. They include firefighting teams, aircraft carriers, manufacturing companies, and nuclear power plants, among others. All of these types of organizations experience failures, of course. Firefighters die, aircraft crash on flight decks, industrial accidents and product recalls occur, and occasionally we even face nuclear disasters. Being an HRO doesn't mean nothing ever goes terribly wrong. But for systems this complex, in environments as dangerous as the ones these organizations operate within, they have a track record remarkable enough for organizational scientists to understand that they don't function like other organizations. They do things differently.

The unique ways in which HROs function have been organized into five principles that summarize the differences in the behaviors of HROs compared to other organizations. These principles encompass how HROs look at such things as failure and the ability to bounce back from it, complexity and operational realities, and who is most capable of dealing with a crisis. These five principles are summarized in Figure 10-1. Each of these principles has its own application in the context of information security, and I will cover these in detail later in the chapter.

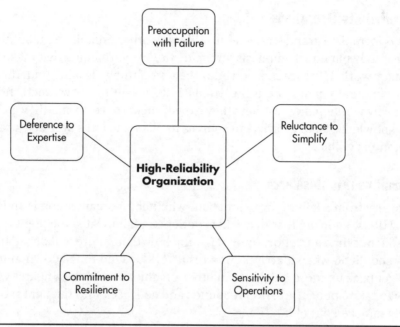

Figure 10-1 *Five principles of high-reliability organizations*

Preoccupation with Failure

HROs obsess over failure, but not for the same reasons as other organizations. Instead of operating on the assumption that failure is a universally bad thing, to be avoided at all costs, HROs treat failure as an unavoidable outcome of doing business, an intrinsic property of their environment. HROs are compulsively driven to identify these failures at all costs, as early as possible. They then try to use small failures as a tool by which they can avoid large disasters.

Reluctance to Simplify

The easiest way to make members of an HRO nervous is to explain the challenges they face in simplistic, dumbed-down terms. By maintaining a healthy respect for the complexity and unpredictability of the environments in which they operate, HROs seek more complicated answers, backed by observation and data. Simple models and frameworks make an HRO wonder what is being left out or ignored, and how that might bite them later.

Sensitivity to Operations

HROs formulate grand strategies just like any other organization, but they differ in that they put equal emphasis on the tactical requirements that make the strategy work. HRO leaders don't do "the vision thing," leaving underlings and subordinates to hammer out the details. HROs want to know exactly how things are really working, not just how they expect them to work, and they gather data and knowledge from a variety of sources to make the links between strategy and operations visible.

Commitment to Resilience

Recovery from a failure says a lot about whether an organization is an HRO or not. HROs, knowing that they will experience a failure at some point for some reason, put time and effort into imagining how that failure will occur and what they should do when it arrives. As a result, HROs tend to fall down more softly and get back up more quickly than other organizations. Like a fighter who knows how to take a punch, an HRO rebounds and gets back into the fight rather than being knocked out of it.

Deference to Expertise

HROs structure themselves around a different decision-making system, one that is more flexible and diverse. Hierarchies are important, but not when they hinder people who know what is going on from acting on that knowledge immediately. By relying on the skills and judgments of the people who are closest to the systems in question, HROs can gather data on potential problems more quickly and respond with more agility to changes in operations.

HROs in Information Security

Since my first encounter with the HRO research literature as a student, I have been struck by how much this body of work has to offer information security. I've observed many companies that behave, from a security perspective, less like organizations committed to surviving in the midst of complexity and existential danger, and more like ones that are complacent and even confident that they are unlikely to ever really get hurt. Even organizations that take security seriously are often plagued by the very deficiencies that HROs have evolved to avoid.

I have been using elements of HRO research in my security work for a long time. Adapting and applying the behavioral lessons of HROs to security programs is a more straightforward project than full-blown cultural transformation. But until recently, I have always used the lessons of HROs in a piecemeal fashion and not as a fully developed model in its own right, one that would be prescriptive and measurable in the context of a security program. My interest and research into people-centric security changed that. As I formulated a model of security culture that could lead to long-term change, I recognized the need for a complementary transformational model. Basing that model on HROs was the natural choice.

Studies in Failure

HRO research is just one branch in a tree of research devoted to how and why systems and organizations fail, and what, if anything, can be done to prevent failure. Are some systems just destined for eventual disaster? Or can catastrophe be avoided through certain enterprise structures, organizational cultures, and behavioral habits? Obviously, Weick and Sutcliffe take a more upbeat stance that, yes, organizations can save themselves from significant failures by learning from and behaving more like HROs. But there are other perspectives.

Sidney Dekker, who I discussed in Part I, is a failure studies expert who has conceptualized drift as a way of understanding how complex systems and organizations experience gradual, entropic decay as the designs of those systems prove unable to keep up with changing environmental and social factors. For Dekker, failure is a sort of byproduct of success. As people make optimizing decisions, compromises in the face of insufficient resources or even simple inertia, the system grows unstable. But rather than being seen as mistakes, these destabilizing decisions look like sound logic in the moment. It is only after a failure incident that the organization is forced to retroactively find and impose responsibility.

Charles Perrow is another failure studies scholar, and his book *Normal Accidents: Living with High-Risk Technologies* was among the earliest efforts to theorize the causes of instability and failure in highly complex technology environments like nuclear energy. Perrow's analysis of these environments is similar to HRO research, identifying principles such as the inevitability of failure, the idea that big failures start small, and that failure is a social rather than a technological problem. Perrow's conclusions are, however, somewhat less encouraging than those of the HRO researchers. He posits that it is more difficult to design around or avoid failures because unpredictable instability is embedded into the fabric of systems that are massively complex and closely linked together.

Highly Reliable Security Programs

Some InfoSec programs already behave like HROs, although they tend to be rare. These programs, which I call Highly Reliable Security Programs (HRSPs), have managed to develop the culture and behaviors of their HRO counterparts in other industries. "Highly reliable" instead of "high reliability" is something of a hedge on my part. I want to emphasize the characteristics and behaviors of HROs within InfoSec programs, but without implying that it's easy to translate those characteristics directly, or to put undue pressure on organizations to suddenly be seen as infallible. HRSPs should, as a goal, simply become more highly reliable than they are today. HRSPs do exist, for instance, in sensitive military and intelligence organizations, as well as some companies that depend so heavily on proprietary or protected information that any security incident can prove deadly, either figuratively or literally. But they are atypical. Taking security seriously is laudable, but it is not the same thing as being an HRSP. High reliability is not about having the most cutting-edge technology or religiously implementing lists of top controls, and it certainly is not about successfully meeting compliance requirements.

High reliability is less about how organizations succeed at security and much more about how they fail at it. In fact, preoccupation with failure is the first principle of HROs, and the value of failure is the first key value in Security FORCE. HRSPs fail in a very particular way, under specific circumstances. More importantly, they expect to fail, and so they prepare for the eventuality in a way that allows them to rebound quickly and gracefully from a fall. Most security programs, even very competent ones, find their capabilities strained when it comes to failure, as many of the recent public breach incidents demonstrate. Their behavioral patterns and habits are concentrated on different priorities. Security FORCE is designed to help InfoSec programs change those habits and behaviors, to adopt new ones that will not only make large failures less likely, but enable better responses to those that inevitably do occur.

Introducing the Security FORCE Behavioral Model

Security FORCE applies the five principles of HROs (depicted in Figure 10-1) as a set of five core values that define an HRSP, adapting these values to security and packaging them within a user-friendly, memorable acronym. These FORCE values, shown in Figure 10-2 and described shortly, drive behavior and influence decision making within the InfoSec program and the entire organization. FORCE values reflect the things that the security program takes seriously.

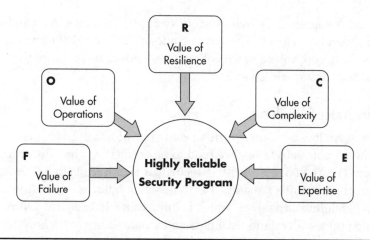

Figure 10-2   *Core values of Security FORCE found in an HRSP*

Remember that organizational culture is the collective values and assumptions of a group of people working at a common purpose, the habits and norms that drive their decisions and activities, often beneath the conscious surface. HRSPs possess a unique culture, one that enables them to perform differently under difficult conditions. Security FORCE identifies the values that are most likely to exist within an HRSP, whether or not that security program considers itself highly reliable. Security FORCE therefore approaches cultural transformation from the other end of the spectrum, from the bottom up. If everyone in an organization behaves toward information security the way that people in an HRO behave, all the time, habitually, then that organization is an HRSP. It doesn't matter if they explicitly think in terms of an HRO-type culture. "HRSP" is not something an organization calls itself, but rather something that it does. When you look like a duck, walk like a duck, quack like a duck, and have the DNA of a duck, you're a duck. Security FORCE defines what it means to be a highly reliable duck.

Five Core Values of Security FORCE

The five core values defined by Security FORCE benefit information security and lead to a typical security program transforming into a Highly Reliable Security Program. An HRSP tends to reduce the number of large security failures that it experiences, and typically will recover from failures that do occur more quickly and with less disruption than its non-HRSP peers. I have developed specific prescriptive behaviors for each Security FORCE value, behaviors that can be observed and encouraged, as well as Security FORCE metrics that can be used to test and assess how closely a program conforms to the behaviors of an HRSP. I summarize these core values in the following sections, and explore them in detail throughout the subsequent chapters.

The Security Value of Failure

Failure may seem like a counterintuitive value for information security, but only because when it comes to failing we tend to be doing it wrong. The security value derived from failure in people-centric security is that it leads to better insights about when organizations fail and what to do when failures occur. Instead of trying to avoid failure altogether, which is impossible, HRSPs use failure as a tool by which they understand weakness and vulnerability in their systems. This value is realized when failures are discovered early and often, so that they can be addressed and corrected while they remain small, instead of waiting for large failures that prove costlier and more disruptive.

The Security Value of Operations

Operations are central to any InfoSec program, but often there is a disconnect between what people in the program think is happening "on the ground" and what is actually going on. A security policy may say something is required, for instance, but the policy ends up being widely ignored. Or compliance with a standard may make a CISO feel like security is functioning more effectively than it really is. HRSPs worry constantly about what is really going on within their organizations. The security value derived from operations happens when the security program increases visibility and focus on operational realities, rather than relying on proxies or assumptions to guide decisions.

The Security Value of Resilience

How an organization's security fails is as important as, if not more important than, whether it fails or when it fails. Security failures are inevitable, but paralysis and disruption as a result of security failures are not. Resilience involves knowing exactly what to do when something breaks, so that you bounce back quickly from the problem. HRSPs constantly think about failure and routinely practice how they will deal with it. The security value derived from resilience, therefore, is gained when a security program not only knows where it is likely to experience failure, but has detailed plans for addressing failure and conducts drills on those plans until handling failure is as natural as handling normal operations.

The Security Value of Complexity

Complex environments, threats, and risks challenge any security program's ability to reduce uncertainty and make effective decisions. But where many organizations meet this challenge by reducing complexity and pursuing simple explanations and frameworks to guide strategy, HRSPs know that oversimplification adds more uncertainty than it removes. Just as assumptions can lead to blind spots, oversimplification can reduce the organization's situational awareness and increase the likelihood of "failures of imagination" resulting from risks that have not been previously considered and resulting in so-called "black swan" events that prove surprising and costly. The security value derived from complexity is harnessed when an organization maintains a healthy skepticism of simple answers and explanations, and prefers nuanced insight to one-size-fits-all explanations.

The Security Value of Expertise

There is no shortage of expertise in information security, but that doesn't mean that the people best positioned to make a decision are always the ones with the authority to do so. HRSPs recognize that rigid chains of command and hierarchical power structures can get in the way of effective operations, especially in a crisis. The security value of expertise is realized by distributing decision authority within an organization to maximize efficiency and impact, taking advantage of the human sensors best placed to respond to new information immediately and take action.

Security FORCE Value Behaviors and Metrics

The purpose of Security FORCE is not merely to describe how HRSPs differentiate themselves from other security organizations. The model is also prescriptive, in that it provides a template for change and transformation that enables more reliable, people-centric security. By breaking down the key values of HRSPs into certain behaviors, we can determine whether the values are being upheld when it comes to enterprise security. Once we have identified these behaviors, we can empirically observe and measure them. And with measurement we can make assessments and assign scores that enable us to compare behaviors and organizations against one another.

Security FORCE Value Behaviors

As I have described throughout the book, organizational culture drives behavior. Culture is the sum total of values and assumptions held by the people who make up the enterprise. An organization's security behaviors, then, are key indicators of that organization's underlying security culture. When a security program functions as an HRSP, when its culture is one that has adopted the principles and values of high reliability, its behaviors will reflect those deep influences and priorities.

Each Security FORCE value has an associated set of observable behaviors that provide evidence of the influence and strength of that particular value within the security program. For security culture transformation, these behavioral indicators are the signs that the transition to people-centric security and HRSP behaviors is taking place. If cultural change is real, if it has penetrated and taken root within the deeply held values and beliefs of the organization, the evidence of that success will be found in measurable changes in daily behaviors of the organization's members. Conversely, if change is superficial and has not influenced embedded values and priorities, this will be observable in the lack of any real behavioral change.

To this end, I have developed two diagnostic tools that can assist you in implementing Security FORCE values. The first is a basic survey you can use to assess whether or not your organization behaves like an HRSP today. The second is a set of measures for each Security FORCE value that you can use to gather empirical evidence regarding how well you manage the Security FORCE value behaviors inside your own environment. Both Security FORCE diagnostic tools can be downloaded from http://lancehayden.net/culture.

I will reserve detailed discussion of the behaviors associated with each Security FORCE value for the subsequent five chapters, where I address each FORCE value at length and provide worksheets for assessing and scoring them. But for purposes of introduction, the behaviors associated with each of the Security FORCE values are listed in Table 10-1.

Security FORCE Value Metrics

Measurement is critical to the success of security culture and behavioral transformation. Another strength of Security FORCE is the inclusion of metrics, tagged to the key value behaviors of the model and designed to assess HRSP-related traits and compare them over time and against other organizations. These metrics provide empirical evidence that the organization is behaving like an HRSP, rather than simply going through the motions of behavioral change.

Security FORCE Value	Key Value Behaviors
Failure	► Anticipate failures
	► Seek out problems
	► Reward problem reporting
	► Share information about failure
	► Learn from mistakes
Operations	► Keep your eyes open
	► Form a bigger picture
	► "Listen" to the system
	► Test expectations against reality
	► Share operational assessments
Resilience	► Overtrain people
	► Create "skill benches"
	► Actively share expertise
	► Encourage stretch goals
	► Practice failing
Complexity	► Don't oversimplify
	► Formalize your assumptions
	► Covet empirical evidence
	► Share the doubt
	► Make every model better
Expertise	► Ask the experts
	► Suppress the egos
	► Allow authority to migrate
	► Share credibility
	► Reward calls to action and cries for help

Table 10-1   *Security FORCE Values and Associated Key Value Behaviors*

As with the specific behaviors associated with the Security FORCE values, I will reserve detailed discussion of the metrics associated with the model for the subsequent chapters. But for purposes of introduction, the metrics associated with each of the Security FORCE values are listed in Table 10-2.

Security FORCE Value	FORCE Value Metrics
Failure	▶ Number of security failure scenarios developed in the past year ▶ Number of security failures (whether or not resulting in a formal security incident) reported in the past year ▶ Ratio of security incidents with no prior failure reporting or indicators in the past year ▶ Ratio of security failure or incident data (reports, root-cause analyses, after-actions, etc.) voluntarily shared outside the information security program ▶ Ratio of security failures resulting in system changes
Operations	▶ Level of security staff coverage for the organization (size of program, breadth of responsibility, systems managed, etc.) ▶ Number of security operations reviews completed in the past year ▶ Ratio of formally documented security operations or processes ▶ Ratio of security operational assessments shared outside the security group ▶ Average time to address operational instabilities
Resilience	▶ Number of security-related training opportunities provided to people, by role or group, in the past year ▶ Number of identified security backup resources available during an incident ▶ Ratio of employees with identified security "challenge" assignments as part of regular performance reviews ▶ Number and type of security knowledge sharing opportunities created in the past year ▶ Number of scenario-based response testing or security war-game exercises conducted in the past year
Complexity	▶ Number, type, and complexity of adopted organizational frameworks ▶ Average time to organizational decisions (from initial proposal, through debate or deliberation, to final resolution) ▶ Average number of data points collected in support of individual organizational decisions ▶ Number of formal reviews of security plans by non-security stakeholders in the past year ▶ Number of outcome and modeling evaluations conducted in the past year

Table 10-2 *Security FORCE Values and Associated FORCE Value Metrics*

Security FORCE Value	FORCE Value Metrics
Expertise	▶ Number of formal knowledge or skill repositories in place
	▶ Number of people with security responsibilities written into their job descriptions
	▶ Number of identified "quick response" scenarios with expedited decision making
	▶ Number of decision owners for security formally assigned in the past year
	▶ Number of cross-functional security-related activities or projects in the past year (initiated internally by the information security program or externally by other stakeholders)

Table 10-2   *Security FORCE Values and Associated FORCE Value Metrics*

The Culture–Behavior Link in HRSPs

The CSCF represents a "top-down" approach to understanding and transforming information security culture. You can use the CSCF to orient yourself broadly in terms of your organization's values and assumptions about security, and to identify areas of competition and potential cultural risk. Transformation using the CSCF is also necessarily broad. The CSCF allows an organization to determine direction and distance, so to speak. It allows an organization, for example, to articulate that it is primarily a Process Culture, and to make the case that it might benefit from traits found in an Autonomy Culture. It's like a real-world map in that you can look at it and decide, "We're too far west. We need to go east."

The CSCF does not tell an organization exactly how to get where it wants to go. "Be more like an Autonomy Culture" is not very helpful if you don't know what that means at a detailed level. The behaviors modeled under Security FORCE are designed to provide the more "bottom-up" perspective on cultural transformation that I discussed early in the chapter. Understanding information security as both culture and behavior is an important insight. As I've stated earlier in the book, an organization cannot change its security culture by just targeting observable behaviors and ignoring the invisible drivers beneath the surface. But at the same time, the organization has to have some idea of what behaviors to look for if it is ever to know whether transformation is successful. This link between top and bottom, between culture and behavior, is at the heart of the relationship between the CSCF and Security FORCE.

HROs and HRSPs do not have to think in terms of culture to accomplish their missions. Their behaviors develop over time, through evolutionary adaptation to hostile environments. It took organizational behavior researchers to observe those adaptations and assign names to the patterns that make them what they are. Highly reliable organizations are often too busy doing what they do, surviving and thriving, to worry about assigning labels like "high reliability" to themselves. But these enterprises are culturally different from others, and their behaviors are a product of that different culture. Which came first is like a chicken and

Only the Reliable Survive

It is difficult to overstate the effort involved in becoming an HRSP, or in maintaining that status on a long-term basis. Organizations are like individuals in a lot of ways. They develop certain habits and worldviews, and they can become very set in their ways. It's about as easy for an organization to say "This year I'm going to become more secure" as it is for a person to say "This year I'm going to get healthy" (or "stop being so stressed," or "write that book I've been thinking about," or whatever). But New Year's resolutions, as they say, are made to be broken. It takes will power, endurance, and dogged effort every single day to live up to our goals.

The habits I see in many InfoSec programs are the ones you can find in most organizations. Pecking order matters, whether or not it is formalized in an organizational chart. People hate to get bad news, especially when they know that turning things around will not be easy or will require that they embrace change. And few things are as comforting as a neatly packaged solution to a problem, whether that solution is a technology product, a neat visual that sums up the world in three slides, or a promise that if you just do these five, or ten, or twenty things, everything will be okay.

HRSPs do their best to reject all of these things, not because they are morally or intellectually superior to other security programs, but because they know deep down that if they don't do things differently, their environment will eventually cripple or destroy them. This means knowing the difference between short-term and long-term necessities, and being able to balance them effectively. It means maximizing both utility and innovation. Like people who find themselves living in inhospitable climates or surrounded by predators, HRSPs adapt or they die. It's never easy being a survivor.

egg question. What both the CSCF and Security FORCE share is the goal of defining and articulating patterns and relationships that exist between cultures, between behaviors, and between both culture and behavior. Together, the CSCF and Security FORCE become complementary exercises in shared visibility.

The values described in Security FORCE often align with individual culture types in the CSCF. Whether an organization or an InfoSec program has a Process, Compliance, Autonomy, or Trust Culture can influence how much resistance or acceptance that organization is likely to experience when promoting the key behaviors of Security FORCE. So understanding and diagnosing the organization's security cultures is an important part of implementing Security FORCE behaviors. In the same way, an organizaton hoping to emulate or become an HRSP cannot really jump into transforming its culture without a deep understanding of the key behaviors that are expected to be found in a more highly reliable InfoSec program. The next several chapters are a detailed examination of those behaviors, starting with the security value of failure in Chapter 11.

Further Reading

- ▶ Weick, Karl E. *The Social Psychology of Organizing.* 2nd ed. New York: McGraw-Hill, 1979.
- ▶ Weick, Karl E., and Kathleen M. Sutcliffe. *Managing the Unexpected: Resilient Performance in an Age of Uncertainty.* 2nd ed. San Francisco: Jossey-Bass, 2007.
- ▶ Perrow, Charles. *Normal Accidents: Living with High-Risk Technologies.* Princeton, NJ: Princeton University Press, 1999.

CHAPTER
11

The Security Value of Failure

The first key value in Security FORCE is failure. In Chapter 10, I discussed how hard it is for information security professionals to embrace failure, while emphasizing its place in people-centric security. In this chapter, I will go into much more detail about just why failure is so valuable to InfoSec programs, what behaviors are associated with accepting failure as a value proposition, and how to measure and incorporate these behaviors into an existing security program.

What Is the Security Value of Failure?

Most of the security programs and leaders I interact with have a special relationship with failure. They fear it and loathe it. To them, failure means that you are not good at what you do, that you have let down your organization and everyone who depends upon it. Failure may also carry harsh personal consequences for your career and your self-image. The idea that failure is not a bad thing is alien to most information security professionals, and attempting to make the case that failure is actually a good thing is likely to get you laughed out of the room. But making that case is exactly what I'm going to do.

Failures are among an organization's most valuable security resources. Until they're not. Then they just might kill you.

"Failure Is Not an Option"

In *Managing the Unexpected* (introduced in Chapter 10), Weick and Sutcliffe talk about a quote from the film *Apollo 13*, a line spoken by actor Ed Harris, playing NASA Flight Director Gene Kranz. "Failure is not an option," Kranz tersely informs his team during the film, setting the stage for the heroic feat of rescuing three astronauts in a crippled spaceship headed for the moon.

Failure is not an option is an informal motto in many security organizations I've encountered, the reasoning being that the stakes are just too high. So it's a bit ironic that the real Gene Kranz never uttered those words during the Apollo 13 mission. The line came from one of the movie's screenwriters, based on a comment that a different mission crew member said as the movie was being researched. The real comment, about how NASA weighed its options continuously throughout the disaster and simply neglected to ever include failing among them, was more nuanced. But that line wouldn't have sounded nearly as cool coming out of Ed Harris.

Failure was obviously an option during the Apollo 13 mission, which failed by definition. No one landed on the moon. The story is legendary because NASA did a heroic job of saving the mission from a much bigger failure, the death of the three astronauts in the crew. To casually say that such an outcome was not a possibility because NASA simply wouldn't allow it is to pretend that we can avoid failure by force of will alone. That may work in the movies, but when the credits roll and the lights come up, most of us in the audience have to go back to reality. In the real world, avoiding failure takes hard, dogged work. This is a lesson that is core to people-centric security.

When I talk with CISOs and security managers and am told that failure is not an option in their organization, or that they have a zero tolerance policy for screw-ups, or any of the other variations I hear on the theme, I understand where they are coming from. But I also try to point out the irrationality of a philosophy that does little more than guarantee you will experience a failure, and probably not just a minor one. It's like repeatedly saying you refuse to be unhappy or insisting that everyone around you must always have a positive attitude. They are impossible outcomes and you just end up lying to yourself about achieving them, or expecting others to lie to you, or both. Eventually that comes back to bite you.

So why do we adopt such a patently false worldview? Probably because most of us have been trained and conditioned to feel bad about failing. This may be more of a uniquely American perspective, but failure gets all tangled up with the idea of losing. We learn that life is a contest, and that business is even more of one. To fail is to lose. And to lose means that other people are better than you. So failure can carry more than just the connotation of making a mistake or having something bad happen. Fail too many times and you actually become a noun, a failure yourself. A loser. A bad person.

Reevaluating Failure

Failure is, at heart, a simple concept. Strip away the moral and cultural judgments that make failure something to be ashamed of, the opposite of a success to be proud of, and you are left with a more basic definition. Failure is the outcome when something does not function as it is supposed to or expected to. It's a state, not a character flaw. In high-reliability organizations (HROs), *failure* is a term associated with the performance of a system and whether or not that performance is consistent and reliable. In a Highly Reliable Security Program (HRSP), which is the InfoSec equivalent of an HRO and the goal of most CISOs, that system can be a specific machine or process, or it can be the entire security program. But whichever system you are considering, the one thing that you can be sure of is that it is not always going to work. Machines break down over time. Software has bugs that get discovered. Security programs are even more complex, for all the reasons I have described in previous chapters. The only sure thing in a security system is that, sooner or later, something is going to fail.

Things do not often collapse spontaneously and catastrophically, not in the physical world and not in information security. It's very rare to have a perfectly viable, strongly designed system that one day suddenly explodes. Most failures occur as part of a continuous process of decay and degradation, the state of the system growing slowly and quietly weaker and less stable until it is no longer able to withstand the pressures of its environment. That final, complete failure, the one that breaks the system and that everyone notices, can certainly come as an unwelcome surprise. But that doesn't mean no one could have seen it coming, if they had looked for signs and clues earlier.

Weick and Sutcliffe refer to big failures as "brutal audits," a description that I find very apropos for information security. So much of our work is compliance-driven these days that the idea of audits has become institutionalized within security programs. Audits are designed to point out discrepancies from an expected norm, usually taking the form of a compliance framework or regime. An information security audit is therefore designed to root out failures, things that are not functioning as they are expected to or as they should. Although you may feel brutalized after your most recent PCI DSS or SOX audit, the fact is that you have had those failures identified by friendly parties, people who are interested in seeing your organization succeed. Pointing out your discrepancies gives you an opportunity to fix them. When a criminal hacker breaks into your systems and exfiltrates all your customer information to sell on the black market, and the story hits the newswires, that's an altogether different kind of audit. Essentially, it has achieved the same result: you are now aware of the shortcomings in your security program, as evidenced by a third party testing it. But that third party is not your friend and could care less whether or not your organization makes things better. They're already done with you.

So the security value of failure doesn't imply that a major breach or incident is valuable, but rather that value lies in understanding the process of slow decay in the stability of your security posture. The ability to identify smaller failures, cracks in the system that appear before it breaks completely, is what is important. HROs and HRSPs are much better than other organizations at finding problems while they are just symptoms of impending failure. Mistakes, missteps, and erosion are all signs of growing weakness in a system. Some of these signs are so small that they are barely visible and the failure causes no real harm, but when small failures start piling up, the signs begin to point to bigger problems that may prove very harmful. Cracks become holes and fissures, and eventually the whole thing gives. The trick to avoiding big security incidents is to correct failures while they remain small and insignificant to the operation of the entire security program. But to correct them, you have to want to find them.

Embracing Failure

Embracing failure as a security value does mean that we desire to fail. It simply means that we know failure of some sort is inevitable, the cost of doing business via the complex systems that we deploy and depend upon in the information economy. Knowing, then, that we cannot help but fail sometimes, at some level, we readjust our outlook on what it means to fail and try to make failure work for us instead of against us. Your InfoSec program may have the most talented people, the most robust processes, and the best cutting-edge technology all working together, but people will make mistakes, processes will be poorly communicated or enforced, and the technology environment will change, creating areas of opportunity for decay. These spaces will grow and expand, compounding one another, until the problem grows too large to ignore.

Even small failures provide clues, pointers to the fact that something is wrong, like the early sharp twinge in an otherwise healthy tooth that presages the cavity that is growing there. Most of us don't pay attention, at least not until the pain has grown constant. We can identify similar symptoms of problems in our security programs. Employees visit websites they are not supposed to, allow someone to tailgate them into a secured area without using their badge, and so forth. The event is a blip, an error, not even something to which one would apply the term failure, with all the baggage that word carries. No one expects that one small deviation to break the system. But in a HRSP, people are much more sensitive to these "weak signals" of failure, as Weick and Sutcliffe call them. They are not huge problems in and of themselves, taken individually. But they are symptomatic of much larger weakness that exists outside of what is visibly obvious.

The heart of highly reliable security is a commitment by the organization to watch closely for insignificant problems, small mistakes and flaws, and to correct and repair those small areas of weakness before they grow too large. Every time something happens that is different from what the organization expected would happen, every time the actual state of a function deviates from the anticipated state of that function, it's considered a failure. That failure represents two things. On the upside, it's an opportunity to learn about, correct, and improve the functioning of the system. On the downside, if it is not addressed, the failure is another incremental step toward the cliff.

When an HRSP embraces failure, it puts mechanisms into place to find, share, and address small problems. An HRSP's security managers tend to obsess over failure, to brood on it, with the same energy and passion that they think about success. That's not the same emotion as the general paranoia that exists throughout the security profession. Paranoia is just fear, often compounded by a sense of powerlessness. Brooding on failure in an HRSP is all about taking action, about finding out whether your paranoia is justified, and then doing something when it is. A CISO in an HRSP is never so paranoid as when everything is going along swimmingly, with no problems to be seen and sunshine on the horizon. He knows that his worst enemy is the complacent assumption that the system is sound. For him, the worst failure is not to have seen the wave coming, not to have put the clues together beforehand. So he looks all that much harder for the problems he knows must be there.

Fail Small, Fail Fast, Fail Often

The optimal failure rate in an HRSP is as close to continuously as possible. Continuous, real-time failure indicates that everything going wrong is detected and identified as it fails. Problems can be addressed with minor course corrections and incremental changes to the system. Decay is never allowed to get a major toehold inside the security program or allowed to last very long. In recent years, the security industry has put a lot of emphasis on compromises that allow attackers to sit on a system or network for months or even years, monitoring, collecting, and exfiltrating sensitive data. The principle is similar to how HROs look at failure in general. The longer a failure state is allowed to continue, the worse the larger problem becomes. Uncertainty is introduced, and grows. You can no longer effectively anticipate system outcomes, and the options available for addressing the problem diminish over time. Of course, none of this may be obvious, or even visible, to those running the system. On the surface, everything appears to be fine. If a major failure occurs, it's all the more disturbing because it feels to everyone involved like things just suddenly collapsed everywhere at once. But that's just because no one saw the rot behind the facade.

It isn't easy to spot small failures. Nor is it easy to adjust to an environment of constant, never-ending bad news, which is why most organizations are not highly reliable over the long term. Paradoxically, the fear of failure that we are ingrained to feel can coexist with equally powerful social norms about being optimistic and upbeat. Nobody likes a downer, and people who are always looking at life as a glass half-empty are seen as negative and even disruptive. We may even create a fantasy where the people who worry about what can go wrong somehow contribute to eventual failure by virtue of a self-fulfilling bad attitude. But the real choice is not whether to "turn that frown upside-down" right up to the point where a catastrophe wipes the smiles off everyone's face. Our choice is whether we want our pain doled out in small, regular doses, manageable pinches that are easily corrected with the control we have over the system but that happen more or less chronically, or we prefer our pain excruciating and all in one burst, as we are ripped apart at the seams by forces we have allowed to grow out of our control, until all we can do is try to clean up the mess afterward.

Embracing failure and the other Security FORCE key values is the essence of organizational mindfulness and cultural maturity. Mindfulness is not some spiritual nirvana, but instead it is the state of being totally and completely aware of everything that is going on and adjusting your actions at such a micro-level that you don't seem to be doing anything at all. Think of Olympic athletes, dancers, martial artists, or virtuoso musicians. One thing observers notice about these people is that they get into "the zone" where everything flows and gives the appearance that their actions are effortless. But we know they are not. Those actions are the process of years of training and practice, until they can adjust what they are doing, correct imbalances or mistakes before most of us even realize they have experienced them. When an organization achieves this state of mindfulness, it may give the impression that it can do no wrong. Every product is a hit, every business move pure genius. Look behind the curtains, and you are likely to see a system so in tune with itself that it doesn't need to wait until after something is finished to know that it is successful. That organization probably knows when things "feel wrong" and has mechanisms in place to correct problems in the moment. I've known a few security teams that could do this. But not many.

Minor Accidents and Near Misses: Tracking the Seeds of Failure

Outside of the security industry, you are much more likely to find an appreciation for identifying small failures. The safety industry, and the government agencies that regulate companies for safety purposes, has a long history of collecting incident data that the security industry would probably find incredible. Federal, state, and local agencies in the United States, as well as national and local governments around the world, are tasked with collecting and collating industrial accident statistics that are used to identify patterns and try to head off larger safety problems before they occur. The Occupational Safety and Health Administration (OSHA), the Bureau of Labor Statistics (BLS), and the National Transportation Safety Board (NTSB) are just three of the many U.S. government agencies that collect and track data about accidents and failure incidents, both small and large, in the companies they regulate.

(continues)

Minor Accidents and Near Misses: Tracking the Seeds of Failure *(continued)*

Some organizations go beyond just collecting routine accident and failure data by attempting to chart and describe the space in which small errors can turn into big, life-threatening problems. The Aviation Safety Information Analysis and Sharing (ASIAS) collaboration between MITRE, the Federal Aviation Administration (FAA), and the aviation industry is one example. The ASIAS system works to identify failure patterns that can point to systemic weakness in the overall aviation safety system. Another organization, the National Near Miss program (www.nationalnearmiss.org), collects information on near-miss failures for both firefighters and law enforcement officers.

Failure Key Value Behaviors

Taking advantage of the security value of failure, and moving toward highly reliable security, depends upon developing a culture and, more specifically, a set of behaviors that enable an organization to embrace failure and begin detecting and correcting mistakes and problems while they remain small and fixable. The Key Failure Value Behaviors defined in this chapter distill the core cultural traits of HRSPs into a measurable set of priorities and activities that will enable an organization to take advantage of failure as a learning experience and a resource, rather than waiting for the catastrophic "brutal audit" that brings disruption and destruction to the system. These behaviors are not hard to understand or even implement, given the benefits they can provide. They are

- ▶ Anticipate failures
- ▶ Seek out problems
- ▶ Reward problem reporting
- ▶ Share information about failure
- ▶ Learn from mistakes

Anticipate Failures

Most information security professionals worry. We know that many things can go wrong, and we fret over what might go wrong. We may even have specific ideas about how things can fail in the information environments with which we are familiar. But worry is different from anticipation. Worrying about some event, such as a security breach, means you believe it *could* happen, but you aren't certain. Anticipating that same event means you *know* it will happen, and you are simply waiting for it to happen, more or less comfortably (depending on how well prepared you feel). When you worry that something could possibly happen, that mental image sits in a balanced tension with the possibility that maybe it won't, which can may make you more complacent. You just can't be sure, so you might hesitate to act.

If you know something is going to happen, you behave differently. If I were to tell you, with 100 percent certainty, that tomorrow an employee will let a hacker tailgate through a locked door and that the attacker will then proceed to steal the plans for your next big product launch, you would take action. You might not prevent the incident, but you would no longer have the luxury of wondering whether or not it would occur. Anticipation spawns action in ways that fear, uncertainty, and doubt do not. Even most risk assessments done today are more functions of worry than of anticipation. We outline our risks, even try to quantify them, but we still operate under the assumptions that they may not happen at all. We think in terms of, "If *x* were to happen, here's what it would mean…"

HRSPs anticipate their worst security failures by flipping that script, by imagining the worst security failures and taking the approach, "*x* is going to happen if we don't…" (for example, "…find the problems creating the conditions for that failure" or "…take action to correct those smaller errors before they get big"). Anticipating security failures means getting people who know together to brainstorm how things can go wrong (and how they probably are already going wrong). It means writing those expectations down so that we can compare them with reality later. And it means creating the investigative mechanisms required to dig into each anticipated worst-case scenario and figure out where the clues and weak signals are today so that we can go find them and correct them.

Seek Out Problems

"Seek, and ye shall find," the verse says, and I've yet to encounter an InfoSec program that could not find problems once it started looking for them. In fairness, I've never encountered a security program that was not looking for problems. Risk assessments, penetration testing, code reviews, and audits all contribute to the search for security failures and the effort to prevent larger failures down the line. But the truth is, most organizations are not doing it enough, in the right way, or for the right reasons to qualify as Highly Reliable Security Programs.

HRSPs seek out failure because they sincerely want to find it. Failure is gold, provided you don't get crushed under an avalanche of it. Most failure seeking that I see today is half-hearted at best, and people are happiest when failure is not actually discovered. That mentality would alarm an HRSP's staff. It would mean they didn't look closely enough, or in the right places. It would mean the threats are still out there, unknown and unaddressed, allowed to grow bigger.

HRSP's cultivate failure-seeking behavior at all levels, by everyone in the organization. The security team cannot be everywhere at once, so they enlist informants all over the enterprise. Security awareness teams train people what to look out for, how to identify problems. And the security program collects and analyzes this data in a systematic and formalized way. Seeking security problems is not the job of specialized testing or audit teams, who usually can identify problems only in specific instances or only after they have reached certain thresholds. HRSP failure-seeking behavior is about trying to capture failure information nearly as soon as someone, anyone, does a double take and says, "Whoa, that was weird!"

Reward Problem Reporting

Few people are going to enthusiastically undertake an activity that doesn't benefit them in some way, much less get excited about volunteering to do something that is likely to hurt them. HRSPs encourage the reporting of failures by using the tried-and-true method of rewarding people for doing it. Security awareness teams, again, are often the frontline troops in any attempt to encourage failure reporting. Not only do these folks represent a primary interface between the security program and the rest of the company, they can also be the best means of putting a more benign and friendly face on a difficult and sensitive topic. A typical employee may feel much more comfortable confiding the fact that there are personal Wi-Fi routers installed around his open-plan workspace to the nice, friendly awareness manager he met at "Security Day" than to the CISO, or even to the geeky, dismissive support technician who fixed his laptop the last time he got a virus.

Rewarding people for reporting security failures means praising people who bring attention to the small gaps in the organization's armor, even if the person who reports that gap is the person who created or caused it. Especially if it is them. This can be an especially bitter pill for security teams to swallow, particularly when the root cause is something a security person would consider stupid or even willfully negligent. But HRSPs keep an eye on the bigger picture here, and that view states that the only thing accomplished by punishing a person for reporting a mistake is to ensure they will never report another one. Highly reliable security is far more concerned with blind spots than with criticizing the source of an invaluable piece of organizational visibility.

Rewards for security failure reporting need to be real and tangible. There are many ways to accomplish this, from building failure reporting into job descriptions and performance reviews, to offering cash or other "bounties" on reporting problems in much the way the security vulnerability market pays out for zero-day exploits, to simply calling attention to and praising people who notice ways to make things better. But however the goal is accomplished, the security value of failure cannot be realized fully unless it is a cultural value that the entire organization practices and believes in.

Share Information About Failures

People reporting about security failures is a way of sharing information with the security program or team. But HRSPs practice sharing information outward, too. Hoarding or even concealing information about security problems, for whatever reason, contributes to the uncertainty and lack of visibility that can allow small problems the space to metastasize into huge ones. Information sharing is another area where the security industry is starting to see more innovation and activity, as a result of high-profile breaches that have prompted (or forced, depending on your political views) government to start getting involved directly. Like it or not, information sharing is only going to get bigger. HRSPs don't mind this trend, because they already believe in sharing as part of the security value of failure.

I hear plenty of reasons why information sharing regarding security failures is a concern. Most of the time, the primary reason has to do with the organization's concern that by revealing incidents or vulnerabilities, it will advertise its weaknesses to potential attackers. This concern has merit in certain situations, but more often it directly contradicts lessons we have learned about how security works in closed versus open systems. Sure, an organization that publicly shares information about an *existing* vulnerability may as well hang a neon sign saying, "Here is where I am vulnerable. I have not fixed the problem, come and get me." But if you know you have a problem, why haven't you fixed it? There may, of course, be legitimate reasons for not sharing information about a vulnerability, such as the inability to fix it. But I would humbly submit, based on a quarter of a century of working in this field, that "we can't fix it" a lot of times is a disingenuous way of saying "we won't fix it," or "we choose not to fix it, because it would be too hard/expensive/ time consuming…"

HRSPs share failure information more freely because they believe what open source proponents believe about security: that more eyes on the problem generates more insight into how to fix it and more pressure to do so. It does not mean that every HRSP publishes the result of every penetration test it conducts or security incident it experiences, down to the IP addresses involved, on a public website in the interest of information sharing. Failures at that level are already a big problem because they were not detected sooner, before they could result in a compromise. Highly reliable security teams are more concerned with sharing information about how the vulnerability got there in the first place, and how it was allowed to go untreated until it reached the breaking point.

Sharing information about security failures requires that the organization set up formal mechanisms by which to exchange data and insights. While most of the information sharing discussions happening in the information security industry today have to do with sharing between separate organizations, HRSPs tend to first look more inward. Facilitating the sharing of information that could prevent a security breach altogether is much more efficacious than struggling over the best way to tell a peer organization when and how you were breached.

Learn from Mistakes

HRSPs see a large part of the security value of failure as being associated with learning opportunities...learning to understand their security programs better, learning to manage anticipated outcomes against actual outcomes, and learning where to take action to keep minor incidents from growing into major ones. Therefore, it is central to highly reliable security that the InfoSec program learn something from every failure it encounters. That may sound trite, but how many times have you seen or heard about a security problem that managed to get identified but not fixed? If we see a security policy being continually violated, how often do we try to learn why that policy is so difficult for people to follow, as opposed to simply handing down sanctions or, worse, just stop enforcing it altogether as unmanageable?

Every failure, no matter how small, has a reason behind it, something that caused a transition from a state of expected functionality to a state of unexpected functionality. In HRSPs, identified failures always trigger change—if not a direct change to people, process, or technology, then at least a change in mindset, to sensitivity. If it can, the HRSP will correct the problem by altering standard operating procedures to accommodate the new expectations that the failure has brought to light. If the HRSP can't do that, it will add the failure to the list of things that can go wrong and to which it must pay more attention in the future.

"That Report Made a Good Paperweight"

Knowing what can or is likely to fail is only as good as your capability to take action on that knowledge. If the organization cannot or will not put the information to productive use, then it becomes impossible to extract value from your failure data. One area I have seen particularly hard hit by this trend is that of vulnerability and penetration testing. It seems that, all too often, doing the test does not translate into doing something with the test.

I've worked with several companies that religiously conducted penetration and posture tests on their security. In each case, the ethical hacker team I was working with or managing would go into the company, do their work, and dutifully present their findings. The audience would get excited or frightened, depending on the findings and whether or not they felt they had known about the likelihood of particular attack vectors working or vulnerable systems being compromised. In all the reports I was involved in delivering, the findings included detailed recommendations for how to correct or otherwise avoid the small failures, errors, and mistakes that had created a space in which the hackers could cause the security posture to weaken or collapse completely. Having shown the customer what was wrong, why, and how to fix it, we would leave, not seeing the customer again for months or years, until the next scheduled test.

There were always a few companies that, upon our return, would suffer the same penetrations, the same failures, as the red team did its work. These were not just similar types of failures, or recurring patterns of vulnerability on differing systems. For some customers, the penetration testers would successfully attack and compromise the same boxes the same way, using the same exploits, as the year before. Nothing had changed at all. No one had corrected anything reported in the previous specific findings. Reasons ranged from the banal ("We didn't have enough time or people to get to that one.") to the terrifying ("That's a production machine that is central to our business, so we can't take it offline long enough to even fix the problem that allowed you to own it.")

One of the fruits of the security value of failure is insight. But insight without action is like apples left to fall from the tree but never picked up and eaten. Soon enough, no matter how much food is sitting around, you're going to starve.

Assessing Your Failure Value Behaviors

Implementing new and different organizational behavior is not as hard as changing the culture that drives those behaviors, but that does not mean the task is easy. You have to identify the behaviors you want to encourage, and then develop ways to assess and measure how prevalent they are and how widely they become adopted. And all the while you have to keep one eye on cultural influences that you may be able to harness to your purpose, or that might resist your efforts toward change by competing directly with the priorities you hope to enshrine.

The Security FORCE Survey

The Security FORCE Survey is a brief data collection instrument designed to assess whether the organization exhibits the behaviors associated with a Highly Reliable Security Program. It consists of 25 statements, divided into sections for each of the five Security FORCE values, mapped to the behaviors associated with each particular value. Respondents are asked to state their level of agreement with each statement. The five statements under Security Value of Failure are listed in the excerpt of the Security FORCE Survey shown in Figure 11-1.

Like the Security Culture Diagnostic Survey (SCDS), the Security FORCE Survey is a generalist tool, suitable for a variety of situations and audiences. It can be used by an information security team to assess behaviors related to the security program

SECURITY FORCE SURVEY

To complete this Security FORCE Survey, please indicate your level of agreement with each of the following statements regarding information security values and practices within your organization. Choose one response per statement. Please respond to all statements.

Statement	Strongly Disagree	Disagree	Neutral	Agree	Strongly Agree
Security Value of Failure					
1. I feel confident I could predict where the organization's next security incident will happen.					
2. I regularly identify security problems while doing my job.					
3. I feel very comfortable reporting security problems up the management chain.					
4. I know that security problems I report will be taken seriously.					
5. When a security problem is found, it gets fixed.					

Figure 11-1   *Security FORCE Survey statements for failure value behaviors*

goals and operations, or as a comparative tool to measure the differences between teams or organizational functions. Security behavior and culture is not unique to the InfoSec team, but applies across the entire organization (although particular cultural traits may vary a lot within the same environment). Highly reliable security also happens organization-wide, or does not, as the case may be. The Security FORCE Survey allows an enterprise to gain visibility into its reliability from a security perspective.

Scoring the Security FORCE Survey

Administering and scoring the Security FORCE Survey is not difficult. The survey can be completed by anyone in the organization, and a wider net is usually better. HRSPs are typically not organizations where security is both highly centralized and relatively isolated, so that people outside security are less aware of how things work. Security FORCE value behaviors must be embedded throughout the organization for the benefits of highly reliable security to be fully achieved. Gathering FORCE value behavior data by administering the survey throughout different areas of the enterprise will yield a much more accurate picture about how often those behaviors occur the further one gets from the official security team.

Once the survey data is collected, the organization aggregates and averages the scores for each statement, for the Security FORCE value the statement represents (Failure, Operations, etc.), and for particular demographic areas of interest (security team vs. other organizational divisions, for example, or between functional roles). Demographic analysis, of course, requires collecting demographic information as part of the survey, which may or may not be possible or desirable for reasons of resource allocation or privacy.

Since the Security FORCE Survey uses a traditional Likert scale, with a range of responses from "Strongly Disagree" to "Strongly Agree," it is possible to assign numerical scores to the data and produce average responses. I would suggest a simple 1 to 5 scale, with lower numbers indicating that the associated behavior is less likely to occur in the organization.

▶ An average score of 4 or above (most responses indicate Agree or Strongly Agree) signifies the organization exhibits behaviors found in an HRSP.

▶ An average score of 3 (most responses indicate the respondent felt Neutral) signifies the organization may or may not behave like an HRSP.

▶ An average score of 2 or below (most responses indicate Disagree or Strongly Disagree) signifies the organization does not exhibit the behaviors found in an HRSP.

In the case of failure value behaviors, then, an average score of 4 or greater indicates that the organization behaves in ways that will make it more likely to discover failures while they remain small and act on them to avoid a major security incident. A score of 2 or below, conversely, indicates that the organization may lack the behaviors associated with an HRSP and may find it difficult to discover the minor problems, failures, and mistakes that are reducing the health and stability of the system.

The Security FORCE Metrics

The Security FORCE Metrics are a set of 25 measures, also mapped to the five Security FORCE values and their associated value behaviors. These metrics can help you measure the success of your efforts to create an HRSP behavioral environment within your organization. Figure 11-2 shows the five metrics for the security value of failure.

You cannot manage what you don't measure, and even survey-based measures of behavior can be difficult to interpret and track over time. The Security FORCE Metrics are based on the artifacts and outcomes that a set of behaviors should produce if those behaviors are prevalent and embedded within an InfoSec program or the larger enterprise. By tracking these artifacts and outcomes, an organization concerned with reliability is given an additional set of evidence to use in comparison with common sense, established policies, and survey results.

SECURITY FORCE METRICS

These metrics can be used to support, verify, and validate Security FORCE behaviors within the organization. These are not the only possible metrics available, but they provide a good baseline. You should alter or adapt these measures as required and appropriate to fit your own program and environment.

Metric	Result
Security Value of Failure	
1. Number of security failure scenarios developed in the past year	
2. Number of security failures (whether or not resulting in a formal security incident) reported in the past year	
3. Ratio of security incidents with no prior failure reporting or indicators in the past year	
4. Ratio of security failure or incident data (reports, root-cause analyses, after-actions, etc.) voluntarily shared outside the information security program	
5. Ratio of security failures resulting in system changes	

Figure 11-2 *Security FORCE Metrics for failure value behaviors*

Even if all of those things indicate highly reliable security behaviors, discrepancies in the Security FORCE Metrics can point out discrepancies that should be explored further.

Using the FORCE Failure Value Metrics

The five FORCE Metrics associated with the value of failure track the identification and management of failures and errors, and serve as indicators of whether those failures are being found early enough to increase the reliability of the InfoSec program. There is no single way to use these metrics, nor do they represent the only performance indicators available to an organization. But they are a starting point for security programs that may not track comparable measures or trends. Metrics work best when they are performed over time, allowing the development of baselines and comparisons of current versus past results. Some of the FORCE Metrics specify measurement intervals, usually on an annual basis. But individual organizations must decide, given available resources and program goals and objectives, what the most appropriate uses and measurement cycles should be for each of the FORCE Metrics.

Number of security failure scenarios developed in the past year   A large part of identifying security failures is anticipating them, and HRSPs will go to great lengths not to fall victim to "failures of imagination," where a breach or incident might have been predicted with a little forethought, but was never considered. Security failure scenarios are simply (but not necessarily simple) brainstormed ideas of events, incidents, or breaches. They are the extensions of the threat models and risk scenarios already undertaken by many organizations, but HRSPs design their failure scenarios with an eye on the details of small failures that will likely occur on the way to the big event. The goal is to develop an idea of the small signs that the big failure is coming. The more scenarios that an organization takes the time to consider and develop over a period of time, the more likely they can spot telltale warning signs early on in the failure cycle.

Number of security failure scenarios (whether or not resulting in a formal security incident) reported in the past year   The purpose of failure scenario development isn't just security team members telling scary stories around a campfire, so to speak. Some failure scenarios are more likely to occur than others, and this metric allows an organization to measure the predictive power and accuracy of its failure brainstorming activities. HRSPs report failures, both small and large, and these failures should be correlated with the scenarios that have been developed internally. If the security team is predicting scenarios with identifiable failure markers, then detecting and managing those minor incidents before the scenario fully develops (or even if a failure does occur, but the signs were noted beforehand), that's a good thing. It shows the enterprise imagination has a healthy awareness of its own weaknesses and can improve those insights.

Ratio of security incidents with no prior failure reporting or indicators in the past year The organization wants to see expected failures being identified and reported, even if a security event proves unavoidable. If, on the other hand, the organization is experiencing security incidents that were never considered, or not observing the minor problems it expects to see associated with an event that does occur, then that's bad. Security incidents should be tracked and correlated with applicable or related scenarios. An organization that doesn't see any incidents coming, or that expects some incidents but gets ones that are completely different, must question its prognostic skills. An HRSP will want this metric to remain very low. Whether or not an incident proves avoidable, the first step in higher reliability is to make it more visible, sooner.

Ratio of security failure or incident data (reports, root-cause analyses, after-actions, etc.) voluntarily shared outside the information security program I made the case earlier in the chapter that information sharing outside the InfoSec program is vital in order to get different perspectives and insights about how security is working within the organization. Sharing security-related information with non-security stakeholders may make some InfoSec team members a bit nervous, but the potential payoff for pushing that comfort zone can be significant. This measure provides a simple gauge for determining whether a security team is emulating the more open, advice-seeking failure behaviors of an HRSP, or is continuing to be insular and closed off from the rest of the organization about security activities and challenges.

Ratio of security failures resulting in system changes It doesn't matter how much the organization sees what's going wrong if it doesn't take action, just as knowing you're driving towards a cliff won't mean much if you don't turn the wheel or hit the brake. Security incidents and data breaches almost always result in system changes, usually large ones. This metric helps the organization understand the extent to which change is being implemented when faced with smaller, more minor failures. Remember that HRSPs aren't just looking to identify small failures. They want to take action while they are still small and the costs of change are less burdensome. Unfortunately, many organizations take just the opposite approach, neglecting to make changes because the problem appears so small. If an enterprise scores low on this measure, that can be an indicator that things do not change until they are forced to, usually as a result of tiny failures adding up to big problems that can no longer be ignored.

Improving Your Failure Value Behaviors

Once you have identified the security behaviors that are most likely to make your security program more highly reliable and have compared the way your organization behaves day to day with these desired behaviors through the survey, measurements, or other means, you are likely to find areas where you want to improve. Improving security behavior does not happen overnight, and it does not happen by fiat. We all know how hard it is to just change our own habits and comfort zones. Changing them for an entire organization is that much more daunting.

Embed the Security Value of Failure into People

People-centric security puts human beings at the top of the security value chain, and they are going to be your first, best source of value when it comes to reaping the fruits of the security value of failure. As I have described throughout this chapter, the real value of failure has everything to do with finding it early enough and often enough to learn from it and change direction before disaster strikes, like a ship's navigator keeping track of currents and wind to make micro adjustments to the ship's course so that it never gets close to danger. Several approaches can be leveraged to make it easier for people to adopt security failure value behaviors.

Reeducate People on What It Means to Fail

Cultural beliefs and assumptions drive behavior, so changing behavior means attacking cultural resistance. Organizations can encourage people to value failure more actively and effectively by redefining what it means to fail in the organization. A key message here should be that not all failures are equal, and that some are actually desirable, since they are destined to happen anyway. By turning small failures into learning opportunities, and reserving fear and avoidance strategies for those big failures that the organization anticipates, a feedback loop can be created. People will understand that there are certain outcomes that are truly unacceptable, that must never happen. Everything else is fair game, so long as it creates an environment of knowledge that can be used to prevent and avoid the unacceptable.

Set Leadership Examples

Few things will encourage a person to behave in a certain way more than seeing other people do it, especially people who that person respects or wants to impress. Organizational leaders like the CISO have enormous power to influence, simply by living up to the ideals and requirements that they set for everyone else. By walking the walk, such leaders encourage imitation. So leaders in the organization, especially security leaders, should be the first to embrace the security value of failure. This means changing the way they deal with failures that occur, but also being more open and transparent about their own failures and those of the security program. When the CISO is seen as welcoming bad news, even needing it to do her job correctly, then people will share it more willingly.

Open Up Communication

The security value of failure only gets realized in an environment of open and free information sharing. Encouraging that sharing, and rewarding people for doing it, is part of the solution. But channels must exist for the message to get through. If failure information, no matter how welcome, never leaves the informal sharing environment of the cafeteria or the water cooler, it will not get codified or distributed in a way that gives the best results. Security awareness teams are often the best positioned to create and manage communications involving the security value of failure. By acting as an interface between stakeholders, they are in the best position to encourage open dialogue, understand challenges, and deconflict problems that may arise.

Further Reading

▶ Paynter, Ben. "Close Calls Are Near Disasters, Not Lucky Breaks." Wired.com. Available at www.wired.com.

CHAPTER 7

The Security Value of Operations

A s indicated in Chapter 10, the second key security value in the Security FORCE Behavioral Model is operations. As with the key security value of failure described in Chapter 11, the FORCE Model challenges us to reconsider our notions regarding what operations means for information security. Of all the Security FORCE values, operations is probably the one that many InfoSec programs think they do best. The industry is increasingly populated with sophisticated (and expensive) security operations centers (SOCs) to monitor activity, combined with dashboards, alerts, reviews, and operational assessments at multiple enterprise levels to maintain security situational awareness. Many companies swear by operational visibility in their information security programs, and with the plethora of available tools, from traditional security event and incident management (SEIM) tools to enterprise risk management (ERM) software to sophisticated threat intelligence systems like OpenSOC, there's a feeling that the options to improve InfoSec visibility are better than they have ever been.

If we were talking about technology only, I would tend to agree. Our tools and capabilities for creating situational awareness around IT infrastructures have evolved to an amazing degree over the years, and are improving all the time. The problem is that operational activities are not limited to technology and infrastructure. They include all the messier components of people and process as well, things like strategies, policies, relationships, and conflicts. If the primary value we derive from the security value of operations is limited to our visibility into technical systems, then we are missing an enormous amount of insight, and probably those very insights that matter most in terms of whether or not our security will be effective in the long term.

What Is the Security Value of Operations?

To be highly reliable, an InfoSec program needs to understand more than just its technology landscape. To behave in ways that will enable the organization to experience fewer severe failures and bounce back more quickly from those that do occur, security teams need more operational awareness than they have today. Technology is one component. Many security programs are at least partly correct in their assertion that they have a good handle on operational awareness. The problem they face is not their ability to observe all the things their tools and methods are designed to monitor, or to interpret the data (usually technical) they are collecting. The problem is their inability to see things they are not looking at, to understand the places where no data is being collected, and to know the difference between what they think is happening (because a policy or a technology control is in place, for example) and what is actually occurring "on the ground" (such as everyone ignoring the policy or finding ways to circumvent the control). Eliminating blind spots like these by redefining the notion of operational visibility leverages and maximizes the security value of operations.

Operational Power

Where does information security exist? Where is it accomplished? Does information security happen in strategy, as organizations decide how to best protect their programs and formulate plans to do so? Does it happen on the wire, as the bits rush by in electromagnetic pulses of data? Does it happen at the interface with adversaries, as threats cross from the theoretical to the real? The answer is that information security happens in all of these places, but none of them can be seen as comprehensively describing an organization's security posture. Security is behavior, a decision being made and a response to that decision. Even when that decision is made by a machine, it is the result of a human decision being made somewhere else, someone deciding on a threshold or building logic into a programmatic response. Security operations, therefore, are inherently people-centric. And Highly Reliable Security Programs (HRSPs) know this. That's why they pay all sorts of special attention to the decision interfaces in their security programs. That's where the magic (black or white) happens.

Decision interfaces at the strategic level are less operational than those made on the front lines of activity. A CISO's decision that his company needs to reduce phishing attacks carries less operational weight than an employee's decision about whether or not to click a link in an e-mail. Power dynamics tend to be turned on their head at the operational level, with the individual user or operator having more influence in the moment than the managers and strategists at higher levels of the organizational chart. One person can destroy an entire business if, at the moment of decision, that person is the one with their finger on the wrong button. HRSPs aren't afraid of being accused of paying more attention to the trees than to the forest. Fires always start small, and HRSPs don't want to wait until half the forest is burning to notice the smoke.

Sensitivity to Operations

The literature about high-reliability organizations (HROs) introduced in Chapter 10 identifies sensitivity to operations as a principle, and HRSPs do their best to be sensitive about what's really happening when security decisions are being made. The idea is tied very closely to the FORCE value of failure, because you can't catch small errors and mistakes if you aren't watching for them at the levels where small failures happen. If the security program's visibility kicks in only when the attackers who have infiltrated your systems for the past nine months start suddenly exfiltrating terabytes of data, that is not the appropriate level of detected failure. And if there was no possible visibility at the level of technology that could have identified failures before that point, it is probably time to start looking at visibility on other levels.

HRSPs are much more comfortable with uncertainty and ambiguity than are more typical InfoSec programs. In their book *Managing the Unexpected*, Weick and Sutcliffe described how one of the greatest inhibitors to operational awareness in HROs is an "engineering culture" that prioritizes and favors certain types of information and knowledge, namely that which is hard, quantitative, formal, and easily measurable, over supposedly softer and "qualitative" information that is less reliable but closer to everyday human experience. These findings are just as applicable to information security, and in Parts I and II of this book I've made the same point regarding the qualitative/quantitative dichotomy in information security professionals.

For HRSPs, qualitative versus quantitative is a false dichotomy. Having access to reams of quantitative data means nothing if those data *don't tell you what you need to know*. And what we often need to know is why things are happening in a certain way, how relationships, motivations, and assumptions are leading people to behave like they do and to make the decisions they make. These are not the sorts of insights one is able to get just by analyzing quantitative data. Instead, HRSPs seek a hybrid form of knowledge. Security professionals who see the word "operations" and immediately think technology products or SOCs, but fail to consider people and process functions such as how people communicate or how they improvise to accommodate conflicting priorities, miss the majority of the operational picture. Technology visibility is important, but so is knowing about how people interact and communicate even when technology is not involved. Operations is never limited to what's going on in one particular area of the organization, such as the network; it is about knowing what is going on everywhere in the organization.

In addition to linking technology operations and other operational functions, an HRSP will explicitly link more people-centric conditions to operational awareness. Operational visibility at the level of human beings is more chaotic and less predictable, but that doesn't mean it's any less real in terms of the organization's security posture. Knowing what is happening at the level of interpersonal and organizational relationships, of politics even, is another important aspect of operational visibility. An organization runs on knowledge, and if full knowledge is not sought out or if a certain type of knowledge is deliberately ignored because it's difficult to acquire or certain stakeholders feel uncomfortable giving it or asking for it, that's a problem, because it means the enterprise doesn't have what it needs to make a fully informed decision.

Expectations and Reality

HRSPs are always worried that things are not going as planned, so they constantly feel the need to test their assumptions. "We have a policy of data classification? Great. Let's go find out how much of our data is actually classified the way the policy says it should be." Or, "The auditors tell us we have the right combination of perimeter controls? Excellent. Let's hire some penetration testers to make sure those controls can really keep people out." Or, "If we are not hearing any bad news from employees, is that because everything is perfect or because employees fear being labeled a troublemaker if they point out that something is broken?"

One big differentiator with HRSPs is that, where other InfoSec programs may view the constant bickering over budget and resources, the political jockeying between divisions and stakeholders, and the silos and fiefdoms of everyday management as intractable problems that can't be overcome, HRSPs view these problems as vulnerabilities to the organization that are as serious as any zero-day vulnerability. Competing values left unaddressed and unmanaged only serve to demonstrate the fragility and instability of the organization's security posture. And when an attack or incident puts stress on that system, it fails.

The security value of operations comes from identifying small failures no matter where they originate. That includes things like interpersonal relationships and organizational rivalries, not just system logs and IT dashboards. Warning signals are warning signals, so HRSPs tend to deploy many more sensors across a much wider spectrum than just IT or information security systems. Knowing that people often say one thing but do something else, HRSPs look beyond official strategies, formal plans, or documented policies. They want to know how the work of security really gets done around the enterprise.

Security Operations "Unplugged"

An information security operations director in one company I worked with had his own way of testing operational reality. Walking around the company, he liked to look out for machines he didn't recognize. It was a decent-sized company, with a large IT operational footprint across multiple physical buildings, and he regularly came across anomalous boxes, sometimes sitting in a data center, sometimes running underneath a desk that nobody owned, and once even one propped up on a couple of telephone directories, sitting lonely and humming in the corner of a common room. When the director came across such a machine, he would ask around to see who owned it. If no owner could be identified, he would see if the machine was registered in the IT asset inventory, which, by the director's own admission, was pretty spotty. Finally, after a day or two, if the director could not find someone to claim the device, he would take action. "I unplug them," he told me, "and wait for the screaming to start..."

The director figured he had done real harm only two or three times in the dozens of times he had resorted to his extreme version of operational review. But he remained unapologetic. "People get angry, of course, and try to get me in trouble. But the fact is, we have a process we try to follow for keeping track of our systems, and when they don't follow it, they put the company at more risk than I ever could. We have to know what's going on under our own roof. I can tell you it never happens twice to the same team."

Operations Key Value Behaviors

Just as with the security value of failure discussed in Chapter 11, there are key behaviors associated with HRSPs that maximize the security value of operations. These behaviors have everything to do with trying to know more about what is really going on in the organization and to use that knowledge to hunt for the small discrepancies, disconnects, and errors that will slowly grow into large-scale security failures. The behaviors that characterize the value of operations include

▶ Keep your eyes open
▶ Form a bigger picture
▶ "Listen" to the system

► Test expectations against reality
► Share operational assessments

Keep Your Eyes Open

According to the old saying, familiarity breeds contempt, and an irony of information security is that we can become so accustomed to certain operational realities, even highly dysfunctional ones, that we begin to take them for granted, maybe even begin to ignore them. Defining culture as "the way we do things around here" does not guarantee that we're always doing things well, or smart, or securely. I've never worked with a security team that couldn't tell me at least one story about something they did that they thought was ill-advised or even dumb, and that they worried would come back to bite them. The difference in an HRSP is not that everything is always done right. HRSPs just worry more about what they are doing wrong, look for those symptoms, and refuse to allow them to go untreated. Dysfunction, complacence, and competing values may or may not result in a direct threat to information security, but bad behaviors create space in which threats can find a foothold and cause problems.

How does an organization keep its eyes open? Let's start by addressing what are the organization's "eyes." How does it "see" what is happening with its security? Don't get hung up on the metaphor. As a key value behavior, keeping your eyes open just means taking advantage of all the sensors and information inputs available to the enterprise and the security program, and implementing more when they are needed. One legacy of the technology branch of the security family tree is the wide variety of tools and products that can be used to generate information security data. Very few security products today don't include data export capabilities of one kind or another. If we think simply in terms of SIEM products, an entire industry of technology systems is available to process and manage this data. If anything, the problem is one of too much information. InfoSec organizations probably complain more about information overload and too much event data to manage than they do about the availability of security data. In some ways, this is the result of relying too much on a single source of visibility. It's as though we've decided that of all our senses, only our eyesight counts, but then we blind ourselves by staring straight into the sun.

HRSPs don't rely on only one sensory input, no matter how sophisticated or data rich it is. Being people-centric by nature, HRSPs also tend to be wary of information and sensors that are abstracted or removed from human involvement. This is not to say that automation is untrustworthy, but only that there's rarely anything that is purely automatic. Either someone has to interpret the results of the automated process or someone has built their own interpretation of things into the process as they automated it. Either way, believing that you have eliminated human involvement is misleading.

So HRSPs look for additional sensors, preferably of the human persuasion. Under these circumstances, many new and interesting sources of data become available, including group meetings, face-to-face conversations, and a host of electronically mediated social interactions, from telephones and telepresence to e-mail and instant messaging. These sources all become potential organizational telemetry streams, along with the documents we create, the performance measures we assign, and the results of evaluations and reviews. Many organizations take these sources of collective sensemaking for granted as mere artifacts of operations, not sources of operational insight themselves. For HRSPs, every one of these sources becomes a tool with which to take advantage of the security value of operations.

Form a Bigger Picture

Information overload is not the only barrier standing between an InfoSec program and the security value of operations. CISOs and security owners also face the related but opposing problem of "information poverty," which happens when an organization's information or information processing infrastructure (not just the IT infrastructure) is not good enough to get, process, and use information effectively. In such an environment, decision making is weakened, starved of its most important fuel. It may seem contradictory to say that a security program could simultaneously suffer from both too much information and not enough information, but if you think about the way security works these days, it actually makes sense. As I've alluded to, we feast on technical and machine-generated information but don't consume enough data from other sources. The result is an operational big picture that is as narrow as our informational diet. The theory of information poverty was first applied to individuals at a socio-economic level, but I've found it applies pretty well to information security too.

We only overcome information poverty by deliberately consuming more varied information and seeking out a bigger picture of operational reality. One difference between traditional notions of information poverty, where people are not given adequate access to information resources by the state or through the effects of economic poverty, and the notion as applied to information security is that the latter tends to starve itself. Like kids who make a face at healthier or unfamiliar foods, InfoSec professionals tend to stick with the things we know and like.

But a good operational information diet is omnivorous, and the first place a truly people-centric security program will look is the area of data-rich interpersonal relationships that exist both within the security program and between security and other parts of the organization.

HRSPs turn relationships into feedback networks. Meetings become sensors. Conversations become telemetry feeds. E-mails and meeting minutes become logs. Enterprise intelligence from these sources is less about the network plane or endpoint activity and more about the cultural plane and political activity. The former may tell you what your users are doing, but the latter helps you understand why they are doing it. Do people know things are failing but are afraid to say so? Does the root of a security problem lie not in an external advanced persistent threat (APT) but in the fact that two rival directors hate one another and covet their VP's job? By making its big picture wider and less dependent on technology infrastructure, an HRSP gives itself more options for operational analysis and response. Competing security priorities and cultures will never come to light on the basis of syslog data—the format and content of that information simply does not lend itself to what drives people to choose their project completion bonus over their security responsibilities, to use an example from earlier in the book. It's like expecting someone in a staff meeting to tell you who is connected to the wireless network by sniffing the air. Different queries require different tools.

People tend to complicate the things they get involved in, which both benefits and challenges the notion of a bigger, wider picture. I think engineers prefer consuming relatively uncomplicated technology data precisely because it is uncomplicated. It's hard to argue with a histogram. The opinions and beliefs tossed around in a staff meeting are trickier, and often the easiest way to deal with them is to make opinion a less-trusted source of security operational insight. We need to use both.

"Listen" to the System

Continuing the analogy of the senses, HRSPs tend to do a better job of "listening" to what their systems are trying to tell them. These organizations are particularly tuned to detecting the small hints and subtexts within an operational conversation that provide evidence of things going wrong. In any conversation, there is more to the process than just the words that are being said. Inflection and demeanor play an important part of interpersonal communication, and organizations have their own versions of hidden meanings, hint dropping, and body language.

"Well, That's Just Your Hypothesis, Man!"

Imagine if we replaced a single word in the InfoSec team's lexicon, changing "opinion" to "hypothesis." We think of opinions as being completely subjective and relatively untrustworthy. (My father, a sailor, had a wonderfully crude aphorism about opinions, invoking certain bodily orifices and implying particular odors that would be inappropriate to quote directly.) A matter of opinion is a matter that can never really be resolved, at least until one party changes their opinion. A hypothesis, however, is something different. It is an opinion of sorts, but one that can be tested. Indeed, it almost must be tested, or why hypothesize in the first place? I complain regularly that information security is insufficiently scientific in its approach to things. So, in the name of the security value of operations, I'm making a challenge. Let there be no more opinions. The next time you hear one, consider it a hypothesis. If you can't convince the person who holds it to test it to your satisfaction, then take it upon yourself to disprove it—with empirical data and repeatable experimentation. We really need to do this more often in our industry. At least, that's my hypothesis.

One of the most common approaches InfoSec programs take toward listening to the system is the use of operational dashboards. Dashboards give (or are supposed to give) an organization a snapshot in time of all the measures and indicators that matter to it. Dashboards are meant to be automated, approaching real-time feedback loops that help us manage against the workings of the system. But dashboards face a classic "garbage in, garbage out" dilemma. If your metrics and indicators are focused on the wrong things, your dashboard is essentially useless. It may be impressive, captivating even, in its sophistication and beauty, but it can lull you into a false sense of visibility and insight. There are many information security–related dashboards marketed on the Web that show amazing views of things like threat sources or vulnerability counts, but most provide relatively little value beyond impressive marketing for their creators.

I'm a critic of what I call *dashboardification*, which is the creation of metrics and dashboards for little other reason than the InfoSec program feels a need or is required to give someone something "operational" to look at. If the security team has not thought hard about what it really wants to know or needs to measure to ensure effectiveness, the result tends to be a histogram built out of whatever data is currently available or most easily collected. That tends to mean technology-based logging, which produces the myopic visibility I discussed in the previous section. The organization may be able to see when a network device or a security product gets overwhelmed with traffic or events, for example, but it will miss when people are hitting their limits, as Clara the software developer from earlier in the book did at the end of her project.

HRSPs use operational data of all kinds, from a variety of sources, in an attempt to manage what is really going on in their systems and not just what is represented in a policy, a diagram, or a technology product dashboard. HRSPs do look to traditional sources of information, from logs to SEIMs to SOCs, but supplement them with people-centric tools such as sentiment analysis of internal communications, "open discussion" sessions built into regular meetings and performance reviews, and anonymous suggestion boxes (physical or digital) where people can bring up problems they feel are important but may not feel comfortable sharing publicly. If dashboards are to be developed, they should be designed to

- ▶ Identify early patterns and signs of operational instability and potential failure for information security, regardless of source (people, process, or technology)

- ▶ Give actionable intelligence about information security operational problems so that the organization can effect incremental changes

- ▶ Include coverage of all systems important to the operational success of information security, not just the systems that are easiest to build dashboards around

HRSPs are constantly worried about whether the complex operational beast they are riding is getting away from them. They want to know when things are beginning to slip out of their control, and they want the ability to call on defined resources to bring things back under control quickly. This means keeping track of required levels of effort and correlating them with availability of resources. Listening to the system means identifying when people, process, and technology operations need more or less management over time and being prepared to meet that demand with as little delay and disruption as possible.

Test Expectations Against Reality

HRSPs test their expectations against reality, another behavior that maximizes the security value of operations. They ask probing questions that avoid taking operational activities for granted: What is the organization's real security posture?

If a people, process, or technology control is tested, will it work as well as it does on paper? When people are faced with information security impacting decisions, especially if they have to juggle competing priorities, will they choose security? And how can we know, empirically and with evidence, the answer to all these questions? HRSPs suspect that things probably won't always go as expected, and they attempt to either confirm or disconfirm that suspicion. This behavioral process begins with the age-old need to document and formalize the InfoSec program itself. Without specific policies, standards, guidelines, and all the rest of the bureaucratic structure that defines the assumptions the security program holds, it is impossible to verify whether or not those assumptions reflect operational reality. Before you can test your expectations and assumptions, you have to know what they are. HRSPs don't look at documentation as just a formality or as a necessary evil, but rather as the code that makes up the organizational OS. Poorly crafted and poorly documented code can cause problems, both for software and for people.

Once you define what you believe is happening or expect will happen, you can test against those expectations. If a policy exists, you can test your expectation that it is enforced. Where standards have been set, you can gather evidence that people and systems do or do not adhere to them. Security teams already perform audits of this kind against certain expectations. A PCI DSS or SOX audit is a test of the expectation that the organization has met the requirements of those regulatory frameworks. A penetration test audits the expectation that networks and endpoints are properly secured against attack. HRSPs do not do things fundamentally differently in this regard; they simply do them more often and in more situations. Those situations include the psychological, behavioral, and cultural dimensions of the organization. We expect, for example, that our developers are completing their security tests on the code they write. How often do we check to make sure that they have enough time and resources to be able to accomplish those tests?

Resources like time, money, and employee allocations (as opposed to the employees themselves) don't think, or exhibit, operational awareness. They don't go where they are needed, but where they are directed. Many organizations undergo annual budget process cycles, doling out cash and headcount based on experiences from the past or predictions about the future over continuous chunks of time. Few organizations review and assign resources in cycles that are closer to operational real time. The result can be scenarios, especially when the system is under duress, where lack of money and people can erode the organization's ability to respond and react. HRSPs work to make resource allocation more operationally sensitive, more capable of flexible response.

Closely related to the idea of flexible resources to meet shifting operational demand is the idea of appropriate resource coverage. It is a tacit expectation that the security organization has enough resources to manage security for the entire organization. This begins with visibility. There's no way InfoSec program staff can manage security operations at a comprehensive level if they don't have sufficient resources to see what those operations entail. Things will be ignored, not out of negligence, but out of necessity. Naturally, no one gets everything they want, and security is not the only organizational function facing resource scarcity. But many information security owners feel as if getting blood from stones is only slightly harder than getting headcount or money from senior management.

Exceptions to the Rules

I have seen the security value of operations embraced in some companies while going unrealized and unrecognized in many others. When organizations really capture that value and understand their operations, it can lift a security professional's heart. When they don't, thinking about the ramifications can scare the hell out of that same professional.

Although I've not come across many HRSPs in the industry, I have encountered a few. One of the best that I consulted for functioned in a highly reliable way, not because the CISO was a business culture wonk or had a degree in organizational behavior. In fact, he wasn't even a CISO. The CIO was responsible for information security in this organization, and he had a small team with which to manage the challenges. He also had a simple, driving principle that informed everything he did and every goal that he set for his team, whether they had direct security responsibilities or not.

"I want my people to go home at night and be with their families," he told me during the engagement. "I don't believe in the whole firefighter thing. You find people who take pride in always having to respond to crises, who will put in 20 hours straight and wear it like some badge of accomplishment. But I think if you had to spend 20 hours straight fixing something that went wrong, that's not something to be proud of."

This CIO had implemented a comprehensive, cascading balanced scorecard performance system that reached from himself all the way down to each individual contributor. The security staff had individual balanced scorecards just like everyone else responsible for IT's contribution to the business, and the company managed those scorecards religiously. The system didn't prevent

(*continues*)

Exceptions to the Rules *(continued)*

things from ever going wrong, but it kept problems manageable by identifying problem trends early in the failure cycle and gave the CIO visibility and choice before things could go off the rails.

At the other end of the spectrum was a company I worked with years ago. On paper, this firm had a comprehensive set of configuration standards that were both strict and highly secure. Everything had to be hardened before it could be deployed. Things were locked down so tightly, in fact, that some internal groups often complained that security restricted some basic business functionality. In a well-intentioned effort to accommodate different business needs, an exception process had been created, one that allowed IT teams with a legitimate business need to alter or ignore the required configurations. By the time I met the CISO, this process had been in place for years. The engagement revealed, among other things, that over time the criteria for getting an exception had slackened considerably, to the point where it had become trivial. As a result, over two-thirds of the systems reviewed did not meet the configuration standards. Years of operational myopia had created a state in which the exception was literally the norm, and the standards that the company expected to be in place were, in reality, outliers.

Share Operational Assessments

The final key value behavior for operations doesn't require that an InfoSec program build anything new or devote resources to additional capabilities, at least not at first. All that is needed is an existing set of operational assessments regarding security within the organization and an open mind. Yet, with so few requirements, this behavior may be one of the hardest to encourage within information security. There are at least two reasons that it is difficult. The first is that security programs hate to share, and the second is that what security programs do share is often not something others want.

InfoSec programs know how to report information, and most do it regularly in some way, shape, or form. But reporting is not the same thing as sharing. To report implies that information is being required or demanded of the security program, that the purpose is for accountability and oversight. Sharing information is a more voluntary activity, performed out of motivations having more to do with collaboration and a sense of common purpose. For HRSPs, one of the first barriers that has been overcome in the process is security's natural instinct of paranoia and mistrust.

HRSPs share operational information and assessments, including information about problems and failures, because they want feedback on their activities, not because they are forced to receive it. And they want that feedback from a variety of sources, not just from those who can obviously benefit the HRSP through budgetary or resource control. Users, other business process owners, partners, and customers are all valuable sources of information that can help the security program understand where a problem or insufficient operational visibility is increasing security risk. This knowledge seeking requires security teams to accept that other stakeholders may not feel the same level of urgency as they do, and to be willing to accept criticism and skepticism about the security team's operational plans and activities. Inviting other people to criticize your hard work is difficult for everyone (trust me, as an author, I know firsthand), but it is also the only way to make that work better.

A more difficult problem to solve in sharing operational assessments involves the quality of those assessments. If the InfoSec program does not do many operational assessments, or does not do them well or in a way that is comprehensible to those outside of security, then sharing those assessments can be a bit of a nonstarter. This is a problem in security information reporting, too. I am often asked to help on the security metrics side by assisting a security team in developing better performance indicators and program measures to present to senior management as part of required reporting. Too often, the security team struggles to show progress, or to lobby for more resources, or even to stimulate the interest of senior enterprise leaders, because their operational assessments are either incomplete or inscrutable to senior business owners. For security programs with inadequate assessment capabilities, this becomes the exception to my earlier statement that this key value behavior doesn't require doing anything new. To effectively share information, you have to make that information accessible to others, both physically and functionally. The good news is that sharing even bad assessments can be useful. If the people from whom you are asking feedback tell you they can't give any because they don't understand your assessments or aren't interested in the information presented, you are immediately provided some useful information that leads to these obvious questions: How can I help you understand them better? What do you care about that I can provide?

Denial Ain't Just a River...

One of the more interesting engagements I've been on involved a side-by-side test of operational visibility and reality. Although we didn't intend it that way, I found that my team was involved with a high-level governance and controls assessment at the same time that a penetration testing team was doing their assessment of the customer company. We were all staying at the same hotel and hanging out together after work each day and, naturally, we began to talk shop. After a few days of onsite work, I mentioned to one of the security engineers doing the ethical hacking that I was pretty impressed with how well the company managed its security. In particular, I was struck by how stringently they compartmentalized things both at the level of information classification and at the level of network segmentation. "Are you kidding?" the engineer smiled. "Their network might as well be flat! We can go anywhere."

As we started trading notes, reality set in. On paper, the company's security infrastructure looked rock solid. Policies defined acceptable activity, standards controlled who could put what where and how they could do it, and guidelines encouraged everyone to make decisions that benefited the protection of organizational assets. In practice, the security the company was so proud of essentially only existed on paper. IT was run in silos, rules were not uniformly enforced, and the business put more emphasis on functionality than security. Like the company mentioned earlier that had excessive exception processes, this company had allowed important operational gaps to develop. More importantly, everyone in the governance interviews either assumed that the infrastructure was working just as it was supposed to, or knew it was not and chose not to say so for reasons of their own.

When it came time to report the findings, some of the management team refused to accept them. "You found isolated problems," they countered. "Every organization has a few problems." Operational blind spots were so pronounced that even when faced with evidence, these individuals found them impossible to reconcile with their assumptions. The alternative was just too disturbing and humiliating to endure, in essence an admission that for years the security team had not been doing its job as well as it believed it was.

Assessing Your Operations Value Behaviors

Like the security value of failure, discussed in Chapter 11, the security value of operations and the other Security FORCE values can be assessed and measured using the Security FORCE diagnostic tools that I have created. The Security FORCE Survey and the Security FORCE Metrics provide empirical evidence of how prevalent and extensive the FORCE behaviors are within an organization and how closely the organization is adhering to the principles of an HRSP.

Scoring the Operations Value Behavior Survey

The Security FORCE Survey includes statements related to the security value of operations. The five statements under Security Value of Operations are listed in the sample of the Security FORCE Survey shown in Figure 12-1.

Remember from Chapter 11 that the Security FORCE Survey uses a Likert scale with a range of responses ("Strongly Disagree" to "Strongly Agree") that allows those conducting the survey to assign numerical scores, such as 1 through 5,

SECURITY FORCE SURVEY

To complete this Security FORCE Survey, please indicate your level of agreement with each of the following statements regarding information security values and practices within your organization. Choose one response per statement. Please respond to all statements.

Statement	Strongly Disagree	Disagree	Neutral	Agree	Strongly Agree
Security Value of Operations					
1. I know that someone is constantly keeping watch over how secure the organization is.					
2. I am confident that information security in the organization actually works the way that people and policies say it does.					
3. I feel like there are many experts around the organization willing and able to help me understand how things work.					
4. Management and the security team regularly share information about security assessments.					
5. Management stays actively involved in security and makes sure appropriate resources are available.					

Figure 12-1 *FORCE Value Survey statements for operations value behaviors*

to the survey responses and produce average levels of agreement among all survey participants:

▶ An average score of 4 or above (most responses indicate Agree or Strongly Agree) signifies the organization exhibits behaviors found in an HRSP.

▶ An average score of 3 (most responses indicate the respondent felt Neutral) signifies the organization may or may not behave like an HRSP.

▶ An average score of 2 or below (most responses indicate Disagree or Strongly Disagree) signifies the organization does not exhibit the behaviors found in an HRSP.

For operations value behaviors, an average score of 4 or greater indicates that the organization behaves in ways that will make it better equipped to understand how things really work within the security environment, and to identify errors and operational patterns that could result in a failure. This increased operational sensitivity not only makes it more likely that the organization will be able to detect small failures while they remain small, but also makes it easier for the organization to detect them. A score of 2 or below indicates that the organization is not behaving like an HRSP, and therefore may lack operational visibility, may mistake what is expected or assumed for what is actually occurring operationally, and may be slower to respond to failures and events than would a more highly reliable program.

FORCE Value Metrics for Operations

In addition to using the assessment scores of the Security FORCE Survey to gauge the security value of operations, an organization can track the Security FORCE Metrics associated with operations to provide additional measures of HRSP behavioral alignment. These five metrics are shown in Figure 12-2.

Using the FORCE Operations Value Metrics

The five FORCE Metrics associated with the value of operations track the organization's capabilities for improved visibility into a broader range of operational information security behaviors, and for identifying discrepancies between what is expected operationally within the InfoSec program and what is actually taking place within organizational systems and processes. As with the other FORCE Metrics, there is no "right" way to measure and the measures I have created, including suggested time intervals, are not exhaustive. The organization should use them and adapt them as appropriate.

SECURITY FORCE METRICS

These metrics can be used to support, verify, and validate Security FORCE behaviors within the organization. These are not the only possible metrics available, but they provide a good baseline. You should alter or adapt these measures as required and appropriate to fit your own program and environment.

Metric	Result
Security Value of Operations	
1. Level of security staff coverage for the organization (size of program, breadth of responsibility, systems managed, etc.)	
2. Number of security operations reviews completed in the past year	
3. Ratio of formally documented security operations or processes	
4. Ratio of security operational assessments shared outside the security group	
5. Average time to address operational instabilities	

Figure 12-2 *FORCE Value Metrics for operations value behaviors*

Level of security staff coverage for the organization (size of program, breadth of responsibility, systems managed, etc.) I've known big companies that had large, centralized InfoSec teams who were responsible for every aspect of protecting systems and data throughout the organization. I've known others of comparable size where the security team was two or three people. Every organization must decide for itself the best structure for organizing information security, but the operational fact is that fewer people cannot observe, explore, or test as much as larger teams, assuming enterprises of equal size. Automation can help, but for reasons I discussed earlier in the chapter, automated security operations carry their own visibility risks. This metric is not prescriptive, and does not imply a magic number for effective security staffing. But it can help an organization understand why operational visibility may be lacking. Like anything else, information security is something of a numbers game, and you can only do so much more with so much less for so long.

Number of security operations reviews completed in the past year This metric does not refer to detailed operational reporting, but rather to overall reviews of InfoSec operational effectiveness. Several respected InfoSec governance frameworks, including ISO 27001, require regular and comprehensive reviews of the security program as a best practice for information security management. Organizations collect a lot of tactical data every day, but it is necessary sometimes to consider all of this from a strategic perspective. Is the data giving us what we need, in terms of visibility and in terms of actionable intelligence or predictive evidence? How can we make InfoSec operations better, or improve and expand sources of visibility?

Most organizations tend to do this sort of review annually, although in large organizations comprehensive reviews may be broken down into components or capabilities and conducted on a quarterly or (more rarely) a monthly basis.

Ratio of formally documented security operations or processes   If managing something you don't measure is a challenge, measuring something you haven't defined is an even greater one. Those familiar with the concept of capabilities maturity models will recognize the benefits of formalizing and standardizing processes and operations within an enterprise. A lack of formal, documented processes makes it difficult to replicate behaviors and share or transfer knowledge. It also makes accurate operational visibility and comparison between what should happen and what does happen nearly impossible. Low ratios of documented processes indicate potential blind spots, spaces where failures can occur and grow larger without anyone noticing. By identifying all the processes associated with information security operations and identifying which are written down, an organization can begin to determine how formalized (and, by extension, how mature) their security program is.

Ratio of security operational assessments shared outside the security group   Measuring how often the InfoSec program shares operational assessments with outsiders is similar to measuring how they share failure data. The goal is to elicit valuable feedback and insight from others who may have other needs, priorities, or concerns. Sharing sensitive operational data about security does not require total transparency. But organizations that seek a higher level of reliability will welcome feedback from interested advisors elsewhere in the enterprise (and maybe even outside of it, in certain cases), and they will track how often this sharing and elicitation of feedback takes place and in what contexts.

Average time to address operational instabilities   When an organization finds a disconnect between what it thinks is happening in terms of information security and what is occurring operationally every day, it has several choices of response. One is to do nothing, for whatever reason seems most logical. Maybe the problem seems small, or maybe everyone already knows about it. Maybe change requires political or senior management support that simply doesn't exist. Another option is to take action to address the discrepancy. In either case, understanding how long this process takes can be valuable to the InfoSec program and to other stakeholders. Improving visibility provides less return on the security value of operations if the average time to fix problems the organization might find approaches forever. In situations where operational instabilities and problems are addressed, then the time necessary to address them becomes another useful InfoSec operations metric to add to the security program's toolkit.

Improving Your Operations Value Behaviors

Attempting to change and improve an organization's operational behavior to function more like an HRSP is likely to meet quite a bit of resistance. It's one thing to point out that we need a new way to look at failure. I don't get a lot of argument among security people when I propose that we need a better understanding of how and why security fails. It's another thing to suggesting tinkering with operations. Security operations not only encompass the single biggest set of regular habits that security programs have built up over time, they are probably the largest collection of activities that we actually feel comfortable with, that we feel like we have a solid lock on accomplishing. Decades of learning the gear, of building technology infrastructure, and of setting up a particular way of auditing and evaluating success have made the security operations center, whether that is an actual physical place or not, into the bastion to which the security program can always retreat when they want to feel like they are on solid, defensible footing. Now comes this Faberge egghead writing a book about something as fuzzy and mutable as culture, telling everyone they need to change because it's not about technology, it's about people. Meh.

So, let's set the record straight. The security value of operations is not about doing operations differently. It's about expanding what operations means and extending our visibility and management practices to other operational areas, specifically beyond technology. The purpose of operational visibility is to know what is happening in security as close to when it happens as possible, and to be able to react to and act upon that intelligence effectively and efficiently. As I've said before, if security was as easy as installing a product into a rack, then we would have automated the problems out of existence long ago. We know this, and we've admitted it publicly as an industry at least since Bruce Schneier coined the phrase 15 years ago that security is less a product than a process. Part of that process is human relationships, and it's about time we added the output of people-centric security infrastructures to our operational monitoring toolbox.

Embed Operations Value into the Security Program

People have an extraordinary capacity to adapt and change. All it takes is an environment, a situation, or a leader that snaps them out of complacency and demands change. Sometimes the impetus for change is painful and threatening, but not every trigger has to be a literal one. The security value of operations can create a space in which information security can thrive and contribute to the greater organization in ways that most CISOs today only dream of. There are few things more impressive than someone who has a complete command of the situation they are in, who can direct action while reassuring others, successfully over time, with the confidence that only comes from absolutely knowing their stuff. We glorify this trait in our leaders, from generals and scientists to CEOs and politicians. You can fake it sometimes, but not always and not forever. The security value of operations means driving that capability home for security leaders by giving them the behavioral resources that create security confidence.

Think More Like Scientists

One of the most important distinctions that I, as a non-engineer, have discovered in my information security career is that engineers are not scientists. For a long time, until I went back to graduate school to become an information scientist, I assumed engineering and the sciences were more or less synonymous. They are not. Engineers take the theories of science and put them to practical purpose. Scientists discover, but engineers build. Security has many engineers, but not nearly enough scientists. Scientists are inherently curious, and not just about how things work. They want to know why they work the way they do, to find the first principles that cannot necessarily be discovered simply by taking apart a system's components. Theory, hypothesis, experimentation, and control groups (as opposed to security controls) are all hallmarks of scientific thinking. They are also the subjects most likely to make me lose my audience when I start talking about them to a group of security engineers. As I stated in the sidebar about hypotheses, we need to start encouraging them much more in the information security profession.

Embrace the "Sharing Economy"

Information sharing is already a big deal at the macro level in security, with industry and government involved in trying to stimulate better collaboration between organizations. We need to push sharing further, down to the internal and even individual level. Not all security information should be made openly available to everyone, but today security is often more about hoarding than sharing. Paranoia, legitimate concerns over vulnerability intelligence, and plain old-fashioned CYA keeps security information under wraps. The effects range from allowing security programs to live in an echo chamber where non-security opinions are rarely heard, to actively hiding operational information the organization needs. The sharing economy works on the idea that making goods and services more freely available actually increases their value. Today that's most visibly performed in the world of consumer goods and services, as with Airbnb, Craigslist, and eBay. But inroads are already being made in applying the idea to information. In some cases, like the open source community, the efforts have been going on for some time, including efforts around security. Other areas, like open government, are new but exemplify the principle that having more eyeballs focused on a problem is often better.

Lighten Up a Bit

The InfoSec profession takes itself pretty seriously sometimes, maybe too seriously. Even if the cybersecurity threat really is one of the greatest facing the world today, it's only one. Major improvements in information security could be achieved if security people would realize—and help their non-security colleagues and constituents realize—that it's a manageable threat, or at least as manageable as many others facing society. Threats to digital assets are no more apocalyptic than threats like disease, crime, or war, all of which we have to face realistically and rationally if we hope to address them. That does not mean downplaying their impact, but it also means putting them into perspective. People and enterprises can take security seriously without being consumed by it. There is no greater threat to a company's security posture than the problem someone knows about but is too intimidated, either by fear of consequence or lack of knowledge, to bring to the attention of the people who can address it.

Further Reading

- Britz, Johannes J. "To Know or Not to Know: A Moral Reflection on Information Poverty." *Journal of Information Science* 30 (2004): 192–204.

- MacDonald, Jackie, Peter Bath, and Andrew Booth. "Information Overload and Information Poverty: Challenges for Healthcare Services Managers?" *Journal of Documentation* 67 (2011): 238–263.

- Schneier, Bruce. *Secrets and Lies: Digital Security in a Networked World.* Wiley: Indianapolis, 2000.

The Security Value
of Resilience

S uppose your organization has maximized the first two key values of the Security FORCE Behavioral Model, failure and operations, discussed in Chapters 11 and 12, respectively. You have set up the requisite operational behaviors and visibility to ensure you can detect errors and mistakes. And you have rebooted your understanding of failure itself, becoming adept at identifying failures while they are still small. What comes next? That's easy: you're going to experience a security incident. Failure is like disease, like sadness, like pain. No matter how good you are at anticipating and avoiding failure, everyone fails eventually. Highly reliable security programs (HRSPs) are no different. They tend to have better track records than other organizations at avoiding failures, but our lessons from firefighting to Fukushima demonstrate that being failure resistant is not the same as being foolproof. But high-reliability organizations (HROs) and HRSPs already know this, which is why they think a lot about what they will do when disaster finally strikes. They embrace the security value of resilience.

What Is the Security Value of Resilience?

Resilience refers to an InfoSec program's ability to experience a major security incident in such a way that the organization not only survives it but comes away better off for it having happened. The experience will still be stressful and will still represent a nonoptimal outcome for everyone involved. But it will be handled expertly and professionally, in a way that maximizes stability during the event and minimizes disruption. And when it's over, the organization will have a better understanding of what happened and why, insight that it will put to use the next time something completely unexpected happens. This is the security value of resilience.

When Bad Things Happen (to Good Organizations)

Even as they seek out small failures that can add up to a big one, HRSPs know they will miss a few. The organizational and technological systems we work within are just too complex to ever completely predict or control. And even if we somehow manage to know everything for a moment, complex systems produce emergent behaviors that continuously throw new sources of uncertainty and risk into the pot. You cannot predict every possible threat and risk, but you can predict that there are threats and risks that you cannot predict. Eventually your organization is going to encounter one.

HRSPs spend a lot of time obsessing over failure, as I have explained previously. But they don't waste time obsessing over the inevitability of failure. Instead, they try to anticipate what they can and they consider what they will do in those instances when anticipation itself fails. At that point, it's a different ballgame with different rules. There's no time for soul searching about how something could have been prevented. All that matters is action and what happens to address the situation. In some ways, resilience is the most important principle of HROs. In the previous chapters I've referenced Karl Weick and Kathleen Sutcliffe's book *Managing the Unexpected* several times. Their choice of title is a reflection of the inevitability of surprise even in organizations dedicated to not being caught off guard.

There is a freedom in accepting the inevitable. When an HRSP, and necessarily the larger enterprise, sincerely internalizes the expectation of a security breach, people are liberated from the terrible constraints imposed by pretending they can dodge security breaches forever. The most important benefit of this new freedom is the ability to put serious thought and resources into what happens during and after the incident. Suddenly incident response and disaster recover planning can take on a whole new meaning, not as contingency planning for nightmares you fervently hope never happen, but as the syllabus for another course in that most valuable of HRSP educational resources: failure.

Incident Response: We're Doing It Wrong

Information security's approach to incident response planning often reminds me of the way people go about preparing their own living will. Some organizations avoid doing it altogether because it reminds them of their own mortality. Others do it but without emotional investment, treating it as a legal and bureaucratic exercise that is necessary out of a sense of fear or due diligence. Rarely do you find someone preparing their living will with a sense of wonder and anticipation, seeing the document as the means to ensure they can meet a universal experience on their own terms. Organizations are not very different, in my experience.

HRO research has always appealed to me because scholars like Karl Weick unapologetically evoke an almost spiritual sensibility on the part of organizations that know how to fail properly. For HRSPs, information

(continues)

Incident Response: We're Doing It Wrong *(continued)*

security incidents are important experiences because they help define and build the character of the organization. You don't want too many of them, but when you have one, you want to squeeze as much value from it as you possibly can. From the self-help aisle of bookstores to the boardrooms of Silicon Valley, dealing with adversity and failure is touted as an important life lesson. There's even an ethical and moral quality to be considered, because if an organization's failure is going to put people at risk or under duress, that organization has a responsibility to make that event count for something.

If that perspective has the more hardcore business types rolling their eyes over "soft" concepts like corporate social responsibility, I get it. Let's instead think about incident response in colder, more rational terms. Not even the most cynical security owner would argue that corporate reputation and brand value are meaningless concepts, untethered from any measure of business success. Security incidents rank among the rare times that an organization is given mass public attention. People are frightened and angry and looking to understand *what are you going to do about this?* Now consider the handling of recent large-scale security events. Did the response serve to help or harm the reputations of the companies involved? The security incident response plan, in many ways, is among the most important marketing campaigns an organization will ever do. If it's little more than a root cause analysis and a severance package for the CISO, that's akin to anchoring your new product launch around the announcement that you've finally figured out why your last product tanked so badly.

Rolling with the Punches

The security value of resilience is about failing successfully. A major information security breach can spawn a variety of responses, from paralysis to proactivity. Think of two boxers. The first is poorly trained and has a "glass jaw." One good punch and he is on the canvas, struggling to get back up again. It may be a while before he is ready to get back in the ring, and he has probably not learned many new skills after being knocked out so quickly. The second fighter is well trained and conditioned from a lot of sparring rounds to take a hit. He appears to be able to weather an impossibly brutal amount of abuse, but never seems to go down.

Even on the ropes, he keeps his wits, looking for how he's going to escape and bring the fight back to his opponent. Even if he loses by decision or technical knockout, he is ready to fight again soon and is able to use the lessons from a ten-round contest to become a better boxer.

One key to HRSP resilience is the attitude that a security failure is just the beginning of the fight, not the end of it. A breach doesn't mean that the organization has failed completely, only that it has entered into a new phase of information security operations, one that was always expected to happen. Focus shifts from trying to predict and prevent to working to respond and recover. These represent separate skill sets and require the security team to quickly shift their strategies and tactics; the first imperative is to not let the incident eclipse everything else the InfoSec program is responsible for. If the response is all hands on deck, then who is left to steer the ship or take care of any of the day-to-day tasks of running it? The entire organization can become disabled. Worse, the panic that ensues creates new spaces for additional failures to manifest unnoticed.

Information security planning and lifecycles don't stop just because your plans go awry. HRSPs take advantage of the value of resilience by remaining calm, by falling back on their training, by bringing in additional resources, and by sticking to the plan they made ahead of time for what to do when other plans fail. Weick and Sutcliffe aptly called it the ability to "degrade gracefully." Resilience is, ultimately, about control. An HRSP has the capabilities in place to assure that even when control is lost, the organization still maintains some ability to influence and determine the pace and tenor of that process. In other words, resilient security programs have worked to ensure that they can at least control how they lose control.

Imagining Failures and Disasters

No organization can develop its capabilities for resilience by fiat. Just declaring in a memorandum or a roadmap that the organization will be resilient does not make it happen. Like every other Security FORCE value, the gains to be had from the security value of resilience only come after a lot of determined, hard work. In this case, much of that hard work involves the security team envisioning all the things that can go wrong and the various ways in which they can go wrong. As much as any other skill, from coding to testing to administration, an active imagination is one of the best attributes to look for in a good incident response manager. An HRSP uses its collective imagination to create a catalog of potential incidents, events, and breaches. Instead of establishing a single, generic incident response plan, HRSPs adopt a scenario-based model, one that considers as many ways that things can go wrong as possible and adapts the incident response strategy to each scenario as appropriate and possible given the information at hand.

Imagining the things that are likely to harm you can feel perverse, even pathological. But an HRSP does not imagine disaster out of a sense of fear. It does it out of an appeal to logic. In a complex system, the opportunities for failure approach the infinite, so an organization that is trying to anticipate failure knows that it will eventually face a situation that it had not previously considered. Logic then dictates that the organization put responses in place to deal with both expected failures and unexpected failures. Planning for expected failures is easier, of course, because you have an idea of the patterns they will take and can specify response resources with more precision. Planning for unexpected failures requires response capabilities that are flexible and able to learn and adapt quickly to novel challenges. The more failures you can add to your "expected" list, either because you thought of them beforehand or because you learned about them from an unexpected failure, the better off you are. But you will always need that capability to manage the unexpected.

Resilience is therefore something of an operational feedback loop itself. An HRSP learns from failure even while attempting to avoid and minimize it. New failures are formally incorporated into the organization's knowledge and memory, so that they become expected failures in the future. HRSPs do not look at security incidents as holes in a dike that must be plugged so that they never ever leak again. When an organization reacts to every security incident by building a new set of policies and restrictions or buying new products, with the goal of making it impossible for that incident to ever repeat itself, the result can be increased rigidity rather than increased security. Just because that one specific security event cannot be repeated doesn't mean one similar to it will not happen or that one completely different won't occur. And having convinced itself that it solved the problem, the InfoSec program risks complacency and a false sense of security. It is much better to treat the incident as a trigger for enterprise imagination and ask, how is this incident similar to others? What patterns can I identify? And what options are available to not only prevent this specific failure from repeating, but make it easier to identify and respond to this general type of failure, preferably before one turns into an incident in the future?

Resilience Under Fire

My favorite Weick journal article is also the first one that I ever read in which he explored the fatal breakdown of a smokejumper team fighting a huge forest fire in Montana. "The Collapse of Sensemaking in Organizations: The Mann Gulch Disaster" still holds lessons for people-centric security. It demonstrates the ways in which catastrophe throws even seasoned professionals into situations so uncertain that their own beliefs and experiences can turn against them, sometimes with fatal results.

The Mann Gulch fire happened in late summer of 1949 and killed 13 smokejumpers as they fled from it up a ridge after the fire grew out of control. The most dramatic point in the event occurred when the foreman of the team, realizing that the fire was going to catch them, began burning a section of the tall grass the team was moving through and ordered everyone to lie down and let the fire pass over them. No one listened and everyone else ran for their lives. The foreman survived, as did two of the firefighters who managed to make it over the ridge in time. The rest died as the fire overtook and engulfed them.

One of the lessons of Mann Gulch was that, in a crisis, what's rational and what's crazy can become confused. People struggling against fear and desperation make emotional decisions if they have not, through training and experience, made their reactions automatic enough to overcome panic. The foreman of the smokejumper team, also the most experienced of the group, had a lot of reactions to fall back on. Knowing that the fire was going to catch his team no matter what, he opted to choose his own ground and create conditions in which he could control what would happen, specifically by clearing a space free of fuel for the oncoming inferno. It made perfect sense. But to everyone else, his command sounded suicidal, essentially an order to lie down and give themselves up to the blaze. Most of the men on the team had not worked with the foreman before, so they didn't know him well enough to comprehend how much experience he had, and thus were unable to understand his actions. The two remaining survivors made it because they were faster and luckier than their companions. But had everyone trusted the foreman's superior instincts and experience, the entire team probably would have survived.

(continues)

Resilience Under Fire *(continued)*

During a security breach, many actions may make sense in the moment. For instance, a common instinct is to stop communicating and circle the wagons until the investigation is complete, or to simply disconnect the affected systems and thus stop the attack. But in some cases, these actions can and will only make the consequences worse. The only way to prepare for a major breach is to actually prepare for it, by imagining it, scoping it out, and then practicing it over and over again until what you have decided are the best courses of action are ingrained, even if they may seem impractical or extreme in the moment. There was a time when war games and red team exercises were something only the military did. Now they are standard operations in most CISOs' toolkits.

Resilience Key Value Behaviors

The resilience value behaviors that an HRSP exhibits enable the organization to fail successfully during an unexpected security incident. These behaviors help ensure that the organization is continuously preparing to meet any failure situation, whether it is one that the organization has previously imagined or one that was never anticipated. The organization must quickly react, adapt, and incorporate lessons from the incident and others to minimize impact while not overcompensating in ways that create risk in other areas. The behaviors that characterize the security value of resilience include

- ▶ Overtrain people
- ▶ Create "skill benches"
- ▶ Actively share expertise
- ▶ Encourage stretch goals
- ▶ Practice failing

Overtrain People

When it comes to training for information security incidents, HRSPs believe "the road of excess leads to the palace of wisdom." In an environment that offers innumerable ways for things to go wrong, you simply cannot have too many skilled and knowledgeable people to help when something inevitably does go wrong. In highly reliable security environments, people know their jobs well, know other peoples' jobs well, and are able to get up to speed quickly in unforeseen situations. Overtraining is not overstaffing. Most organizations cannot afford to keep more people around than they need normally, just in preparation for the day when adequate is not enough. But organizations can afford to maximize the people they do have, to encourage and even demand that their skills are optimized against extraordinary as well as typical system stressors.

People-centric security takes the approach that investment in and development of human capital to support the protection of information assets and IT systems are just as important, if not more important, than investing in more traditional capital expenditures on security. Human capital is broadly defined as the value of an employee's knowledge and skills, and human capital theory has been widely applied across industrial and educational contexts. At the core is the idea that investments in people are similar to investments in other large-scale infrastructures. If you invest significantly and wisely, you get better and more productive organizational systems. Skimp on people and, like cheaping out on building materials or IT systems, you end up with structural weakness that makes you less competitive and more prone to breakdown.

During a security incident, an organization's resilience is going to depend on its ability to engage the problem by applying lots of potential solutions very quickly, identifying patterns and more and less successful responses to events on-the-fly. Even with the best preparation, security incidents are going to confound and distract. Response teams that barely understand how systems work in the best of times will be ill prepared to understand how they work as they are collapsing. And as incidents suck in other systems and functions, including those totally outside the normal purview of InfoSec, only a combination of skills and experience will be able to manage them.

HRSPs try to build collaborative incident response capabilities that can learn and grow even while in the middle of a full-blown attack and breach. This requires committed, engaged people who have worked to build cross-functional, interdependent knowledge. It isn't easy and it isn't cheap, especially considering that the more valuable the human capital is to one organization, the more fungible those skills and talents are on the open market. But for security programs concerned with effectively managing large failure events, no threat is more disturbing than not having resources capable of responding to it effectively.

Exploring Human Capital

Human capital has been the subject of a great deal of research and, in some cases, critique. But today it is widely accepted in fields as diverse as education, human resources, and public policy. I have not even scratched the surface of human capital theory in describing the training environment of HRSPs. There are lots of books on the subject and its applicability throughout organizational management. Two good introductory sources of information for those interested in exploring the topic further are the Human Capital Institute (www.hci.org) and the Deloitte report *Global Human Capital Trends 2014* (available from Deloitte University Press, http://dupress.com).

Create "Skill Benches"

Training and skill building alone don't give an organization everything that it will need in a crisis. It only provides the raw materials for the security value of resilience. An HRSP still needs to direct and structure its human capital so that it can be brought to bear effectively during a security incident. Formally designated skill benches throughout the InfoSec program and beyond provide a flexible support structure that can adapt to changing circumstances before, during, and after an incident.

A *skill bench* is, at heart, just a plan combined with a list of people with specific expertise. The bench functions as a workaround for personnel shortages that emerge during an incident. If only one or two employees have a set of skills, technical or otherwise, then a breach that involves their expertise can tie them up for days or weeks. What happens to their regular duties and responsibilities during that time? If they do not directly support or are not directly affected by the security event, it's likely they will be neglected or even ignored completely. That's not effective operational management. If, on the other hand, the organization can call on a bench of similar talent and skill, even if those individuals are not as fully capable as the employees who do the job full time, calling in the bench resources can blunt the impact of the crisis. Like a reserve parachute, the skill bench may not work quite as well as the main chute, but it will ensure that you aren't killed on impact.

HRSPs create skill benches by first mapping out the roles and requisite job skill requirements for every information security function, and probably several non-security ones, that could reasonably be involved in an incident. The resulting expertise map is used to assess probable skill shortages and bottlenecks resulting from specific security incidents in the organization's incident catalog. Contingency plans are then devised with particular triggers to guide the security team in identifying likely incident patterns and applying skill bench resources based on predetermined need. Again, none of this is easy. Contingency planning is complicated and is as much art as science. Organizations are fluid and environments are dynamic, so the skill bench must be kept current over time. People on the bench have to know they are part of it and be provided the training and education necessary to keep their capabilities viable. But like every other behavior involving the security value of resilience, HRSPs choose to undertake the challenge because they want to know that when a major event happens, it will feel more like a bad day at the office and less like the end of the world.

Skill benching can be a perfect opportunity for outsourcing, especially in resource-strapped enterprises. It's very likely that a security incident will motivate senior management to free up funds and support that are simply not available in other, more normal circumstances. But building an externally supported bench does not let an HRSP off the hook for advance planning. Like backup sites in disaster recovery and business continuity planning, the organization should give itself options for hot, warm, and cold staffing before an incident. You don't begin preparing a hot disaster recovery site the day the flood takes out your datacenter. An outsourced bench staff needs to be on call immediately, not only to ensure that the response is timely, but to negotiate and take advantage of "I may have a problem someday" vs. "I need someone here now!" pricing differentials.

Actively Share Expertise

You may have noticed by now that every one of the Security FORCE values includes a behavior devoted to sharing information and insight. For the security value of resilience, that sharing is of expertise, which flows naturally out of the first two key behaviors. But expertise sharing extends beyond just letting everyone know who has Active Directory skills or who has been trained in incident forensics. Expertise sharing also means opinion and imagination sharing across the organization during a security event. It's about bringing the full weight of enterprise human and intellectual capital to bear on successfully managing a security crisis.

Reflex and instinct may, during a security incident, drive people to embrace action over thought. As in the case of the Mann Gulch disaster (see the earlier sidebar), when a 30-foot-high wall of fire is coming at you, the option that seems least wise is to stop and think about what to do. The wisest option would seem to be to run for your life. But as the victims soon tragically discovered, stopping and listening to the foreman is exactly what they should have done. The same holds true in information security. It feels better in the midst of an uncertain situation to be doing something, anything, that seems like positive action. But if our situational awareness is insufficient to know what the best action is, we may find that taking action works against us. In a crisis situation there is a fine balance between reflex and reflection. It pays to remember that gut instincts can be misleading and sometimes we need to question them, particularly in those instances where we have little experience or training with what we are facing.

During a security incident, it is imperative that an organization examine all the options available and choose (albeit quickly) the best moves to make. However, when expertise has been relegated to silos and individuals have only their own limited experience to rely on, the chance of making bad decisions goes up. Even worse, crisis often motivates people to act like they know what's going on, either because they don't realize the extent of their own ignorance about the situation or to reassure others into supporting their actions. HRSPs try to avoid decisions based on bravado or narrow insights. Their goal instead is to create just enough room for collecting different analyses and opinions across a variety of stakeholders before decisions get made, what *Managing the Unexpected* refers to as "conceptual slack." It's a tricky balance between snap judgment on one side and vacillation on the other. For an HRSP managing a security event, though, taking a few hours to gather alternative frames of reference and contrary viewpoints may mean not wasting orders of magnitude more time going down the wrong path and then having to retrace their steps.

Encourage Stretch Goals

The security value of resilience is not reaped simply by giving members of an organization plenty of training. Taking classes and achieving certifications do not make a person a seasoned practitioner. If those new skills are not put to use, they atrophy and degrade. For that reason, HRSPs motivate and encourage their members to put their training to work, preferably by taking on challenges that will prepare them for the more intense tempo of a security incident.

Stretch goals are used widely in information security and performance management more generally, although they can sometimes be more about wishful thinking or an attempt to squeeze out a few more ounces of productivity than about really stretching someone's abilities. Challenges in the context of HRSPs and resilience are meant to achieve the latter, to strain and stretch the employee's capabilities in the same way we strain and stretch our bodies through exercise. We want our teams to be stronger and more limber so that they are better prepared to face adverse conditions during an event. But instead of physical prowess (although that can be necessary as well—security incidents tend to be exhausting physically), the objective is cognitive and even emotional strength and stamina.

The key resilience value behaviors described in this chapter provide ample opportunities for challenging stretch goals, to the point where such goals are practically a structural feature of the security value of resilience. Having trained and organized skilled people to function as both primary and reserve resources during a major security incident or event, HRSPs will encourage them to engage and participate across the security program landscape. Rotations through other InfoSec and IT functions, opportunities for leading or joining projects and initiatives, and virtual team building exercises that bring together folks on the skill benches and their primary-duty colleagues are all means by which an HRSP can foster an environment of collaborative excellence.

Most importantly, however, stretch goals have to be rewarded. Compensation for going above and beyond one's usual responsibilities does not always have to be financial in nature, and in some cases money can be less effective than other means of motivation. Remember that the goal is to form a tightly knit operational team that can effectively handle a crisis. If we take lessons from other crisis management fields, those with a high degree of professionalism and esprit de corps, the best performers are not necessarily the best paid. As important as money is, HRSPs work to make people feel valued and appreciated for their contributions. Company-wide recognition, opportunities to mentor or work on interesting projects, and formal inclusion of stretch goals into performance reviews (which can also have a financial benefit in the long term) are good alternative ways to encourage people to go above and beyond the call of duty.

Practice Failing

How do you get to Carnegie Hall? the old joke goes. *Practice!* It's something of a universal life lesson that no one is just naturally a virtuoso. If you want to be the best at something, you have to put in the long, hard hours to train and prepare, repeating the same exercises again and again until they are pitch perfect and inscribed in muscle memory. It's true for musicians, it's true for athletes, and it's true for HRSPs. Failing is pretty much the one event that information security teams most often think about, stress about, and wonder if they are ready for. You would think we might practice a bit more than we do to get ready for our big night onstage!

Some of the problem goes back to the points I made about the security value of failure in Chapter 11, namely that we hate the thought of failure and we engage it with about the same enthusiasm as we do death and taxes. But, as I've also pointed out, security incidents are as inevitable as death and taxes, so we should be ready for one when it comes. Without practice, a security incident is new and unfamiliar and frightening, maybe overwhelmingly so. Even with practice, security incidents will include things that are new and scary, so making as much of our response as possible routine and familiar amid the chaos frees up cognitive resources that we can devote to solving problems. Returning again to Chapter 11, I talked about how the movie *Apollo 13* misquoted the "Failure is not an option" line. NASA never ruled out failure. In fact, they practiced failing all the time. The very first Apollo mission ended in tragedy in 1967 when three crew members died in a fire. A board of inquiry was highly critical of NASA's operations leading up to the accident, and afterward NASA began paying a lot more attention to safety and preparing for future accidents. As Nick Gardner describes in his book *Mistakes*, throughout the rest of the Apollo program, NASA teams spent time between launches dreaming up disaster scenarios and running simulations of them against one another as tests. The Apollo 13 rescue plan, in fact, was the outcome of one of these scenarios.

HRSPs treat failure practice the same way that they treat training: you can never have enough. You might not be able to get all you want or all you need, but practice in the form of war games, scenario planning, and security incident drills is considered high value and an excellent use of time and money. Practicing failure is not, however, the same thing as penetration testing or compliance audits, although these can be factored into a practice exercise. Testing and audits are data collection mechanisms, not experiential exercises. Practicing failure does not mean identifying where a cybercriminal can compromise your production servers. Practicing failure means simulating exactly what happens when that criminal actually compromises those devices. How does the organization find out? How does it respond? How does it deal with the outcomes? Practicing failure involves understanding this entire process in detail and figuring out where the response to the security incident fails in and of itself. After many iterations, that response becomes much better, and eventually becomes habit, professionalized into just another operational process.

The Unrecovered Country

Estonia worries a great deal about the security value of resilience. The Baltic nation has an impressive history of digital adoption, as well as concerns over cyberwarfare, having been hit by one of the earliest examples of it in 2007. More recently, the Estonian government has embarked on a program designed to manage the country's digital service infrastructure even if the country is hit by another massively debilitating cyberattack.

Under the rubric of the "Data Embassy Initiative," Estonia has begun planning for the migration of computer data and resources to other countries in the event of an emergency. In situations where an attack takes out or denies government services hosted inside Estonia, those resources can quickly and effectively migrate abroad, primarily to predesignated data embassies run from inside Estonia's physical embassies around the globe. The strategy is for government capabilities to continue to function, including paying salaries and providing services for citizens, while the crisis on the home infrastructure is resolved.

An initial test by the Estonian government of the digital continuity system was promising but also demonstrated the incredible intricacies that exist even in well-designed and well-managed digital infrastructures. The tests conducted in partnership with Microsoft found technical problems, legal problems, and management problems, some of which had been considered ahead of time and some which were complete surprises. As the official government report stated, "it...became clear that no matter what, textbook readiness is impossible to achieve."

Among the specific findings and recommendations of the exercise were two that clearly echo the material in this chapter. One finding determined that due to improper or missing system documentation, it was often the case that working knowledge of a system was limited to "only a small number of experts" and created gaps in the potential for digital continuity during an incident. One of eight key recommendations of the report was even more to the point. It stated that "operational procedures should be prepared and tested in advance rather than in a crisis." The full report can be found on Estonia's English version of the Ministry of Economic Affairs and Communications website at www.mkm.ee/en (search for "Data Embassy Initiative").

Assessing Your Resilience Value Behaviors

Use the Security FORCE Survey and Security FORCE Metrics to determine how well your organization adheres to the key value behaviors for resilience and to provide empirical evidence of those behaviors.

Scoring the Resilience Value Behavior Survey

The Security FORCE Survey includes statements related to the security value of resilience. The five statements under Security Value of Resilience are listed in the sample of the FORCE Survey shown in Figure 13-1. As with previous chapters, scoring assumes Likert responses normalized on a 1–5 scale:

▶ An average score of 4 or above (most responses indicate Agree or Strongly Agree) signifies the organization exhibits behaviors found in an HRSP.

▶ An average score of 3 (most responses indicate the respondent felt Neutral) signifies the organization may or may not behave like an HRSP.

▶ An average score of 2 or below (most responses indicate Disagree or Strongly Disagree) signifies the organization does not exhibit the behaviors found in an HRSP.

SECURITY FORCE SURVEY

To complete this Security FORCE Survey, please indicate your level of agreement with each of the following statements regarding information security values and practices within your organization. Choose one response per statement. Please respond to all statements.

Statement	Strongly Disagree	Disagree	Neutral	Agree	Strongly Agree
Security Value of Resilience					
1. I feel like people are trained to know more about security than just the minimum level necessary.					
2. The organization has reserves of skill and expertise to call on in the event of a security incident or crisis.					
3. I feel like everyone in the organization is encouraged to "get out of their comfort zone" and be part of security challenges.					
4. I feel like people are interested in what I know about security, and willing to share their own skills to help me as well.					
5. The organization often conducts drills and scenarios to test how well we respond to security incidents and failures.					

Figure 13-1   *FORCE Value Survey statements for resilience value behaviors*

For resilience value behaviors, an average score of 4 or greater indicates that the organization behaves in ways that will enable it to respond more quickly and more effectively to security incidents. The organization will have prepared for a variety of possible incidents in advance and put mechanisms into place to deal with unexpected incidents that had not been considered. The response will be more effective given the presence of resources ready to address problems in a coherent way. A score of 2 or below indicates that the organization does not behave like an HRSP and is less likely to "fail gracefully" and recover quickly from a security incident. It is more likely to lose control of the failure process and give into panic or paralysis when faced with new or uncertain security incident scenarios.

FORCE Value Metrics for Resilience

The FORCE Value Metrics for resilience, providing additional measures of HRSP behavioral alignment, can be found in Figure 13-2.

Using the FORCE Resilience Value Metrics

The five FORCE Metrics associated with the value of resilience capture an organization's capacity for crisis in the face of an information security failure such as a major data breach. All are suggestions and non-exhaustive, and should be used, adapted, or supplemented as appropriate.

SECURITY FORCE METRICS

These metrics can be used to support, verify, and validate Security FORCE behaviors within the organization. These are not the only possible metrics available, but they provide a good baseline. You should alter or adapt these measures as required and appropriate to fit your own program and environment.

Metric	Result
Security Value of Resilience	
1. Number of security-related training opportunities provided to people, by role or group, in the past year	
2. Number of identified security backup resources available during an incident	
3. Ratio of employees with identified security "challenge" assignments as part of regular performance reviews	
4. Number and type of security knowledge sharing opportunities created in the past year	
5. Number of scenario-based response testing or security war-game exercises conducted in the past year	

Figure 13-2 *FORCE Value Metrics for resilience value behaviors*

Number of security-related training opportunities provided to people, by role or group, in the past year   Companies give their InfoSec teams information security–specific training, usually. And they give training in the form of awareness education across the enterprise, most likely. If security really does affect a company as a whole, then the whole company should be trained on it to some degree, and beyond just the basics of knowing when or when not to click an email link. Many organizations today treat proficiency with standard office productivity software as a required skill. Mere awareness that word processing or presentation development is a thing is not enough. Security knowledge and skill should be on the same level, and the organization should provide everyone with access to it. Not everyone in HR will need or want to know how encryption works or how to configure a firewall. But some might. And having skilled people in non-security roles can both help to prevent failures as well as to make an organization more resilient in the face of one. If the organization limits security skills development to just the InfoSec team, this can be an indicator that resilience may be impaired when that team faces a breach that no one else is able to understand.

Number of identified security backup resources available during an incident   Spreading around information security skills and knowledge can lead to more than just an informed and capable workforce. The organization can dramatically improve resilience by formally identifying some of these people as backup resources that can be called upon during an incident, a sort of "volunteer fire department" or "Army Reserve" for the InfoSec program. Knowing who and where these people are, or if they even exist, is a good measure of crisis capacity for an organization, which will directly impact the organization's ability to respond and recover quickly from an incident.

Ratio of employees with identified security "challenge" assignments as part of regular performance reviews   This metric does not mean the organization must find ways to make people directly responsible for security or take on security-related tasks they do not understand or want to pursue. Security challenge assignments begin where the minimum baselines of training and awareness end. Organizations should work creatively to make assignments practical and valuable, to make completing them worth an employee's time, and they should be comparable and equal to other performance goals, not extra responsibilities. Assignments can range from taking an extra optional security training course all the way through shadowing a member of the InfoSec team for a day. The point is to (gently) push people's comfort zones and expose them to the fact that the organization takes information security seriously enough to ask them to devote work time to it and then rewards them appropriately come time for performance appraisals.

Number and type of security knowledge sharing opportunities created in the past year   Teaching information security skills and encouraging individual efforts to improve security knowledge should be supplemented by fostering the sharing of those skills and that knowledge. Like the challenge assignments, organizations should be creative with how they develop knowledge sharing for InfoSec, and doing so does not imply or require significant expenditures of time or money. But the organization should track its efforts and use that metric as a gauge to understand how and to what extent the diffusion of security capabilities is taking place within the enterprise in order to leverage increases in the value of resilience that are realized when collective knowledge is required during a failure event.

Number of scenario-based response testing or security war-game exercises conducted in the past year   This metric is very straightforward and, unlike the previous measures, is directed primarily at the InfoSec program. The organization should track efforts to anticipate and simulate failure scenarios as part of its resilience strategy. If it is not practicing failing on a regular basis and not feeding the resulting data and insights back into security in general, and incident and crisis response plans in particular, then the resulting low scores for this measurement are a good indicator that the organization is not as prepared for a major information security event as it could otherwise be.

Improving Your Resilience Value Behaviors

People are the cornerstone of the security value of resilience, and improving their behaviors is about providing more opportunities for them to realize their personal goals, while also meeting strategic objectives of the entire firm. Unlike with the security values of failure and operations, which asks an organization to rethink its approach to those things, the security value of resilience exhibited by an HRSP in the face of information security incidents is probably not as controversial. Most everyone will agree, especially today, that the ability to weather a security crisis, and look competent publicly while doing it, is an unqualified good thing. It's how you get there that's tricky.

The major obstacle an organization is likely to face in realizing the security value of resilience is not skepticism about training or practicing incident response scenarios. Few managers, at least in public, would downplay these important elements of operational readiness. The most likely pushback the InfoSec program will face is the availability of resources, including time, money, and people, necessary for the organization to behave like an HRSP. The theme of competing priorities runs throughout this book, and that competition will impact people's decisions about where they spend their time, money, and political capital. Improving resilience means shifting limited resources from something else, often something tangible and current, deprioritizing that thing in favor of improved readiness for events that will inevitably happen but cannot be accurately predicted. That can be a tough sell.

I've found that among the best ways to make the case for the security value of resilience is to tie that value to other, more intuitive enterprise priorities. Don't make it about improving resilience. Make it about improving functions and decisions that will result in better resilience, which brings us back to the idea of human capital and people-centric security. Resilience is only one of the positive benefits of training and improving people's expertise, skills, and work experiences. The most admired companies today, the ones that end up on the lists of best places to work, have in common their emphasis on creating a meaningful place to be employed. The value of resilience includes opportunities for human improvement inside the InfoSec program, but with much wider possibilities for the organization as a whole.

Embed Resilience Value into the Security Program

The two biggest changes necessary to move an InfoSec program toward becoming an HRSP in terms of the security value of resilience do not involve convincing people that more effective incident response is good. As I mentioned earlier, that's pretty much a given. The changes that are required involve getting people to take more active ownership in cross-functional security responsibilities and overcoming organizational anxiety over an inevitable security incident.

"A Security Incident? I Want In!"

Elite teams of heroes, sacrificing themselves doing a job nobody else can do or would want to, is exactly the opposite of how you want people to see the employees who respond to security incidents, or to see themselves if they are those people. HRSPs spread the ownership of major failure events around, and not in order to lay blame or hold people accountable. If you train and prepare well for something, even something horrible, there's a certain sense of accomplishment and even pride that comes with putting that preparation to the test. First responders in a disaster scene don't come onsite hoping to find other people to do the job.

They jump in and take action, providing the resources and services they have trained and committed themselves to provide. Security incidents should trigger this same level of, if not enthusiasm, determination. People who have worked to contribute to the value of resilience want to help because they are confident they can. It's a cultural trait that must be nurtured and constantly reinforced through the behaviors defined throughout this chapter.

Make Security Incidents Mundane

It will be much easier to get people involved in responding to security incidents when they look at such incidents as a test of skill and not an existential threat. A problem I have with the "you've already been hacked" narrative in information security today is that it teaches the wrong lessons about the banality of security failures, namely that you can't do anything about them (except, of course, buy the products and services of the firms using the narrative). A better approach, a more HRSP-oriented approach, would be to accept the inevitability of failure but reject the inevitability of helplessness in the face of it. What should make a security incident mundane is that it is expected, anticipated to some degree, planned for, and documented so that the results can be fed into a process of organizational learning and improvement. In an organization running an HRSP, "we had a security incident" is, ideally, on the same level as "revenue growth was flat in Europe" or "we had a supply chain issue in Asia" or "the company had to deal with a product lawsuit." These happen all the time and are rarely front page headlines, although no one would argue they can be big problems. But as such, they are crises to deal with, to analyze, to respond to, and to move on from with as little disruption as possible.

Further Reading

- Gardner, Nick. *Mistakes: How They Have Happened and How Some Might Be Avoided*. BookSurge, 2007.

- Maclean, Norman. *Young Men and Fire*. Chicago: University of Chicago Press, 1972.

- Weick, Karl E. "The Collapse of Sensemaking in Organizations: The Mann Gulch Disaster." *Administrative Science Quarterly* 38:4 (1993): 628–652.

The Security Value
of Complexity

Resilience, the ability to gracefully weather failure even after every attempt to detect and prevent it has been unsuccessful, is something of an overarching objective of the Security FORCE values. If resilience is the overarching goal of the FORCE Model, then complexity should be thought of as the soul of FORCE. The security value of complexity infuses and informs everything else, a way of looking at the whole world differently. Research into accidents, breakdowns, and HROs grew out of and in tandem with research into complex systems. The emergence of complexity in social and technological environments was, in fact, a primary catalyst for studying the inevitability of failure in the face of these systems' emergent and unpredictable behaviors. For HROs and HRSPs, working with, not against, complexity is fundamental to improving their reliability.

What Is the Security Value of Complexity?

Complexity isn't simple. That's a terrible cliché, but not a bad definition. According to the Santa Fe Institute, a major research center devoted to the science of complexity, the term *complexity* is usually defined differently across various disciplines. Fundamentally, complexity involves emergent behaviors that grow out of interactions between the different elements of a system. Neil Johnson, the author of *Simply Complexity*, riffs on "two's company, three's a crowd" and makes the case that complex systems begin when binary ones end. My favorite definitions of complexity come courtesy of Warren Weaver, who, along with Claude Shannon, developed the field of information theory. In his 1948 article "Science and Complexity," Warren sketched out three levels of complex problems:

▶ **Problems of simplicity**   Complexity at the level of two, three, or four variables, which is to say not that complex at all and easy to predict with relatively unsophisticated analytical methods

▶ **Problems of disorganized complexity**   Complexity at the level of millions or billions of variables, operating at random so that no one variable is predictable but average behaviors can be accurately analyzed

▶ **Problems of organized complexity**   Complexity in which large numbers of variables interact, but in nonrandom ways, and those organized relationships within the system make behaviors unpredictable using normal analysis

When Weaver published his article about the differences between disorganized and organized complexity in 1948, he anticipated that organized complexity would be the big challenge for science in the coming century. It certainly is for information security today. Security programs have for the longest time behaved as if they were dealing with problems of simplicity. Now that they are realizing that's not the case, they are turning to techniques like big data that promise to turn security into a problem of disorganized complexity. But that won't work either, at least not completely. The security value of complexity begins with the recognition that information security is an environment dominated by problems of organized complexity. Those problems cannot be easily measured, or even measured with difficulty, using traditional methods. They may not be predictable at all. HRSPs start by accepting that possibility and incorporating its implications.

Dumbing It Down

Humans are biologically and evolutionarily programmed to simplify things. Identifying patterns, shortcuts, and heuristics is one of the ways that we have survived over our history as a species. As people began to come together in collective and then organized groups, they brought their tendency to simplify complex and diverse information inputs with them, now intensified by the need to create shared consensus and agreement. Cut forward a few millennia and our current world of frameworks, common criteria, and best practice methodologies is much easier to understand. Like their lone ancestors, companies and enterprises thrive by simplifying the paralyzing stimuli they must deal with into categories, labels, scenarios, and triggers that allow them to make decisions under conditions of chaos.

Go too far down the simplicity track, though, and you end up in a place where you have removed so much nuance and detail from the abstractions you have created that they become meaningless. Everything gets reduced to the small set of variables necessary to make it a problem of simplicity, and thus easily analyzed and acted upon. Run into something new? Just dump it into the closest category bucket. Instead of focusing on what might make it different, look for the things that make it the same. Otherwise, how can we act on it? Is it secure or vulnerable? Is it compliant or non-compliant? Is it a technical control or a process control? If someone reminds a group of people that something can be both of these things, or even all of them, they are reminded of the practical qualities of information security: *We have to draw the line somewhere.* And drawing that arbitrary line, whether it represents divisions of cells on a heat map or perimeters on a network diagram, involves an assumption. The organization assumes the division reflects reality, and it assumes risk against the probability that it does not.

The security value of complexity is not a rejection of simplification, which is impossible, but instead a healthy sense of skepticism and mistrust. We dumb things down because we have to at times, not because we want to. There is always a trade-off, and every act of simplification brings concomitant risk along with it. HRSPs fight to keep simplifications from taking over by engaging in them hesitantly, by questioning and critiquing them repeatedly, and by trying to re-complicate them continuously. Allowing simplicity is like allowing vulnerability. Sometimes you must do it for business reasons, but you're never happy about it. And as soon as you can, you try to correct the problem.

Growing Uncertainty

When security teams and other organizations oversimplify, they start putting too much stock in labels, categories, and representations. In fact, they may start trusting their classifications and models so much that they stop paying close attention to the real world those things represent. Empirical evidence can become less important than what the model says is real. This is especially true when political or cultural forces have a vested interest in the representation. If the organization has invested significant effort in compromise and in developing consensus and cooperation among stakeholders, criticizing that common frame of reference may be seen as threatening. Take the example of a penetration test, where an organization receives a report of vulnerabilities. The findings come back with problems classified by severity, perhaps using Common Vulnerability Scoring System (CVSS) scores. Tasks and maybe even blame are doled out as a result, with some teams being assigned severe problems that have to be fixed immediately, while other teams are assigned less problematic vulnerabilities and are given more leeway. Now imagine the hell that breaks loose when someone argues that a commonly found "minor" vulnerability is actually as bad as the severe ones and should be prioritized, tripling the workload of the teams who thought they had the easier assignment. Screaming matches and appeals to senior management ensue. Whether or not the vulnerability in question is really that dangerous gets lost in the noise. The model drives the argument.

Linguists and philosophers have, for a long time, explored the idea that words very literally have power. They are not just tools of description, but actions themselves with the ability to shape thought and drive behavior. In *Managing the Unexpected*, Weick and Sutcliffe cite Benjamin Whorf, a linguist, who demonstrated the power of labels in his examination of "empty" gasoline drums at an industrial site. Used drums, which had once been filled with fuel, were processed once the gasoline had been drained. These now-empty drums, Whorf found, were treated less carefully than ones that still contained liquid. Workers equated the idea of an empty drum with something devoid of flammable material, which made them less likely to take safety precautions with it. But in reality, a full container of gasoline is safer than one that has no liquid left in it, due to the explosive nature of vaporized gas. Returning to the penetration test example, I have seen plenty of organizations that allowed vulnerabilities to go unmitigated for years because classifying them as "minor vulnerabilities" came to be interpreted as nonthreatening even when they existed widely throughout the network.

Every time we simplify something to make it easier to conceptualize or manage, we create uncertainty. To reduce complexity, we have to leave things out, lump things together, make blurry edges artificially sharp. Our pictures become clear because we no longer have to focus on so many messy details. It's an incredibly useful process that makes decision making more efficient. It's also an illusion. The hidden aspects are not eliminated, just put into the background. They keep functioning, but we choose not to see them in favor of the things we've brought to the foreground. Although we are not focusing on the hidden aspects, they may still affect us, and we won't realize it because we've placed them into our blind spot. HRSPs worry about that to no end.

CVSS, Heartbleed, and the Uncertainty Challenge in Scoring Systems

Scoring systems are useful. We need them. I use them myself for both of the measurement frameworks I propose in this book. But they are imperfect and should never be treated as empirically measuring some objective reality. They are metaphors describing something (performance, risk, etc.) in terms of something else (a number, a rank, or a label). We usually invent scores when something is too difficult to measure directly and we have to create an approximation. Even seemingly objective scores, like in sports, hide as much as they reveal. The Texans beat the Cowboys by 14 on Sunday? Well that proves the Texans are a better team, right? Highly unlikely, as I'm sure some Cowboys fan will point out to me someday in person.

Blogger Michael Roytman explores similar problems in the context of information security, specifically vulnerability severity scoring in the wake of the Heartbleed OpenSSL vulnerability of 2014. His post, "CVSS Score: A Heartbleed by Any Other Name" was written in May of that year. While technology and mainstream media outlets were throwing around terms like "catastrophic" and "worst vulnerability ever," Heartbleed was officially given a CVSS score of 5.0 out of 10, classified as medium severity. The score reflected a combination of factors inherent to CVSS calculation and included

(continues)

CVSS, Heartbleed, and the Uncertainty Challenge in Scoring Systems *(continued)*

an analysis that the vulnerability, while highly exploitable, was of relatively low impact. The score seemed so out of touch with reality that the National Vulnerability Database (NVD) took the apparently unprecedented step of issuing a caveat warning about it. The NVD pointed out that, even though some local system resources might not be directly affected, the vulnerability could be used to gain sensitive information that might lead to other attacks.

The point of the attention that Roytman and the NVD brought to the CVSS, and which I illustrated through my football analogy, is that any scoring system is a product of simplification. We use them to reduce our uncertainty about a decision or analysis, such as who played a sport better (the highest-scoring team) or which vulnerability to prioritize for fixing (the ones with the highest CVSS scores). But you cannot reduce real-world complexity to a small set of data points without simultaneously increasing uncertainty as well. If your algorithm is good, you reduce the uncertainty you want while introducing uncertainty you don't really care about in that context. If your algorithm is flawed, you confuse yourself about the very thing you are trying to make more clear, a problem worth thinking about. You can find Michael Roytman's complete analysis of CVSS scoring challenges on the AlienVault blog page at www.alienvault.com.

Ignorance Is Risk

Deliberately choosing to ignore some things in favor of emphasizing others may be a uniquely human skill. And as long as we remember what we have chosen to ignore, we manage the trade-off quite well. It's when people and organizations go for the full-on bliss, neither remembering nor really caring to know what they have chosen to disregard, that they open themselves to danger. HRSPs use ignorance as a tool, but as a powerful, dangerous tool, one that must be managed consciously and carefully so that it doesn't cause harmful accidents. Assumptions are the containers in which HRSPs store and manage the things they deliberately ignore. And like any other dangerous materials, they are subject to strict rules regarding how they are treated.

HRSPs do not like to create new assumptions that they then have to manage. HRSPs tend to simplify things as infrequently and as carefully as they can, and when they do choose to dumb things down, they try not to go overboard, no matter how easy that might make their lives. That means HRSPs minimize the number of assumptions they have to deal with and maintain a healthy sense of cognitive dissonance, always holding both the simplification and the assumption in balance, using the former but never forgetting the latter. It's like the suspension of disbelief when watching a movie or reading a good novel. You know what you imagine is happening isn't real or doesn't make logical sense, but you accept it for a little while in order to absorb the experience and everything it offers. Then the lights go up in the theater or you lay the book down on your desk, and it's back to reality.

People in HRSPs are like the people you know who love to rip apart the movies and novels others enjoy, to point out every flaw in plot or inconsistency of detail. They enjoy killing a good buzz by pointing out things like the observation that the hero's gun seemed to have an unlimited supply of bullets during the final shootout. But instead of shutting down these cynics, HRSPs invite their comments, even when they are inconvenient or annoying. Security teams focused on the value of complexity know that the problem that ultimately impacts them will probably not be coming from the place they are looking. They suspect it will come out of their blind spot, so they are fanatical about reminding themselves where that spot is and what they have shoved into it. Those assumptions are the vulnerabilities in their mental security systems, and they try to test and address them as much as the ones in their technology products.

My Heat Map and I Have Boundary Issues

One of the best illustrations of the power and danger of labels and categories in information security is the heat map that so many security programs use to measure and express security risk. I must preface this example, as I do when I speak about it to customers or at conferences, that I have nothing against heat maps per se. But I have big issues with using heat maps unselfconsciously and without thinking as much about what the heat map leaves out as what it contains. HRSPs use heat maps too, but they never lose sight of the fact that you end up packing a disproportionately large quantity of assumptions and uncertainty into these visualizations compared with other available risk management techniques.

(continues)

My Heat Map and I Have Boundary Issues *(continued)*

The following illustration shows a simple heat map, representative of heat maps I have seen used throughout information security organizations around the world. The X-axis is the company's estimate of the frequency of security risk or events, while the Y-axis is the company's estimate of the impact of any particular risk or event. Increased frequency and/or likelihood tends to raise the perceived risk level, thus increasing the overall risk severity score. Many organizations use different scores than high, medium, or low, but it really doesn't matter in the end what terminology is used, as we'll see. Usually, the cells representing high scores are colored red, the medium scores yellow, and the low scores green. These scores are then used to make decisions regarding resource allocation and time allotted to address the risk or fix the vulnerability. There may be variations on this theme, but heat map–driven risk assessments have been and remain an accepted best practice (or at least a totally acceptable practice) in the information security industry.

Impact				
Medium	High	High	High
Medium	Medium	High	High
Low	Medium	Medium	High
Low	Low	Medium	Medium
Low	Low	Low	Medium

Frequency

I could comment on the somewhat intriguing practice of assigning any security risk or vulnerability a "green" color, but it reminds me so much of Benjamin Whorf's "empty" (and thus presumably "safe") gasoline containers that I feel like I've already addressed it. Instead, let's focus on the assumptions and uncertainty that congregate around the heat map's artificial boundary lines.

The next illustration breaks out a section of nine cells from the middle three rows in the upper right area of the heat map. I've also labeled the boundaries between cells in ways I have found pretty typical in the heat maps I have seen. Frequency is separated into four probability thresholds of 25 percent each. Impact is defined by numerical scores from 0 to 10, with 10 being the most severe. Usually, these scores will be tied back to a category key that indicates financial loss, loss of service or access, or some other direct impact. Most organizations I've seen use heat maps use them to build or populate remediation plans, assigning the highest severity risks to be fixed the quickest and gradually moving down the severity stack until everything is addressed or the organization runs out of time, money, or personnel (usually the latter). By examining three unique risks, labeled A, B, and C and classified using the heat map shown in the illustration, we can start to get an idea of just how much uncertainty is involved with heat maps and how these labels can result in large blind spots of potential risk.

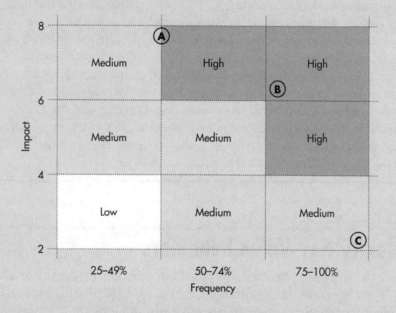

Risk A comes in with a frequency estimate of 50 percent likely to occur and an impact score of 7.9. According to a literal interpretation of the heat map, Risk A is a high-severity risk (often colored red on a heat map). But heat maps are not literal measurements of risk, and the boundaries between severity

(continues)

My Heat Map and I Have Boundary Issues *(continued)*

are arbitrarily drawn up by the people interpreting them. The organization builds an approximation of reality, which then becomes tempting to use in place of actually exploring reality. If Risk A, during the assessment calculations, had been rated just one percentage point of frequency lower, becoming 49 percent likely, it would have immediately been categorized as medium severity (and shaded yellow). Is a risk of 50 percent/7.9 that different from one of 49 percent/7.9? In terms of risk treatment, if the InfoSec team is given a deadline of six months instead of six weeks to fix the problem, then the difference in categorization implies a significant difference between the two estimated risks.

Risks B and C are variants of this same phenomenon. In the case of Risk B, it falls within a high-severity risk cell bracketed by other high-severity risk cells, but had it been estimated slightly less impactful and slightly less likely during the assessment calculations, it would have fallen into the medium-severity risk cell to its lower left on the heat map. How do we differentiate between Risk B and other high-severity risks that may be less likely or more damaging, or between it and a medium-severity cousin just across the boundary? Risk C is rated 100 percent likely, but its impact score makes it medium severity. In this case, the organization may decide it has to accept unavoidable damage from one risk in order to protect against one that might never happen. Heat maps encourage, even demand, this category-centric thinking, sometimes at the expense of common sense. HRSPs refuse to allow their models to tell them what's really real.

Complexity Key Value Behaviors

Environments of organized complexity resist our attempts to identify predictive patterns. Thus, the complexity value behaviors that an HRSP will encourage are less about looking for those patterns and more about reminding ourselves that they can be misleading or impossible to accurately identify. I described the security value of complexity earlier as the soul of an HRSP because embracing it results in an attitude of cautious self-doubt that is fundamental for successful people-centric security. Security fails because organizations forever overestimate their understanding of the systems that they create, and underestimate those systems' capacity to do something completely unexpected. We do this out of a desire to make reality simpler and easier to analyze and explain, when we should be trying to make our explanations more complex and harder while stretching ourselves into more sophisticated analyses. The behaviors that characterize the security value of complexity include

- ▶ Don't oversimplify
- ▶ Formalize your assumptions
- ▶ Covet empirical evidence
- ▶ Share the doubt
- ▶ Make every model better

Don't Oversimplify

With training for resilience, discussed in Chapter 13, the road of excess leads to good places. But with simplification, the road of excess is paved with good intentions and only leads downward. Simplicity is seductive and alluring. It promises better results for less work, all while delivering an aesthetic quality that appeals to our artistic and even spiritual natures. But too much simplicity ends up making us oblivious and indifferent to a great deal of risk we may never notice until the aftermath of an incident. Oversimplification happens when an organization is not careful enough about how much reality it is willing to give up in the name of efficiency.

HRSPs greet promises of simplicity like they would greet a salesperson who walks through the door promising that their product does more, does it better, and costs less. HRSPs take the marketing brochure with a large grain of salt and start asking hard questions. They actively and aggressively distrust and challenge attempts to boil down complex systems and processes into easily digested labels, categories, or pictures. Instead of emphasizing how much work a simpler approach saves them, an HRSP wants people to consider how much has to be hidden away from view in order to achieve that level of reduced complexity. Sacrifice too much reality to the model and you destabilize your ability to respond to your own system.

InfoSec programs that leverage the security value of complexity avoid oversimplification first by changing their attitude about complexity, much the same way that security programs that embrace the security value of failure first change their attitude about failure. Simplicity increases uncertainty in security, and oversimplifying creates risk. Therefore, an HRSP simplifies only when there is a clear need for it and a clear understanding of what is being hidden for the sake of simplification. In an HRSP, people are conditioned to pay attention to what is being ignored and to point out the assumptions that have to be accepted in order for a simplified model or framework to even work. A similarity between the security value of complexity and the security value of operations is that both are concerned with comparing what is believed with what is real. A security framework may do wonders at describing some theoretical future state, along with the 10, 20, or 100 discrete elements that get you there. HRSPs worry about the current state and how the million discrete elements already in play will influence those the framework prioritizes.

Formalize Your Assumptions

Assumptions are organized collections of uncertainty, dedicated to a specific purpose. They are mental tactics that allow us to accept things as true without any proof. Assumptions allow us to take a shortcut around problems of evidence by ignoring our lack of it. Scientists make assumptions all the time. Groups and individuals making assumptions can do so temporarily, to work through part of a problem, or they can do it permanently by transforming those assumptions into biases and prejudices. Just because something is an assumption, or even a prejudice, that does not automatically make it untrue. It just means that those who make it have little or no empirical evidence to support their assertion of belief.

By virtue of their desire to reduce the number and degree of simplifications they engage in, HRSPs naturally try to reduce the number of assumptions that have to be factored into security decisions. When HRSPs do make assumptions, they attempt to formalize them. This includes identifying them, documenting them, and making that documentation available to others. A successful audit is cause for celebration, but the security team will also be considering everything it has accepted at face value, from the competence of the auditor to the comprehensiveness of what was tested.

Formal, documented assumptions provide both a paper trail for when things go wrong and an opportunity to identify new sources of data and insight. They allow the organization to track and manage uncertainty around security decision making, which is one proxy for security risk. Formal assumptions are also a very valuable, but much underutilized, complement to security frameworks, regulatory regimes, and program plans and strategies. Comparing and rating these organizational tools according to the amount of reality they force you to ignore to reap their benefits has security as well as economic value, similar to the value of understanding the total cost of ownership over the life of the whiz-bang new product line that salesperson has come to pitch to you.

Covet Empirical Evidence

Coveting something means more than just wanting it. It means wanting it very much, to the point of obsessiveness. Recognizing the security value of complexity, HRSPs covet data and evidence because they are never satisfied with how little or how much they know about their threat environment, their security posture, and their decisions in regard to both. It's not just a question of metrics, performance indicators, or dashboards. HRSPs want evidence-based security management and scientific levels of justification, even when they know those things may not be possible with the information at hand.

One reason that HRSPs covet empirical evidence is an inversion of an argument used by many traditional security professionals, namely that security effectiveness is very difficult to measure because it's impossible to prove a negative. If you put in security technology and don't get hacked, you can't prove you didn't get hacked because you put in the security technology. This "logic" has been the basis of any number of measurement and metrics arguments I have found myself drawn into, and it would seem to make sense. How can you prove something that you did prevented something that never happened? But as presented, it's a false choice, predicated on the assumption that the underlying measurement of security effectiveness is the absence of security failure. And, as I've discussed at length in this section of the book, that's an impossible and meaningless definition that even the security industry no longer believes. But the argument still gets made.

The security value of complexity cannot be realized as long as information security programs insist on trying to understand their complex systems using only limited sources and types of data and evidence. Ignoring information because it is hard to collect or measure, or because we trust machines more than we trust people, is to accept a deliberate handicap. Low-hanging fruit eventually all gets picked. If you want more to eat, you're going to have to work a little bit (or a lot) climbing higher into the tree.

Limiting the data we use to support our InfoSec program means limiting the vocabulary we can use to discuss our program and the security it provides or facilitates. When we limit our ability to describe and discuss security, we limit the ways we are able to think about it. That leaves information security very vulnerable to disruption by anything novel, and these days it feels like everything in the threat world is novel. HRSPs work hard to think in terms of questions that need to be answered, not data that are easily available. Wanting something because it's cheap and mediocre doesn't work for security evidence any more than it does for consumer or industrial products. Not all luxury is about status or ostentation. HRSPs covet quality evidence because it gives them capabilities they can't find in the commodity brands. Good empirical evidence answers important questions and allows security to compete more effectively in the organization.

Evidence and Falsifiability

Hitchens' Razor is an axiom named after the late journalist and skeptic, Christopher Hitchens, who coined it from a Latin proverb. The axiom states, "What can be asserted without evidence can be dismissed without evidence." In other words, if you make a claim for something and you can't provide any supporting data, I am free to refute your claim without any supporting data of my own. The responsibility of proof is placed on the party making a particular claim. When helping with security measurement, I encourage CISOs and security managers to make Hitchens' Razor a core tenet of their programs, both offensively and defensively. You can't expect enterprise support or resources if you cannot back up your security claims with evidence, but neither do you have to accept arguments against the need for security when they are not supported by data.

Another interesting concept regarding evidence and truth is that of *falsifiability*, which originated with Karl Popper, a philosopher of science. Popper's argument was that for a theory to be truly scientific, it must be capable of being proven false through empirical inquiry. You have to be able to test a theory. If you can't test it by observation or experiment, then the "theory" is just a meaningless statement. Take two examples from security. If I tell my information security vendor that I don't need the vendor's product because I have no security vulnerabilities, that's a falsifiable statement and thus has scientific meaning. My vendor could do a penetration test, and if they found a vulnerable system, my theory that I have no security vulnerabilities would be instantly invalidated. That's science. But if my vendor tells me my system has been hacked, I just don't know it yet, that's not something I can test empirically. No matter how many times I find no evidence of attack, I can't disprove the theory that there might be one that I missed. So I can never prove the vendor's "theory" wrong. That may be a great marketing technique, but it's not rational science.

Share the Doubt

HRSPs run on skepticism and an obsession with taking nothing for granted. They worry that they aren't finding their failures, that they don't know what's really going on operationally, and that their models and frameworks are missing the information they need to stay safe and secure. As this section outlines, there are quite a few habits and behaviors that these organizations adopt to overcome their doubts and fears, and one of the most important is sharing those doubts inside and outside of the security program.

Simplification happens for many reasons, and one of them is that an organization relies on an experience base that is too limited. If everyone shares the same skills, background, and experiences, the chances increase that everyone will look at a problem in the same way. Diversity benefits psychological ecosystems in the same way that it benefits biological or technological ones. When you add people with different backgrounds and opinions to the mix and encourage them to interact, you get more ideas and more nuanced views of the environment and the challenges it offers. Specialists are very valuable when it comes to engaging on a specific, targeted problem, like what to do about a software flaw in widely deployed software. If you bring in a bunch of experienced software engineers, they can deconstruct that problem quickly and effectively. That's what they do. But if you ask that same specialized group of software engineers to brainstorm the five biggest security threats to your organization, you should not be surprised if all of their replies are software related. After all, that's what they do.

HRSPs encourage broader experience and value general knowledge as much as specialized skills. Jacks and Jills of all trades are welcomed for their ability to mix and mash up different concepts and insights into new knowledge. This includes coming up with novel ideas as well as novel problems with existing ideas. HRSPs apply the security value of complexity to skepticism and doubt by encouraging everyone to poke holes in theories, spot logical and conceptual flaws, and relate challenges they see in other areas to the ones under discussion.

It is not enough to just bring together specialists from different areas, as well as generalists, and let them talk. HRSPs understand that social norms and politics may impede frankness even in such brainstorming groups, so they deliberately and officially give these participants the space and freedom to question and criticize each other's ideas and arguments. Whether these interactions are conducted in person through focused group activities or by remote and asynchronous peer review systems or some other means, structures have to be created to ensure that everyone feels safe and welcome while sharing. This becomes a leadership responsibility for the organization, to emphasize that the goal of the process is to harness the collective wisdom of the organization for the benefit of everyone.

Make Every Model Better

As predictors of real phenomena, models are kind of meant to be broken. You build one, test it against reality, and realize that it's pretty flawed, so you reject that specific model and go about creating a new one. That process has been at the core of scientific inquiry for pretty much the entire history of science. Models are pretty poor substitutes for the rich complexity of a real system, be it weather, the stock market, or organizational culture. On the other hand, models allow us to describe and deconstruct those systems much more easily and cheaply than if we had to describe or re-create the whole thing with complete accuracy. It's a trade-off. We can squeeze plenty of insight and predictive power out of even an imperfect model, but compared to reality, most models possess a potential for improvement that approaches infinity.

A career in information security has brought me to the conclusion that the modeling capabilities and skills of most InfoSec programs are pretty unsophisticated. We build models all the time, and we use models everywhere, but we rarely question or even consider the assumptions on which our models are based, and we don't do much to test those models or attempt to make them better. Heat maps are models, annual loss expectancy is a model, and compliance frameworks are models, but in many cases, we have been using the same models, almost as is, for decades. When we do improve a model, it's often more about making the model "quantitative" or "prettier" than about testing its assumptions or the results we get from it. The thing is, bad models make for bad security. And imperfect models that never change or are never updated because they are never tested for accuracy are not good models.

HRSPs know that models must grow and evolve to stay relevant, especially when they are being used for decision support. Luckily, models are generative if you allow them to be. They produce the raw materials necessary for improving the model, namely the results of the model and the errors in those results, as a function of their operation. Any model that is developed should be accompanied by a formal set of assumptions that defines what the simulation has to leave out in order to work, and HRSPs already make a habit of this behavior, as I've described. Next, any predictions or insights generated by the model must be tested against the system being simulated. Did the model predict an event or a level of loss? Did that really occur? If yes, then great, we can begin looking at how the model might be expanded to predict other system behaviors. If no, then that's okay too, so long as we can go back and decide where to change our assumptions and tweak the model based on the real outcomes.

Assessing Your Complexity Value Behaviors

Use the Security FORCE Survey and Security FORCE Metrics to determine how well your organization adheres to the key complexity value behaviors and to provide empirical evidence of those behaviors.

Scoring the Complexity Value Behavior Survey

The Security FORCE Survey includes statements related to the security value of complexity. The five statements under Security Value of Complexity are listed in the sample of the FORCE Survey shown in Figure 14-1. As with previous chapters, scoring assumes Likert responses normalized on a 1 to 5 scale:

▶ An average score of 4 or above (most responses indicate Agree or Strongly Agree) signifies the organization exhibits behaviors found in an HRSP.

▶ An average score of 3 (most responses indicate the respondent felt Neutral) signifies the organization may or may not behave like an HRSP.

▶ An average score of 2 or below (most responses indicate Disagree or Strongly Disagree) signifies the organization does not exhibit the behaviors found in an HRSP.

For complexity value behaviors, an average score of 4 or greater indicates that the organization behaves in ways that will minimize oversimplification and reduce risks associated with blind spots and unrealized assumptions regarding the organized complexity of the information security environment. An average score of 2 or below indicates that the organization does not behave like an HRSP

SECURITY FORCE SURVEY

To complete this Security FORCE Survey, please indicate your level of agreement with each of the following statements regarding information security values and practices within your organization. Choose one response per statement. Please respond to all statements.

Statement	Strongly Disagree	Disagree	Neutral	Agree	Strongly Agree
Security Value of Complexity					
1. I feel like people in the organization prefer complex explanations over simple ones.					
2. I feel like people are open to being challenged or questioned about how they arrived at an answer.					
3. The organization always has plenty of data to explain and justify its decisions.					
4. People from outside the security team are encouraged to participate and question security plans and decisions.					
5. The organization formally reviews strategies and predictions to make sure they were accurate, and adjusts accordingly.					

Figure 14-1 *FORCE Value Survey statements for complexity value behaviors*

and is more likely to oversimplify the information security environment and the challenges the security program faces, and may create and increase risk and uncertainty by not making assumptions explicit, by not collecting sufficient evidence to support assertions or decisions, and by using outdated or flawed frameworks and models.

FORCE Value Metrics for Complexity

The FORCE Value Metrics for complexity, providing additional measures of HRSP behavioral alignment, can be found in Figure 14-2.

Using the FORCE Complexity Value Metrics

The five FORCE Metrics associated with the value of complexity assess how well the organization manages uncertainty and avoids oversimplification in the information security program. These measures are intended to be applied broadly across people, processes, and technology. Some of the metrics themselves represent complex and highly uncertain aspects of InfoSec, and may require necessary simplification to collect and analyze. All are suggestions and non-exhaustive, and should be used, adapted, or supplemented as appropriate.

Number, type, and complexity of adopted organizational frameworks   Organizations should understand how dependent they are upon different conceptual frameworks and models used to manage information security for the business. Collecting data on the number of frameworks or models used, along with analysis of how they

SECURITY FORCE METRICS

These metrics can be used to support, verify, and validate Security FORCE behaviors within the organization. These are not the only possible metrics available, but they provide a good baseline. You should alter or adapt these measures as required and appropriate to fit your own program and environment.

Metric	Result
Security Value of Complexity	
1. Number, type, and complexity of adopted organizational frameworks	
2. Average time to organizational decisions (from initial proposal, through debate or deliberation, to final resolution)	
3. Average number of data points collected in support of individual organizational decisions	
4. Number of formal reviews of security plans by non-security stakeholders in the past year	
5. Number of outcome and modeling evaluations conducted in the past year	

Figure 14-2   *FORCE Value Metrics for complexity value behaviors*

work, can help the organization decide how much uncertainty it is accepting. Using too many constructions that are overly simplistic or poorly understood and applied can produce results that obscure more insight than they reveal. The organization should understand if its frameworks and models are conceptual, descriptive, or technical, and whether assumptions for each construct have been fully and formally documented. An analysis of complexity should also be performed on frameworks and models, although this is necessarily a loosely defined term. At a minimum, frameworks and models should be assigned complexity ratings that result from how many inputs a framework or model allows, how many assumptions are necessary for it to function correctly, and how much variability is allowed in the results. Oversimplified frameworks and models tend to limit inputs and results, while requiring users to ignore large numbers of potential influences, in order for the construct to work properly.

Average time to organizational decisions (from initial proposal, through debate or deliberation, to final resolution)   Put very simply, how long does it take the organization to make a decision on average? Are decisions thoughtful and deliberated, with debate and input coming from many different areas? Or do they get made quickly, by a few people close to the decision itself, perhaps then "rubber stamped" through other areas of the organization? Just because a firm makes decisions quickly or without wide consensus does not mean that it is losing out on the value of complexity. But if an organization's decision-making process tends to be fast and not very rigorous, this could be a sign that oversimplification is more likely to occur during that process.

Average number of data points collected in support of individual organizational decisions
This measurement is another one that may be highly variable in its collection and analysis. A data point can refer to just about anything that goes towards supporting a particular decision, although I define the term as a specific item of empirical (observable) evidence that is collected and presented in order to influence a decision maker. The more data points that an organization can reasonably and efficiently collect, the better. If an organization is making its decisions on only a few data points, it is likely that the value of complexity is not being fully realized or exploited.

Number of formal reviews of security plans by non-security stakeholders in the past year
Like the other FORCE Metrics concerned with sharing information and collaborating on information security decisions, this measurement assesses how well an information security program is asking for feedback, assumptions,

and criticisms from other stakeholders in the firm, especially ones who may see different organizational priorities as being more important than InfoSec. The more reviews subjected to outside review and scrutiny, the better the chance that inaccurate or incomplete assumptions can be identified regarding how security will function.

Number of outcome and modeling evaluations conducted in the past year   If the frameworks and models used by an organization are not subject to review and assessment on a regular basis, they run the risk of losing their relevance and accuracy. Equally important, evaluating the effectiveness of models and frameworks by comparing expectations with results is the only way by which these constructs can be shown to be accurate in their predictive or descriptive capabilities. Basing information security on a model that consistently delivers inaccurate results creates risk, but unless that model is audited to ensure that the results it produces match what really occurs, it is very unlikely that inaccuracies or errors in the model will ever be detected. Every model or framework used by the organization should be evaluated periodically to ensure it is still meeting the organization's needs.

Improving Your Complexity Value Behaviors

Returning to Warren Weaver and the idea of organized complexity, it is difficult to understate the significance of his differentiation between types of complexity. The security industry today has become very concerned with complexity, but I believe that it may not appreciate how enormous is the size of the wrench that is thrown into the analytical gearbox when a system moves from disorganized to organized complexity. The promise of big data has been touted as being able to find patterns that will allow us to predict system behavior in aggregate, even when we cannot predict the behavior of individual system components. But that assumes disorganized complexity, where everything in the system follows the same rules, which can be determined. When complexity starts organizing itself, you get different rules in different parts of the system, and the distribution of organization may itself be random. That's not a system with a million things behaving individually according to complicated rules. It's a system composed of millions of those systems, all doing their own thing but impacting each other. It may be possible to analyze that too, but Weaver's point was that we haven't discovered how to do it yet.

HRSPs don't try to discover how to analyze and predict systems of organized complexity. They simply try to find ways to survive and thrive within those systems.

They do this by facing the implications head on. You will never understand exactly why your security systems behave the way that they do. You may understand a technology product pretty well, but people are part of that system too, and once they get involved, all bets are off. You can manage against the complexity, but you will always inevitably be surprised by emergent behavior. Instead of hoping things work the way they predicted, HRSPs spend a great deal of time and effort thinking about the ways they won't.

Improving complexity value behaviors can, paradoxically, be liberating. When you accept that you are not in complete control, you can stop putting so much effort into convincing others that you are. It opens up avenues for collaboration and cooperation that are fruitful and even pleasant, breaking down barriers between the silos of the organization and inviting people to work together to master their complex, surprising environments. People are problem solvers by nature, and people-centric security devotes itself to solving not only the problems that come from specific threats or vulnerabilities, but also the problems that come from the lack of interaction and sharing of information that keeps people locked into risk-inducing behaviors in the first place. Complexity is the most direct link between the Security FORCE Behavioral Model and the Competing Security Cultures Framework, addressing the relationships between human beings that cause complexity to become organized to begin with.

Embed Complexity Value into the Security Program

Giving up illusions of control and breaking down barriers between groups will challenge any security program. Specialization plus politics equals turf, and taking and holding territory is another thing that people have become good at over the life of our species. Many of us will not give up those instincts easily, whether they concern our homes, our job titles, or our ideas. But so many of our security problems today emerge from exactly these behaviors that it is nearly impossible to find a more appropriate candidate for organizational change. To thrive, maybe even to survive as a field, information security will have to grow more in the next decade than it has in its entire history. It is already starting to do so, but the changes that have to happen are nothing short of incredible. Five years ago, when I talked to publishers and security practitioners about wanting to write a book on culture and the sociological aspects of security, I got weird looks and suggestions that maybe I should get a job in academia. Today when I mention these topics I can even manage to get some hard-core engineers and practitioners to nod their heads in agreement.

Security has hit an inflection point where we realize just how little we know about why our systems work or don't work. In the scramble to come to grips with that knowledge, we are all taking a crash course in the security value of complexity. Some security programs will harness it better than others, put it to more productive use. And some of those programs will do it so well that they find themselves morphing into HRSPs.

Think Bigger

Thinking bigger means thinking about bigger goals, bigger challenges, and bigger stakes. Information security is one set of organized complexities living within a larger complex system. The boundaries between the subsystems—between security and other business groups, or between technology and people—are both real and imaginary. Security teams can tap into the value of complexity by practicing something they do well in a lot of other contexts: deliberately ignoring things. We make assumptions in our models and our frameworks, foregrounding or deemphasizing things as necessary. Information security can do the same thing at a program level. We can try ignoring organizational boundaries and divisions in favor of assuming that the entire enterprise functions as a single organism. How would or should that change the purpose and behavior of the security program? Or perhaps we could assume that the contributions and objectives of other organizational stakeholders are equal to our own, ignoring our own feelings that security must be given priority. How would that change our behavior? Would it encourage us to be more inclusive and complementary in our own activities?

We can build such new security behavioral models without forgetting, or even believing, the assumptions that we make. All we have to care about is giving ourselves a more sophisticated insight into how the entire system works, one that might even improve our analytical and predictive capabilities for managing and growing our own programs. At the same time, learning these behaviors can also make the entire organization better. Information discovery and sharing are central to HRSP activity, something that should be clear from the behaviors described for each of the Security FORCE values. No one in an organization can or should hold a monopoly on information, even those tasked with securing it.

Accept What We Already Know

An irony of the security value of complexity is that people already know they are not in control. The idea that the world is capricious and unpredictable, and human beings even more so, is embedded in human belief and culture. We can try to outwit or control nature, but most of us accept that we are small beings in a big universe. We need to embed that same resignation into our security programs.

Being resigned to the innate unpredictability of the world is not synonymous with despair. If anything, it can mean the opposite. I think that some of the sense of defeatism I mentioned early in the book, which I see permeating the information security field today, results from our repeated frustration and horror watching the control we thought we had be swept away like dust. If you have your best-laid plans and all your hard work invalidated in the most brutal way imaginable a few times, you can be forgiven for thinking the world's out to get you. But it's not. It's just that there are more things in heaven and earth than are currently dreamt of in our philosophy. When a thousand things can happen, but day in and day out you insist there are only three, you are bound to be regularly surprised and disappointed. It's about expanding our sense of what's possible.

Further Reading

▶ Johnson, Neil. *Simply Complexity: A Clear Guide to Complexity Theory.* Oxford: Oneworld Publications, 2009.

▶ Popper, Karl. *The Logic of Scientific Discovery.* New York: Basic Books, 1959.

▶ Weaver, Warren. "Science and Complexity." *American Scientist* 36:536 (1948).

▶ Whorf, Benjamin. "The Relation of Habitual Thought and Behavior to Language." Available at http://languageandhistory-rz.wikidot.com.

The Security Value of Expertise

Over the years that I managed penetration testing engagements, I ran into a curious phenomenon regarding expertise. Expertise should be something respected for its own sake. If you know your stuff, that knowledge should invite respect from others. At least that's how it's supposed to work. One of the reasons consultants and specialists (such as penetration testers) are hired and paid premium rates is the assumption that they know more than the organizations that hire them about their particular areas of expertise. That's why my team of security engineers was routinely hired to test customers' information security infrastructure for vulnerabilities. Our team would engage a customer, the engineers would run their reconnaissance and primary scans, perform secondary exploitation, own whatever systems they could, and then report flaws and findings. The expectation was that we would uncover things our client didn't know were there, because we were the experts. But over and over, as we would begin to report the vulnerabilities we had identified to the technical groups in charge of the information security infrastructure, they would be unsurprised. Sometimes my team would find things that these groups had told us we would find before we even started the first probes. And often they would be positively happy that the engineers had managed to break into and own a critical system. "We knew all about this," would be the general explanation for why something so bad made them feel so good. "But no one listens to us. We had to pay big money to outside experts to prove it. Now that you guys found the same problem, management will have to listen to us."

Expertise is not just about knowing something well. It's also about proximity. Being close to something can make you uniquely qualified to judge it. But being local is a double-edged sword. Organizations exist and succeed by managing a delicate balance between the local and the global, between strategy and tactics. The further up the hierarchy one gets, the more important becomes big-picture, generalized expertise. You have to know a little bit about an awful lot to manage a complex, distributed organization. But as broad expertise increases, narrow expertise tends to be lost. A CISO who started out as a brilliant security engineer back in the day probably finds she no longer has the time to focus on the details she once knew inside and out. Now she has different set of knowledge and skills, more focused on managing people and politics than individual systems (that level of management is pushed downward to subordinates). Organizational charts are really just the technical blueprints for organizational delegation, maps of decision flows within an enterprise.

Problems with enterprise effectiveness begin when hierarchies and organizational charts stop mapping dynamic flows of information and authority, and instead begin to show only the locations and boundaries of power centers.

The corrupting influence of power is a people-centric problem across all organizations. Ego and greed may supplant duty and responsibility. When people care more about their personal status and position than they do about the success of the organization, instability can result. In the case of information security, this creates uncertainty and risk, especially when something goes wrong.

Security FORCE is about improving organizational effectiveness, particularly in the face of crisis, by bringing to the foreground the priorities and behaviors that enable more highly reliable results. Expertise is too important to an organization's performance to squander its value or limit its availability when it is most needed.

What Is the Security Value of Expertise?

Power and authority are not inherently or inevitably bad things. They are requirements for just about any large-scale collective activity. If everyone is doing their own thing, under their own authority and subject to their own whims, then it's only by luck that something collective happens at all. The danger that power and authority pose to organizations is twofold: first, individual power may become more valued culturally than collective expertise and responsibility; and second, the authority to make decisions may become a privilege that is reserved only for those with power.

HRSPs take advantage of the security value of expertise by fighting the urge to value power over knowledge and skill. They recognize that power is relative and that authority is a commodity the organization has to put to good use. Power can be mismanaged and it can be wasted, just like money, electricity, or time. When optimized, authority flows through the organization to the places where it is needed, when it is needed. Expertise defines where and when those needs exist, and it means making authority more fluid so that decisions can be made by the people closest to the problem and with the best information regarding how to address it.

Filter Your Water, Not Your Information

Most people are trained from a very young age to respect authority. Parents, teachers and coaches, bosses, politicians, and professional experts of all stripes are all held up as people we should respect, listen to, and obey. We rebel against some of them, express disdain and skepticism for others, but most of us have authority figures in our lives to whom we defer. They may have direct power over us, like our employer, or they may have a different sort of power. I have not lived under my parents' authority since a long time ago, but that doesn't mean they cannot still exercise some part of their authority over me, even if it's only to make me feel a little guilty for not calling or visiting more often. And when they ask me for advice about something, even in situations where I'm strongly against what they may want to hear, I have a hard time just bluntly giving my opinion. Unlike my colleagues, or even some of my close friends, when it comes to Mom and Dad, I try not to hurt their feelings with my honesty.

The problem with sparing someone's feelings by not being completely honest is that it does not help them to make the best decisions. When filtering my opinion for my mother's sake, the consequences are usually small. She may buy a low-quality appliance against my advice because she wants to save some money. But in security programs and other organizations, filtering the information I give to the people who are senior to me can have more dire effects. I may be reluctant to share or disclose bad news or problems I believe exist. I may do this for many different reasons. Maybe I assume that, because they are upper management, they must be more competent or knowledgeable and already know what I know. Maybe I know that's not true and that there is real reason for concern, but I worry that pushing bad news up the chain of command could hurt my career or invite unwanted attention. Whatever the reason, and whoever's responsibility it is for those filters being imposed in the first place, information filtering is a dangerous practice for any organization. Being told that everything is fine, or even that it's not as bad as it really is, works only until an event or situation comes along that exposes the lie behind all the fake optimism. Then everyone is left to figure out how things went from utopia to the zombie apocalypse overnight.

Structural Authority vs. Structural Knowledge

HRSPs try to mitigate the risks that come when expertise and local knowledge are suppressed, either unintentionally or by design, by authority and power. They know that where someone sits in an organizational chart may have very little correlation with how much that person knows about a particular situation, especially something like an information security failure. Expecting that visibility into a security incident will correspond to how high someone sits in the management hierarchy only makes it likely that the organization will be flying relatively blind. Power and expertise tend to be two separate but interactive systems within any enterprise. Power, embodied in authority structures like job titles, organizational charts, and management chains, defines who can make decisions. Expertise, embodied in knowledge structures like individual and team experience, available skills and training, and the informal and situational information that only exists when people work closely to the systems themselves, defines what decisions need to be made.

Striking a balance between organizational authority and organizational knowledge often is difficult. People without power and organizational stature can end up feeling (and being treated) like they are invisible, even if they know more about what's really going on than anyone else. And the higher someone rises in the hierarchy, the more they may be tempted to feel superior instead of just senior. The problems that arise when one structure has more say than the other are not just theoretical. In *Managing the Unexpected*, Weick and Sutcliffe cite the official report on the problems at NASA that led to the accident that destroyed the *Columbia* space shuttle. One key cause of the tragedy was that NASA, over the years, had developed a chain-of-command structure that overrode all other sources of information, including the technical knowledge and experience of NASA's own engineers. As a result, problems were downplayed and ignored until they turned into catastrophe.

In an HRSP, the goal becomes one of never allowing the influence of one structure to outweigh or overcome the influence of another. What this usually means in practice is protecting expertise and knowledge from becoming subservient to authority and power. Experience and insight "from the trenches" should always be valued and respected, even when (and maybe especially when) it contradicts what senior leaders think or what they want to hear. This is accomplished by assigning expertise and knowledge its own brand of authority, the same kind of authority that we reserve for other specialists and professionals we call upon in life. If you visit a mechanic and he tells you that you need a new transmission, or if you see a doctor and she tells you that you need to go on medicine for some illness you have, you may not like the news. But you are unlikely to ignore them, even if you own the garage in which the mechanic works or are a board member of the doctor's hospital. Ignoring or downplaying security problems reported by your InfoSec team just because you have enough power to do so is, to use a technical term, dumb.

Optimally, decisions in an HRSP are routed to the points where authority and expertise intersect. They can move back and forth between the knowledge structure and the authority structure. In some cases, it is a matter of quick response, like when factory workers can shut down an assembly line if they see a problem. In others, it is a matter of who has the best visibility and insight. Senior members of an organization are not without their own specialized expertise, all jokes and pointy-haired cartoon characters aside. Some decisions may impact multiple sets of stakeholders and need to be made not by a technician but by a politician.

Bob and Clara Revisited: Migrating Authority

Early on in the book, I introduced Bob and Clara. Bob was the safety officer in my vendor conference who triggered an evacuation over burnt bacon. Clara was the software developer who got her project done on time but found out later the corners she cut on security resulted in a security vulnerability in her company's product. Both of these individuals represent experts who made decisions. And both are examples of how and why authority to make particular security decisions often need to migrate to the person in the organization who has the best expertise to make that decision.

In Bob's case, authority moved the right way. It went down the chain of command to find the best person to make the call. The company had already thought about these scenarios and, at least in the case of physical safety, practiced a system of marrying up power with expertise. Bob was the recognized expert, so the decision was his and everyone deferred to him, even the executives running the event. The fact that Bob's evacuation order proved unnecessary was both fortunate and beside the point. Imagine if one of the company's VPs had decided that Bob was overreacting and countermanded his directive in the interest of time, only to have people hurt or even killed in a real fire. That scenario is more like what happened after the sensitive document was discovered in the breakout room during the conference, albeit without such physically dire consequences. Whether because of an absence of identified expertise or some other reason, the decision to chastise the audience and move on rather than investigate a serious lapse in security migrated to the senior executive in the room, who did not apparently have the expertise to recognize the severity of the problem.

For Clara, authority moved the wrong way. It should have gone up the chain of command. Clara's decision was not between finishing her security testing or finishing the project on time. That was only the immediate scenario. Instead, Clara had to decide between two specific enterprise risks. One risk was the impact on the firm of potentially delaying an important product release. The other risk was the future impact on the firm should a vulnerability be discovered in the product. Those risks cut across multiple stakeholders and parameters, including financial ramifications, legal liabilities, and impacts on the corporate brand, to name a few. Clara did not have the expertise to make that decision, although by default she had the authority. The expertise to deal with decisions regarding enterprise risk is just what you would hope to find in senior management, who have wider visibility and more insight into consequences at the corporate level. But the people best positioned to make that call were never informed, in part because Clara was afraid that in bringing the bad news to management she would be punished instead of rewarded. And so she was, along with everyone else, but only after it was too late to ask for help.

Waiting for the Big One

In organizations in some sectors, like commercial aviation, healthcare, and the military, process and procedure can approach almost religious status. Policies, procedures, and checklists can evolve to cover almost every conceivable scenario that the organization has dealt with or has been able to think of. Members and employees of these organizations can become so indoctrinated into standardized ways of doing things that those ways become unconscious ritual. In many cases this works, sometimes exceptionally well. Atul Gawande's book *The Checklist Manifesto* demonstrates the positive side of checklist-driven activity, and Gawande makes a strong case for meticulously following standardized procedures. But what happens when something takes place that you have never experienced before and have never thought of? What happens when there is no checklist? The irony of all that useful standardization is that it can, in certain scenarios, make a bad situation much worse. When everyone is used to doing things exactly a certain way, not being able to do it that way can cause paralysis. The system may lock up, literally and figuratively. Information security struggles with this balance, between the unarguable value of defined processes and checklist procedures and the danger of turning those same checklists into a crutch that relieves people of the responsibility to think and adapt.

Bureaucracy is a fantastic stabilizer, like organizational concrete that can fix processes in place so that they last decades, even centuries. But concrete is rigid and not very adaptable once it hardens. That's why we have wrecking balls. Bureaucracy can also be battered and crushed into dust. Some companies do just that after a serious security incident. The CISO is fired (or a CISO is hired, if there wasn't one before). The existing organizational chart and technology infrastructures may get torn down and replaced. Perhaps the entire security program is moved into another part of the enterprise. But if at the conclusion of that process all that results is a new bureaucracy, a different structure with the same rigidity, what's really changed? It's like rebuilding after an earthquake. If you don't change the fundamental principles and try to make buildings less susceptible to unforeseen shocks, you're starting out on borrowed time.

HRSPs use expertise and authority to make their organizations less prone to shocks like structural engineers use base isolators or reinforced concrete to make their buildings earthquake resistant. There is certainly structure in an HRSP. People have roles and superiors and subordinates. Policies and processes define activity. But when put under stress, the organization adapts by finding the right combination of knowledge and authority to respond. Unlike a building, where physics and mechanics determine which pieces shift and which absorb, in an organization the resistance is accomplished through processes and networks of people, along with all the knowledge and skill they possess. They allow the organization to temporarily shift and reconfigure itself, managing the stresses and forces it encounters without collapsing.

The Road to Damascus

Eric Schlosser's book *Command and Control*, about nuclear accidents during the Cold War, is must reading for any security professional, particularly for people like me who are interested in how competing cultures create risk. But more immediately, *Command and Control* speaks to the security value of expertise. In describing the 1980 Damascus, Arkansas, incident, a deadly accident at a nuclear missile silo in Arkansas, Schlosser recounts story after story within the crisis where breakdowns in decision and authority flows added to the danger and uncertainty of the incident. All along the way, the very nature of the military's rigid command system, controlled through meticulous attention to procedure and checklists and obsessively deferential to seniority and rank, built up organizational pressures that were as dangerous as the fuel vapors that caused the physical explosion.

Schlosser writes in great length about the dependence of the missile crews on checklists, which precisely defined every aspect of missile crew activity and maintenance. Addressing every (supposedly) imaginable detail of the care and servicing of the ICBMs the Air Force owned, checklists structured just about every aspect of life for the crews on duty. But when a socket from a socket wrench a maintenance crew member was using during a routine procedure fell into the silo and punctured one of the missile's fuel tanks, the Air Force soon found out it faced a situation for which it had no checklist. Without a checklist, the missile crew and their superiors literally did not know what to do and had to go about building a brand-new checklist to deal with a crisis they were already in the middle of. As authority migrated upward, commanding officers refused to take any action until the checklist was in place and procedures established once again. Reality for them was the process. The brown haze of fuel vapor building up in the silo only existed locally.

At the bottom of the chain of command, some local experts chafed under the restrictions placed upon them as they watched the danger building in the silo by the minute. In some cases the airmen and technicians obeyed the orders they were given, some doing so even as they questioned the decisions of their superior officers. At other times they rebelled against the orders they were receiving from people who were far away and more concerned with issues of public relations and politics, instead favoring local expertise that might save their friends' and colleagues' lives. In the end, no one escaped unscathed. One crew member died and many were injured, an outcome that would likely have been less catastrophic if authority had been delegated to the local level. Some crew members were punished because they took it upon themselves to exercise local authority anyway by disregarding orders they thought made no sense. The entire incident served as a demonstration that you simply cannot plan for everything, that when facing a completely novel scenario, one where no script or checklist exists, the importance of reconfiguring organizational expertise and authority to meet the new challenge can mean the difference between life and death. It's a lesson as valuable for HRSPs as it is for nuclear missile crews, to be sure.

Expertise Key Value Behaviors

The secret of organizational expertise is that everyone possesses it. Expertise is not limited by rank in the hierarchy or salary or political status. It's not even limited to a single person at a time. Expertise is an organizational capability, a byproduct of human capital. By definition, everyone in an organization is an expert in something, possesses some specialized knowledge about his or her job functions that no one else possesses (except perhaps others who hold the same position). This even applies to people who don't do much work at all—it often takes a great deal of skill to avoid doing anything. HRSPs utilize the security value of expertise to make their organizations more supple and nimble, especially when facing an incident or a crisis event that they have not encountered previously.

HRSPs want to function in a stable and predictable way just like any other organization, but during a security incident they also want to be able to reconfigure themselves, or at least their information and authority flows. Instead of slowly and inefficiently forcing information up the chain and decisions back down, expertise and authority are combined wherever they are most needed. It's a process that cannot be accomplished if it is not embedded in culture, in mutual respect and trust that overcome natural desires for control and power, which is probably why it is one of the hardest sets of behaviors for an HRSP to maintain over time. The behaviors that characterize the security value of expertise include

- ▶ Ask the experts
- ▶ Suppress the egos
- ▶ Allow authority to migrate
- ▶ Share credibility
- ▶ Reward calls to action and cries for help

Ask the Experts

Strange as it may seem, given the large amount of media coverage of information security breaches and given the high level of importance being placed on information security by many sectors of society, I regularly encounter situations where the people in an organization who know the most about security are not the ones who get asked for input about it. This often happens not because of any deliberate policy, but as a result of the basic disconnect I described earlier with regard to hiring external pen testers. Companies know they have security experts, hired and trained to perform that role. But when the communication of expert knowledge has to be channeled up through successive layers of management, the temptation by those layers to shape and control the message can be overwhelming. I've met very few board members or senior executives who do not want to be told if there is a serious problem in the organization, yet I've also met more than a few front-line and middle managers who actively avoid having to tell higher-ups when such a serious problem exists.

There are also cases where experts aren't asked for input because their expertise is, or seems to be, so operational or specialized that most people can't or don't understand it. It's human nature to downplay the importance of things that we do not fully comprehend, as well as to pretend we know more about them than we do when we make our decisions. It cuts both ways. I've talked to security engineers and administrators who are convinced that senior managers are "clueless suits" who have no business running a company because they don't know the "obvious" answers to information security issues. If the security engineer or administrator can see the problem so clearly, how can the executive not? From the executive's standpoint, the engineer or administrator may come across as a parochial specialist, convinced that information security is the most important thing in the company, when in fact it is just one more variable in a complex business equation.

In an HRSP, expertise is valued for its own sake and forms the organization's cognitive capability to deal with the failure, operations, resilience and, especially, complexity that must be managed to create effective security. HRSPs are always trying to find new sources of expertise and find out what they know. At higher levels in the bureaucracy that means understanding different stakeholder positions and requirements so as to better adapt security to the business. At the lower levels it means identifying who can tell you the most about whatever it is you may need to know, regardless of that person's rank or political clout. Whether the person is the patch analyst who understands all the things that can go wrong updating even vulnerable software, the security guard who knows which entrances are most susceptible to tailgating, or the administrative assistant who is not even part of the InfoSec program but knows the passwords of half the executive staff because they keep giving them to her against company policy when they are too busy to do something themselves, all these people possess privileged knowledge that is independent of their level of privilege.

Suppress the Egos

Naturally, some organizations are more egalitarian than others. In the best cases, the idea of pulling together as a team is not just a cliché. That doesn't necessarily mean there is no rank or organizational hierarchy, although companies have experimented with going down that path too. Fostering a more communal workplace environment is in vogue these days, which includes approaches such as adopting open floor plans, abandoning performance reviews, and launching internal campaigns to create a sense of community and even family inside the organization. Sometimes these approaches are less than sincere, and they don't always work even when they are sincere, but their growing popularity reflects a sense that promoting trust and a sense of shared purpose adds enterprise value.

Equality doesn't mean that everyone gets paid the same salary, has the same job title, or does not have to take orders from anyone else. Rather, equality means that no one in the organization is considered any more vital than anyone else. A customer told me a great anecdote that illustrates this perfectly, about a meeting in which the customer's CEO discussed a new compensation plan. Under the new plan, the number of employees receiving bonuses was going to be expanded greatly. One employee expressed some concern that the company was rewarding people who had nothing to do with the core business and didn't deserve the same bonus as the people in more mission-critical roles. The CEO responded by holding up his hand to show the watch on his wrist, then asked the employee to point out which parts of the watch were not "mission critical" and could therefore be thrown out.

Getting rid of egotism in business is like getting rid of security vulnerabilities in commercial software: an admirable but not very realistic goal. HRSPs do not attempt to suppress ego altogether or to discourage a sense of pride in individual accomplishments, but they do understand that egotism can lead to arrogance and arrogance can make a security problem exponentially worse. No one in a modern organization is responsible for all the success, no matter how talented they are. HRSPs try to make another cliché reality, that security is everyone's responsibility. Many organizations invoke this phrase when they want to emphasize that everyone has to follow security policies no matter what position they hold or where they work. HRSPs use the phrase as a mantra reflecting the security value of expertise. If you know more about your individual job than anyone else in the organization, then you know best about how security works in the context of that job. The security value of expertise means that you have a responsibility to share your knowledge with the rest of the enterprise and that other people have a responsibility to respect what you know and ask for your insight. It doesn't matter if that person is your colleague in the cube next door or the chairman of the board.

Allow Authority to Migrate

There are a few prerequisites for the key behavior of allowing authority to migrate within the organization: knowing where expertise exists and asking for help from those who possess it, and suppressing the egotism that might make those requests more difficult. Once more, it's important to differentiate between a completely open authority structure, where one's expertise defines one's power, and an adaptable structure, where the organization can deliberately loosen the controls and free up decision authority if necessary. HRSPs do not have to be any more democratic than any other security program. What they do better is to recognize that there are some scenarios, usually security events that turn the normal order of things on its head, where a rigid command-and-control hierarchy is not the best approach and is more likely to exacerbate the situation. In these cases, the organization restructures temporarily to meet the new challenges. Authority goes to where it's going to be of most immediate use, and expertise defines where that is.

Allowing authority to migrate means that, under certain circumstances, actual decision authority will be delegated elsewhere within the organization, usually downward to the individuals and teams closest to the affected systems. For information security, this might mean placing a lot more power in the hands of the CISO to proactively respond to an incident. More likely still, it means allowing front-line managers and engineering teams to make executive decisions about what needs to be done in a crisis. Under these challenging circumstances, senior leaders will stay in constant contact, offering their support and any advice they can provide, but they will stay out of the way while the people closest to the work make the decisions. For many organizations, just the suggestion of this arrangement is enough to make people uncomfortable, but time and time again, from NASA to nuclear missile teams to commercial enterprises, when senior leaders insist on micromanaging fluid and immediate crisis scenarios, the results are rarely good. Time simply does not afford the luxury of sending information about what's going on up and down the chain of command. Often, by the time one piece of information reaches a point where someone can make a decision, the situation has changed again and that decision no longer makes sense.

The key to marrying authority with expertise in the enterprise is to identify the subject matter experts you may need before the crisis occurs, so that looking for the right people to take the helm is not a matter of blind guessing or luck of the draw in the midst of extreme circumstance. And senior leaders don't just hand over the reins and say "call me when you're done." They stay on top of the situation and monitor it, putting themselves at the ready for when circumstances require authority to migrate back to them. During a security incident, you probably don't want the CEO deciding whether or not a particular server needs to be taken offline any more than you want the server's administrator to make the call about whether or not to alert the press.

Share Credibility

Authority and credibility are tightly coupled. Those without the latter tend to lose the former. HRSPs do their best to ensure that expertise is recognized and respected throughout the organization, that it brings with it the credibility necessary to make people accept that a designated person can be safely given authority during an incident or event. Ensuring that expertise is recognized and respected is accomplished in part by putting effort and resources into building human capital, as I have discussed previously. People's training, skills, and experience have to be officially recognized and supported for this to function. In a crisis, people at all levels of the organization have to trust that their fellow members not only are willing to help, but possess the ability to help. If one group thinks another group is incompetent, the likelihood is low that the first group is going to follow the latter group's lead when disaster looms. In my recounting of the Mann Gulch fire in Chapter 13, I described how several of the smoke jumpers balked at the foreman's order to start another fire, lie down, and let it pass over them. Because the team had not worked together extensively, the foreman lacked credibility despite his extensive experience, and failing to defer to his superior expertise cost several men their lives.

There is no simple process for sharing credibility inside an organization. It is a cultural trait, defined first by the belief that expertise means something important to the enterprise, and then by everyone demonstrating a healthy level of respect and deference to those who possess expertise. Since everyone possesses some level of specialized expertise, this means that deference has to become something of a universal attribute. It must be constantly nurtured and reinforced through action and example. This can be more easily accomplished in smaller companies, or even family-owned firms where the sense of personal stake is more a feature of everyday life than it is in public companies. But every organization that wishes to be highly reliable needs a level of deference to expertise. If it can't be achieved through emotional appeals, it needs to be done structurally, embedded into meetings, performance reviews, and training programs. When everything goes to hell, the last thing the organization can afford is for people to be questioning whether or not the people who are best positioned to do the job are the best people for the job.

Reward Calls to Action and Cries for Help

Part of the security value of expertise for individuals and organizations alike comes from knowing what expertise you have and what knowledge you're lacking, and then reacting appropriately in the moment. HRSPs go out of their way to reward not only teams and people who take action based on their expertise, but also people who realize that authority needs to migrate and thus ask others for help. Like the other key behaviors, knowing when to act and when to defer to others requires both a solid awareness of where knowledge and expertise exist within the organization and the ability to decide which situations call for what kind of authority. Trust and credibility are crucial here, because not every decision in the midst of a fluid situation is going to be the best one. The real question is not whether a decision was right or not, but whether the right person made it. Anyone can screw up, even an expert, but migrating authority to the proper expert to make a decision is going to increase the organization's odds of choosing the best path forward. There is no greater test of character for an HRSP than to reward someone for making the wrong decision at the right time.

We tend to reserve our admiration and respect for people who take charge in a crisis, showing their strength and mettle when others around them are panicking. But the bold play isn't always the smart one. Egotism and arrogance can turn heroism into foolhardiness as easily as fear and lack of confidence can paralyze. Both are irrational responses, and neither gets great results. HRSPs expect the organization to remain levelheaded. Sometimes that means to charge ahead, but it can just as easily mean to fall back and request reinforcements. HRSPs reserve their praise and reward for the times when expertise and authority are properly aligned and brought to bear on a problem or a failure. The measures of success are much less about individual personalities and more about what was likely to bring about the best outcome for the entire system. As anyone who has ever had to admit that they are in over their head understands, expressing your weakness and limitations and asking someone else for help often takes a lot more courage than forging ahead on your own. Senior leaders can be especially prone to taking the latter course, often because they fear damaging the formidable reputations that they have built over many years. But what makes HRSPs work differently than other security teams is exactly their ability to put the security and stability of the enterprise ahead of any individual insecurities or personal concerns.

"We're Changing the World"

One of my favorite books in policy studies is James Scott's *Seeing Like a State*. Scott, a Yale political scientist and anthropologist, sets out to describe why so many of the large-scale attempts at social engineering in the 20th century failed, often terribly. Enormous collective projects, sometimes by authoritarian regimes with near total control of their citizens, have attempted to transform entire nations in relatively short time spans. From the Soviet Union to China, and from Tanzania to Brazil, countries have tried to collectivize, to industrialize, and to create entire cities and societies from nothing.

(continues)

"We're Changing the World" *(continued)*

When these projects didn't work, the results ranged from the merely epic failure to complete horror, including famine, displacement, and suffering on a massive scale. Some nations were set back a generation as a result of the hubris and determination of their leaders to create or re-create a national utopia. Even when the results were less disastrous and the outcome limited to failed civil and engineering projects that never quite seemed to take, the costs remained huge. For Scott, the cause of these failed nation-building projects was fairly simple. States, whether embodied by a dictator or a government, become victims of their own grand vision when they lose the connection between that vision and the everyday knowledge and practice of the masses of people who actually comprise the state. Scott called this ignored and marginalized practical knowledge *metis*, and it represented the common, everyday skills and experiences of individuals. In the context of HRSPs, expertise is quite similar to metis, and organizations neglect it at their peril.

Thankfully, many of the massive collectivist schemes of the last century appear to be products of their place and time. But that doesn't mean we've solved the problem. The 21st century has seen its share of large social engineering errors, at the level of both countries and organizations, some of which echo the clashes between theory and practice described in *Seeing Like a State*. In the worst cases, the result is war, regional instability, and global financial crises. But things don't have to get that bad to see Scott's causes and general effects on a smaller scale in reorganizations, acquisitions, and failed enterprise implementations that somehow always seem to work better on paper than they do in real life. Often, the reason these projects crash and burn is the same disconnection between authority and knowledge, between high-level and local experience, that I have discussed in this chapter. The edifices that are built are not flexible and adaptable enough to withstand the tremors and shocks they must endure, a fate that HRSPs try to avoid by harnessing the security value of expertise.

Assessing Your Expertise Value Behaviors

Use the Security FORCE Survey and Security FORCE Metrics to determine how well your organization adheres to the key expertise value behaviors and to provide empirical evidence of those behaviors.

Scoring the Expertise Value Behavior Survey

The Security FORCE Survey includes statements related to the security value of expertise. The five statements under Security Value of Expertise are listed in the sample of the FORCE Survey shown in Figure 15-1. As with previous chapters, scoring assumes Likert responses normalized on a 1 to 5 scale:

▶ An average score of 4 or above (most responses indicate Agree or Strongly Agree) signifies the organization exhibits behaviors found in an HRSP.

▶ An average score of 3 (most responses indicate the respondent felt Neutral) signifies the organization may or may not behave like an HRSP.

▶ An average score of 2 or below (most responses indicate Disagree or Strongly Disagree) signifies the organization does not exhibit the behaviors found in an HRSP.

For expertise value behaviors, an average score of 4 or greater indicates that the organization behaves in ways that will allow authority to migrate and join up with the expertise needed to make effective decisions under stress. A score of 2 or below indicates that the organization does not behave like an HRSP and is more likely to experience problems of bureaucratic rigidity or lack of adaptability

SECURITY FORCE SURVEY

To complete this Security FORCE Survey, please indicate your level of agreement with each of the following statements regarding information security values and practices within your organization. Choose one response per statement. Please respond to all statements.

Statement	Strongly Disagree	Disagree	Neutral	Agree	Strongly Agree
Security Value of Expertise					
1. I know exactly where to go in the organization when I need an expert.					
2. I think everyone in the organization feels that monitoring security is part of their job.					
3. In the event of a security incident, people can legitimately bypass the bureaucracy to get things done.					
4. People in the organization are encouraged to help other groups if they have the right skills to help them.					
5. I feel empowered to take action myself, if something is about to cause a security failure.					

Figure 15-1   *FORCE Value Survey Statements for Expertise Value Behaviors*

that keeps the expertise necessary to understand a problem separated from the authority necessary to act on it.

FORCE Value Metrics for Expertise

The FORCE Value Metrics for expertise, providing additional measures of HRSP behavioral alignment, can be found in Figure 15-2.

Using the FORCE Expertise Value Metrics

The five FORCE Metrics associated with the value of expertise describe an organization's success at ensuring that expert knowledge is identified, effectively managed, and coupled with the power to act locally where decision making is required in a given situation. They track the location of expertise and migration paths of authority and, where these things do not exist, offer insight into how to increase the value of expertise for the InfoSec program. As with all the FORCE Metrics, these measurements and indicators are suggestions and non-exhaustive, and should be used, adapted, or supplemented as appropriate.

Number of formal knowledge or skill repositories in place   An organization cannot hope to migrate authority to the right decision makers if it does not know where expertise, knowledge, or specialized skills currently exist. Knowledge and skill repositories are often the domain of enterprise knowledge management

---

SECURITY FORCE METRICS

These metrics can be used to support, verify, and validate Security FORCE behaviors within the organization. These are not the only possible metrics available, but they provide a good baseline. You should alter or adapt these measures as required and appropriate to fit your own program and environment.

Metric	Result
Security Value of Expertise	
1. Number of formal knowledge or skill repositories in place	
2. Number of people with security responsibilities written into their job descriptions	
3. Number of identified "quick response" scenarios with expedited decision making	
4. Number of decision owners for security formally assigned in the past year	
5. Number of cross-functional security-related activities or projects in the past year (initiated internally by the information security program or externally by other stakeholders)	

Figure 15-2   *FORCE Value Metrics for expertise value behaviors*

professionals, and these groups are a great place to begin if the information security program is starting fresh. At their most simple, these repositories are simply lists and databases of the knowledge and skills currently existing within an organization. Sources can include training and education records, job descriptions, or crowd-sourced and self-selected repositories (a previous employer of mine, for example, allowed everyone in the corporate directory to add their skills and knowledge to their directory profiles, then made this information searchable as part of the directory).

Number of people with security responsibilities written into their job descriptions   Nothing says "I'm responsible for this…" like explicitly writing it into a job description. For the information security team, these inclusions are likely taken for granted. In fact, if the InfoSec program doesn't score 100% on this metric, then that may be the first place to start. But the organization should not stop there. Anyone responsible for technology management certainly should have something about security built into their job requirements. As enterprise security culture matures, security responsibilities should become more widespread and more specific across all job descriptions, replacing the current practice of making people responsible for undergoing security training periodically, which is not the same thing. The point is to achieve more than just accountability. If a company makes an employee responsible for some aspect of information security as a job requirement, it takes on responsibility of its own to make sure the employee is trained to do that job. The more specific and comprehensive these responsibilities get, the more they can feed into a functional repository of expertise the firm can leverage.

Number of identified "quick response" scenarios with expedited decision making   This measurement collects data regarding how many "decision fast lanes" exist within the organization. A quick response scenario is one that has already been identified and analyzed such that, should it occur, authority immediately migrates to a predetermined locus of expertise, be that a group, a functional role, or an individual. Think of these scenarios as parallel structures to the incident or disaster scenarios that the organization creates in anticipation of security events. In fact, a quick response scenario can be as basic as an addendum to an existing incident or disaster scenario that specifies how authority migrates during that incident. A useful application of this metric is to determine how much coordination an organization will have to do should a security incident occur. If a fast lane has not been established beforehand, the organization can assume that information will have to travel from the point of origin or discovery of the incident through the entire chain of authority and back before action can be taken, even if local experts already know the best response.

Number of decision owners for security formally assigned in the past year   A corollary indicator with ties to both the assignment of security responsibilities and the assignment of ownership for assets and risk, decision owners are defined as the people in an organization with the authority to take action in response to a security event. Decision owners may be local, for instance, a system administrator with the authority to immediately restrict access of an unrecognized user account on his machine. Or they may be more removed from the immediate incident but local to other concerns, like the firm's general counsel, who is responsible for deciding when the organization notifies the authorities or the public about the security breach that the unknown user account represents. The purpose of this metric is to capture and make available where these decision points exist. If no decision owners are assigned, this again is a strong indicator that the organization will need to take precious time to determine or create these information and authority flows in the midst of a crisis.

Number of cross-functional security-related activities or projects in the past year (initiated internally by the information security program or externally by other stakeholders)   This measure assesses the sharing and coordination of expertise both within the InfoSec program and between InfoSec and other groups and functions of the organization or beyond (partners, vendors, regulators, etc.) Cross-functional activities are those developed with the intent of fostering the exploration and sharing of expertise between different units. They may be training sessions or knowledge sharing workshops, but the emphasis should be on two or more different groups coming together to share knowledge, not one group disseminating content or teaching another. These latter activities, while useful, do not foster the two-way exchange of information that facilitates the value of expertise. Cross-functional insights are attained when all the groups present have a chance to challenge and collaborate with each others as equal partners. But these activities do not have to be overly formal or burdensome. Any opportunity for groups to observe how others manage and do information security, especially when they do different things or do things differently from one another, is a useful exercise.

Improving Your Expertise Value Behaviors

All of the Security FORCE values have psychological components, requirements that an organization's members change the way they think about its values in order to achieve more highly reliable security. But embracing the security value of expertise can be difficult to encourage behaviorally, as it challenges the way we look at ourselves and compare our own sense of value with that of others. As a FORCE value, leveraging the security value of expertise means facing up to the idea that some people are smarter and more capable than you are, and that they may be better positioned for success in certain situations. It also means accepting that in other situations, the smartest, most-capable person in the room may be you, which can be an equally scary prospect.

When emotion is taken out of the equation, though, the logic becomes very simple. Response during a crisis of any kind, including security incidents, requires a combination of knowledge about circumstances and the power to take action on information about the problem. Inefficiencies that result from having to negotiate between the people who have the knowledge and the people who have the power degrade the response capability of the system as a whole; therefore, negotiations of this type are unambiguously bad if they reduce response time and effectiveness, or make things worse. It is a uniquely human problem, found only in complex social systems where ego and personal agendas have to be factored into the mix. It's not a problem we find in technology systems, where software and hardware components know their place and function unimpeded by ego or politics. Organizational programming such as culture is more complicated, so our solutions have to be more sophisticated too.

Embed Expertise Value into the Security Program

Building better conduits between expertise and authority flows requires a combination of process, culture, and a desire by members of an organization to overcome barriers to their own success. As we have seen, actions and decisions happen more efficiently when they have become habit. So HRSPs try to create habits of behavior that make sharing expertise, credibility, and authority easier. But they also focus on promoting the cultural values that enable those habits to become ingrained. This combination can be difficult to get right, but when that is achieved, the result can be stunning: an organization that has a clear command-and-control structure under normal conditions but is able to reconfigure itself quickly in a crisis, like some sort of advanced material, adapting to stress, shifting strength and reaction to where it is most needed, then returning to its original form once the crisis has passed.

Make Everyone a Sensor

I have a number of humble sensors in my home. My smoke alarms are inexpensive commodity appliances designed to be nearly invisible. Timers and alarms of all sorts are scattered throughout my house. Even the natural gas I use to cook with is embedded with tiny molecules of chemical, probably methyl mercaptan, that gives the otherwise odorless gas its familiar sulfur smell that alerts me of a leak (although technically, in this case, my nose becomes the sensor). I am far more powerful and evolved than any of these devices. But when they trigger, they instantly demand my full attention. Under certain circumstances, I depend upon them for their expertise.

HRSPs take that idea and run with it. Lance Spitzner likes to talk about "human sensors" within the organization, and I think it's a great analogy, one that has been explored throughout the HRO research literature as well. People are the most sophisticated sensors that any organization will ever hope to field, capable of far more than the relatively dumb stimulus-trigger logic of even sophisticated technological sensors. An organization that cares about the security value of expertise will never ignore any potential source of useful data. It won't care where that source sits in the pecking order, so long as it's close to the action in any given situation. The challenge an HRSP cares about is how to query all these sensors effectively, how to find the expertise, to ask those experts what's happening, and maybe even give them authority to take action.

Create Decision Fast Lanes

Information needs to travel. We even talk about information pipes, conduits, and highways. When those become congested or roadblocks are erected, to extend the metaphor, communication breaks down. Decisions are just a specialized form of information. Knowing that they may face scenarios where the distance between knowledge and authority needs to collapse quickly, HRSPs try to create shortcuts ahead of time, like evacuation routes or HOV lanes in the physical world. As a result of other Security FORCE behaviors, the organization will already have considered many failure scenarios, and part of those considerations will be plans and capabilities for quickly marrying up expertise with power. By predefining contingencies in which authority will migrate, the organization gets an immediate jump on things. As I mentioned earlier, this is not about senior management removing themselves from the equation. During a security incident or any other crisis, organizational leaders in an HRSP will remain intimately involved, but in a supporting role until such time as a decision must be made that requires their own personal expertise.

A lot of the discussion about authority migration involves top-down movement, because power tends to be concentrated at the higher levels of the organizational chart. But authority may need to flow upward as well, especially in cases where lower-level decision makers may not have all the big picture data needed to make decisions that have larger or more political ramifications. In these cases, decision fast lanes will have to overcome different obstacles. Instead of convincing managers to give up power temporarily to those further down the hierarchy, upward authority migration often has to overcome the filtering of information and suppression of bad news that prevents senior leaders from understanding the risks they may be facing.

Value Expertise from the Top Down

The security value of expertise often highlights what goes on at the lower ends of the organizational chart, but the truth is that harnessing that value starts with enterprise senior leaders. One of the best things a leader can do is to accept their own relative powerlessness over, and ignorance about, much of what goes on in their environment. Setting a humble example for others, particularly subordinates, can be tough. Much of our traditional ways of thinking about business puts individualism on a pedestal. But like the home of Percy Shelley's king, Ozymandias, the desert is littered with broken pedestals and the remnants of once invincible empires. The myth of the indispensible CEO has been pretty thoroughly busted. Even the best executive leaders accomplish what they do only because they do so in partnership with others. Yet that myth remains resilient and enduring in industry culture, often perpetuated by those who tend to benefit from it.

Earlier in the chapter I referenced Schlosser's *Command and Control*, with its descriptions of dysfunctional Air Force power dynamics that contributed to a bad accident almost literally going nuclear. Let me end the chapter by pointing out that the military is also one of the best examples of an organization that lives and sometimes dies by the value of expertise. The Damascus accident notwithstanding, the U.S. military orchestrates some of the most efficient marriages of knowledge and authority imaginable, and any good general knows that sometimes you have to depend on the fact that the squad on the ground is the only one that can make the call, and then let them make it.

Further Reading

▶ Gawande, Atul. *The Checklist Manifesto: How to Get Things Right.* New York: Metropolitan Books, 2009.

▶ Schlosser, Eric. *Command and Control: Nuclear Weapons, the Damascus Incident, and the Illusion of Safety.* New York: The Penguin Press, 2013.

▶ Scott, James C. *Seeing Like a State: How Certain Schemes to Improve the Human Condition Have Failed.* New Haven, CT: Yale University Press, 1998.

16

Behavior and Culture: Mastering People-Centric Security

I n Chapter 8 I discussed how to implement a security culture diagnostic project, including how to get support for the project, how to execute the project, and how to interpret and use the results collected from the Security Culture Diagnostic Survey (SCDS) instrument. Chapter 9 made the point that diagnosing and measuring security culture is not the same thing as improving and transforming it. Now that I have presented both the Competing Security Cultures Framework (CSCF) and the Security FORCE Behavioral Model in depth, we can consider how these two complementary frameworks can be combined to create comprehensive people-centric security transformation.

What Does Security Culture Transformation Mean?

I have discussed security culture transformation in several contexts and at several levels during the course of the book. Transforming security culture can refer to a number of outcomes, including changing existing security culture types to different ones (for example, from a Process Culture to an Autonomy Culture); encouraging or discouraging specific cultural traits and behaviors within a security culture type (for example, focusing on how risk is managed or how failure is handled); or growing and developing a behavior-based security culture around a desired model (for example, Security FORCE and highly reliable security programs). These results are all forms of security culture transformation. But they don't capture the more structural process of transformation. When attempting to get stakeholder buy-in for people-centric security, it is helpful to also have a supporting story to explain what transformation means in terms of the hows and whys of the process.

Describing Transformation in Terms of Cultural Capabilities Maturity

A useful way of telling a story about the process of transforming organizational culture in general, and security culture specifically, is to discuss transformation in the context of a capabilities maturity model. Maturity modeling first developed at the Software Engineering Institute of Carnegie Mellon University in the 1980s as a way of evaluating and managing software engineering capabilities. Since then capability maturity modeling has expanded beyond its roots, and maturity models have been built and deployed as more general business process improvement tools across a range of industries and functions, including traditional software development, other information technology functions, and even human capital and resources. As such, maturity models will likely be familiar to many stakeholders involved in people-centric security transformation, even if they are not directly associated with the InfoSec program.

Capability maturity models focus on the visibility and measurability of a "capability," such as a business process or function, and whether the insights gained from observing and measuring the capability are effectively used to improve it over time. At the lowest level of maturity, the organization performs the capability in a way that is poorly understood, informal, and hard to repeat systematically. At the highest level, the organization has mastered the capability to the point where it not only knows how to perform it in a way that is well understood, formalized, and easy to repeat systematically, but also actively improves and optimizes how it performs the capability based on regularly collected measures and data. Scales and definitions vary with the type and creator of the maturity model, but the scale is usually a variation of a 0-to-5 scale or 1-to-5 scale.

People-centric security transformation involves both cultural change and behavioral change. But transformation only happens as the organization gets better at understanding itself and taking action on those insights. The CSCF and the Security FORCE Behavioral Model are tools that work within this structure of increasing maturity and awareness, both contributing to improved maturity and benefitting from that maturity as it grows. Communicating this process helps people understand how the organization's security culture is changing and the benefits that the organization will get from transformation.

The Cultural Capabilities Maturity Model: Formalizing Cultural Maturity

I have developed my own maturity model, the Cultural Capabilities Maturity Model (CCMM), to facilitate communication and to give InfoSec programs another tool by which to tell the story of people-centric security. Like the FOXTROT case study and model of the financial impact of culture on security incident losses in Chapter 8, the CCMM is meant to be one more way to demonstrate to stakeholders what the security culture transformation project is intended to accomplish. Note that the CCMM is not limited to only information security culture. It can be used to describe organizational culture much more broadly. But I will limit the discussion here to its utility in the context of a security culture transformation project. Figure 16-1 shows the CCMM.

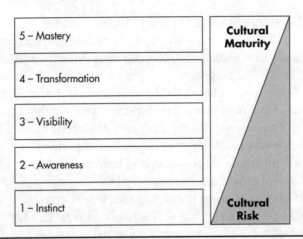

Figure 16-1   *The Cultural Capabilities Maturity Model*

The CCMM, like other maturity models, divides cultural capabilities into five levels of proficiency. At the lowest level, culture is not understood well at all and people in the organization operate on a form of instinct, reactively, without much insight into why the organization works the way it does. Returning to the iceberg metaphor from Chapter 3, they are like people above the surface of the iceberg who have no idea what is beneath the waterline or why the iceberg moves in the direction it does. At this level of cultural maturity, risk and uncertainty are high. The organization cannot identify cultural deficiencies or competing priorities that may negatively impact performance. At the top level of the CCMM, the organization has mastered its own culture to the point where it not only understands why people behave as they do, but can shape and drive behavior as necessary, quickly and efficiently, to meet just about any challenge. They are like people who have mapped the entire iceberg above and below the surface, calculated its mass and density, and created mechanisms to tow and push it in different directions. Cultural risk at this level is low, as the organization has a full understanding of its culture–performance linkages and can easily adjust to challenges.

Table 16-1 describes the specific organizational proficiencies that exist at each level of the CCMM.

CCMM Level	Organizational Proficiencies
5 **Mastery**	▶ Organizational culture is formally managed as a defined business process. ▶ Cultural measurement and evaluation are automated within various systems. ▶ "Optimal" cultural and behavioral traits are identified and embedded in business processes. ▶ Culture, behavior, and performance are formally linked, regularly measured, and systematically reviewed.
4 **Transformation**	▶ Resources are officially devoted to cultural transformation and behavioral change efforts. ▶ Cultural and behavioral interventions are regular processes. ▶ Culture and behavior are measured over time to capture the outcomes of ongoing efforts and interventions. ▶ Members of the organization are evaluated and held accountable on the basis of cultural performance as well as other performance measures.
3 **Visibility**	▶ Behaviors and cultural traits are formally measured and analyzed. ▶ Cultural and behavioral patterns are observed and correlated with specific decision processes. ▶ Cultural risks that impact business decisions are identified and documented. ▶ Formal strategies are developed to reduce cultural risk, implement desired cultural traits and behaviors, and transform undesirable ones. ▶ Cultural impact on performance is seen as a strategic consideration.
2 **Awareness**	▶ The need to analyze decisions and outcomes is understood. ▶ The need to identify and change problem behaviors is recognized. ▶ First attempts are made to formalize and encourage desired behaviors and cultural traits. ▶ Policy and training are seen as proper ways to promote desired decisions.
1 **Instinct**	▶ Decisions are based on habit and "how we always do it." ▶ "Gut reactions" control responses to challenges or changing conditions. ▶ Decision analysis is rare or nonexistent. ▶ Behaviors are learned and transmitted informally from person to person, not formally documented or analyzed. ▶ Politics and individual emotions are key decision drivers.

Table 16-1 *Organizational Proficiencies Within CCMM Maturity Levels*

Supporting Security Culture Transformation with Security FORCE Projects

Just as the SCDS is a means of identifying and evaluating competing security cultures within the CSCF, I've designed the Security FORCE Survey and Security FORCE Metrics to be diagnostic tools for use in evaluating how closely an organization's behaviors align with those of a Highly Reliable Security Program (HRSP). I have touched on the survey and metrics in relation to each specific FORCE value in the preceding chapters. This chapter looks at how to pull everything together to create a simple scorecard that can be used to quickly show stakeholders and management the results of Security FORCE behavioral assessments.

The Value of a Security FORCE Project

Implementing and running a Security FORCE project has a lot in common with running a security culture diagnostic project, which I discussed in Chapter 8. The two are, ideally, closely related. In developing the CSCF and SCDS, I saw the need for a parallel model that could allow security programs to address people-centric security at the behavioral level, which can be more tactical and concrete than culture. The culture–behavior links within the high-reliability organization (HRO) research, discussed in Chapter 10, provided just what I needed to create my Security FORCE Model. Security FORCE projects can and should be used in conjunction with SCDS projects to address cultural transformation both from the top down and from the bottom up. I will discuss SCDS and FORCE alignments later in the chapter.

Managing a Security FORCE Project

Project management issues for a Security FORCE analysis parallel those I enumerated for SCDS projects in Chapter 8, but it never hurts to review. Understanding the similarities and differences between the projects will be especially valuable when the projects are conducted separately to avoid redundant work or stakeholders' perception of redundant work when activities are similar for both types of projects.

Costs and Schedules

Projects cost money and time, and implementing a Security FORCE project to complement your SCDS project will add to those costs. One way to overcome the challenge is to take advantage of scale and combine SCDS and FORCE work into a single project or program plan. Even if the projects will be undertaken separately, budgetary and operational planning over the course of quarterly or annual cycles can ensure resources are available for the complete set of projects in advance. This way the organization can take advantage of the fact that most activities for an SCDS project require the same tools and capabilities as a Security FORCE project (including survey-based data collection, interviews and project reviews, and linking both projects to people-centric security transformation efforts). If resources are tight, the modular nature of both SCDS projects and Security FORCE projects allow them to be conducted separately, perhaps annually or semiannually. The good news about people-centric security and transformation is that there is literally no rush. Cultures take time to change.

Leadership Support and Engagement

An old security industry friend of mine recently gave me some excellent advice, about this book no less. "A CISO isn't going to listen to you just because you have a good idea," he told me. "You have to tell him specifically how his program will directly benefit from your good idea."

I've worked hard to live up to my friend's guidance in these pages by showing the concrete ways that culture and behavior can impact security bottom lines. Even if you are reading this and finding yourself agreeing with me on every point, you would do well to keep his words in mind. Do not just expect your people-centric security program's benefits to be self-evident, to speak for themselves. You will have to constantly reinforce those benefits, to recruit management buy-in through them, and to message them to every stakeholder group whose support you require.

I have especially tried to pack these chapters, including the "Further Reading" sections at the end of each, with more evidence for the approaches I propose. These frameworks and techniques have been widely and productively applied in industries other than information security. They are new only to information security, but there is nothing in information security that would keep them from working here too. One of the selling points for senior leadership engagement is simple innovation, the opportunity to put new ideas to work on the organizational and people side, just like a CISO looks to leverage innovation in technology. The innovation spin can even help sell the inevitable risks to any security project, including transformation projects. We're not trying to keep up with the problem; we're trying to get ahead of it. And getting ahead of tomorrow's security failures is probably worth some rational experimentation with new techniques today, especially since, once again, they aren't even that new. You're just taking the tested work of others and bringing it home.

Stakeholder Engagement

Stakeholders for Security FORCE projects will tend to require the same care and feeding as SCDS project stakeholders. Users, other managers and business owners, and even external stakeholders such as customers or auditors may have an interest in or be able to add value to a project. Part of the outreach program to carry forward a people-centric security message includes not only recruiting participants effectively to gain support and excitement for the project, but also sharing information regarding findings and behavioral change strategies.

Security FORCE can sometimes be a bit of an easier sell to stakeholders due to its more tactical nature and focused attention on observable activity. Stakeholders can often determine whether it's better to lead with Security FORCE or with SCDS and full cultural transformation. Either way, the journey ends in the same place.

Respondents and Data

All of the considerations and caveats of SCDS projects apply to Security FORCE projects. Before conducting the survey, the organization should determine in advance who will receive the survey (a sampling of respondents or blanket delivery to everyone in the organization?), how metadata and demographic information will be collected, and what the end goals of the project are. Tools for administering and analyzing the Security FORCE survey are the same as those for the SCDS. The survey can be delivered on paper, by PDF form, or online, whichever is desired and appropriate within the organization. As with the SCDS, respondents should be trained prior to taking the Security FORCE survey.

It is also worth reiterating my points on demographic data and privacy from Chapter 8. Collecting demographic data about respondents can provide a wealth of information to make the analysis of Security FORCE values and behaviors more sophisticated and rich. But collecting such data also brings questions of privacy and anonymity in both conducting the survey and storing response data. InfoSec programs should consider how they will ensure that respondents feel safe and comfortable in giving honest responses to the survey or in reporting Security FORCE Metrics to management. In some cases, personally identifiable information may be protected by policy, regulation, or law. If the organization decides to collect or track respondent data in any way, it is advisable to seek approval and advice from the Human Resources and Legal departments before doing so.

The Security FORCE Scorecard

Chapters 11 through 15 described each of the Security FORCE values, including key behaviors for each of the five FORCE values: failure, operations, resilience, complexity, and expertise. Each chapter included the specific Security FORCE

Survey statements and Metrics associated with the value discussed in the chapter. Together, these individual statements and measures make up the complete Security FORCE Survey and Security FORCE Metrics. The survey and metrics are available as full-size, customizable, downloadable documents for use by security organizations online at http://lancehayden.net/culture, along with instructions for how to use them.

Scoring the FORCE Survey Questions, Revisited

The Security FORCE Survey includes statements related to each FORCE value, as described in the preceding chapters. Each Security FORCE value has five associated statements designed to measure, at a high level, the prevalence of key behaviors for that FORCE value and the alignment of behaviors with those found in HRSPs. When scoring the survey for each value, recall the following:

▶ An average score of 4 or above (most responses indicate Agree or Strongly Agree) signifies the organization exhibits behaviors found in an HRSP.

▶ An average score of 3 (most responses indicate the respondent felt Neutral) signifies the organization may or may not behave like an HRSP.

▶ An average score of 2 or below (most responses indicate Disagree or Strongly Disagree) signifies the organization does not exhibit the behaviors found in an HRSP.

Pooling Your FORCEs

After collecting Security FORCE data from the survey responses, organizations will want a quick, high-level way of presenting results. The Security FORCE Scorecard is a simple representation of Security FORCE Survey results that can be used to present findings and analysis to stakeholders and senior management. The Scorecard, illustrated in Figure 16-2 and also available at http://lancehayden .net/culture, provides several representations of the survey scores, including

▶ Average scores for the presence and strength of each Security FORCE value from 1 through 5

▶ A histogram showing all five Security FORCE value scores for side-by-side comparison

▶ A spider chart showing all five Security FORCE value scores for "shape" comparison

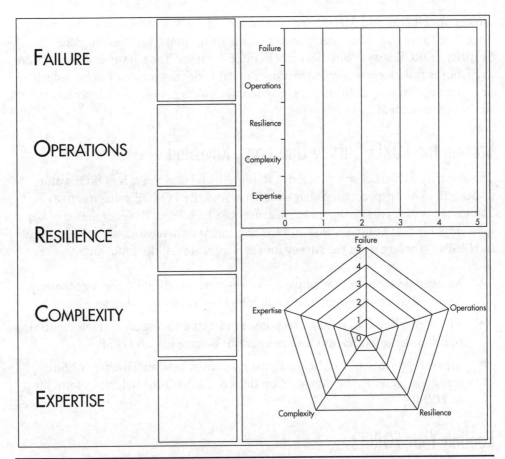

Figure 16-2 *Blank Security FORCE Scorecard example*

Security FORCE Metrics and the FORCE Scorecard

The Security FORCE Scorecard does not incorporate the results of any Security FORCE Metrics. This is a deliberate omission, for several reasons. Security FORCE Metrics are important components of the model, but they do not lend themselves as easily to inclusion in an easily developed and easily explained scorecard. Instead, the Security FORCE Metrics are designed to operate in the background of the Security FORCE Model, providing empirical evidence to support or challenge Security FORCE Survey responses, and to allow for more detailed and granular measurement of specific FORCE values and behaviors over time. The following are things to consider when comparing the Security FORCE Scorecard to Security FORCE Metrics:

▶ Use the Security FORCE Scorecard to simplify (always carefully, with all assumptions made explicit) the presentation of FORCE Value results.

▶ Use Security FORCE Metrics to support and validate Security FORCE Scorecard results for stakeholders and security owners who require more specific details.

▶ Use the Security FORCE Scorecard primarily as a diagnostic of attitudes and perceptions among members of the organization.

▶ Use the Security FORCE Metrics primarily as a diagnostic of actions and operations that are actually taking place within the organization.

"Are We a Highly Reliable Security Program?"

Having conducted a Security FORCE Survey and collected Security FORCE Metrics results, it will be tempting to make a judgment regarding whether or not the organization can claim to function as an HRSP. Highly reliable security does not exist in a single point in time or as the result of people's perceptions. HRSPs are highly reliable precisely because they remain highly reliable over extended periods of operation within hostile or dangerous environments. No organization can claim to operate as an HRSP on the basis of a single diagnostic data point. HRSPs can only be judged longitudinally, over time and over multiple assessments and evaluations. These assessments must be compared and correlated with the frequency and severity of security incidents and failures as well, compared against historical data or against industry expectations and standards of how secure an organization should be. Unfortunately, today, there are few such standards or expectations beyond "more reliable than we are today..."

It may be helpful to consider several scenarios against which to compare claims of HRSP behavior. Each of the following three examples represents an example organization that has conducted a Security FORCE project using the FORCE Scorecard.

GEORGE G, LLP

GEORGE G, LLP, is a boutique advertising and marketing company, specializing in online campaigns. With a multinational presence and sophisticated technology companies for customers, GEORGE G takes a proactive approach to protecting customer intellectual property and strategies. As part of a security culture assessment, GEORGE G implemented a company-wide Security FORCE Survey. The resulting Security FORCE Scorecard is shown in Figure 16-3.

Interpreting on the basis of the Security FORCE scores, GEORGE G would seem to lack several of the behavioral attributes of an HRSP. Only in the area of the security value of operations did company employees express a perception that tracks with highly reliable security. Does that mean that GEORGE G is not reliable and is on the verge of a major security incident? Certainly not. No single diagnostic tool can provide such predictive evidence. But GEORGE G management would have some cause for concern about these scores, particularly those for Failure and Expertise, if HRSP behaviors were among their goals.

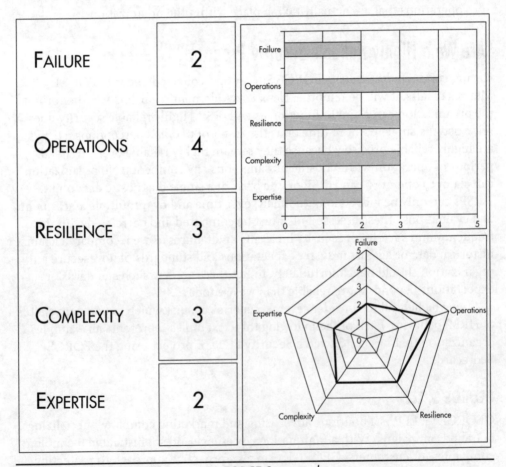

Figure 16-3 *GEORGE G, LLP, Security FORCE Scorecard*

HOTEL INDIA, Inc.

HOTEL INDIA, Inc., manages a chain of unique lodging establishments, including traditional hotels, B&Bs, and hostels, in 19 countries. HOTEL INDIA undertook a security culture improvement initiative as part of a larger security training and awareness program, following several security incidents within both the corporate and customer-facing networks. The results of HOTEL INDIA's Security FORCE Scorecard are shown in Figure 16-4.

Is HOTEL INDIA an HRSP? It certainly would seem to be when its Scorecard is compared to the Scorecard for GEORGE G. Perception of the company's behaviors indicates that many of the Security FORCE behaviors are strong.

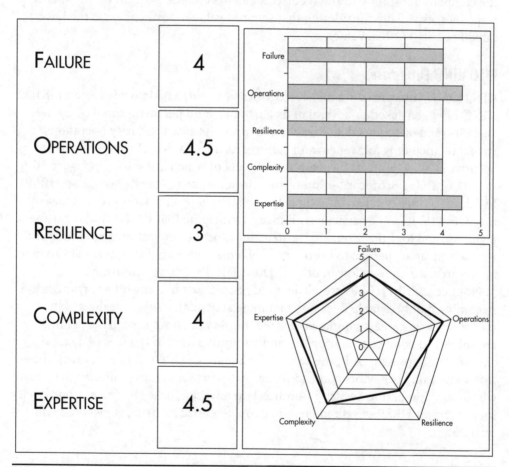

Figure 16-4   *HOTEL INDIA, Inc., Security FORCE Scorecard*

This is a situation where the Security FORCE Metrics could prove valuable in determining to what extent company perceptions match up to reality. If the Security FORCE Metrics results were poor—for example, if no activities or artifacts could be produced to validate claims or perceptions of behavior—the information security team might be forced to consider other reasons that the FORCE Survey scores were so high. Were people afraid to respond honestly for some reason? Is security awareness out of sync with security operations?

If Security FORCE Metrics for HOTEL INDIA validated the results of the FORCE Survey, then it may be that the company's InfoSec program is operating as an HRSP, the recent events notwithstanding. After all, even an HRSP will eventually experience a failure (and embrace its lessons). In this case, reexamining the company's response to the security incidents could shed light on the survey responses, especially considering that security value of resilience was the lowest-rated Security FORCE value.

KILO KING Enterprises

KILO KING Enterprises is a midsize logistics firm with a nationwide network. KILO KING has been asked by several of its customers and partners, spooked by the current trend of serious data breaches, to assess its entire security operations structure, including awareness and culture. As a result, KILO KING undertook a Security FORCE project, the Scorecard results of which are shown in Figure 16-5.

KILO KING's Scorecard is interesting. In some areas, it behaves like an HRSP. In others, it does not, leaving a lopsided behavioral profile. How are we to assess these results? It is not particularly difficult to imagine that KILO KING's business, planning, and logistics would drive an environment of operational readiness and reliance on smart people to overcome problems. But why, if the scores are so high in one area, are they so low in others? Don't HRSPs behave uniformly?

Not necessarily. HRSPs are made up of people, just like any other organization. Becoming highly reliable does not guarantee staying that way, nor does high reliability in one area guarantee the same in every area. All security programs are subject to competitive priorities and cultural drivers in the face of dynamic and uncertain pressures. In the case of the Security FORCE values, it turns out that some value behaviors come more easily to certain security cultures that exist within the Competing Security Cultures Framework. These alignments, and what they mean for HRSP development and people-centric security, are where I will turn now.

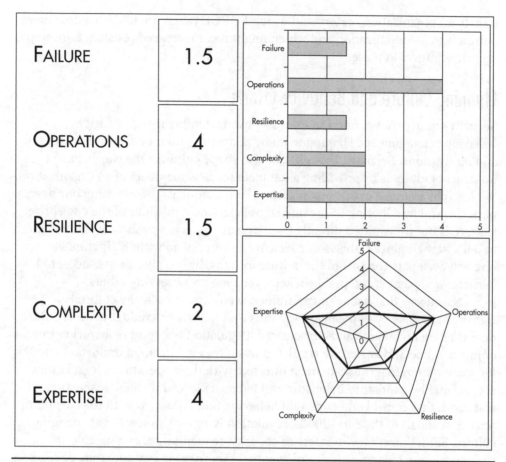

Figure 16-5   *KILO KING Enterprises Security FORCE Scorecard*

CSCF and Security FORCE: Aligning Culture and Behavior in People-Centric Security

In the same way that individual personality traits in people naturally predispose them to certain behaviors, different information security culture traits can make an organization more naturally predisposed to certain behaviors. A Process Culture, with its hierarchies and formality, is going to excel at certain activities more than an Autonomy Culture, which will have its own strong suits. One advantage of the Security FORCE model is that it can be aligned with the CSCF to help an organization understand which FORCE values are likely to come more naturally to an organization and which might meet increased resistance, given the security cultures in place.

Chaining Culture and Behavior Efforts

Security culture transformation exerts a powerful influence on security behaviors, changing and shaping them by addressing their underlying causes and motivations. Behavior, though, can also shape culture. One way behavior influences culture is by providing a template for new members of an organization. We learn by example in our organizational environments, by watching our peers perform, and by adhering to the official policies and guidelines of the enterprise. Culture is not transmitted directly from person to person as such. It is not enough to tell a new employee "this is our security culture, so go with it." That new hire will acclimate (or not) to the culture in steps, by learning what is accepted behavior and what is acceptable belief, over time, by observing others.

A second way that behavior can influence culture, specifically cultural transformation, is by imposing new habits that quickly or gradually replace older ones that are no longer valued or desired. Regulation is a good real-world example of this practice. Industries are regulated when they are deemed important enough for some reason that the state must interfere with their operations. Regulations are essentially mandatory behaviors and habits, enforced through inspection and audit, that control and constrain behavior. Sometimes, as with the corporate finance scandals of the early 2000s, regulation is explicitly directed at changing culture. Sometimes, as with safety or security, regulation seeks a specific effect such as fewer accidents or harmful events. In these cases a culture may develop around the regulated behaviors, creating a culture that takes those things seriously. Industries like energy and aviation already have decades of experience in this organic cultural growth, while industries like information security are just beginning to experience it.

Reinforcing "chains" of culture and behavior, illustrated in Figure 16-6, perpetuate values and priorities within an organization. These chains can function more or less unconsciously, below the level of deliberate analysis. Or they can be deliberately forged and shaped through visibility and effort. To extend the metaphor a bit, how we manage culture and behavioral chains also says a lot about whether they will act to the organization's benefit, like an anchor to a foundation, or will imprison and drag down the organization, like Marley's ghost in *A Christmas Carol*.

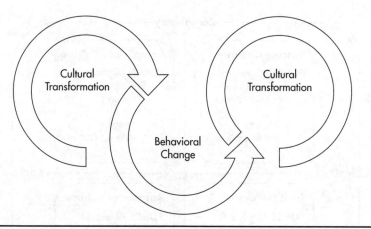

Figure 16-6 *Culture and behavior "chains"*

Using the SCDS and FORCE Independently

There is nothing to stop a security stakeholder or CISO from using the SCDS and the Security FORCE model independently of one another. The Security FORCE model is just one proposal for behavioral adaptation, actually, although I think it is uniquely suited to information security. But I kept the two frameworks separate because I did not want to imply that improving the Security FORCE value behaviors is the only way to improve InfoSec culture. It is not. Organizations in heavily regulated environments, or those with strong security training and awareness programs in place, may already have built into their security operations behavioral models that they wish to adapt and apply to the CSCF. ISO 27001, COBIT, ITIL, and some NIST standards, to name but a few, all attempt to address behavior changes. Where these frameworks are already implemented and well understood, they may serve as useful complements or alternatives to Security FORCE.

General Alignments Between Security FORCE and the CSCF

With the exception of security value of complexity, which applies to everything in people-centric security, each of the Security FORCE values can be grounded in one of the quadrants of the Competing Security Cultures Framework. Figure 16-7 illustrates this basic alignment. An important caveat to point out once again is that these are models, not perfect reproductions or infallible crystal balls. They make assumptions and contain uncertainty. They should be used as tools, to identify connections and guide discussion and assessment, and should not be

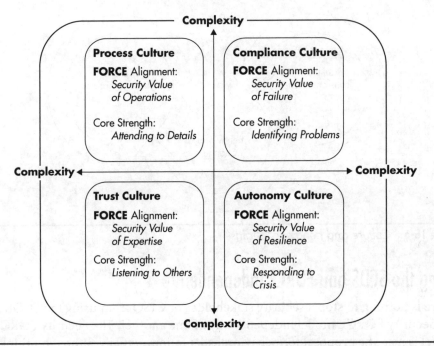

Figure 16-7   *Security FORCE values aligned to CSCF quadrants*

expected to answer all the organization's questions. But when used as a means to understanding, not as a substitute for it, these models can be highly effective in helping implement a more people-centric program.

In the following discussion I'll address the Security FORCE values a bit out of order, going instead by the CSCF quadrants, to make the alignments easier to follow, and addressing the security value of complexity, which has no direct cultural alignment, at the end.

Process Cultures and the Security Value of Operations

Process cultures are all about the details. Setting standards, documenting policies and configurations, and making sure people know where they fit within the hierarchy are all highly valued priorities for Process-focused security programs. The overarching need to manage and coordinate activities, and to have a high degree of visibility into those activities, is what differentiates a Process Culture from the other three security culture types.

This sense of prioritizing visibility and standardized management is what makes a Process Culture particularly adept at realizing the security value and key behaviors of operations from the Security FORCE Model. The security value of operations incorporates the active understanding of how things work and when they are working differently from the way they are expected or assumed to work. A Process Culture will more naturally prioritize the analysis and documentation of operational functions needed to see and compare these differences and to detect deviations while they are minor.

The security value of operations also puts a premium on assessing and sharing operational information, behaviors that also lend themselves to a Process Culture, one in which organizational boundaries and bureaucratic communication channels tend to be established by default. These can often be utilized as readily available processes for formally and safely disseminating operational assessments and eliciting feedback from other stakeholders in the business.

Compliance Cultures and the Security Value of Failure

While Compliance Cultures certainly concern themselves with a fair share of information security details, including operational activities, their often single-minded focus on successful audits makes them especially sensitive to the consequences of not meeting that goal. The result is a culture that takes the security value and key behaviors of failure more seriously than other security cultures, even if they don't think about it consciously in terms of the Security FORCE Model.

Anticipating worst-case scenarios in an organization with a strong Compliance Culture is easy, since the organization's perspective on the world can be a bit binary: either we passed or we failed. Failure is easily defined and its possibility is ever present, as the audit cycle never ends. Each successful evaluation leads straightaway into the possibility that the next one won't go so well, and the organization must always maintain vigilance, learning from mistakes to prevent their recurrence.

That vigilance extends to the other key failure behaviors of seeking out problems before they manifest, rewarding people for finding and reporting problems, and sharing information about security failures. In some organizations, these behaviors may even read like a job description for the internal audit function. Compliance security cultures embed these same values, this same preoccupation with failure, across the security function.

Autonomy Cultures and the Security Value of Resilience

Security incidents throw everything into confusion, challenging every type of security culture within an organization. But of the four cultural types identified within the CSCF, Autonomy Culture most prizes and even encourages initiative and independent action in the face of uncertainty. Perhaps the fact that Autonomy Cultures tend to be almost uniquely suited to the chaotic conditions of an incident helps explain why they tend to be rare in information security. Organizations view security incidents as something that should never happen, and encouraging the kind of culture that thrives in those situations may seem like tempting fate.

The security value and key behaviors of resilience begin with the explicit acceptance that every organization will experience security incidents of some kind or another, including damaging public breaches that throw everything into crisis. This acceptance of risk and uncertainty is easier to internalize in a culture that already accepts change as a constant and views independent thought and action as a requirement. Spreading training, skills, and responsibilities around to a wider variety of people, enabling multiple people to do a job, and encouraging them to stretch themselves are central to the more entrepreneurial bent of people in an Autonomy Culture.

That same startup mindset can make it easier for people to accept mistakes and incidents in an Autonomy Culture, too. Falling down in these environments counts more as on-the-job training for success than proof of incompetence or personal failure. This can be a productive psychology for an organization attempting to recover gracefully and with confidence in the aftermath of a security incident.

Trust Cultures and the Security Value of Expertise

Trust cultures take no one for granted. Every person in the organization is valuable human capital, necessary for the success and growth of the enterprise. For security specifically, that means traditional security awareness and beyond, to the point where members of the organization are the human sensors, firewalls, and response systems that act as a parallel infrastructure complementing and extending technology.

The security value of expertise leverages people as sources of both knowledge and action, and its key behaviors drive decision making into the fabric of the organization. These priorities and behaviors demand trust, and without it, organizations will not be able to allow authority and decisions to be pushed down and around the organization to where circumstances require them. A Trust Culture that values people based not on rank or position but on their abilities to contribute to the goals of the enterprise will instinctively gravitate toward the security value of expertise. Those behaviors will come more easily and be more sustainable over time.

Complexity Everywhere

Complexity has no direct alignment. Every one of the CSCF culture types must address complexity and work within its influence, and no particular culture is better or worse at dealing with it. At best, it can be said that each security culture type concerns itself with a particular flavor of complexity and develops its own culturally specific methods for dealing with it.

Tacit assumptions, the temptation toward oversimplification, and the need for empirical data are the realities of every security culture. The presence of and tensions between these realities may even be at the root of some of the competition between security cultures in the CSCF. That's why each CSCF culture type needs to accept and manage the complexities they face and to coordinate and share their evidence and their doubts among those who may have a different cultural outlook.

Nowhere does the need for coordination on issues of complexity demonstrate itself more than on the issue of models. Each security culture type will have its favored models, the lenses through which that culture looks at the world of security and of the organization writ large. Process models, audit frameworks, agility and innovation methodologies, and human capital management structures will exist side by side within an InfoSec program, with their relative strength and influence constrained only by the relative power of that culture within the security program. They must be brought together, made more transparent, and improved if the organization is to achieve high reliability and true, transformative people-centric security.

Taking Advantage of Cultural-Behavioral Alignments

Paths of least resistance are wonderful things. Especially when you find them among other paths of almost ridiculous resistance. Another beneficial use of the CSCF and the Security FORCE Model is to combine them into a compass of sorts, a navigational aid that can help a security program know where potential problems might lie. Like a "here be dragons" sketch over unknown territory, cultural–behavioral alignments can identify the areas on the people-centric security map where danger lurks, hidden below the waves.

In any given point in time, culture is going to trump behavior, just like the iceberg metaphor suggests. But when people can direct and concentrate behavior in particular areas to particular ends, you can multiply its effect. People have known this at least since Archimedes' time ("Give me a lever and a place to stand, and I shall move the earth"), just as people have known, for at least as long as there have been bricks to build them with, the frustration of banging our heads against walls. The trick is to know the difference between a fulcrum and a wall.

When Culture Makes Behavior Easier

If your people-centric security transformation includes both cultural and behavioral elements, you should be looking at how to take advantage of force multiplication. Your cultural diagnostics can help you. The combination of SCDS results and security culture mapping helps your organization understand the security values and priorities most prevalent inside your organization. Those cultural insights can guide you as you plan behavioral strategies as part of your program.

Imagine that you have conducted a security culture assessment using the SCDS. The assessment reveals that your organization has a particularly strong Compliance Culture. After administering the Security FORCE Survey, you decide that your organization's behaviors supporting the security values of both failure and expertise need improvement. Some stakeholders suggest an immediate inclusion of those behaviors and their relevant metrics in the company's security awareness program.

The thing is, the effort required to improve those two behaviors may not be the same. Because of the natural alignment between a Compliance Culture and the security value of failure, the organization may see immediate gains in its effort to improve behaviors supporting the security value of failure, while its effort to improve behaviors supporting the security value of expertise could prove less effective. Without insight into cultural–behavioral alignments, the disconnect might not make sense and the entire effort could end up tainted and discredited.

One alternative to dividing resources between different challenges is to put all your efforts into one particular challenge where you think you can make the most gains. If the security value of failure is seen as important and the Compliance Culture is likely to find it more acceptable, the organization could work to improve just that area and take advantage of the cultural–behavioral alignment. Significant improvement on the Security FORCE Survey and Metrics resulting from the program could then be used to demonstrate the value and effectiveness of overall cultural transformation efforts, and the resulting goodwill could be applied to improving the security value of expertise, which might prove more difficult.

When Culture Makes Behavior Harder

Knowing how cultural alignment and influence make a transformation job harder can be just as impactful as knowing how they reduce resistance to change. There may be times when the organization decides on a strategy that focuses less on finding the path of least resistance and easy wins, and more on addressing the really difficult, intractable culture problems that are holding back performance.

Consider a company that has experienced a couple of bad, and badly managed, security incidents. CSCF assessment reveals a process-heavy security culture with very little priority given to the values of Autonomy. A Security FORCE Survey shows that the organization is lacking in several behaviors it needs to improve to be closer to becoming an HRSP. But, feeling a strong need to improve its capabilities for incident response at a macro level, the firm embarks on a strategy designed to get more value out of resilience and its associated key behaviors.

The relative weakness of Autonomy Culture–related security values perhaps helps explain why the company struggles to respond flexibly and reliably with every incident. That weakness also shows the challenges the company is likely to face trying to improve resilience behaviors whose underlying motivations conflict with the way the firm looks at security. Once again, a choice is implied: treat everything the same, or focus on specific areas?

Instead of following a path of least resistance in order to more easily secure a win, as with the prior example, this company may choose to tackle the biggest conflict first, because the security value of resilience is seen as the most critical value in the path to become an HRSP. But just like the prior example, this insight allows the company to devote resources to a specific outcome based on a nuanced understanding of the effort involved to achieve it. Rather than cultivating every Security FORCE value and just hoping for the best, understanding cultural alignments allows InfoSec programs to achieve more targeted, and ultimately more effective, outcomes.

Blending Security Culture Diagnostic and Security FORCE Projects for Improved Cultural Maturity

Exploring and analyzing the alignments between CSCF/SCDS and Security FORCE projects should be part of every people-centric security transformation project. Addressing the linkages and potential conflicts between different security cultures and the behaviors necessary for highly reliable security is perhaps the single best reason to use the two frameworks in tandem. Together they allow an organization to understand what is going on both above the surface of organizational awareness and below it, and to grasp where lines of force and influence between the two intersect. The insights won't always be perfect, but as with any other model, they can be put to use and, over time, improved to make security culture transformation more effective and mature.

The idea of implementing one overarching security culture transformation project is somewhat misleading. In all likelihood, most organizations will implement

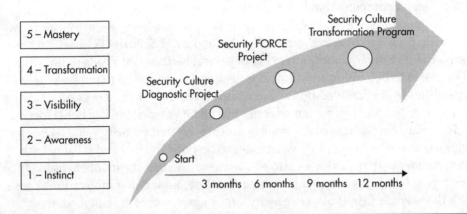

Figure 16-8 *Security culture transformation and people-centric security programs*

something more like a transformation program, made up of a series of projects over time, as shown in Figure 16-8. Insights from one initiative are digested by the organization—for example, the cultural types and conflicts discovered during an SCDS project—which in turn point to immediate options for cultural or behavioral change. At the same time, the increased visibility and proficiency gained through the execution of consecutive projects allows the organization to plan better, ask better questions, and test the results of past initiatives. This in turn increases cultural capability maturity for the InfoSec program and the overall organization as people get better at mastering people-centric security.

Further Reading

▶ Bush, Marilyn and Donna Dunaway. *CMMI Assessments: Motivating Positive Change.* Upper Saddle River, NJ: Addison-Wesley, 2005.

▶ Curtis, Bill, William E. Hefley, and Sally A. Miller. *The People CMM: A Framework for Human Capital Management.* 2nd ed. Boston: Addison-Wesley Professional, 2009.

▶ Paulk, Mark C., Charles V. Weber, Bill Curtis, and Mary Beth Chrissis. *The Capability Maturity Model: Guidelines for Improving the Software Process.* Boston: Addison-Wesley Professional, 1994.

Leadership, Power, and Influence in People-Centric Security

"Anyone can hold the helm when the sea is calm." Roman author Publilius Syrus probably wasn't thinking about information security when he wrote those words sometime in the first century B.C., but his maxim can be applied to leaders in any crisis situation. The quotation always makes me think of the CISOs, InfoSec directors, and data protection managers I have worked with throughout my career. I've known many good, skilled folks responsible for securing the information assets of their organizations. But managerial competence is not the same as inspired (and inspiring) leadership, in information security or anywhere else. All it takes is one bad storm to show you the difference between an Admiral Lord Nelson and a Francesco Schettino, the infamous *Costa Concordia* captain.

The sea of information security is not calm today, and most everyone expects the storms to get worse before they get better. If we are to realize people-centric security in the coming years, our industry is going to need all the Admiral Nelsons that we can get.

A Crisis of Leadership

How important is leadership to information security as a profession? To explore that question, I performed that most loosely scientific of all inquiries: I asked the Interwebs. Operating on the assumption that information security leadership is embodied in the position of CISO, just as other types of corporate leadership are embodied in the positions of other members of the C-suite, I fired up Google. My search was simple: "CISO" and "leadership." I repeated the search for each of five other common C-suite roles: CEO, COO, CFO, CIO, and CTO. Figure 17-1 shows the results, in millions of hits (or not, in the case of CISO).

Wow! 300,000 hits surprised me. Thinking (hoping) that maybe "CISO" is, as they say, not the preferred nomenclature, I tried searching on "CSO" instead. The new search returned 500,000 hits, but the presence in those hits of everything from chief sales officers to chief strategy officers made me less confident of the number. Given once again that this is not exactly a rigorous scientific experiment, one has to be careful about reading too much into it. But at the very least it implies that if people are thinking as much about leadership in information security as they are in other management areas, they are not putting those insights online to be indexed by Google. The order-of-magnitude difference between CEO leadership hits and the next largest group is not surprising. A CEO can easily find abundant resources online about CEO leadership. But even compared to the resources available online to chief information officers and chief technology officers who are looking for role-specific leadership resources,

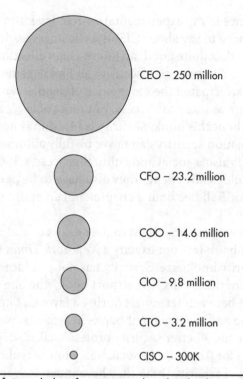

CEO – 250 million

CFO – 23.2 million

COO – 14.6 million

CIO – 9.8 million

CTO – 3.2 million

CISO – 300K

Figure 17-1   *Millions of Google hits for "CXO" plus "leadership"*

CISOs live in a bit of an informational desert. Five of the first ten hits actually refer to the same source: the (ISC)[2] book *CISO Leadership: Essential Principles for Success.* What gives?

The CISO as a Business Leader

I think that the results of my Google searches just demonstrate the uncomfortable truth that many InfoSec programs have to live with every day: that traditionally they have not been considered central to the business. Likewise, CISOs have not been considered equal partners in the C-suite in most organizations, notwithstanding the bone of "chief" designation many are thrown. Security leadership traditionally has not been considered synonymous with business leadership, not even to the degree that CIOs and CTOs are considered business leaders. That has made it much easier to ignore basic leadership principles when it comes to CISOs and their work. That has to change. And it is changing, as the consequences of security failures have begun to blast their way into the boardroom in unprecedented ways.

Given its prominence in my experimental search, I went to *CISO Leadership* to see what it might have to say about CISOs as business leaders within their organizations. The book is quite good, an interesting collection of contributed works by 20 experienced information security and management professionals. Published in 2008, it anticipated the emergence of people-centric security and the centrality of culture as a key to success. But most of all, it echoes the themes I have explored throughout this book. Security leadership is not about technology, and successful information security can never be fully automated. Because information security is also a social and cultural process, CISOs can't succeed if they are only technologically adept. They also have to be people savvy (*CISO Leadership* contributor Billi Lee built a chapter and an entire management model around the term "savvy").

Unfortunately, and without any slight to the editors of and contributors to *CISO Leadership*, the book was not exactly a *New York Times* bestseller. Very few information security books are. Security has not produced many of what a professor colleague of mine calls "the airport book," the one you buy as you browse the bookstore between terminals during a layover. I know I've bought my share of leadership and management books in airports, particularly the titles I thought would make me a better security professional. Today, most CISOs know they can learn a lot from other executives. But the reality is that almost no executives outside of security think they have much to learn about business leadership from CISOs.

Business Leaders as Security Enablers

The fact that non-security executives typically do not look to information security executives for insight into how to do their jobs better is a cause for concern because non-security executives have a lot of influence on how information security gets done, or doesn't, in their organizations. It's a classic asymmetrical power relationship. The business enables security to function at the discretion of the business, but not the other way around. A CEO or CIO can interfere with the function of information security, sometimes directly and officially, depending upon reporting structures. But it's much more rare to see a CISO or security director with the power to unilaterally tell another business function, say Finance or IT, how to run its affairs, even if there is a direct security stake in those operations. Instead, security executives often have to work by proxy, recommending and guiding up the chain of command to influence those with the power to make such decisions.

Security Power Dynamics

The power dynamics of information security leadership reflect something of a trend in the evolution of business leadership in general, as executive-level recognition and prestige have moved out from the traditional locus of business operations. The first wave of evolution saw the rise of the chief information officer and chief technology officer to the ranks of CEO, COO, and CFO. Despite the difference in titles, both of these executive positions evolved to address the growth of technology and IT products within companies. These are areas of expertise that are outside of the experience of traditional management but are increasingly central to business success. As Figure 17-2 shows, this evolution has continued into a third wave of more information-centric leadership recognition. Roles like chief privacy officer and even chief risk officer have evolved, like the CISO role, to address new challenges around the management of corporate

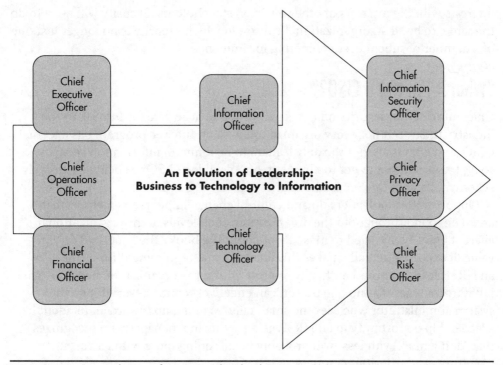

Figure 17-2   *An evolution of executive leadership*

information and knowledge assets. (As a side note, I attempted to use both "CPO" and "CRO" in my Google "leadership" search experiment, but neither is a universally known acronym. I ended up with more insight into naval noncommissioned officers and life sciences researchers than privacy and risk leadership.)

If information is key to the business, then maintaining the integrity and security of the information supply chain is, by definition, a key business enabler. One of the recurring takeaways from *CISO Leadership* is the need for CISOs and other security leaders to grow beyond the management of technology infrastructures. Indeed, my interpretation of several of the chapters is that too much focus on technology management actually holds a CISO back. The most successful security leaders will be those who can manage people and culture, both those within security's sphere of influence and, even more importantly, those outside of it. Competing security cultures come to exist in many cases because the InfoSec program cannot or does not operate within the bigger picture of the organization. Other CXOs have had more time to figure out how to merge their interests with the interests of other business stakeholders. Security will need to do the same, to build an organizational culture in which security is no longer just one of a number of subcultures competing for influence.

"What if I'm Not a CISO?"

Chief information security officer is the symbolic head role for InfoSec in the industry today. But not every organization with an InfoSec program has a formal CISO, and CISOs are not the only leaders to be found in information security, so it's important not to get too hung up on mistaking CISOs as being exclusively synonymous with InfoSec leadership.

Opportunities for leadership and cultural change in people-centric security are to be found throughout the organization, at all levels of the organizational chart, a point I have tried to make throughout the book. The Security FORCE value of expertise actually makes this idea a formal requirement for HRSPs. In an HRSP, leadership and authority migrate within the organization because an HRSP recognizes that no one person can effectively control everything. The system administrator who sees the small failures piling up toward an incident has a leadership opportunity in an HRSP, as does the line manager who recognizes that "doing more with less" will probably mean "doing more with less security" as cultures and priorities compete.

It's little more than a platitude to breezily say everyone is responsible for security, especially if most people have neither the authority nor the resources to live up to that responsibility. But it's also an excuse when people absolve themselves of responsibility for security just because they are not part of the InfoSec program. We live in an information society, and information is central to the success of just about every firm. Protecting it is about protecting the business itself. Most employees of corporations are not accountants or law enforcement officials, but that does not mean they are relieved of their responsibility to prevent fraud or criminal activity. Most employees don't work for HR, but they still have a duty to report harassment or abuse. And organizations have their own obligation not only to make the exercise of these responsibilities possible, but also to encourage it. People-centric security in an enterprise must live up to these same standards if companies today are going to see today's security challenges become more manageable.

CISO Leadership Resources

My Google search may not have turned up as many resources for CISOs and security leaders as it did for other CXOs, but that doesn't mean there were no resources. There are several venues and forums for CISO networking, mentoring, and knowledge sharing out there, including (ISC)², which was behind *CISO Leadership*. Many security professionals know (ISC)² as the organization that offers Certified Information Systems Security Professional (CISSP) certification, but (ISC)² also hosts events such as the Information Security Leadership Awards. In addition to (ISC)², the Information Systems Security Association (ISSA) hosts regular CISO Executive Forums, and organizations such as CSO (www.csoonline.com), the Argyle Executive Forum, the Tech Exec Networks (T.E.N.), and the EC-Council hold events dedicated to information security leadership development.

The resources and organizations listed are those I am aware of that put a specific focus on CISO leadership. Of course, there are many other organizations, including ISACA, the SANS Institute, and a number of industry-focused Information Sharing and Analysis Centers (ISACs), that provide opportunities for information security training, mentoring, and professional networking in support of InfoSec programs and leadership.

Leadership in People-Centric Security

As previously noted, not every information security leader is a CISO. Security leadership can be found in unexpected places, and not every organization has elevated information security to a CXO level of recognition. If this book has made a point of anything, it's that successful security is a cultural trait. Even a CISO can only do so much if he or she is trying to do it in a culture that doesn't value or prioritize the CISO's job. But wherever InfoSec ownership exists, under whatever title it is given, someone will have ultimate responsibility for protecting the organization's data, information, and knowledge. To be successful, that person will have to stand up and take hold of the helm in the midst of the gale.

You Don't Lead Machines

Security is people. I made the point early in the book that if you throw out all your technology, you still have an organization to manage. That's an important lesson for security leaders, including CISOs. As long as security leaders are viewed primarily as managers of technology, there will be less opportunity and less expectation for them to lead the business. People-centric security is about more than simply incorporating people into information security infrastructures or simply managing the people in the information security program. People-centric security is about leading the entire organization into a new relationship with the business value of information assets, just like CIOs did over the past couple of decades with IT. As IT moved from the back office to the back pocket, CIOs went from technology managers to corporate leaders.

Information security leadership needs to bridge that same gap between technology and those who use it. When CISOs (or other organizational InfoSec leaders) are seen as managing the relationship of the entire organization (meaning all the people in it) with information security, those leaders' roles and status within the organization will change, just like CIO roles changed as IT became more ubiquitous. Because managing people and culture puts security leaders on equal footing with other leaders of the organization, it lets them bring their own unique insights to bear on how to motivate people and make them productive and successful, even in the face of adversity. That's something technology management, no matter how sophisticated the technology, cannot achieve. You can manage a rack of servers or switches, but you can never inspire it, never lead those devices to become something more than what they are.

Influence and Transformation

The influence and leadership skills necessary for security culture transformation are developed as evolution, not upheaval. They are variations on existing themes of management and organizational behavior that have existed for a long time, and have their origins outside of InfoSec. CISOs and security leaders have to keep doing what they have always done, managing and directing the technology and processes that are required to protect corporate information. But the industry's leadership will have to grow too, both in terms of size and in terms of scope. For all the disruption and stress in the security world today, it's actually a great time to be thinking about becoming a security leader.

That being said, CISOs and other leaders are going to find that more is being asked of them than ever before, and many of the new needs will be in the area of soft skills. Russell Reynolds Associates, an executive leadership and strategic consulting firm, conducted a recent study of CISOs and identified a number of new skills that will be called for in the next generation of information security leadership. These include innovation and agility, the ability to think strategically while simultaneously educating and influencing others in the organization, and a capability for attracting top talent to the enterprise. Basically, these are all the same skills one would expect from those who are responsible for leading the entire business, not just locking down parts of it.

To be certain, there are already CISOs working in the industry today who fit the bill, who wield the influence and have mastered the skills of an executive leader on par with other C-levels. But these leaders are not universal, they are not widely available, and they do not come cheap. The security industry is going to have to grow a new generation of them. The training programs for security professionals are going to have to start looking less like computer science and engineering degrees and more like MBAs. And we're going to have to go outside of security and outside of technology to round out our skills. I'm waiting for the day that I meet a CISO who rose up through enterprise marketing or, even better, came from an anthropology or a psychology background. When these individuals become more than exceptions and outliers, things will get really interesting.

Adapting the CSCF and Security FORCE Model to Leadership

Measuring leadership traits can be viewed differently than measuring the traits of an organization's members' behaviors or its overall culture. For one thing, leaders in an organization have a disproportionate amount of power to influence and affect behavior and culture. That alone can make it beneficial to understand how they look at the world and how they engage with their environment. As a result, some organizational culture and behavior models, including the Competing Values Framework, have been adapted to specifically address leadership qualities within the model.

I could easily add an entire section to this book by extending the CSCF and the Security FORCE Model to measuring leadership traits and indicators, but that would be a tad premature, given the relatively nascent state of both security culture transformation as a legitimate approach to information security management and the professional development of the CISO in our industry. I hope that the state of information security leadership matures quickly enough that I can perhaps address how to measure it in a future edition of *People-Centric Security*. For now, I will simply address the ways that the existing models can be adapted to a leadership-specific assessment. The materials are already there. The approach to collecting and interpreting the data is all that really has to be reconsidered.

The CSCF, SCDS, and Cultural Leadership

Assessing cultural leadership against the Competing Security Cultures Framework involves a more introspective approach to the model. Instead of using the Security Culture Diagnostic Survey as an instrument to measure the culture that people in the organization feel they inhabit, corporate executives and organizational leaders can use the tool to analyze the example and tone that they set themselves for the rest of the organization. What beliefs do they bring into work with them every day that will influence how subordinates and members of the organization make security-related decisions? What values and priorities do they promote in the examples that they set that are then emulated down the organizational chart?

An organization can conduct a basic security leadership assessment by administering the SCDS only to members of the executive staff, or even the board of directors, and then interpreting and mapping those results as they would for a wider security culture assessment. Identifying cultural conflicts at the executive level can go a long way toward explaining why they exist elsewhere. For CISOs or security stakeholders who are trying to get buy-in for a larger security culture transformation initiative, this can be an excellent way to start. It may even provide the security team with a breakthrough in support. The impact and importance of culture is often more widely discussed and accepted at the executive level than it is in technical or operational business units. Putting security into the terminology of corporate culture can provide a novel marketing technique by which an InfoSec program can differentiate the initiative.

The Security FORCE Model and Behavioral Leadership

Similar to adapting the CSCF to organizational leadership, adapting the Security FORCE Model to organizational leadership takes a more top-down approach to the model that emphasizes commitment and example setting. Given the more tactical nature of the FORCE Model, it is usually wise to tie behavior back to culture anyway, focusing on the organizational cultures that create high-reliability security. A capability to stop more incidents before they occur and to better manage those failures that do happen is likely to get the attention of any executive these days, so the FORCE Model can be leveraged as a sort of a behavioral "how to" guide for senior management. Encouraging and fostering these behaviors will make their jobs easier in the long run.

Instead of looking for cultural conflicts, using Security FORCE for leadership assessment focuses on how senior executives motivate, reward, and sanction individual behaviors that are invisibly reducing or expanding the space in which security incidents can happen. Gauging the individual attitudes of senior enterprise leaders toward failure, operations, and sharing decisions and information can result in valuable insights about where security problems are likely to happen. And once again, using Security FORCE can give a security team a hook they may not have previously had when dealing with non-security leaders. The origins and pedigree of Security FORCE and HRSP behaviors exist outside of InfoSec, in HRO research, and were developed as a means of improving general enterprise performance. By adapting them, CISOs and security leaders are not using parochial "by security, for security" methodologies, but rather products of research into optimizing overall business value and company performance. Empirically supported by academic analysis and industry studies, this research and the models it has produced speak directly to the core goals of everyone on the executive staff, not just those tasked with information security.

Further Reading

- ▶ Comyns, Matt, T. Cook, and J. Reich. "New Threats, New Leadership Requirements: Rethinking the Role and Capabilities of the Chief Information Security Officer." Available at www.russellreynolds.com/.

- ▶ Fitzgerald, Todd, and M. Krause, eds. *CISO Leadership: Essential Principles for Success* ((ISC)² Press Series). New York: Auerbach Publications, 2008.

Securing a People-Centric Future

I t's a people-centric world. That can be easy to forget in a society that is dominated by, even obsessed with, technology. We talk about the Internet of Things, fantasize and fret about robots and artificial technology, even look forward to the "singularity" that will occur when humans and machines finally come together to create a new species. To hear us talk, you might sometimes think that the entire world is about the centrality of technology. And maybe at some point in our future, technology really will eclipse people societally or even evolutionarily. But we are not there yet. For my own part, I'm skeptical that we will ever reach that point. It's an end that has been predicted almost since human beings invented technology, and certainly since they started thinking about it and using it. But for our immediate future, and certainly for the practical future of anyone in information security, it's still a human's world. We may embed technology ever more deeply into our lives, and even our bodies, but inventing, deploying, and using technology are things people do to and with machines, and not, for the most part, the other way around. And securing technology is up to people as well. Technology won't do that for us. Without people, there is no security, nor any need for it. So let's look ahead to the challenges still to come in a people-centric future.

The Security of Things

If you want to pick the best metaphor to embody the challenges information security faces in the future, it's probably the whole "Internet of Things" (IoT) or "Internet of Everything" (IoE) trope. Various estimates put the number of networked devices operating by 2020 in the high tens of billions, typically 50 to 75 billion or more. Compare that with estimates of the number of networked devices operating today, which clocks in at under 10 billion. So in less than a decade potentially, we'll be looking at anywhere from a fivefold increase to an order of magnitude's worth of growth in the number of nodes on the global network, all with some degree of intelligence, all taking in, storing, and pumping out data. Just from a sheer numbers game, that's several brave new worlds' worth of opportunity for bad guys of all stripes.

The purpose of this chapter isn't to jump on either the hype bandwagon or the FUD (fear, uncertainty, and doubt) bandwagon, both of which have established regular pick-up routes throughout the industry these days. The vendors hyping the IoT/IoE concepts, either as a good thing or a scary one, have enormous financial stakes in the metaphor. I've been in the industry long enough to have heard promises of a paperless society and intuitive home appliances made and then fade, only to be picked up and repeated again a few years later. And yet I still use paper and I still have a home that is relatively dumb. So my eyes roll a little more easily when I hear grandiose claims about how thoroughly different and digital my life will be in ten years. But I also realize how different and digital my life is today compared to a decade ago, which convinces me that things are going to continue to change radically for the world. I may not be able to upload my consciousness to the cloud in the next decade, but then again I may not have to drive my own car. That's pretty impressive no matter how you look at things.

Social Security

Setting aside the fact that digital saturation is a geographically and demographically variable phenomenon, and not everywhere or everyone on the planet is connected to the same degree, what are the implications of the Internet of Everything? I get a kick out of the thought of "securing the IoE." If everything is networked, then you are not securing a network; you are securing everything. Reality is your attack surface. Consequently, information security starts to look less like an IT challenge and more like a societal one. Like disease and medicine. Like war and diplomacy. Like ignorance and education. You don't solve these problems, or even manage them. You live with them as best you can, and by "you" I mean everyone. Technology plays a huge role in that effort; many technologies in fact. But the center of the universe shifts, like a Ptolemaic paradigm giving way to Copernicus. People don't move to the IoE. The IoE revolves around people.

Security in an IT system that is slowly approaching a level of complexity that rivals human society is going to be equally complex. I know security managers and CISOs for whom security is essentially synonymous with the SANS Top 20 controls, or the PCI DSS standard, or a set of NIST special publications. Those constructions are all very useful, but it's a bit like saying that a person's life is synonymous with the data in their Facebook profile. As much as things may feel that way at times, it's an illusion, a digital representation of an analog phenomenon too complex to fully get your arms around. If information security is to succeed in the digital future, it's going to have take a more analog approach.

As Many Securities as Things to Secure

There is no one single "security" to create and manage. We already have to specify between physical, information, and IT security if we want to be clear, even though the overlap in these fields is enormous. And within information security, the term I prefer, there are enough subdisciplines and specializations that one could spend a rich and productive career inside the information security field and never venture outside the world of cryptography, or IPS signatures, or audits. "Security" is whatever the people talking about it mean when they say it…because security is people.

I don't expect people-centric security to become the dominant way of thinking about our field and industry. But I do want to add it to the list of conceptual toolkits that we can choose from, because up until recently, InfoSec professionals generally have thought of people, if at all, as obstacles to be worked around, or perhaps as children in need of education so that they don't do something stupid, or even as actual threats living within the organization's walls that have to be rooted out and eliminated. But security is not meant to work *around* people. It's meant to work *for* them. Our profession would benefit a lot from embracing that idea. And we can start by thinking about these different kinds of security by thinking about different ways that security can exist as an information challenge as well as a more tangible one. Context and nuance are creating new and specialized InfoSec phenomenon depending on what is being secured, and how, where, and why it must be protected.

Information

I use the term *information security* to refer to what I think of as the "traditional" focus of our profession because it encapsulates other information-related specialties. Information security includes IT security because IT can't do anything if there's no information for the technology to process. But information security also implies every kind of information that may exist, from paper records to human knowledge. When I think about information security, I am forced to consider things that are not technology-specific, and that always makes me think of people. Information always implies use. Some user (human or otherwise) has to be informed by it to make it information.

Applying a user-centric idea to security helps put a people-centric spin on the control and protection of information, which is at the core of our work. The people-centric future of security will see information diffusing throughout a network that is more vast and vastly different than anything we have today. But information will remain a fundamental commodity, and ensuring the confidentiality, integrity, and availability of it will still be a central responsibility of the security profession. The difference is that we will no longer be able to call the shots on who gets what information and how. When our computers, our homes, our cars, our clothing, and even objects inside our bodies all become smart and interactive, people will find things to do with those infrastructures that defy control. Security will have to change accordingly, moving from dictating and limiting how people can behave to understanding and accepting many new information behaviors and figuring out how to protect the users from those who would abuse them.

Infrastructure

In graduate school I became fascinated by the field of infrastructure studies, the body of scholarly research into the underlying structures that make society function. These structures can be physical or organizational, with both influencing and operating on one another. What interested me the most was the concept that infrastructure, by definition, exists in the background, invisible to most people, having become so common that it has faded from our consciousness...at least until it breaks down (making it a lot like culture in that sense). If you realize you have stopped noticing the electrical and telephone wires strung by the side of the road, the ductwork in your office building, or the wireless access points and telecommunications equipment that gives you the Internet access you are enjoying over coffee, then you know what I'm referring to.

In a world that is exponentially more connected through information technology, countless infrastructures will have to be considered from a security perspective. Consider SCADA and other industrial control systems that control things like utilities and refineries. Securing these systems today remains a pretty specialized area of information security expertise, as obscure to most security professionals as they are scary when you hear what a successful attacker can do to and with them. If the IoE even fractionally lives up to the hype, it will create infrastructures with physical safety implications that make SCADA security look quaint. And we won't be dealing with pipelines or installations that can be isolated and fenced off from the public. Society will be the infrastructure and every single person a potential conduit or hub of activity. Security cannot take on that challenge with the tools we have today.

Identity

There are aspects of information security that are not fully understood right now but will become central to the profession in the future. Ask a CISO today about "identity" and she will likely talk about identity management, the processes and technologies that enable an organization to control users and their access. But the concept of identity and what it means in a digital age is swiftly evolving into a sister discipline of information security, one that will exert immense influence on information security's direction and requirements in the coming decades. Identity systems have become one of a few boundary lines in society where the virtual or symbolic meets the physical. Identity can be stolen, mass produced, and used both to create business value or ruin it. How our society will address the question of what it means to be someone within it and how that process can be managed, manipulated, or subverted are going to be important questions for security professionals to grapple with as we move forward.

Security has already seen one wave of disruption from these new identity challenges, even if we have not explicitly recognized it as such. Personally identifiable and personally contextual information is central to most of the recent massive corporate security breaches. Both types of information are tied to unique individuals and are of interest to thieves because they allow them either to steal an identity (personally identifiable) or to cash in on an existing one, such as by releasing personal photos or e-mails (personally contextual). Security has tended to treat personal information similarly to how a bank treats money: as something you lock up in a vault to keep safe. But identity is much more complex than mere cash; it is inherently people-centric, and will require the information security profession to completely reexamine how it deals with the challenges of safeguarding identity. Some organizations are already exploring identity as a novel phenomenon in the digital age. For example, the Center for Identity at the University of Texas is working on concepts of identity that use terms like "ecosystems" and "physics" instead of just "technology" and "policy." Such research is beginning to recognize that one's identity, rather than being an attribute or a characteristic of a person or a system, is itself a complex system. Managing that complexity and the emergent behaviors that come with it will bridge fields as diverse as engineering, law, information security, sociology, and philosophy.

Privacy

Related to both information and identity, the concept of privacy is growing in interest and importance, and would have even if the massive surveillance programs revealed by Edward Snowden had never come to light. Bruce Schneier's latest book, *Data and Goliath*, is on its way to being one of the best-selling privacy books ever written, and the fact that its author is a security professional is telling. But Schneier's book is only the latest in a large literature of scholarly privacy and surveillance studies extending back at least as far as Michel Foucault's *Discipline and Punish*, with its powerful metaphor of the panopticon and its all-encompassing visibility into everyday activities. Many of these works were written by researchers and theorists who were people-centric, focused as much on societal and organizational aspects of privacy as they were on information and technology systems.

Security will need to bring our considerable expertise to bear here, because with so many aspects of privacy being mediated by technology and digital information systems, the protection and control of systems is more important than ever. But once again, technology and system-level controls will never be enough to address what is fundamentally a challenge at the social level. If information security cannot create people-centric innovations as well as techno-centric ones, we will only ever play a supporting role in what history may remember as one of the pivotal points in human civilization.

Framing People-Centric Security

This book is about giving organizations and security professionals a new language and new tools with which to discuss and improve information security. This language and these tools directly address a corner of the people–process–technology triangle that has been traditionally neglected by the profession and the industry. People-centric security is not necessarily more important than the other two corners, although I think a case can be made to that effect, but it is equally important, and any InfoSec program that does not include people-centric approaches that are taken as seriously as process or technology is not going to have long-term success. When you have a three-legged table, there's no way to skimp on one leg and expect the resulting piece of furniture to be stable. It just doesn't work.

Security Soft Power

In foreign affairs, the concept of *soft power* refers to a nation's ability to get things done by convincing other nations to work with it, rather than by bribing them or resorting to military force. Soft power is also used to change public opinion through less direct and coercive channels. Joseph Nye, the political scientist who coined the term soft power, has commented that credibility is the most valuable and rarest resource in an age of information.

I could not agree with Nye more. The single greatest weakness I see in InfoSec programs, security vendors, and security professionals is a lack of credibility. No one doubts that security is important, but the security industry struggles to make the case for just how important it is, where resources should be allocated, or what constitutes effectiveness. The result is that security is naturally drawn into cultural competition with others who, no matter how critical they believe security to be, don't believe security is as critical as the things they care about. If security cannot make itself more credible in these conflicts, failures and breaches will continue to happen.

Security affairs need a soft power approach, an alternative to coercive policies and automation that attempts to force people to take security seriously without ever really convincing them of why they should. That sort of approach only works until those people can figure out how to get around the constraints, either directly or by undermining them within the organization. People-centric security concentrates on understanding how organizations think and behave as individuals and collectively, and crafting approaches to security that work with these social and organizational forces rather than against them.

Three Takeaways from the Book

At the risk of oversimplifying hundreds of pages into a short list, there are three core ideas that any reader of this book should have embedded into their brain after turning the final page:

▶ People are the most important system to secure.

▶ Strong culture equals strong security.

▶ Failure is a feature of complex systems, not a flaw.

People Are the Most Important System to Secure

An organization without technology is still an organization. An organization without people is not. This basic truism implies that any organization thinking about security must think about where people fit into those efforts. You simply cannot automate people out of the equation when it comes to security. This is not because people are so insidiously clever that they will always find a way to adapt around your controls (but they are and they will). It's because completely automating human judgment and adaptability out of the equation ends up creating a security infrastructure that is more rigid and brittle than the alternative you are trying to prevent. The people that make up any organization are its messiest and most complex system. It is much better for security to leverage this system in support of security than to unrealistically attempt to constrain it. People-centric security is about elevating the status of this system dramatically across the organization.

Strong Culture Equals Strong Security

Culture as people-centric software is a metaphor I led with at the beginning of the book. If an organization can make its culture more secure, then there is less need to try to automate poor security out of the organization by using tools and programs that will never be as sophisticated as the one they are trying to control. By the same token, if an organization's security culture is weak and buggy, if it constantly competes or conflicts with other routines and processes running things, that organization is going to have problems. The security profession has always talked about security as a challenge that can only be addressed through a combination of people, process, and technology. We've also always tended to reverse those three things in order of importance. This has to change. The Competing Security Cultures Framework is about bringing together different ways of looking at security to create stronger, more balanced security cultures overall.

Failure Is a Feature of Complex Systems

Security has, at times implicitly and at other times explicitly, devoted itself to stopping security failures. That is probably one of the reasons it can be so frustrating to be a security professional. You feel like your job is futile, and in that sense it is. You cannot prevent failure in a complex system because the nature of complexity is emergence, and some of the things that emerge from such a system are decay, entropy, and breakdown. The opportunity for information security is to realize that we are now managing a system that has grown beyond our capability to control it. That's frightening and exhilarating at the same time. Our information systems and technologies will enable us to do things pretty soon that would have been considered fantasy (or nightmare) just a few years ago. We have long passed the point where we can make the outcomes of using these systems predictable, but we can still make those outcomes more reliable. The Security FORCE Model and the Highly Reliable Security Programs that it is designed to encourage are all about managing failure in complex systems, not by preventing it but by understanding it, keeping it as small as possible, and bouncing back quickly when it's not.

Putting People-Centric Security to Work

When considering how to implement people-centric security within your own organization, it's important to understand ahead of time what you want to accomplish. There is a lot of material in this book and a lot of ways to put it to use. I have laid out the book comprehensively, an all-in approach that combines culture with behavior, diagnosis with activity. And that approach is certainly a good one to take if your organization has the commitment and desire to transform security culture across the board. But it's also important to note that not every organization can afford or wants to do that.

Two Models, One Goal

The CSCF and the Security FORCE Model are both means for transforming organizational security culture. The CSCF is more of a top-down approach, diagnosing different cultures and building transformation strategies around this macro view of security and the way it interacts with other organizational goals. Security FORCE is more bottom-up, addressing specific behaviors as a backdoor method of cultural change. Optimally, they work together. Separately, they can still work.

In the absence of reasons not to, I recommend beginning with the CSCF, using the framework as a diagnostic instrument to identify areas of conflict between security and other organizational priorities and between unique security priorities themselves. An organization may find the insights generated by the CSCF to be revelatory, identifying areas where the organization says one thing but believes something else, or realizing that one priority always trumps every other priority the organization professes to hold dear. Even if a CSCF analysis does not lead to a full-blown security culture transformation plan, knowing what the organization believes about security shines light on how it behaves toward security.

I tend to recommend the Security FORCE Model as a starting point for organizations that are focused primarily on program self-improvement, organizations who would like to change their culture but require something a bit more tactical to begin with. Moving toward the behaviors of an HRSP can create powerful changes in an InfoSec program, but those changes probably will not extend very far beyond the InfoSec program. Improving the FORCE behaviors may enable the CISO to run a tighter ship, but it won't help that CISO convince others that security is just as important as cultural drivers like profit or productivity. And because the model is behavioral, any cultural change it creates is slower, the result of changing habits more than changing beliefs.

People-Centric Security Strategies

Whether you are a CISO, a security awareness manager, or a different security stakeholder entirely (maybe not even part of the security program), any attempt at people-centric security requires a strategy and a plan before you begin. The strategy can be transformational or behavioral, exploratory or directed. But whatever strategy you choose, you should have a basic idea of what you want to accomplish before you dive in. The following are just a few example strategies that might provoke some thoughts or ideas.

Improving Board and Business Stakeholder Engagement

Improving organizational culture and behavior may not be central to information security managers today, but the concept gets a lot of traction at the board and senior executive levels. Most of the research I've applied in this book comes from people who work with company leadership teams as their primary research partners and consulting customers. While it's no guarantee that including cultural transformation will get executives to pay more attention to security, it does provide another approach to CISOs who are struggling to find common ground with business stakeholders. And as a form of the soft power I discussed earlier in this chapter, the CSCF can be a powerful way of encouraging security teams and these other business stakeholders to talk about their priorities using a common framework, one that gives everyone a voice in the security process and a means of listening too.

Supercharging Security Awareness

Security awareness programs, as I've said, remain the most people-centric of all security efforts within an organization, the front line between the InfoSec program and everyone else. As both champions of security and security educators, training and awareness teams can benefit extensively from both the CSCF and the Security FORCE Model. In fact, I have a hard time imagining security culture transformation starting without the active participation of the security awareness team. It can happen, but it's much harder. People-centric security has the potential to elevate and extend the reach of these professionals and the service they provide to the organization as a whole.

People-Centric Incident Response

The visibility into cultural threats and risks provided by the CSCF and the determination to keep failure small and keep response resilient embodied in Security FORCE both offer innovative benefits to organizational incident response capabilities. Too often, root-cause analyses and incident response planning unnecessarily limit themselves to the immediate, technical components of detection and mitigation. The result is an incident response capability that misses the reasons that the organization drifts from non-failure to failure states to begin with. By incorporating CSCF and Security FORCE principles into incident response planning, organizations can change the game by changing their basic understanding of what an incident means and what it implies for an organization seeking to keep it from happening again in the future.

Conclusion

This book is a culmination of both a quarter-century of my direct experience with how people do information security all over the world, in a variety of organizations, and ten years of specific work theorizing and researching ways to put "people" in their rightful place at the front of the "people, process, and technology" triad that InfoSec programs claim is the core of successful security. I reject the idea that we are beleaguered defenders about to be overrun by the hostile enemies outside our walls, and that change is required because security has fundamentally failed. There have certainly been colossal and disturbing failures, and there will continue to be. But I prefer to think of our profession as adolescent, faced with the same leap into maturity that every other profession (such as insurance, law, and even IT) has faced.

It's scary growing up. You have to start thinking about things that are much more difficult and complicated than what you have had to deal with throughout your childhood. But most adults probably would not want to go back to their days of being a kid. Maturity brings opportunity and reward on a grander scale. That's where information security is today, facing challenges bigger than any we've had to face before and needing tools that we've not used before to meet those challenges. The rewards are enormous if society gets information security right. But that's not why we have to do it. We have to do it because we can't go back to the way it was, any more than you can go back to childhood, even if you wanted to. As society becomes increasingly dependent on technology and information, threats to technology and information become threats to society—not "meteor from the sky obliterates all life" threats, but "crime, disease, and war make life miserable" threats. Bad things will always happen, but we have to learn to deal with them, adapt, and manage. That, too, is a lesson we learn as we get older. This book certainly doesn't have all the answers, but I hope that it helps at least a few people in this profession that I have enjoyed for so long answer some of their own tough questions.

Further Reading

▶ Foucault, Michel. *Discipline and Punish: The Birth of the Prison.* New York: Vintage Books, 1995.

▶ Schneier, Bruce. *Data and Goliath: The Hidden Battles to Collect Your Data and Control Your World.* New York: W.W. Norton, 2015.

▶ University of Texas Center for Identity. Information available at http://identity.utexas.edu

Index